Critical Infrastructure Protection

IFIP – The International Federation for Information Processing

IFIP was founded in 1960 under the auspices of UNESCO, following the First World Computer Congress held in Paris the previous year. An umbrella organization for societies working in information processing, IFIP's aim is two-fold: to support information processing within its member countries and to encourage technology transfer to developing nations. As its mission statement clearly states,

> *IFIP's mission is to be the leading, truly international, apolitical organization which encourages and assists in the development, exploitation and application of information technology for the benefit of all people.*

IFIP is a non-profitmaking organization, run almost solely by 2500 volunteers. It operates through a number of technical committees, which organize events and publications. IFIP's events range from an international congress to local seminars, but the most important are:

- The IFIP World Computer Congress, held every second year;
- Open conferences;
- Working conferences.

The flagship event is the IFIP World Computer Congress, at which both invited and contributed papers are presented. Contributed papers are rigorously refereed and the rejection rate is high.

As with the Congress, participation in the open conferences is open to all and papers may be invited or submitted. Again, submitted papers are stringently refereed.

The working conferences are structured differently. They are usually run by a working group and attendance is small and by invitation only. Their purpose is to create an atmosphere conducive to innovation and development. Refereeing is less rigorous and papers are subjected to extensive group discussion.

Publications arising from IFIP events vary. The papers presented at the IFIP World Computer Congress and at open conferences are published as conference proceedings, while the results of the working conferences are often published as collections of selected and edited papers.

Any national society whose primary activity is in information may apply to become a full member of IFIP, although full membership is restricted to one society per country. Full members are entitled to vote at the annual General Assembly, National societies preferring a less committed involvement may apply for associate or corresponding membership. Associate members enjoy the same benefits as full members, but without voting rights. Corresponding members are not represented in IFIP bodies. Affiliated membership is open to non-national societies, and individual and honorary membership schemes are also offered.

E. Goetz and S. Shenoi
Editors

Critical Infrastructure Protection

Eric Goetz
13P, Dartmouth College
Hanover, New Hampshire
USA

Sujeet Shenoi
University of Tulsa
Tulsa, Oklahoma
USA

Critical Infrastructure Protection

Edited by E. Goetz and S. Shenoi

p. cm. (IFIP International Federation for Information Processing, a Springer Series in Computer Science)

ISSN: 1571-5736 / 1861-2288 (Internet)

ISBN: 978-1-4419-4531-0 eISBN: 978-0-387-75462-8
Printed on acid-free paper

9 8 7 6 5 4 3 2 1
springer.com

Contents

PART III CONTROL SYSTEMS SECURITY

PART IV NETWORK INFRASTRUCTURE SECURITY

PART V INFRASTRUCTURE INTERDEPENDENCIES

PART VI RISK ASSESSMENT

Contributing Authors

Rune Ask is a Senior Consultant at Det Norske Veritas, Oslo, Norway. His research interests include information security, risk assessment, vulnerability assessment and information technology management.

Dan Assaf is a candidate for the Doctor of Juridical Science (S.J.D.) degree at the University of Toronto, Toronto, Canada. His research interests are in the intersection of law, economics and security, in particular, the regulation and governance of security.

Uwe Beyer is the Department Head of Process Intelligence and Head of Security at the Fraunhofer Institute for Intelligent Analysis and Information Systems, Sankt Augustin, Germany. His research interests include new security technologies, future C3 systems and large-scale software architectures.

Roy Campbell is a Sohaib and Sara Abbasi Professor at the University of Illinois at Urbana-Champaign, Urbana, Illinois. His research interests include security, distributed operating systems and ubiquitous computing.

Rodrigo Chandia is a Ph.D. student in Computer Science at the University of Tulsa, Tulsa, Oklahoma. His research interests include SCADA security, computer security and open source software development methodologies.

Rocky Chang is an Associate Professor in the Department of Computing at Hong Kong Polytechnic University, Kowloon, Hong Kong, China. His research interests include network security, measurement, operations, management and economics.

Adrian Chavez is a Computer Software Researcher and Developer at Sandia National Laboratories, Albuquerque, New Mexico. His research interests include critical infrastructure protection, cryptology and algorithm design and development.

Guanling Chen is an Assistant Professor of Computer Science at the University of Massachusetts-Lowell, Lowell, Massachusetts. His research interests include wireless networks and computer security.

Steven Cheung is a Computer Scientist at SRI International, Menlo Park, California. His research interests include network security, intrusion detection, alert correlation and sensor networks.

Henrik Christiansson is a Senior Scientist at the Swedish Defence Research Agency, Stockholm, Sweden. His research interests include information assurance and critical infrastructure protection.

Daniel Cross is an M.S. student at the Information Security Institute, Johns Hopkins University, Baltimore, Maryland. His research interests include critical infrastructure protection, network security and digital forensics.

Kenneth Crowther is a Research Assistant Professor in the Department of Systems and Information Engineering at the University of Virginia, Charlottesville, Virginia. His research interests include risk analysis of regional and multiregional interdependent systems, geodatabase systems and regional strategic preparedness.

Robert Cunningham is the Associate Leader of the Information Systems Technology Group at MIT Lincoln Laboratory, Lexington, Massachusetts. His research interests include intrusion detection, analysis of malicious software and automated fault detection in mission-critical software.

Anita D'Amico is the Director of Secure Decisions, a division of Applied Visions, Inc., Northport, New York. Her research interests include situational awareness and visualization, information security, cognitive task analysis and technology transition.

Bruno Dutertre is a Senior Computer Scientist at SRI International, Menlo Park, California. His research interests include formal methods, software architectures, and the application of theorem proving and model checking techniques to the engineering of high-integrity systems.

Scott Dynes is a Senior Research Fellow and Project Manager with the Center for Digital Strategies at the Tuck School of Business, Dartmouth College, Hanover, New Hampshire. His research interests include the economics of cyber security and infrastructure protection, policy issues and risk management.

Janica Edmonds is a Visiting Assistant Professor of Mathematics at the University of Tulsa, Tulsa, Oklahoma. Her research interests include information assurance, formal methods and distributed system verification.

Felix Flentge is the Area Head of Multimodal Software Engineering at Darmstadt University of Technology, Darmstadt, Germany. His research interests include human-computer interaction (especially in crisis situations), software engineering, and modeling and simulation.

Martin Fong is a Senior Software Engineer at SRI International, Menlo Park, California. His research interests include the design, implementation and deployment of extensible software security systems.

James Ford is a Faculty Associate (Research) at the University of Texas at Arlington, Arlington, Texas. His research interests include medical imaging, artificial intelligence and computer security.

Michael Freeman is an Assistant Professor in the Department of Defense Analysis at the Naval Postgraduate School, Monterey, California. His research interests focus on the causes of terrorism, the relationship between democracy and terrorism, and U.S. foreign policy.

Regis Friend Cassidy is a Computer Software Researcher and Developer at Sandia National Laboratories, Albuquerque, New Mexico. His research interests include information assurance, digital forensics and malware analysis.

Rajni Goel is an Assistant Professor of Information Systems and Decision Sciences at Howard University, Washington, DC. Her research interests include information assurance, digital forensics, control systems security and data mining.

Eric Goetz is the Associate Director for Research at the Institute for Information Infrastructure Protection, Dartmouth College, Hanover, New Hampshire. His research interests include information security and critical infrastructure protection, and developing business and policy solutions to counter risk.

Jesus Gonzalez is a Security Analyst with CITGO Petroleum in Houston, Texas. His research interests include network infrastructure security and intrusion detection.

John Goodall is a Senior Analyst at Secure Decisions, a division of Applied Visions, Inc., Northport, New York. His research interests include information visualization, human-computer interaction, socio-technical design and computer network defense.

James Graham is the Henry Vogt Professor of Computer Science and Engineering at the University of Louisville, Louisville, Kentucky. His research interests include information security, digital forensics, critical infrastructure protection, high performance computing and intelligent systems.

Yacov Haimes is the Quarles Professor of Systems and Information Engineering and Director of the Center for Risk Management of Engineering Systems at the University of Virginia, Charlottesville, Virginia. His research interests include systems engineering, risk analysis and risk management.

Mark Hartong is a Senior Electronics Engineer with the Office of Safety, Federal Railroad Administration, U.S. Department of Transportation, Washington, DC, and a Ph.D. student in Information Technology at George Mason University, Fairfax, Virginia. His research interests include software engineering, software systems safety, information security and forensics, and control systems security.

Matthew Henry is a Senior Staff Member at Johns Hopkins University's Applied Physics Laboratory in Laurel, Maryland. His research interests include risk in interdependent systems, coordination of distributed agents and multi-objective control.

Jeffrey Hieb is a Ph.D. candidate in Computer Science and Engineering at the University of Louisville, Louisville, Kentucky. His research interests include information security, honeypots, digital forensics, critical infrastructure protection and secure operating systems.

Justin Hoeckle is an M.S. student at the Information Security Institute, Johns Hopkins University, Baltimore, Maryland. His research interests include digital forensics, incident detection and response, and malware analysis.

Stig Johnsen is a Senior Research Scientist at SINTEF, Trondheim, Norway. His research interests include information security, SCADA systems, integrated oil and gas operations, and plant safety.

Tim Kilpatrick is an M.S. student in Computer Science at the University of Tulsa, Tulsa, Oklahoma. His research interests include SCADA systems security, network forensics and portable electronic device forensics.

Jason Kopylec is a Senior Software Engineer at Secure Decisions, a division of Applied Visions, Inc., Northport, New York. His research interests include visualization, interaction design and cyber infrastructure protection.

Michael Lavine is an Adjunct Assistant Professor at the Information Security Institute, Johns Hopkins University, Baltimore, Maryland. His research interests include mobile forensics, critical infrastructure protection, information assurance policy and homeland security.

Chenyang Lian is a Scientist at Fair Isaac Corporation, San Rafael, California. His research interests include dynamic modeling, interdependency analysis of critical infrastructure systems and economic sectors, risk analysis of disasters and catastrophic events, and risk management of terrorist attacks.

Ulf Lindqvist is a Program Director at SRI International, Menlo Park, California. His current research focuses on the real-time detection and correlation of computer misuse in critical infrastructure systems.

Eric Luiijf is a Principal Consultant at the Hague Centre for Strategic Studies and TNO Defence, Security and Safety, The Hague, The Netherlands. His research interests include information assurance and critical information infrastructure protection.

Xiapu Luo is a Ph.D. student in Computing at the Hong Kong Polytechnic University, Kowloon, Hong Kong, China. His research interests include network security, denial of service attacks, covert channels and network management.

Fillia Makedon is the Chair of Computer Science and Engineering at the University of Texas at Arlington, Arlington, Texas. Her research interests include bioinformatics, pervasive computing, cyber security, human-computer interaction, sensor networks and image analysis.

Marcelo Masera is a Scientific Officer at the Institute for the Protection and Security of the Citizen, Joint Research Center of the European Commission, Ispra, Italy. His research interests include the security of networked systems and systems-of-systems, risk governance, and control systems and communication systems security.

Bruce McMillin is a Professor of Computer Science at Missouri University of Science and Technology, Rolla, Missouri. His research interests include critical infrastructure protection, formal methods, distributed systems, parallel algorithms and software engineering.

Michael Miller is a Software Engineer with BAE Systems, Mawson Lakes, Australia. His research interests include information assurance and critical infrastructure protection.

Suvda Myagmar is a Ph.D. student in Computer Science at the University of Illinois at Urbana-Champaign, Urbana, Illinois. Her research interests include systems security, wireless communications and information retrieval.

Igor Nai Fovino is a Researcher at the Institute for the Protection and Security of the Citizen, Joint Research Center of the European Commission, Ispra, Italy. His research interests include system survivability, formal methods for security assessment, secure communication protocols and privacy-preserving data mining.

Zvia Naphtali is a Research Scientist at the Institute for Civil Infrastructure Systems and an Adjunct Clinical Assistant Professor of Public Administration at New York University's Wagner Graduate School of Public Service, New York. Her research interests involve the use of geographic information systems in environmental health and justice, urban planning and civil infrastructure systems.

David Nicol is a Professor of Electrical and Computer Engineering at the University of Illinois at Urbana-Champaign, Urbana, Illinois. His research interests include computer and communications systems security, high performance computing, parallel algorithms, and modeling and simulation methodologies.

Paul Oman is a Professor of Computer Science at the University of Idaho, Moscow, Idaho. His research interests include various aspects of information assurance, especially securing real-time systems used in critical infrastructure assets.

Mauricio Papa is an Associate Professor of Computer Science at the University of Tulsa, Tulsa, Oklahoma. His research interests include distributed systems, information assurance, and network and SCADA systems security.

Sandip Patel is an Assistant Professor of Information Science and Systems at Morgan State University, Baltimore, Maryland. His research interests include information security and secure SCADA communications.

Ronald Pawlowski is a Senior Research Engineer at Pacific Northwest National Laboratory in Richland, Washington. His research interests include modeling, simulating and securing process control and SCADA systems.

Matthew Phillips received his M.S. degree in Computer Science from the University of Idaho, Moscow, Idaho. His research interests include SCADA systems security, reliability and survivability.

Carlos Restrepo is a Research Scientist with the Institute for Civil Infrastructure Systems at New York University's Wagner Graduate School of Public Service, New York. His research interests include environmental health, sustainable development, risk management, and infrastructure policy and protection.

Eric Robinson is a Senior Research Scientist at Pacific Northwest National Laboratory in Richland, Washington. His research interests include cyber security and adaptive systems.

Neil Robinson is a Researcher at RAND Europe, Cambridge, United Kingdom. His research interests include critical infrastructure protection, cyber crime and information assurance.

Randi Roisli is the Chief Information Security Officer with Statoil AS, Stavanger, Norway. He is an information security professional with fifteen years of experience in the oil industry.

Jason Rubin is an M.S. student at the Information Security Institute, Johns Hopkins University, Baltimore, Maryland. His research interests include computer security, network security, vulnerability analysis and digital forensics.

William Sanders is a Donald Biggar Willett Professor of Engineering, Professor of Electrical and Computer Engineering and Director of the Information Trust Institute at the University of Illinois at Urbana-Champaign, Urbana, Illinois. His research interests include secure and dependable computing, and reliable distributed systems.

Joost Santos is a Research Assistant Professor in the Department of Systems and Information Engineering and Assistant Director of the Center for Risk Management of Engineering Systems at the University of Virginia, Charlottesville, Virginia. His current research interests include probabilistic risk analysis and the dynamic modeling of disruptions to interdependent economic systems.

Roberto Setola is a Professor of Automatic Control and Director of the Complex Systems and Security Laboratory at University Campus Bio-Medico di Roma, Rome, Italy. His research interests include interdependent infrastructure modeling and analysis, control strategies for complex systems, non-linear estimation, mobile robots and biomedical systems.

Sujeet Shenoi, Chair, IFIP Working Group 11.10 on Critical Infrastructure Protection, is the F.P. Walter Professor of Computer Science at the University of Tulsa, Tulsa, Oklahoma. His research interests include information assurance, digital forensics, critical infrastructure protection and intelligent control.

Jeffrey Simonoff is a Professor of Statistics at New York University's Stern School of Business, New York. His research interests include categorical data, outlier identification and robust estimation, smoothing methods, computer intensive statistical methodology and applications of statistics.

Sankalp Singh is a Ph.D. student in Computer Science at the University of Illinois at Urbana-Champaign, Urbana, Illinois. His research interests include the evaluation, quantification and validation of computer security.

Jill Slay is a Research Leader with the Defence and Systems Institute, University of South Australia, Mawson Lakes, Australia. Her research interests include information assurance, critical infrastructure protection and forensic computing.

Kevin Snow is an M.S. student at the Information Security Institute, Johns Hopkins University, Baltimore, Maryland. His research interests include computer security, network security, digital forensics and information warfare.

Nils Svendsen is a Ph.D. student at the Norwegian Information Security Laboratory, Gjøvik University College, Gjøvik, Norway. His research interests include the modeling and simulation of critical infrastructures, graph theory, cryptography and coding theory.

Han Tang is an M.S. student in Computer Engineering at Missouri University of Science and Technology, Rolla, Missouri. Her research interests include information security in distributed systems and formal security models for cyber-physical systems.

Yajuan Tang received her Ph.D. degree in Radio Physics from Wuhan University, Wuhan, China. Her research interests include statistical signal processing, optimal control and time-frequency analysis.

Jason Trent is a Computer Software Researcher and Developer at Sandia National Laboratories, Albuquerque, New Mexico. His research interests include control systems security, digital forensics and hardware-software interaction.

Jorge Urrea is a Computer Software Researcher and Developer at Sandia National Laboratories, Albuquerque, New Mexico. His research interests include control systems security and digital forensics.

Alfonso Valdes is a Senior Computer Scientist at SRI International, Menlo Park, California. His research interests include intrusion detection and scalable methods for visualizing anomalous and malicious activity in computer networks.

Lorenzo Valeri is a Researcher at RAND Europe, Cambridge, United Kingdom. His research interests include information technology policy, security and privacy.

Duminda Wijesekera is an Associate Professor of Information and Software Engineering at George Mason University, Fairfax, Virginia. His current research is in information, network, telecommunications and control systems security.

Marianne Winslett is a Research Professor at the University of Illinois at Urbana-Champaign, Urbana, Illinois. Her research interests include information security and scientific databases.

Stephen Wolthusen is a Professor of Information Security at the Norwegian Information Security Laboratory, Gjøvik University College, Gjøvik, Norway, and a Lecturer in the Department of Mathematics at Royal Holloway, University of London, London, United Kingdom. His research interests include the modeling and simulation of critical infrastructures using combinatorial and graph-theoretic approaches as well as network and distributed systems security.

Bradley Woodworth is a Senior Research Scientist at Pacific Northwest National Laboratory in Richland, Washington. His research interests include complex adaptive systems and security solutions for critical infrastructures.

Yurong Xu is a Ph.D. student in Computer Science at Dartmouth College, Hanover, New Hampshire, and a Research Assistant at the University of Texas at Arlington, Arlington, Texas. His research interests include wireless sensor networks and information security.

Zhenyu Yan is a Ph.D. student in Systems and Information Engineering at the University of Virginia, Charlottesville, Virginia. His research interests include Bayesian data analysis and hierarchical analysis, and their applications in risk analysis.

Michael Zhivich is an Associate Research Staff Member at MIT Lincoln Laboratory, Lexington, Massachusetts. His research interests include program analysis and the automated detection of security vulnerabilities.

Rae Zimmerman is a Professor of Planning and Public Administration and Director of the Institute for Civil Infrastructure Systems at New York University's Wagner Graduate School of Public Service, New York. Her research interests include the sustainability and security of urban infrastructures, risk assessment and management, and environmental planning and policy.

Preface

The information infrastructure – comprising computers, embedded devices, networks and software systems – is vital to operations in every sector: information technology, telecommunications, energy, banking and finance, transportation systems, chemicals, agriculture and food, defense industrial base, public health and health care, national monuments and icons, drinking water and water treatment systems, commercial facilities, dams, emergency services, commercial nuclear reactors, materials and waste, postal and shipping, and government facilities. Global business and industry, governments, indeed society itself, cannot function if major components of the critical information infrastructure are degraded, disabled or destroyed.

This book, *Critical Infrastructure Protection*, is the first volume in the new annual series produced by IFIP Working Group 11.10 on Critical Infrastructure Protection, an active international community of scientists, engineers, practitioners and policy makers dedicated to advancing research, development and implementation efforts related to critical infrastructure protection. The book presents original research results and innovative applications in the area of infrastructure protection. Also, it highlights the importance of weaving science, technology and policy in crafting sophisticated, yet practical, solutions that will help secure information, computer and network assets in the various critical infrastructure sectors.

This volume contains twenty-seven edited papers from the First Annual IFIP Working Group 11.10 International Conference on Critical Infrastructure Protection, held at Dartmouth College, Hanover, New Hampshire, March 19–21, 2007. The papers were selected from fifty-one submissions, which were refereed by members of IFIP Working Group 11.10 and other internationally-recognized experts in critical infrastructure protection.

The chapters are organized into six sections: themes and issues, infrastructure security, control systems security, network infrastructure security, infrastructure interdependencies and risk assessment. The coverage of topics showcases the richness and vitality of the discipline, and offers promising avenues for future research in critical infrastructure protection.

This book is the result of the combined efforts of several individuals and organizations. In particular, we thank Rodrigo Chandia and Mauricio Papa for their tireless work on behalf of IFIP Working Group 11.10. We gratefully acknowledge the Institute for Information Infrastructure Protection (I3P), managed by Dartmouth College, for nurturing IFIP Working Group 11.10 and sponsoring several of the research efforts whose results are described in this volume. We also thank the Department of Homeland Security and the National Security Agency for their support of IFIP Working Group 11.10 and its activities. Finally, we wish to note that all opinions, findings, conclusions and recommendations in the chapters of this book are those of the authors and do not necessarily reflect the views of their employers or funding agencies.

ERIC GOETZ AND SUJEET SHENOI

I

THEMES AND ISSUES

Chapter 1

ON THE SECURITY IMPLICATIONS OF DISRUPTIVE TECHNOLOGIES

Neil Robinson and Lorenzo Valeri

Abstract This paper summarizes the results of a study that explored the security implications of the use of "disruptive technologies" in various economic sectors. Robust evidence of the security challenges associated with deploying advanced technologies was gathered by bringing together internationally-renowned experts with firsthand experience involving major case studies. Policy recommendations in the context of the European i2010 strategy were also articulated. This paper focuses on three technologies: Voice over Internet Protocol (VoIP), Radio Frequency Identification (RFID) and Internet Protocol version 6 (IPv6). It examines the security challenges related to the three technologies, and analyzes security issues that apply more generally to disruptive technologies.

Keywords: Disruptive technologies, security implications, VoIP, RFID, IPv6

1. Introduction

This paper summarizes the main results of a study undertaken by RAND Europe for the Information Society and Media Directorate-General of the European Commission. The goal of the study was to collect and analyze robust evidence on the security challenges involving the deployment and use of disruptive technologies.

Information and communication technologies (ICTs) are seen as the engine for sustainable growth and employment in Europe. This is the central message of the "i2010 Strategy" put forward by the European Commission in 2005. Its push for a "Single European Information Space" is based on faster broadband connections, seamless interoperability, and rich content and applications. The European Commission's communication that detailed the i2010 Strategy emphasized that "trustworthy, secure and reliable ICTs are crucial for the wide take-up of converging technologies" [10].

Robinson, N. and Valeri, L., 2008, in IFIP International Federation for Information Processing, Volume 253, Critical Infrastructure Protection, eds. E. Goetz and S. Shenoi; (Boston: Springer), pp. 3–14.

Coined by Harvard professor Clayton Christensen, the phrase "disruptive technology" refers to new technologies that unexpectedly displace the position of established technologies [5, 6]. An important element of these technologies is their potential for "creative destruction" and the resulting market impact [19]. Disruptive technologies displace leading technologies even though they may initially perform worse than existing technologies. Organizations often tend to focus on established technologies because they know the market, and have mechanisms in place to develop services and applications. Many organizations initially dismiss disruptive technologies, only to be surprised when the same technologies mature and gain massive market share. A good example is telephony, which was originally conceived as a short-range application. But it evolved and expanded, and completely disrupted the incumbent telegraph industry.

Given the ramifications that the successful deployment of disruptive technologies can have on global society, there is the need for appropriate awareness activities, self-protection mechanisms, and effective responses to attacks and system failures. Consequently, the RAND study focused mainly on the security challenges faced by organizations during the deployment of disruptive technologies and the steps taken by them to address the challenges. Five technologies were investigated. Of these, three were already stipulated by the European Commission: Voice over Internet Protocol (VoIP), trusted computing and Internet Protocol version 6 (IPv6). The remaining two technologies, Radio Frequency Identification (RFID) and wireless microwave access (WiMAX), were selected by RAND as good examples of disruptive technologies.

The study employed a multi-stage approach to investigate and identify security challenges for the five technologies. It involved a Delphi exercise, literature review, case studies and expert workshops. This was done to overcome the limited historical evidence base regarding the implementation of these technologies. The multiple case study approach was used as the primary research method to allow for the provision of more compelling evidence which would help support the conclusions and policy recommendations. This paper presents the results for three of the five technologies examined in the RAND study: VoIP, RFID and IPv6. It discusses the security challenges related to these three technologies as well as the security issues that apply more generally to disruptive technologies.

2. Voice over Internet Protocol Case Study

This case study considered the implementation of VoIP in the U.K. network of HSBC Bank, one of the world's largest financial institutions. Any new ICT implementation in HSBC, such as VoIP, must satisfy the key tenets of HSBC's technology strategy: standardization, self sufficiency, centralization and careful timing of technology adoption [17]. The VoIP implementation initiated with a pilot effort involving approximately 40 HSBC branches. The effort was undertaken by a corporate technology implementation team, which included two security experts. Key characteristics of the implementation were the creation of virtual local area networks (VLANs) and the use of a consistent, organization-wide IP traffic allocation plan.

2.1 Risk Assessment

A formal risk assessment study was conducted by the IT security team and the overall project team early in the implementation effort. The study identified 23 risk areas. VoIP-related risks were categorized as follows:

- **Telephony End Point Attacks:** Eavesdropping on unencrypted network traffic, denial of service (DoS), Dynamic Host Control Protocol (DHCP) starvation, and attacks against IP handsets.
- **IP Telephony Server Attacks:** Viruses, worms and Trojans – typical attacks against servers connected to IP networks (Cisco Call Manager in this case).
- **Application Attacks:** Unauthorized access to the telephone system, toll fraud and telephony fraud using interfaces to the public switched telephone network. Other security issues included server organization, robustness, access control and vendor knowledge about voice communications, with a specific focus on QSIG signaling. QSIG is a signaling protocol used in enterprise voice and integrated services networks, typically between private branch exchanges (PBXs) [9].

The nature of the VoIP implementation with its separate VLANs for voice and data meant that other security considerations, especially those relating to availability, had to be met. Chief amongst these was the need for a contingency center capable of dealing with sites that were 100 km or more apart. Other availability issues came with the specific solution that was devised, e.g., managing the requirement for staff to make adjustments within the constraints of the solution.

HBSC also developed a traffic allocation plan to reduce congestion and mitigate the risk related to availability. As the VoIP implementation was carried out, HSBC staff began to appreciate that a higher level of security practices had to be undertaken with particular attention to servers, especially VoIP servers that carry both voice and data. HSBC staff were aware that users would not accept the same level of quality for voice communications as they did for e-mail communications, which suffers from occasional outages, low reliability and periodic non-availability. Finally, HSBC staff had to comply with various national and international regulations concerning the retention of communications data, which was possible with their new PBX solution.

2.2 Analysis

This case study illustrates that VoIP is a highly disruptive technology from the end-user and market perspectives, but at present is viewed less so within large corporations. In the case study, HSBC adopted a "wait and see" attitude;

it did not deploy the technology throughout its global organization as there was no clear business case.

VoIP deployment can act as a catalyst for important changes in numbering and addressing within an organization. However, by moving to a single technology other risks appear, especially those relating to reliability. Another challenge highlighted in the case study was meeting regulatory requirements across different legal jurisdictions. VoIP might be too secure in some cases, preventing regulators from undertaking the desired level of monitoring. Interoperability was also a large concern, particularly with regard to consumer use of VoIP software and applications. Security is a key element when addressing interoperability between different products.

3. Radio Frequency Identification Case Study

Airbus is a leading aircraft manufacturer with 434 deliveries and a turnover of 26 billion euros in 2006. The company maintains cooperative efforts and partnerships with major companies around the world; it has a network of more than 1,500 suppliers in 30 countries [2].

For this case study, Airbus collaborated with LogicaCMG, which operates the RFID Competency Center, and Kortenburg, which produced RFID chips to implement a fully-integrated solution for tracking and tracing of tools, instruments and spare parts. As a result, all Airbus tools and toolboxes are now equipped with RFID microchips, offering electronic support for tool loan and repair management. The microchips contain data about tools as well as shipping, routing and customs information.

The RFID solution was motivated by the desire to provide better, quicker service by improving the efficiency of the tool loan business. The tool loan business was chosen because it was a separate organizational division, and thus a relatively "safe" environment for experimenting with new technology [1, 18].

The RFID chips contain a variety of administrative data, including shipping information, serial numbers, receipt dates, last check numbers, check codes and original laboratory identifiers. The RFID solution is seamlessly integrated with Airbus' SAP business application software leading to the instant availability of data, which provides a great degree of transparency throughout the supply chain. Suppliers are able to verify that tools are genuine; this reduces the risk of unapproved tools entering the supply chain. Engineers do not need to delve through paperwork to discover the status of tools. The resulting optimization of the supply chain of repair tools has significantly reduced aircraft turnaround times.

3.1 Security Concerns

Data access and modification, and access to the backend system are possible only via authorized access by checking user rights. Only certain types of equipment can directly read and write to the RFID tags.

Data and system availability concerns were met by having the product serial number printed on the protective casing of the chip, allowing technicians to revert, if necessary, to manual handling. To maintain data integrity at the highest level, the complete destruction and revocation of a tag must be ensured if it is removed from a part or tool. Thus, counterfeit parts cannot be equipped with tags from scrapped components. Manufacturers check the tags to prevent unapproved parts entering the supply chain; therefore each tag must have a valid serial number.

Airbus performed extensive tests on the RFID tags to identify defects and evaluate interference during commercial aircraft operations. RFID devices used on aircraft must be of high integrity, and the radio frequencies must be stable. Tags were exposed to severe conditions followed by read-write tests. Safety tests included temperature changes, chemical and liquid exposure, humidity, lightning-induced transient susceptibility, electrostatic discharge, shock and vibration, and fire impact. None of the physical conditions had negative effects on the read-write functionality or data integrity; nor did the hostile test environment cause defects in the tags.

Government authorities are working on airworthiness approval and regulatory policy for passive RFID devices used in civil aircraft. In cooperation with a European airline, Airbus performed in-flight tests of RFID tags carried on Airbus A320 aircraft. No defects were encountered during 6,000 flight hours on 12 aircraft. The tags were approved by the German Airworthiness Authorities (LBA) after this successful test, paving the way for future approval and certification of the technology.

In 2005, the U.S. Federal Aviation Administration issued a policy memo on the safety aspects of passive RFID use in aircraft [11]. The memo suggested that data regarding parts should be accessible anytime, anywhere, by anyone and should respect data protection rights. Furthermore, round-the-clock verification of the information held on a tag must be possible from a secure central database.

The use of RFID accelerated goods receipt and quality inspection processes mainly due to the rapid availability of accurate data. The easier, faster and improved flow of information between all participants in the supply chain led to process acceleration, and, thus, to faster loan tool re-availability. The technology was deemed to be reliable; nevertheless, additional reliability was achieved by adjusting the appearance and layout of the serial numbers on toolboxes.

3.2 Analysis

RFID is perceived as a controversial technology by the general public. The use of RFID in a supply chain environment is certainly not a controversial application, but one where the technology is being deployed very widely. In the case study, RFID was used only in a "safety-critical environment" in a relatively safe organizational area or "testbed."

In a logistics environment, the transmission of RFID data over open networks such as the Internet is of less concern than in an environment where the data is of a personally identifiable nature. In Airbus' case, availability was the primary concern, not confidentiality. Clearly, as RFID applications increase, privacy issues associated with transmitting data over open networks will come to the fore.

Policy makers have an opportunity to promote appropriate and secure applications of RFID by encouraging research and development efforts related to security parameters for RFID infrastructures and by supporting efforts focused on addressing consumer perceptions related to RFID use. For example, initiatives such as the ongoing EU consultation on RFID should be encouraged and its results disseminated as widely as possible [13].

While the case study did not explicitly consider consumer concerns about RFID applications, other significant challenges were encountered. These included ensuring synchronization and concurrency of datasets (which are equally relevant to logistics and consumer applications of RFID). Obviously, failure to address these issues would wreak havoc on an RFID implementation. Another challenge deals with data being transmitted over open, potentially unreliable networks such as the Internet. The question is whether the data on a RFID chip ought to be complete or merely a serial number referencing a complete record held elsewhere.

Consideration of RFID as part of an open network (rather than a closed network as in the case study) is critical to identifying future challenges. The accessibility of the data in an RFID system is a key to realizing the benefits of the technology, with the caveat that such a system must be made as secure as possible to minimize data leakage.

4. Internet Protocol Version 6 Case Study

This case study investigated the deployment and use of IPv6 in a Defense Research and Education Network (DREN) trial. DREN is a U.S. Department of Defense (DoD) information network [8], which is part of the High Performance Computing Modernization Program (HPCMP), an effort to leverage cutting-edge technologies across the U.S. government. DREN connects 4,500 users across the U.S. It has ten core nodes and 100 smaller "service delivery points," all connected in a wide area network via high capacity optical links provided by Verizon [4].

The implementation of IPv6 in DREN was done to ease the DoD-wide transition to IPv6. HPCMP was not required to build a formal business case for its implementation, and there was no risk/reward threshold to be overcome before the decision to go ahead was taken. Undertaking the pilot effort was also seen as a way to identify best practices before the technology was rolled out more widely in DREN and within the DoD as a whole. It was crucial to understand the strengths and weaknesses of the technology, especially given the aggressive timetable for transition within the DoD. This was thrown into sharp relief by the need to identify the security risks inherent in a dual-stacked deployment of the technology. The DREN implementation operates two distinct IPv6 networks: a test network (DREN IPv6 Pilot) and DREN2, the rollout of IPv6 on the production network.

During the case study, emphasis was placed on having the most up-to-date equipment, which was critical to successfully deploying IPv6 on DREN. Experiments have shown that comparable performance is obtained for IPv4 and IPv6, despite claims of increased efficiency in IPv6's processing of datagrams. However, systems administrators must understand the complexities of operating in a dual-stack environment. Because of the requirements for either dual stacking or tunneling, the end-to-end paradigm is undermined during the transition period between IPv4 and IPv6. Another technical facet is that many IPv6 features (including its security benefits) will not have much of an impact until a significant portion of the Internet uses IPv6.

4.1 Security Concerns

The rollout of IPv6 in the DREN test network was simply a matter of enabling IPv6 on a new network. However, deploying IPv6 in the production network was more complicated and involved a significant planning effort. A team was formed to coordinate deployment across fifteen sites with the goals being to minimize workarounds and dual-protocol operations on the final dual-stack network – fewer tunnels and translators would make for a more robust and stable network. The well-known CMU SEI process for technology transition planning [15] was adopted by the project managers. The result was a set of transition plans in seven functional areas: IP transport and infrastructure, infrastructure services, network management, security, applications, "planning for the future," and the high-performance computing community.

Training sessions were conducted to assist staff during the transition; this also helped coordinate deployment and manage risk. The security of a dual-stacked environment is equal to that of an IPv4 network, and an IPv6 version of the IPv4 security strategy was deployed to manage risk. This case study is somewhat unique in that no cost-benefit study or risk assessment was undertaken. Network managers at HPCMP sites were responsible for carrying out the IPv6 plan for deployment. Ideally, the network protocol would be transparent to most network terminal users, so the term "user" in this case study refers to programmers who write applications to manage network resources or exploit protocol features.

Several general lessons were derived from the deployment. These included the importance of thorough planning, meaning that the margin for error was minimal or non-existent. The involvement of a broad range of stakeholders was crucial, especially those with security interests. Obtaining vendor support for IPv6 was also important; the demands placed on vendors by HPCMP for full IPv6 support was a significant motivator for them to upgrade their equipment and network management tools. However, some vendors offered less than complete support, and a number of tools and applications were incompatible with IPv6. The absence of a vendor schedule for delivering IPv6-ready applications along with new generations of equipment was a particular challenge, especially concerning IPSec. More than 90% of the IPv6 products did not support IPSec. In fact, if systems are deployed inappropriately, IPSec communications can bypass traditional defenses, leading to the insertion of worms and viruses in secure links. Management of IPSec was difficult due to the absence of tools. Although HPCMP has not observed reduced security or an increase in attacks after deploying IPv6, it is clear that additional resources are required to maintain the security of DREN in a dual-stack environment.

4.2 Analysis

IPv6 can significantly increase the overall reliability and stability of public IP networks, and its DREN deployment was important as a precursor to the widespread use of IPv6 in U.S. government agencies. Lessons learned include the need to run a dual-stack environment with additional resources and the importance of engaging the vendor community, especially with regard to IPSec support. A heterogeneous network environment using both IPv4 and IPv6 during the transitioning from IPv4 to IPv6 may introduce other risks that undermine end-to-end security (e.g., tunneling between IPv4 and IPv6 affects IPSec). The need to maintain the same level of security during the transition period may also have second-order effects such as the need for additional resources.

The case study highlighted the narrow margin for error available to an organization deploying IPv6, and the need to effectively manage the transition, especially with respect to vendor expertise in IPSec.

The involvement of security personnel in the early stages of the IPv6 deployment eased the transition; this underscores the need to incorporate security in the core of any implementation or use of a disruptive technology. Organizations must be aware that vendor support for IPSec is limited, and must be prepared to negotiate with equipment suppliers to ensure that the appropriate security functionality is in place. Also, because the security benefits of IPv6 are realized more fully when it is used widely, it is important that policy makers encourage the pervasive use of the new protocol.

The case study did not consider the implementation of IPv6 in mobile environments. Given the DoD's massive investment in the area, it is extremely important to explore the challenges related to IPv6 in mobile environments. In addition to traditional security issues, it is critical to investigate the impact of IPv6 on the availability of applications and services in fast-moving mobile environments (e.g., command and control activities involving the use of 3G phones with wireless interfaces).

5. Analysis of Disruptive Technologies

The selected technologies are not inherently disruptive; rather, the disruption comes from how they are used [7]. This means that several of the lessons learned should apply to the larger set of emerging technologies.

A focus on "disruptive innovations" as a concept is recommended. More attention needs to be placed on defining what constitutes a "good" implementation. Effort also needs to be directed at attempting to pre-empt disruptions, for example, by exercising foresight, planning and evaluating scenarios, raising awareness, and engaging stakeholders [12].

Exploring the issues and impact of disruptive innovations based on one case study per innovation means that the results are a reflection of just a single application of the technology. Finding the right case studies to apply new technologies is not easy. Clearly, few, if any, mature applications exist of new technologies. Additionally, some case studies (e.g., RFID and IPv6), even if they are interesting and well motivated, do not represent the wider use of the technology in other applications. Positive experiences with new technologies lead to competitive advantages that are not always shared. Negative experiences for which solutions have not been found are often not shared by the affected organizations. Nevertheless, case studies are important because they help draw valuable insights on the disruptive effects of new technologies.

Recognizing the potential security challenges of disruptive technologies helps clarify what needs to be done to benefit from the new opportunities, and to avoid unnecessary risks. By considering the security challenges early, it is possible to move away from viewing security as an add-on. This ensures that all the issues, including the role of security, are fundamentally addressed from the outset.

6. Conclusions

Several observations can be made regarding the security challenges posed by the deployment of disruptive technologies in the case studies. The case studies show that it is important to include security in the business case when considering a new disruptive technology. In all three studies, the organizations involved did not make a business case either because the deployment was not mature enough or because a business case was not deemed necessary. In the case of VoIP, despite a business strategy of centralization and simplification, the organization did not elect to deploy the technology in a widespread fashion due to the absence of a clear business case. In the case of IPv6, it is questionable if a satisfactory business case could have been made given that none was required and that the deployment was mandated by the organization's heads.

This shows that doubt exists about the worth of disruptive technologies, despite the relative maturity of some of the technologies. But this is not entirely unexpected: organizations tend to favor the prevailing technology until an inescapable "tipping point" is reached. However, an organization's perception of a disruptive technology from a business perspective may parallel its view of how the technology contributes to the organization's overall security posture. Unfortunately, this could lead to a poor implementation of the disruptive technology, which translates to a poorer security posture.

The security implications of transitioning to a new technology must be considered very carefully. In the IPv6 case study, the security implications of an organization's transitioning from one technology to another was highlighted. The need to keep IPv4 and IPv6 running together until the use of IPv6 was widespread enough to take full advantage of its security features undermined the end-to-end nature of the security mechanisms built into the IPv6 protocol.

Infrastructure reliability is a challenge when using disruptive technologies. With VoIP, reliability is a major concern in distributed geographies where the technology requires a massive degree of centralization to achieve economies of scale. Even in the case of privately-owned networks, reliability concerns are high and, although the economic possibilities offered by centralization of telecommunications at a regional level are attractive, the risks cannot be underestimated, particularly from denial of service attacks and natural disasters. Despite the hype, VoIP is regarded as suitable only for home-user communications where best-effort transmission is acceptable.

This challenge is also true for RFID when data is passed over the public Internet. The problem of ensuring that safety-critical data arrives when it should over a best-effort network is an important issue to any organization deciding to implement an RFID system using elements of public IP networks for data transmission. (The same concern has been raised for SCADA systems where electronic networks are used to transport control information for electric power stations, oil and gas pipelines, and public utilities.) Of course, with the increasing use of personal data in RFID systems, thorny security and privacy questions will no doubt arise.

Many security challenges are technology specific, but we can also conclude that some challenges apply to multiple (or all) disruptive technologies, even those not covered in this study. First, unexpected risks arise from "mission creep." As new technologies are implemented, their utility increases. This is unavoidable and, in a sense, is exactly what makes such technologies intrinsically disruptive. As applications of the technologies increase, new and unknown security issues often arise.

The convergence of nanotechnology, biotechnology, material science and information technology will surely have unexpected multi-disciplinary security consequences. For example, personal privacy could be infringed when implementing aspects of human genome research, or physical safety might be compromised by telemedicine-enabled applications.

Privacy may be even more at risk. Although privacy is often at odds with security, there may be a need to introduce a common set of principles for privacy as well as information security (e.g., extending or amending the OECD network and information security principles). There could be a need for an effective ombudsman or trusted third party to act in cases where technology has breached privacy guidelines.

Network integrity and reliability are also critical issues. Many disruptive technologies rely on a global information infrastructure to one degree or another. Sensor networks built on a nanotech-enabled infrastructures will mean that networks will become ever "smarter," with the consequence of increasing frailty and fragility [14].

Finally, security challenges could also arise from social quarters not merely from technological vulnerabilities. Consider the case of genetically modified (GM) crops. The technology has existed for some time and the economic case is sound. But social and environmental factors will ultimately decide whether or not the technology will flourish.

References

[1] Airbus, Airbus applies RFID technology to supply of aircraft spare parts (www.airbus.com/en/presscentre/pressreleases/pressreleases_items/09_18_03_RFID_technology.html), 2003.

[2] Airbus, Airbus corporate website (www.airbus.com), 2007.

[3] T. Alves and D. Feldon, TrustZone: Integrated hardware and software security, White Paper, ARM, Cambridge, United Kingdom (www.arm.com/pdfs/TZ_Whitepaper.pdf), 2004.

[4] J. Baird, DREN IPv6 pilot network for HPC users, presented at the *Supercomputing 2004 Conference*, 2004.

[5] J. Bower and C. Christensen, Disruptive technologies: Catching the wave, *Harvard Business Review*, vol. 73(1), pp. 43–53, 1995.

[6] C. Christensen, *The Innovator's Dilemma*, Harvard Business School Press, Boston, Massachusetts, 1997.

[7] C. Christiansen and M. Overdorf, Meeting the challenge of disruptive change, *Harvard Business Review*, vol. 78(2), pp. 67–76, 2000.

[8] Department of Defense, Defense research and engineering network definition (www.hpcmo.hpc.mil/Htdocs/DREN/dren-def.html), 2004.

[9] ECMA International, QSIG home page (www.ecma-international.org/activities/Communications/QSIG_page.htm), 2006.

[10] European Commission, i2010: A European Information Society for Growth and Employment, Communication from the Commission to the Council, the European Parliament, the European Economic and Social Committee and the Committee of the Regions, COM(2005) 229 Final, Brussels, Belgium (europa.eu.int/eur-lex/lex/LexUriServ/site/en/com/2005/com2005_0229en01.pdf), 2005.

[11] Federal Aviation Administration, Policy for passive-only radio frequency identification devices, U.S. Department of Transportation, Washington, DC (www.airweb.faa.gov/Regulatory_and_Guidance_Library/rgPolicy.nsf/0/495367dd1bd773e18625715400718e2e?OpenDocument), 2005.

[12] Foresight Programme, Cyber Trust and Crime Prevention Project (www.foresight.gov.uk/previous_projects/cyber_trust_and_crime_prevention/index.html), 2005.

[13] P. Gabriel, RFID consultation website: Towards an RFID policy for Europe (www.rfidconsultation.eu), 2007.

[14] M. Handley, Why the Internet only just works, *BT Technology Journal*, vol. 24(3), pp. 119–129, 2006.

[15] L. Heinz, TransPlant: Helping organizations to make the transition, *News @ SEI*, vol. 4(4), Software Engineering Institute, Carnegie Mellon University, Pittsburgh, Pennsylvania (www.sei.cmu.edu/news-at-sei/features/2001/4q01/feature-4-4q01.htm), 2001.

[16] M. Hines, Worried about Wi-Fi security? (news.com.com/Worried+about+Wi-Fi+security/2100-7347_3-5540969.html), 2005.

[17] HSBC Holdings, IT strategy (www.hsbc.com/1/PA_1_1_S5/content/assets/investor_relations/HSBC_Investor_day_6.pdf), 2003.

[18] Logica CMG, Case study: Airbus takes RFID into the spare parts supply chain (www.logicacmg.com/file/4017), 2005.

[19] J. Schumpeter, Creative destruction, in *Capitalism, Socialism and Democracy*, Harper, New York, pp. 82–85, 1975.

Chapter 2

CYBER SECURITY: ARE ECONOMIC INCENTIVES ADEQUATE?

Scott Dynes, Eric Goetz and Michael Freeman

Abstract Protecting national critical infrastructure assets from cyber incidents is an important challenge. One facet of this challenge is that the vast majority of the owners and operators of critical infrastructure components are public or private companies. This paper examines the threats faced by for-profit critical infrastructure entities, the incentives and drivers that influence investment in cyber security measures, and how policy initiatives might influence cyber preparedness in critical infrastructure entities.

Keywords: Information security, economic incentives, government policy

1. Introduction

Critical infrastructures are vulnerable to cyber incidents. According to one study, thirty hackers with a budget of $10 million "could bring the United States to its knees. [Terrorists] are now powerful enough to destabilize and eventually destroy targeted states and societies" [8]. In a government exercise, simulated hackers took control of power grids and 911 systems in nine U.S. cities [12]. *The Washington Post* reported that "U.S. analysts believe that by disabling or taking command of the floodgates in a dam or of substations handling 300,000 volts of electric power, an intruder could use virtual tools to destroy real world lives and property" [6].

In launching the National Strategy to Secure Cyberspace [11] in February 2003, President Bush demonstrated the concern about "the threat of organized cyber attacks capable of causing debilitating disruption to our Nation's critical infrastructures, economy or national security," noting that "disruption of these systems can have significant consequences for public health and safety," and emphasizing that the protection of cyber systems has become "a national priority" [2].

Dynes, S., Goetz, E. and Freeman, M., 2008, in IFIP International Federation for Information Processing, Volume 253, Critical Infrastructure Protection, eds. E. Goetz and S. Shenoi; (Boston: Springer), pp. 15–27.

President Bush's Executive Order on Critical Infrastructure Protection [1] established the National Infrastructure Advisory Council (NIAC), which was charged with determining the risk terrorists might pose to critical infrastructures and how the government might best reduce those vulnerabilities. In its final report, the NIAC concluded that market forces, where they are free to operate, would be the most effective means to promoting a greater level of information security [10].

Given this desire to raise the general level of information security for critical infrastructures, the question becomes one of how to bring this about. This challenge must be viewed in the context that the vast majority of the owners and operators of critical infrastructure assets are non-governmental (public, non-profit or private for-profit) entities. In all cases, managers face similar incentives and drivers in utilizing limited resources to achieve their business objectives. The question thus becomes to what extent is information security perceived as a business objective. If the investment by businesses does not meet societal needs, government may be required to take regulatory or legislative action. Arguments against stricter information security regulation often cite market forces as being effective societal cyber security drivers, but the evidence does not completely support this position.

To gain a grounded perspective on this issue, we examine the main economic drivers of cyber security and assess how they can improve the security postures of industry and government organizations. The action of these economic drivers, if better understood, could help shape a framework for evaluating cyber security and investments in cyber security. We approach this problem by examining theoretical economic incentives and drivers for public and private firms to invest in information security. We follow with field studies of firms, looking at the actual practice of cyber security investment. We conclude with a discussion of the effectiveness of market forces, and possible policy mechanisms that could drive entities to do better.

2. Cyber Security Investment

This section discusses theoretical and practical approaches to making cyber security investment decisions. These are by no means the only approaches; rather, they are representative of those found in each domain. We begin by framing the issue of what companies hope to achieve through investments in cyber security.

2.1 Cyber Security: What is Adequate?

What does it mean for a firm or other entity to have an "adequate" level of cyber security? A rational approach to defining "adequate" involves identifying the entity's risk by examining the vulnerabilities, the probabilities of successful exploitation of the vulnerabilities, the cost of the outcomes if the vulnerabilities are exploited, and the cost of mitigating the vulnerabilities. The incentives for security arise from the possible costs and other losses that are uncovered.

While the insight into the risk from this process is likely better than that from more heuristic methods, even a strict application of the process can result in an overly narrow and localized view of information security risk.

Consider the security management of a home computer. Most individuals use their home computers to surf the web, send and receive email, and do word processing. From this purely local viewpoint, the incentives for users to protect their machines are to maintain connectivity and to protect the data they value. If a user does not store valued data on his/her machine, no security measures may be adopted until the machine is infected with a virus that interferes with the user's limited use of the machine. There is little incentive to invest in security against viruses, Trojans, worms and other malware unless they affect the user's ability to use the machine. The user is typically not concerned about the probable induction of the machine into a bot network that may cause harm to others.

The Broad View Consider the situation of a global information risk manager of a financial firm. Her focus is not merely on keeping her firm's machines free of viruses and worms; it is also on assuring the availability of her firm's services and on the integrity and security of data as it is being held internally, at business partners, and passed between her firm and other enterprises. She has a much broader view of what is being protected: her firm's business processes, her customers' data, her local machines and network, all of which may be viewed as sources of risk to business processes. Consequently, she invests in information security at a level consistent with this view. Her incentives are different from those of the home user: she needs to protect her clients' data (money) internally, she needs to assure that clients' data is protected by her business partners, and she must ensure that her firm is regarded as a secure entity by other businesses that interact with her firm.

In the case of most firms, the definition of what is being protected lies between these two extremes. We hypothesize that absent external forces such as regulation, the relative information security stance assumed by an organization is correlated with the inclusiveness of what is being protected. For example, within a particular industry sector, some firms would consider that protecting their local machines, applications and data is adequate. Other firms would adopt a more extensive view of what needs to be protected by ensuring that their communications and data transactions with members of their extended enterprise are secure.

External forces such as regulation will affect this correlation. Returning to our financial sector example, regulation can have the effect of making the local good and the sector good the same. This is the result of regulation imposed on industry as well as network effects: if a financial institution's security is inadequate, then other financial institutions will not conduct business with it because they realize that the institution's level of security affects their own level of security. In this case, the minimum acceptable level of security is that which also meets a sector good. This is especially true in a sector that relies heavily on user trust, which can be eroded across a sector by a security breach at just one institution.

Incentives and Public Welfare So far we have examined what entities might reasonably do in their self interest from the individual firm and sector points of view. What might constitute an adequate level of information security from the viewpoint of a government, and what relationship does this level of security have with the security level that firms might reasonably adopt? Ultimately, the question is: are there adequate incentives for firms to adopt security postures that are in line with the public welfare?

The government is primarily interested in addressing vulnerabilities that would threaten the ability of the infrastructure to deliver critical services and goods to the population [11]. The government is concerned with systemic risks that have not manifested themselves to date. Because of the different nature and low probability of these risks, it may be the case that rational firms will never adopt a level of information security that would address the vulnerabilities that underlie the risks. Put another way, the types of information security desired by the government may be different from those that individual firms might consider. It is reasonable to assume that information security solutions needed for the public welfare are different (and possibly more stringent) than those required by firms.

This is not to say that there is no overlap between a sector's interests and the government's interests. It is likely that the financial industry's interests and the government's interests are closely aligned. In other instances, the aims will be different, as in the case of control systems used by power sector companies. The government would like to see more secure control systems, but the companies see little or no economic incentive to upgrade. In our discussion we will address mechanisms that promote the adoption of better security measures in cases such as this.

2.2 Optimal Level of Investment

Every firm will adopt some level of information security. A minimum level of information security investment is required simply to do business and to be credible with potential customers and suppliers. We call this the security baseline β. This baseline level would be different for the various business sectors and, perhaps, for different business sizes.

At or above the security baseline is an optimal level of investment for the firm (see, e.g., [7]). The argument is that the optimum level of cyber security investment is where the marginal costs of increased information security equal the marginal decrease in costs due to events such as virus attacks, hacking and break-ins. This argument represents a definition of the optimal level of investment in information security. Figure 1 graphically relates the minimal level of spending with the local optimal level of spending. Note that the minimal level β will always be less than or equal to the local optimal level of spending O_L. Within an organization, the optimal level of spending occurs when an

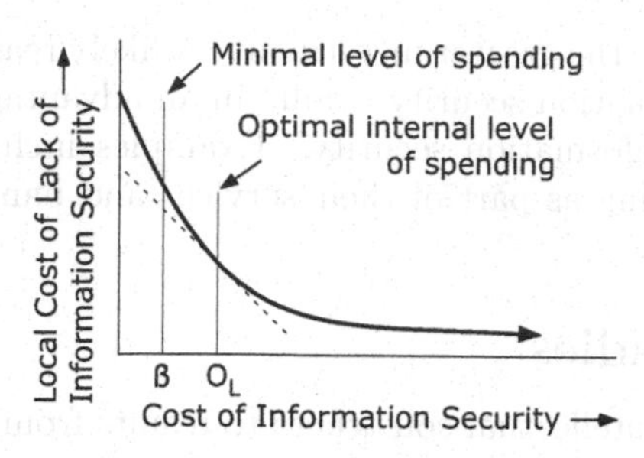

Figure 1. Optimal level of local information security investment O_L (after [7]).

increase in security results in an equal decrease in costs due to security lapses. Taken literally, this optimum corresponds to a largely local view of what to protect. This is because the vast majority of firms have not experienced cyber events that have had significant external costs.

If organizations are to use such a method, they need assessments of the costs incurred due to a lack of information security, their spending on information security, and the marginal rates of return for changes in spending. In reality, while an organization may know how much it spends on cyber security, estimating the true cost of information security lapses is a much more difficult proposition. Some costs are fairly concrete (e.g., the time spent to rebuild systems and recover data); other costs are less tangible (e.g., theft of intellectual property and loss of future business due to brand damage). Surveys such as those done annually by CSI/FBI include such costs, but they are more indicative of trends rather than providing accurate estimates of true economic costs (mainly because survey respondents estimate their losses without applying consistent metrics or guidelines).

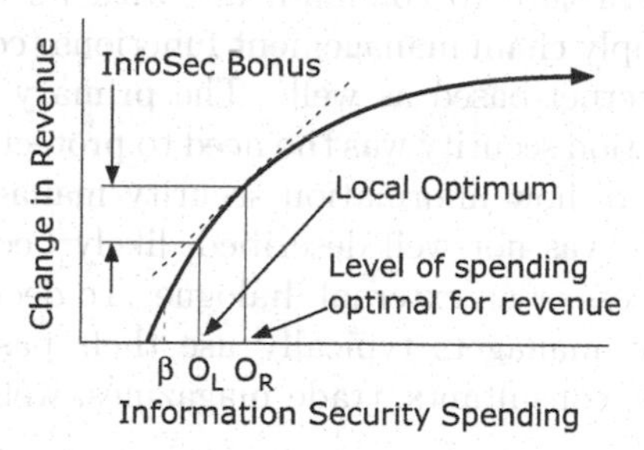

Figure 2. Revenue change as a function of information security investment.

If there are economic incentives for investing at a level higher than that required for a local optimum, what would they look like? Any economic incentive would imply that increasing information security would result in greater profits, either from increased revenue or reduced costs. The case of increased revenue leads to the scenario shown in Figure 2, where the curve in Figure 1 is plotted on new axes to show the change in revenue as a function of investment in information security. Increased revenue (and profits) would result in a new optimal point reflecting the greater investment. A likely reason for this scenario is that increased information security results in an advantage over competitors with lesser levels of information security. Examples include email providers that offer virus screening as part of their services and banks that offer secure online services.

3. Field Studies

We now turn from intellectual constructs to results from field studies, which have been motivated by a desire to understand how firms actually invest in information security: drivers, incentives, and how risk is identified and managed. The field studies involved identifying a "host" organization, and typically conducting interviews with the CIO, the manager of information security, a supply chain executive, and a supply chain relations manager of the host. We would ask the host to introduce us to a few key suppliers that it interacted with using the information infrastructure; we then conducted similar interviews of the suppliers.

Our field studies involved more than fifteen companies and interviews with dozens of people. Details of the case studies are provided elsewhere [3, 5]. In the following, we present pertinent results from the case studies. The results are organized around the drivers of information security investment, the degree of interconnectedness and dependency on the information infrastructure, and the resilience of the organization to cyber events.

3.1 Manufacturing Sector

The host was a manufacturing conglomerate; we conducted interviews at its electrical and automotive business units. The host is very dependent on the information infrastructure to communicate with its customers, and was working to move its supply chain management functions (communications with its suppliers) to be Internet-based as well. The primary driver of the firm's existing level of information security was the need to protect its internal network and data. The process of how information security managers arrived at their current level of security was not well described, likely because it was not the result of a rational process or an external dialogue. To decide on the base level of information security, managers typically use their past experience, input from trusted colleagues, consultants, trade magazines, web research and other mass media.

The main drivers for the adoption of additional information security measures are government regulation and customer requirements. While more than one firm mentioned Sarbanes-Oxley as shining a spotlight on their internal information security procedures, none said that their level of information security increased as a result of Sarbanes-Oxley (although there was frequently a shift in focus or reallocation of resources as a response). On the other hand, every firm described itself as being responsive to customer requirements for improved security. In the manufacturing sector, customer demands mainly come in the form of questionnaires, some of which are quite extensive. The firms viewed these questionnaires as representing a qualification for business. As a group, the interviewed firms made little or no demands on their suppliers for levels of information security, although one supplier said that it would introduce such requirements in the near future. Most of the firms viewed information security as a cost and as a qualifier. The director of IT at one supplier thought that information security provided a competitive advantage because customers felt more comfortable doing business with them as a result of their information security focus. With this exception, none of the interviewees felt that information security would ever become a competitive advantage in the manufacturing sector. Details of the risk the host faced as a result of using the information infrastructure to manufacture and deliver its products can be found in [4].

3.2 Oil and Gas Sector

The field study host was a mid-sized refiner of specialty petroleum products. Unlike the situation in the manufacturing sector, business operations at the refinery would be largely unaffected by an Internet outage. Supplies are typically ordered by telephone with a lead time of weeks, and product orders, while usually communicated via the Internet, could easily be handled via the telephone as well. However, the plant's process control systems (PCSs) rely on an information infrastructure. PCSs are commonly used in refineries, pipelines and electric power generation and distribution systems; they comprise sensors, actuators and logic systems required to operate and monitor industrial processes. The dependence of the refinery on the PCSs is very high; it is not feasibly to operate a refinery manually.

From interviews with the V.P. of refining and the manager of information security, it was clear that there is little perceived economic incentive to invest in a more secure PCS; the lens that the VP of refining adopted was, "How will a more secure PCS help me make a better product?" There were few if any questions from customers about PCS security; the major driver is long-established regulations related to required redundancies in critical systems. During our interviews, two additional PCS security drivers emerged, both centered on assuring business continuity. The first concerned motivations arising from the threat of PCS cyber incidents. The VP of refining allowed that he was concerned that an event could shut his plant down, but it had never happened before, and he had never heard of such a thing in the industry. As a result, he could not justify investments to mitigate the risk. He emphasized that even if a malicious cyber event were to disrupt operations at a major refinery, he would be reluctant to invest in better PCS security because his was not a major refinery and would not be subject to the same risk. However, he would be inclined to invest in security if similar-sized refineries were to be attacked.

The second driver resulted from a risk mapping exercise conducted under a research project supported by the Department of Homeland Security [13]. This effort focused on creating a mapping between IT and business risk at the refinery. The mapping clarified the business consequences that would result from various PCS security incidents. As a result of this activity, the VP of refining stated that he understood how investing in security would help him make a better product: he could make more of it due to increased resilience. As a result, we conclude that the economic and market drivers for increasing PCS security at this refiner are low. While latent drivers do exist, a greater level of transparency into actual PCS security incidents at other refineries would be required for these drivers to become effective. The drivers and incentives for major refineries are somewhat different, leading to a more proactive and global view.

3.3 Financial Sector

The field study involving a financial institution is not yet complete; however, we have interviewed multiple CIOs and global risk managers of firms in the financial sector. There are two main information security drivers in financial firms: government regulations and internal concern for brand and reputation. Unlike firms in the manufacturing and oil and gas sectors, the reputation of financial firms for being secure is of critical importance, both for the firm and its customers. Financial firms are also prime targets for break-ins; Willie Sutton famously said that he robbed banks because that's where the money is [14]. Financial institutions have a very large economic incentive to assure the security of their information. As a result, financial firms are very proactive about security and business continuity. Global risk officers think quite broadly about risk. For example, one risk officer mentioned that his biggest concern regarding cyber security was a lack of imagination: he and his staff cover known cyber risks, and spend serious effort on "blue sky" thinking about what is possible, but he is concerned that he is not clever enough. The attention to detail extends to business partners. Whereas the manufacturing firm above depended on business partners to have "reasonable" levels of information security, and not be proactive about assuring that this was the case, the financial institutions we interviewed were very proactive. The institutions had a set of security practices that they expected their business partners to adhere to, and they ensured that the partners adhered to the practices by conducting audits. This practice is not industry wide, as indicated by a recent data theft case involving a third-party processor for Visa [9].

Finally, financial institutions are completely reliant on the information infrastructure. Trillions of dollars are transferred electronically each day, and the vast majority of customer cash withdrawals occur via ATMs. Without electronic communications, banking activities would be severely disrupted.

3.4 Investment Practices

Based on our interviews, we have identified three approaches that firms employ to make cyber security investments.

Sore Thumb Paradigm In this paradigm, decision makers prioritize their information security efforts and investments based on the attacks and incidents that cause the organization the greatest "pain" (i.e., costs in terms of dollars and manpower). Security investment decisions are generally made based on incomplete risk information (e.g., from industry publications and peer groups) and not on detailed risk assessments. The sore thumb approach is common in smaller companies (where there may be close personal relationships between information security managers and the executives who authorize security spending) and in sectors that are less reliant on IT for business operations. This mainly reactive approach provides many opportunities for improvement.

IT/Business Risk Paradigm This paradigm involves a certain degree of implied risk management methodology to rank information security initiatives, with the goal of reducing the risk to IT components and processes. The information for these efforts typically comes from IT managers and staffers within the organization who relay security issues that they have identified internally or from other industry sources. The director of information security then prioritizes responses based on estimates of the likelihood and cost of successful attacks, and the cost to mitigate vulnerabilities. Directors use this process to varying degrees of rigor. The IT risk portion of the paradigm seeks to protect the network, servers, desktops, i.e., hardware devices. This is not directly a risk management approach, although elements of managing risk – identifying costs and potential consequences of incidents – are employed. The business risk portion explicitly examines how information security risks might impact business processes. The assets protected might include the ERP system and the customer order system, i.e., business processes. The security initiatives, therefore, relate to ensuring business continuity. The IT/business risk paradigm can be reactive and/or proactive.

Systemic Paradigm This paradigm is sufficiently different that it cannot be placed on a continuum that encompasses the above strategies. In this paradigm, information security efforts are inseparable from business strategy. Decision makers incorporate information security at every step of IT process development to enable a business strategy. In fact, it makes no sense to even think about IT-enabled business without having information security baked in; it also makes no sense to have "naked" information security initiatives that are not developed as part of some business process. The prioritization and funding of information security initiatives are not treated separately; budgets for IT projects automatically include security considerations. This paradigm is clearly proactive.

The first two approaches could all be present in an organization. The sore thumb approach is often a tactical response to security incidents such as a virus infection. The presence of the IT risk and business risk strategies in firms is more subtle. As a firm's view of information security matures, it is also possible to move a firm from IT risk to business risk, possibly through an exercise that maps IT risk to business risk.

4. Are Economic Incentives Enough?

If we adopt the theoretical treatment of economic drivers discussed earlier, where economic drivers are defined by increased net revenue, the results of our field studies suggest that the role economic factors play in information security varies from sector to sector and within sectors. In general, economic factors are more prevalent in investment decisions in the financial sector than in the manufacturing sector. The motivation for companies to invest in information security comes from best practices, government regulations, brand/reputation protection and customer demands. Best practices are derived largely from trade publications, industry associations and from regulations. A subset of these best practices forms a baseline for information security investment; managers can invest in this baseline set of security capabilities without further conversations with higher management. This is regarded as a cost of doing business.

While firms comply with government regulations, the great majority of them believe that existing regulations have a negligible effect on the quality of information security. In fact, many feel that the efforts spent on complying with Sarbanes-Oxley and similar regulations detract from efforts to develop effective security capabilities. One director of information security commented that he now has to spend time assuring that the door to his data center is of a certain thickness rather than working on business continuity planning.

Protecting brand and reputation is an important driver at larger firms. This is an economic driver as brand and reputation are related to the viability of the firm. The drivers behind brand and reputation protection offer insight into the differences in the stature of information security in various industry sectors. Manufacturers gain their competitive advantage from pricing, speed of design and development, and reliability in meeting schedule commitments. While information systems play an important role in creating these advantages, an information security failure at a supplier does not necessarily impact the level of trust customers have in the supplier (there are exceptions, e.g., the intellectual property of customers held by suppliers is of critical importance to the customers).

In the financial sector, brand reputation for security is paramount, and financial firms invest accordingly. One information risk manager we interviewed said his firm would invest essentially unlimited funds to make the information security risk disappear. The last element, responsiveness to customer requests, is interesting from several perspectives. First, the willingness of a firm to modify its information security practices for a potential customer is likely to be a competitive advantage, which is an economic incentive. Next, responsiveness to customer requests gives customers influence over the information security environment in which they operate. As noted above, most firms regard these customer requests as qualifications. For example, potential suppliers to a major oil company must complete a questionnaire about their information security practices. Interviewed firms said they regard these questionnaires as a set of qualifications, and strive to meet all the qualifications. This mechanism can (and should) be used by firms to manage the risks they face due to their interdependencies with other firms.

4.1 Systemic Risk Management

A central theme of our field studies was the emergent risk due to the interdependencies of Internet-mediated business processes. As noted above, the ability of business sectors and critical infrastructures to provide quality services is dependent on the availability of the information infrastructure. With the exception of the financial sector, the field studies indicate that firms generally do not consider inter-firm risk. Examining the systemic risk of their dependence on the information infrastructure enables organizations to better address their risk. The risk can be reduced by addressing the vulnerabilities and/or by increasing the resilience of business processes in the face of cyber events. For intra-firm processes, this would require interactions with partners in the extended enterprise, along with joint actions to address the systemic risk that emerges from business interdependencies. It is clear that this can be accomplished. The willingness of firms to accommodate customer requests for particular information security practices indicates that firms would be receptive to addressing shared risks with customers and potential customers. The enabling activity is for the customer to communicate the desired action to the vendor; the precursor to this is the customer taking a systemic view of its cyber risk.

Unfortunately, understanding the systemic risk may not be enough. In the case of the VP of refining at our field study partner, the realization of a risk was not enough to cause an investment to mitigate the risk. He was challenged to see the rationale of investing against a threat that to his knowledge had never occurred; moreover, even an attack against a large refinery might not drive him to action. This point of view was reflected in other interviews: managers are disinclined to invest against hypothetical threats. Investing in physical security is reasonable because break-ins and physical theft are common; the threats are tangible. Investing in PCS security is much harder as the threats are less tangible and it is unclear to some managers whether the threats are real. This is not to say that attacks do not occur: according to Eric Byres, there have been more than 150 PCS security incidents. The reason that this is not well-known is that there are incentives to not share this information; knowledge that a firm has experienced a PCS attack could damage its reputation. The same situation is true for other types of cyber events. Managers would be much more apt to invest against threats that they knew had been exploited or are in a class that had been exploited. Processes that determine systemic risk will certainly detail how to rationally invest in information security to reduce the exposure to largely intangible risks. Knowledge of the range of actual attacks would make important risks more tangible, and more likely to be mitigated.

4.2 Proper Policy Role

We have noted that the government is promoting the development of protection against information attacks that have been hypothesized, but have never been seen. The government is trying to manage the risk by proactively reducing the vulnerabilities prior to suffering any consequences. The difficulty is that most firms are averse to making security investments against events that have never occurred, even if they might worry about them. Many firms are reactive in their investments, responding to actual vulnerabilities. Implicitly, they are not managing risk, but closing known vulnerabilities.

One recent policy effort to remedy this was taken in California, which passed a data breach notification law (AB 700, better known as SB 1386) that required the notification of persons whose personal information was or may be accessed inappropriately. Prior to this law, personal data theft was not broadly reported, resulting in an environment where security investments were not a priority. Since the enactment of the law there have been many reports of data breaches, which have resulted in greater awareness of the issue and in investments to protect against such breaches. Essentially the data breach notification law resulted in the sharing of information that transformed what was for many a hypothetical threat into a known reality. This is certainly a proper role for government policy.

5. Conclusions

Our studies indicate that latent market forces exist for increased cyber security in critical infrastructures. Firms are incented to assure that their business processes are resilient in the face of cyber events, internally as well as externally. By adopting methods for examining their systemic risk to cyber events, firms can become aware of the risks they face due to their interdependencies with other firms. Acting to address these risks will make their own business more resilient; as a result, their business sector will also become more resilient. Thus, latent market forces result in the protection of critical infrastructures.

The government has at least two roles to play. First, by enacting policies that result in disseminating information about cyber incidents, the government can help activate the latent market forces. Secondly, market mechanisms will serve to address the government's concern about critical infrastructures only to the extent that these concerns are aligned with business concerns. If the government is concerned about risks that are not concerns of individual firms, endogenous economic forces are not present, and the government will have to address these risks in other ways.

Acknowledgements

This work was partially supported by the Institute for Information Infrastructure Protection (I3P) under Award 2003-TK-TX-0003 from the Science and Technology Directorate of the U.S. Department of Homeland Security.

References

[1] G. Bush, Executive Order on Critical Infrastructure Protection, The White House, Washington, DC (www.whitehouse.gov/news/releases/2001/10/20011016-12.html), October 16, 2001.

[2] R. Dacey, Critical Infrastructure Protection: Challenges and Efforts to Secure Control Systems, Report GAO-04-628T, U.S. General Accounting Office, Washington, DC, 2004.

[3] S. Dynes, Information security and health care – A field study of a hospital after a worm event (mba.tuck.dartmouth.edu/digital/Research/Research Projects/InfoSecHealthCare.pdf), 2006.

[4] S. Dynes, E. Andrijcic and M. Johnson, Costs to the U.S. economy of information infrastructure failures: Estimates from field studies and economic data, presented at the *Fifth Workshop on the Economics of Information Security*, 2006.

[5] S. Dynes, H. Brechbühl and M. Johnson, Information security in the extended enterprise: Some initial results from a field study of an industrial firm, presented at the *Fourth Workshop on the Economics of Information Security*, 2005.

[6] B. Gellman, Cyber-attacks by al Qaeda feared, *The Washington Post*, June 27, 2002.

[7] L. Gordon and M. Loeb, The economics of information security investment, *ACM Transactions on Information and System Security*, vol. 5(4), pp. 438–457, 2002.

[8] J. Lewis (Ed.), *Cyber Security: Turning National Solutions into International Cooperation*, CSIS Press, Washington, DC, 2003.

[9] L. Loeb, CardSystems solution becomes a cautionary tale, *eWeek*, July 21, 2005.

[10] National Infrastructure Advisory Council (www.dhs.gov/xprevprot/committees/editorial_0353.shtm).

[11] National Infrastructure Advisory Council, The National Strategy to Secure Cyberspace, The White House, Washington, DC (www.whitehouse.gov/pcipb/cyberspace_strategy.pdf), 2003.

[12] Public Broadcasting Service, PBS Frontline: Hackers (www.pbs.org/wgbh/pages/frontline/shows/hackers), 2001.

[13] J. Watters, Analyzing corporate risks with RiskMAP, presented at the *Second I3P Process Control Systems Workshop*, 2006.

[14] Wikipedia, Sutton's Law (en.wikipedia.org/w/index.php?title=Sutton%27s_law&oldid=119669553).

Chapter 3

GOVERNMENT INTERVENTION IN INFORMATION INFRASTRUCTURE PROTECTION

Dan Assaf

Abstract Critical information infrastructure protection is the subject "du jour." An important part to addressing the issue is to answer the question whether the private sector or the government should be responsible for protection. The choice of governing arrangement – government provision, private provision or any combination thereof – is essential to ensuring an adequate level of security. This paper discusses how the market for critical information infrastructure protection may be susceptible to various market failures, namely public goods, externalities and information deficits. The presence of these market failures suggests that government intervention in the market is necessary. Whilc this paper does not present a specific regulatory model or a set of regulatory tools to address these market failures, it asserts that understanding the market failures inherent in critical information infrastructure protection is a key element to designing a successful regulatory policy. Failure to understand and acknowledge the reasons for the inability of the private sector to provide adequate protection can impact a nation-state's security and render it vulnerable to attack.

Keywords: Critical information infrastructure protection, cyber security, market failures, government regulation

1. Introduction

Critical information infrastructures (CIIs) have become viable targets for adversaries, and it is extremely important to secure them in order to mitigate the risk from information warfare attacks. In the United States, as well as in other developed countries, most critical infrastructure assets are owned and operated by the private sector. As markets around the world undergo liberalization and privatization, the private sector is rapidly increasing its ownership of critical infrastructure assets in developing countries. With this in mind it

Assaf, D., 2008, in IFIP International Federation for Information Processing, Volume 253, Critical Infrastructure Protection, eds. E. Goetz and S. Shenoi; (Boston: Springer), pp. 29–39.

could be inferred that the market should be left to its own devices to provide critical information infrastructure protection (CIIP). However, there are certain instances when the government should intervene in the market. One instance is when the market cannot provide or under provides the good it is supposed to provide, a phenomenon referred to as "market failure" in neo-classical economic theory. Another is when the government intervenes in the provision of the good (although the market can provide the good) due to paternalism or based on values such as distributive justice or corrective justice.

While the protection of CII assets is an essential part of a country's national security efforts, the potential targets are usually private companies. But companies are self interested by nature, pursuing business objectives such as the maximization of profits and shareholder value instead of public values such as national security. This raises some interesting questions. Should the government intervene in the provision of CIIP although this negates the market-based approach of non-intervention? Should the government leave a national security issue – where a failure could have catastrophic consequences – in the hands of self-interested private firms?

This paper sheds light on the nature of the market for CIIP. It examines whether there is a need for government intervention. The analysis provides a possible answer to why the American policy of endorsing a "hands-off" approach and keeping faith in the market has been ineffective so far [2]. The market for CIIP has characteristics that indicate market failures, specifically, public good characteristics, presence of externalities and informational problems. These market failures call for government intervention to correct them. Furthermore, the market failures are cumulative. This point is key as it affects the choice of remedy – regulatory tools that address market failures.

The following section discusses the free market notion and the limited role that government should play in it under neo-classical economic theory. Next, the neo-classical economic justifications for government intervention are highlighted and applied to CIIP. Finally, the paper asserts that a new model is required to govern CIIP, one that calls for a more active role for the government. While a specific model is not presented, the paper stresses the importance of understanding the nature of the market for CIIP in the analysis of solutions.

2. Role of Government in a Market Economy

Neo-classical economic theory, based on Adam Smith's classical notion of the Invisible Hand [18], suggests that government intervention is required only when market failures are present. In other words, a market failure must be demonstrated in order to justify intervention.

Market failures that are most commonly demonstrated include monopolies, public goods and asymmetric information. More than one failure can be present in a market at the same time. For example, a market can be subject to the presence of both public goods and externalities [19]. Any of these market failures can justify government intervention.

3. Public Goods and CIIP

A public good is a phenomenon whose presence may demand government intervention in the market. It has two distinct, albeit related, characteristics. First, it is non-excludable; second, it is non-rivalrous in consumption [16]. Typical examples of pure public goods are clean air, radio broadcasts, street lights and national security.

When a good is non-excludable, either it is impossible to exclude non-payers from using it, or the costs of excluding non-payers are high enough to deter a profit-maximizing firm from producing that good. Non-rivalrous consumption means that the consumption of the good by one individual does not affect the ability of any other individual to consume it at the same level. Non-excludability and non-rivalry in consumption lead to a distorted outcome: consumers refrain from paying for the good and become free-riders. Thus, the market is not likely to produce and/or supply these goods and, when it does, it will do so in a sub-optimal manner. Government intervention is required to ensure the optimal production of these goods.

3.1 Is CIIP a Public Good?

Two propositions are central to justifying government intervention in CIIP on the grounds of public good: the national security proposition and the cyber security proposition. The first proposition is more intuitive and captures the essence of CIIP. National security is a (pure) public good; CIIP is an essential component of national security; therefore, CIIP should be regarded as a (pure) public good. The second proposition is less intuitive. Cyber security has some of the characteristics of a public good; therefore, the market for cyber security can be subject to failure. By itself, this proposition is unlikely to provide sufficient justification for government intervention.

3.2 National Security as a Public Good

National security is a classic example of a public good [12]. It is both non-excludable and non-rivalrous in consumption. Once it is provided, it is extremely difficult to exclude certain individuals from the security that is generated, and one individual's use of it does not detract from the amount consumed by others. This is the economic reasoning for the provision of this good by central government (there are other non-economic reasons for this as well). But what exactly is national security? Threats are no longer exclusively directed at nation-states. Corporations around the world are experiencing an escalation in threats and security incidents [11]. The new threats include information warfare, cyber crime and economic espionage, among others. The list of potential actors now includes terrorists, rogue states, hackers, competing corporations and international crime syndicates. The increasing reliance of public and private actors on information flow and information technology, which have led to interdependencies between the public and private sectors, have contributed to the growth and evolution of these threats.

This situation has contributed to a change in what needs to be protected. In the past, national security involved protecting the nation-state and its institutions. Today, the definition of what needs to be protected is much broader, and it includes private entities whose activity is essential to a nation-state's economic and national security. Thus, the protection of CII assets is an important component of a nation-state's security, which, in turn, is a (pure) public good. Hence, it is important to include CIIP as an integral component of a national security strategy.

But the ability of the private sector to provide CIIP at an optimal level is questionable. It is likely that the private sector can provide protection at some level, perhaps at a level that protects its systems against criminal activity or unsophisticated industrial espionage. However, it is doubtful that the private sector can, on its own, protect against well-targeted information operations orchestrated by nation-states and terrorist groups. The private sector cannot provide an adequate level of security required to address sophisticated threats (for one, it cannot meet the high costs associated with an adequate level of security). This is a characteristic of a public good. Thus, the assertion that adequate levels of CIIP cannot be provided by the market, coupled with the adverse effects of inadequate CIIP on national security, calls for government intervention in the provision of CIIP.

3.3 CIIP as a Public Good

CIIP is a segment of what is generally known as cyber security (this is explicitly stated in Section 3(3) of the United States Cyber Security Information Act of 2000). Cyber security is considered to be a public good, although not a pure public good. It has strong public good characteristics – it is non-rivalrous in consumption and it generates positive externalities [7]. But it is not considered to be a pure public good because it is, at least to some extent, excludable.

One of the characteristics associated with the provision of public goods is the generation of positive externalities, which, in turn, leads to the creation of the free-rider problem. Therefore, the presence of positive externalities frequently points to the existence of a public good. Several scholars have addressed this concept in relation to cyber security. Jean Camp, for example, discussed the creation of positive externalities by the provision of security in a networked world [5].

The positive externalities in information security may be attributed to two sources. First, firms derive some benefits from other firms' reports of security breaches in their information systems and networks. The benefits include important information about attack methods, critical flaws in software that were exploited, etc. Second, there are positive spillovers from the actual implementation of cyber security policies and mechanisms by individuals or firms.

Consider the case of a distributed denial of service (DDoS) attack. If computer users adequately secured their systems, the chances of their systems being used for DDoS strikes would be substantially lower. Hence, one user's security would generate positive benefits for the entire community. While the public enjoys increased security, the first users do not fully capture this benefit and, therefore, do not have an adequate incentive to protect their computers.

Powell models this as a prisoner's dilemma game and shows that, without coordination, users would make an inefficient decision (i.e., not secure their computer systems) [14]. Powell argues that cyber security is not a pure public good. He analyzed various surveys taken in the financial services industry, examining how businesses in the sector protected themselves against cyber terrorism. This included information about the investments made by companies in cyber security, their concerns about providing security, and whether they used security protocols. Powell concluded that "there must be enough of a private return to cyber security to cause firms to invest so much in it," and, hence, the market for cyber security is not failing.

Powell's conclusions are controversial for several reasons. An argument can be made, for example, that the financial services industry is not a good exemplar for the incentive structure related to investments in cyber security, because the benefits it derives from security investments are high relative to other critical infrastructure sectors. This is because the financial services sector relies heavily on online transactions and on maintaining consumer trust, which could easily be lost due to a security breach. Moreover, the threats that financial institutions defend against are not necessarily the same as those that chemical facilities face. Financial institutions are also very good at quantifying monetary losses and have experience in "return on investment" calculations for cyber security.

But even if we accept Powell's conclusions, they only point to the importance of distinguishing between the two propositions discussed above. More importantly, they point to the need to give more weight to the national security proposition. By failing to acknowledge this distinction, scholars risk oversimplifying the threats to CIIs. Upon considering the cyber security as a public good proposition alone, the conclusion that the market is working may seem quite plausible. However, after the national security proposition is added to the equation, the uncertainty disappears. Arguing for government intervention on the grounds that cyber security is a public good seems to be somewhat less convincing than arguing for intervention on the grounds that CIIP is a part of national security, and is thus a public good. This is why it would probably be harder to convince decision-makers to intervene in the general market for cyber security than it would be to convince them to intervene in the market for CIIP.

4. Negative Externalities

The second market failure identified by neo-classical economic theory is the presence of externalities in the market. An externality occurs when a decision by one actor in the market generates benefits or costs for other actors, which are not taken into account by the externalizing actor when making the decision. Externalities could be either positive (generating benefits) or negative (generating costs). Consequently, market demand and/or supply are distorted, leading to socially inefficient outcomes.

A common example of a negative externality is a factory that pollutes the air in its vicinity. The pollution is a cost conferred on the people living nearby, a cost which the factory (and its end consumer) do not fully incur. When making the decision about the optimal quantity of goods to be produced, the factory's executives do not take into consideration environmental costs, and an above-optimal, inefficient quantity is produced. If the factory were required to internalize the costs conferred on its neighbors, it would not produce the same amount of goods.

According to the Coase Theorem [6], externalities can be avoided or corrected if voluntary exchanges take place. Coase asserted that where transaction costs are negligible, a voluntary exchange will take place and externalities will be internalized without the need for government intervention. In the polluting factory example, the factory and its neighbors would reach an agreement imposing the costs on the party that could internalize them in a least-cost manner. That is, if the costs generated for the neighbors were higher than the benefits derived by the factory from polluting, the neighbors would pay the factory to stop polluting. If the benefits derived by the factory were higher than the costs generated for the neighbors, the factory would pay the neighbors to relocate. However, as negligible or zero transaction costs are very rare, most parties affected by an externality cannot reach an agreement and government intervention may be warranted.

Justifying government intervention in the market for CIIP on the grounds of externalities seems intuitive, as discussed below. First, however, it is useful to discuss the important concept of interdependencies in critical infrastructures [15]. The term critical infrastructure interdependency emphasizes the correlation existing between the state of one infrastructure and the state of another. Power grids, telecommunication networks, banks, transportation, etc. are all interdependent. Thus, an attack on a communications network may have a debilitating impact on a power grid and vice versa. The fact that critical infrastructures rely on other critical infrastructures means that a disruption of one could lead to cascading failures in other critical infrastructures [20].

Following the notion of interdependency, a cyber-interdependency occurs when an infrastructure's operability relies on its information systems. Computers and automation systems are indispensable to operations in every critical infrastructure. Failure of information systems would lead to a failure of practically every critical infrastructure.

Thus, interdependency is a striking characteristic that leads to the phenomenon of externalities. Consider the case where executives of an Ontario-based energy company, which supplies all the electricity to Toronto, have to determine the level of security in their information systems. The chief information security officer (CISO) presents them with two options that differ in the level of investment required: (i) high-level security measures that would cost the company 0.5 million dollars and provide a 70% probability that the

Table 1. Total expected cost for high and low security levels.

Level of Security	Cost of Security	Probability of Breach	Cost of Breach	Expected Loss	Expected Cost
High	$0.5M	0.3	$1M	$0.3M	$0.8M
Low	$0.0M	0.7	$1M	$0.7M	$0.7M

company's information systems would not be breached; and (ii) very basic, free security measures, which only provide a 30% probability that the company's systems would not be breached. If the losses that the company would incur from a security breach are estimated at 1 million dollars, the decision that the executives face naturally involves some uncertainty. The uncertainty deals with the likelihood of a security breach. Under rational decision-making, the executives would compare the expected utility of each of the options presented to them.

The data and expected costs for the company are summarized in Table 1. Clearly, under a profit maximizing assumption, the executives would opt for the second strategy – a lower and cheaper level of security. It is not worth it for the company to invest more in security. Therefore, upon applying a cost-benefit analysis, the executives would choose the option that maximizes the company's bottom line.

This is where the externalities problem arises. The executives only took into account the expected loss to their company. They disregarded the interdependencies that exist between their company and other critical infrastructures – that a security breach in their information systems would spill over to other critical infrastructures and negatively influence their operations, inflicting losses on them. These additional losses did not factor in the cost-benefit analysis.

This conclusion is further strengthened by Kunreuther and Heal [10], who show that in an interdependent security problem where one compromised agent can contaminate others, investment in security can never be a dominant strategy if its cost is positive. The lack of incentive to consider the influence on other interdependent stakeholders underlines the need for government intervention.

The problem of negative externalities is not unique to CIIP; it also applies to the broader discipline of cyber security. When one decides not to install security software on one's computer, one puts one's own computer at risk as well as numerous other computers, because an unsecured computer could be used as a "zombie" in DDoS attacks. Externalities are, therefore, a problem inherent to CIIP and to cyber security in general. This supports the need for government intervention.

5. Information Deficits and CIIP

One of the basic assumptions underlying competitive markets is the availability of full or perfect information, or, at least, the availability of information required to make choices between alternatives. Therefore, the third justification for government intervention in a market is the presence of imperfect or asymmetric information [13].

A simple example involving imperfect information is the used automobiles market, where sellers usually possess superior information regarding their cars than potential buyers. Information deficiencies can cause a market failure. In the used automobiles market, they may lead to an adverse selection effect – the crowding out of high-quality car sellers by sellers of low-quality cars (lemons). The result is a "market of lemons" – a market comprised solely of low-quality cars [1]. Akerlof [1] discussed several possible solutions to the problem of information asymmetry, all of which are based on the private market. However, in some circumstances, there is a need for government intervention to correct a failure and induce more efficient exchange.

The application of informational problems to CIIP (and cyber security) is somewhat counterintuitive, mainly due to the reduction in information costs in the Internet era [9]. However, the reduction in information costs is not pertinent in the context of cyber security and, more precisely, to the market for CIIP. One of the most important elements of cyber security and CIIP is information flow between all stakeholders: owners of critical infrastructure assets, state agencies, and other entities (e.g., US-CERT) who share information about flaws, threats and vulnerabilities.

The informational problem in the market for CIIP is that private owners of critical infrastructure assets are reluctant to share important security information with other owners and with the government. Thus, information is not shared optimally by all the stakeholders.

There are a number of reasons for the reluctance of stakeholders to share information with their counterparts. On the horizontal axis (i.e., among critical infrastructure owners), companies are reluctant to share information that may constitute valuable intellectual property. Also, there is a concern that released information could be manipulatively exploited by competitors (e.g., a competitor could pass certain information to the media to damage the company's reputation).

Consider a scenario involving the CISO of an American bank who discovers that a security breach in the bank's information systems has resulted in the theft of data about millions of customers. The breach was due to a security flaw in software used by almost every American bank. The "right" thing to do on the part of the bank is to report the incident (including the vulnerability that enabled the breach) to other bank CISOs and to the regulator. All the other banks could then fix the flaw and, thus, enhance the security of their computer systems. However, the benefit to the other banks entails a potential additional loss to the first bank. The other banks could pass information about the breach to the public, severely damaging the reputation of the reporting bank, leading to loss of clients and, ultimately, loss of business [17]. Clearly, the fear of losing its reputation would play an important role in the affected bank's decision about sharing the information.

On the vertical axis (i.e., between critical infrastructure owners and the government), information sharing is also flawed. The private sector is hesitant to share information with the government for several reasons. First, companies fear that information disclosed to the government will find its way to the public or, even worse, to competitors because of freedom of information laws. Some countries, including the United States and Canada, permit special exemptions to these laws for information regarding critical infrastructures that is shared with the government, but the problem of trust has not been resolved. Second, any leaks of this information could result in civil suits against companies for negligence. Third, companies fear that sharing information with the government could result in increased regulation. In particular, disclosures may induce the government to set security standards and regulations that could prove rather costly [4].

Similarly, the government should provide the private sector with valuable information (usually intelligence information) concerning cyber security. However, the government's inclination to maintain secrecy by classifying information, and to share information on a very narrow, need-to-know basis do not allow for efficient sharing [8]. Analogous to the incentives underlying information sharing between industry actors, security agencies tend to believe "that the risks associated with disclosure are greater than the potential benefits of wider information sharing" [8]. In economic terms, it seems that the government feels that the marginal costs of releasing the information are higher than the marginal benefits. This means that the optimal amount of information regarding the cyber security of critical infrastructures is not generated.

The reluctance to share information is quite costly. As Aviram and Tor [3] argue, sub-optimal information sharing can inflict social costs, especially in network industries, due to the fact that information sharing is crucial for compatibility, which in turn is a key component for producing positive network effects. The inability or reluctance of critical infrastructure owners to share information about vulnerabilities with other owners, along with the harsh consequences of attacks that exploit these vulnerabilities, produce immense social costs.

Indeed, the issue of information sharing on both the horizontal and vertical axes is not a clear case of information asymmetry, but rather a case of information deficit. There is not enough information available to all the stakeholders to enable them to make optimal choices on the basis of the information. This hampers the decision-making processes of the various actors, and leads to inefficiencies in the provision of CIIP. Consequently, there may be a case for government intervention.

6. Conclusions

The market for CIIP and, to a certain extent, the broader market of cyber security appear to be susceptible to a number of market failures, namely public goods, externalities and information deficits. The economic analysis presented is rather straightforward, but it sheds light on why the "hands off" approach taken by certain governments in their policy toward CIIP has been largely ineffective in reducing the vulnerability of CIIs to attack.

Some market failures are remediable through voluntary, private action. But as we have seen, private action is sometimes ineffective. The presence of three market failures in the market for CIIP suggests that government intervention in the market is necessary. There are instances when government intervention could be limited in scope (e.g., when the regulatory instruments employed are more compatible with the market system). In other instances, collective action is required, and stronger regulatory intervention is warranted and is in the public interest. This paper has not presented a specific model, or a set of tools, for regulatory action. However, understanding the market failures inherent in the protection of CIIs is a key element in designing a successful regulatory policy. Failure to understand and acknowledge the reasons for the inability of the private sector to provide adequate protection affects a nation-state's security and renders it vulnerable to attack.

One point should be stressed. When advocating a new governing arrangement, arguing for regulation based on public goods, externalities or information deficits alone is insufficient as the regulatory tools used to remedy one market failure may not work on the other failures. Therefore, all three justifications for government regulation should be acknowledged, and integrated regulatory tools should be designed and put in place.

References

[1] G. Akerlof, The market for "lemons:" Quality, uncertainty and the market mechanism, *The Quarterly Journal of Economics*, vol. 84(3), pp. 488–500, 1970.

[2] P. Auerswald, L. Branscomb, T. La Porte and E. Michel-Kerian (Eds.), *Seeds of Disaster, Roots of Response: How Private Action Can Reduce Public Vulnerability*, Cambridge University Press, New York, 2006.

[3] A. Aviram and A. Tor, Overcoming impediments to information sharing, *Alabama Law Review*, vol. 55(2), p. 231, 2004.

[4] L. Branscomb and E. Michel-Kerjan, Public-private collaboration on a national and international scale, in *Seeds of Disaster, Roots of Response: How Private Action Can Reduce Public Vulnerability*, P. Auerswald, L. Branscomb, T. La Porte and E. Michel-Kerjan (Eds.), Cambridge University Press, New York, pp. 395–403, 2006.

[5] L. Camp and C. Wolfram, Pricing security, in *Economics of Information Security*, L. Camp and S. Lewis (Eds.), Kluwer, Boston, Massachusetts, pp. 17–34, 2004.

[6] R. Coase, The problem of social cost, *Journal of Law and Economics*, vol. 3, pp. 1–44, 1960.

[7] C. Coyne and P. Leeson, Who protects cyberspace? *Journal of Law, Economics and Policy*, vol. 1(2), pp. 473–495, 2006.

[8] B. Crowell, Too many secrets: Overclassification as a barrier to critical information sharing, Testimony to the Markle Taskforce on National Security in the Information Age, Subcommittee on National Security, Emerging Threats and International Relations, House Committee on Government Reform, U.S. House of Representatives, Washington, DC (www.fas.org/sgp/congress/2004/082404crowell.html), August 24, 2004.

[9] N. Elkin-Koren and E. Salzberger, *Law, Economics and Cyberspace*, Edward Elgar, Cheltenham, United Kingdom, 2004.

[10] H. Kunreuther and G. Heal, Interdependent security, *Journal of Risk and Uncertainty*, vol. 26(2/3), pp. 231–249, 2003.

[11] R. Mandel, *The Changing Face of National Security: A Conceptual Analysis*, Greenwood Press, Westport, Connecticut, 1994.

[12] P. McNutt, Public goods and club goods, in *Encyclopedia of Law and Economics, Volume I – The History and Methodology of Law and Economics*, B. Bouckaert and G. de Geest (Eds.), Edward Elgar, Cheltenham, United Kingdom, pp. 927–951, 2000.

[13] A. Ogus, *Regulation: Legal Form and Economic Theory*, Clarendon Press, London, United Kingdom, 1994.

[14] B. Powell, Is cyber security a public good? Evidence from the financial services industry, *Journal of Law, Economics and Policy*, vol. 1(2), pp. 497–510, 2005.

[15] S. Rinaldi, J. Peerenboom and T. Kelly, Identifying, understanding and analyzing critical infrastructure interdependencies, *IEEE Control Systems*, vol. 21(6), pp. 11–25, 2001.

[16] P. Samuelson, The pure theory of public expenditure, *The Review of Economics and Statistics*, vol. 36(4), pp. 387–389, 1954.

[17] B. Schneier, *Secrets and Lies: Digital Security in a Networked World*, John Wiley, New York, 2000.

[18] A. Smith, *The Wealth of Nations*, Bantam Classics, New York, 2003.

[19] M. Trebilcock and E. Iacobucci, Privatization and accountability, *Harvard Law Review*, vol. 116(5), pp. 1422–1453, 2003.

[20] U.S.-Canada Power System Outage Task Force, Final Report on the August 14, 2003 Blackout in the United States and Canada: Causes and Recommendations, U.S. Department of Energy, Washington, DC (reports.energy.gov/BlackoutFinal-Web.pdf), 2004.

II

INFRASTRUCTURE SECURITY

Chapter 4

SECURITY OF INFORMATION FLOW IN THE ELECTRIC POWER GRID

Han Tang and Bruce McMillin

Abstract The confidentiality of information in a system can be breached through unrestricted information flow. The formal properties of non-deducibility and non-inference are often used to assess information flow in purely cyber environments. However, in a "cyber-physical system" (CPS), i.e., a system with significant cyber and physical components, physical actions may allow confidential information to be deduced or inferred. This paper conducts an information flow analysis of a CPS using formal models of confidentiality. The specific CPS under study is the advanced electric power grid using cooperating flexible alternating current transmission system (FACTS) devices. FACTS devices exchange confidential information and use the information to produce physical actions on the electric power grid. This paper shows that even if the information flow satisfies certain security models, confidential information may still be deduced by observation or inference of a CPS at its cyber-physical boundary. The result is important because it helps assess the confidentiality of CPSs.

Keywords: Cyber-physical systems, power grid, information flow, confidentiality

1. Introduction

Major critical infrastructures such as the electric power grid, oil and gas pipelines, and transportation systems are cyber-physical systems (systems with significant cyber and physical assets) [5]. These infrastructures incorporate large-scale distributed control systems and multiple security domains. This paper focuses on the security analysis of the cooperating FACTS power system (CFPS), which is a representative cyber-physical system (CPS).

The CFPS consists of the electric power grid (generators, loads and transmission lines) and several flexible alternating current transmission system (FACTS) devices. These FACTS devices are power electronic flow control devices that stabilize and regulate power flow. Coordinated under distributed control, they

Tang, H. and McMillin, B., 2008, in IFIP International Federation for Information Processing, Volume 253, Critical Infrastructure Protection, eds. E. Goetz and S. Shenoi; (Boston: Springer), pp. 43–56.

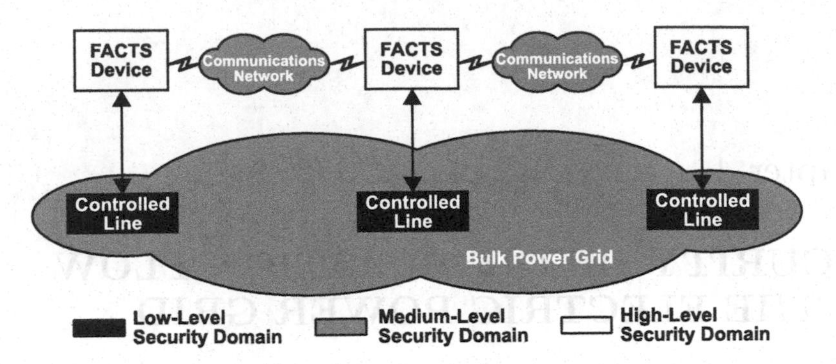

Figure 1. Cooperative FACTS power system (CFPS) network.

can be used to mitigate cascading failures such as those that occurred during the 2003 United States blackout (when a few critical lines downed due to natural causes resulted in cascading failures in the power grid).

Security is of paramount concern within a CFPS as malicious actions can cause improper operation leading to exactly the types of failures that the CFPS is designed to prevent. Confidentiality, integrity and availability are vital concerns in a CFPS. Much work has been done on ensuring integrity and availability, but relatively little on guaranteeing confidentiality. Information about the state of the power grid can divulge the locations of critical lines; a malicious action on one or more of these transmission lines can cause a cascading failure [3]. Thus, preventing the disclosure of information related to the state of the system is critical to reducing the vulnerability of the power grid.

This paper focuses on the confidentiality of CFPS information and its dependence on physical actions by FACTS devices. In particular, it analyzes the flow of information between CFPS components using several prominent security models [6–9, 14].

2. Background

Figure 1 presents a CFPS network with FACTS devices that cooperate by passing messages over a communications network. Each FACTS device controls the power flow on one line (controlled line) that is part of the bulk power grid. In this work we assume that the communications network is secure and that FACTS devices are secured using physical controls.

2.1 FACTS Devices and CFPS

FACTS devices are power-electronic-based controllers that can rapidly inject or absorb active and reactive power, thereby affecting power flow in transmission lines. A FACTS device (Figure 2) consists of an embedded computer that relies on a low voltage control system for signal processing. The embedded computer, which depends on low and high voltage power conversion systems for rapidly switching power into the power line, incorporates two software com-

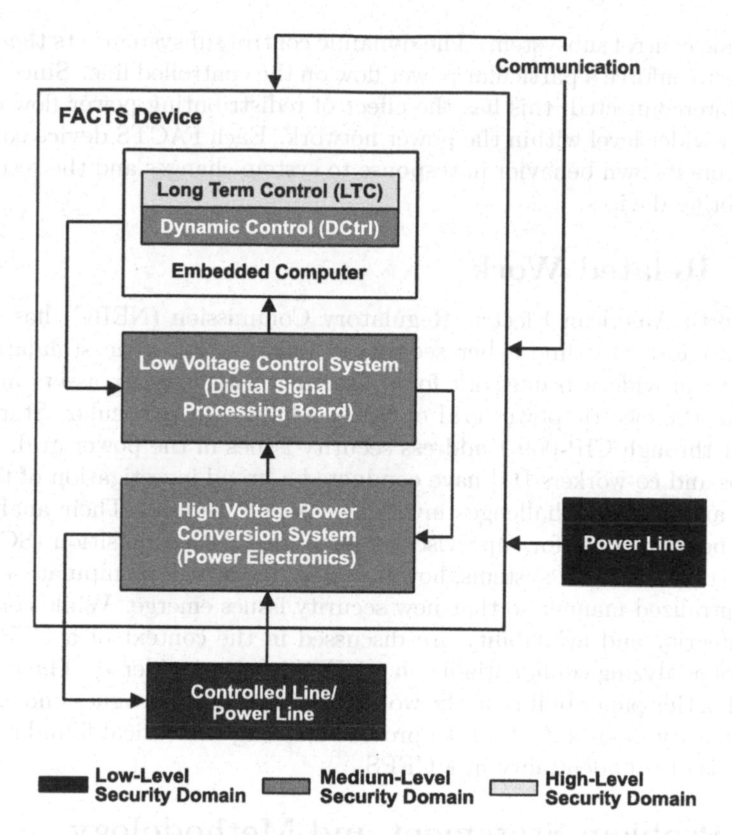

Figure 2. FACTS device.

ponents, the long term control (LTC) and the dynamic control (DCtrl) subsystems.

A FACTS device changes the amount of power flowing in a particular power line (controlled line). A unified power flow controller (UPFC) device [4, 11] is a FACTS device that can modify the active flow of power in a line. The FACTS devices considered in this paper are UPFC devices.

Coordination of multiple FACTS devices is crucial. When transmission lines are down (due to a naturally-occurring fault or a malicious attack), the remaining power flow overstresses the power grid. In such a situation, too much power may flow over lines of insufficient capacity. This causes the lines to overload and trip in a domino effect, resulting in a large-scale power outage [3]. The FACTS devices, in coordination, can stop this domino effect by rebalancing power flow in the grid by modifying the flow in a few key transmission lines [1].

FACTS devices operate autonomously, but they depend on information received from their participation in a CFPS to determine their response. The CFPS uses a distributed max-flow algorithm [1] for the LTC subsystem to rebalance power flow. The LTC runs on embedded computers located in different FACTS devices to compute a FACTS device setting that is communicated to the dynamic control subsystem. The dynamic control subsystem sets the power electronics to enforce a particular power flow on the controlled line. Since power lines are interconnected, this has the effect of redistributing power flow over a regional or wider level within the power network. Each FACTS device continually monitors its own behavior in response to system changes and the responses of neighboring devices.

2.2 Related Work

The North American Electric Regulatory Commission (NERC) has spearheaded an effort to define cyber security standards [10]. The standards are intended to provide a framework for protecting critical cyber assets and ensuring that the electric power grid operates reliably. In particular, Standards CIP-002-1 through CIP-009-1 address security issues in the power grid.

Phillips and co-workers [11] have conducted a broad investigation of the operational and security challenges involving FACTS devices. Their analysis is based on best practices for supervisory control and data acquisition (SCADA) systems. Unlike SCADA systems, however, FACTS devices manipulate a CFPS in a decentralized manner so that new security issues emerge. While confidentiality, integrity and availability are discussed in the context of a CFPS, the problem of analyzing confidentiality in a CFPS is not considered. The research described in this paper builds on the work of Phillips and colleagues and engages various security models [6–9, 14] to provide a strong theoretical foundation for the analysis of confidentiality in a CFPS.

3. Problem Statement and Methodology

While the information flow between FACTS devices is secure, the confidentiality of information can still be compromised at the cyber-physical boundary by observing controlled lines in the bulk power grid. At some point, the settings of FACTS devices are exposed to the local power network via the actions of FACTS devices on physical power lines (controlled lines). This situation is not unique to a CFPS. Many critical infrastructure systems have similar elements: intelligent controllers that communicate with other controllers and make decisions using a distributed algorithm. The CFPS examined in this work is a model system, and the results developed here should be applicable to a wide range of cyber-physical systems.

3.1 Problem Statement

Decisions in a CFPS are made cooperatively. The analysis in [11] indicates that FACTS device settings and control operations are treated as confidential information. The results of the analysis are summarized in Table 1.

A CFPS has three security levels (Table 2). In the high-level security domain, a computer network is employed by the LTC for communications. In the medium-level security domain, the dynamic control and power electronics

Table 1. Confidential information in a CFPS (adapted from [11]).

Data	Type	Source	Function
Dynamic Control Feedback	Digital	Dynamic Control	Obtain and pass computed setpoint changes to prevent oscillations
Data Exchange with FACTS Neighbors	Analog and Digital (Ethernet)	Neighbor FACTS	Data needed to implement the distributed max-flow algorithm

Control	Type	Source	Function
Control Exchange with FACTS Neighbors	Digital (Ethernet)	Neighbor FACTS	Information needed for cooperative agreement on FACTS changes

Table 2. Security levels in a CFPS.

Security Level	Security Entities	Reasons
High-Level	Long Term Control, Parameters of the Entire CFPS	Contains critical information for the distributed control algorithm and computed settings with a global view of the power grid
Medium-Level	Dynamic Control, DSP Board, Power Electronics	Contains settings received from high-level entities and generates local settings according to local control algorithms
Low-Level	Controlled Line, Local Power Network	Open access to some power lines or information about a part of the power grid can be obtained

subsystems have implicit communications with other FACTS devices. In the low-level security domain, power line settings create implicit communications in the power network. Implicit communications occur when the power setting of a controlled line is changed and the power flow in the system is redistributed correspondingly. A confidentiality breach occurs when an observer in the low-level security domain can observe or deduce information in a higher-level security domain.

The following assumptions are adopted in our work:

- **Assumption 1:** Messages sent by the LTC subsystem are legitimate and correct. Note that LTC security is outside the scope of this paper.

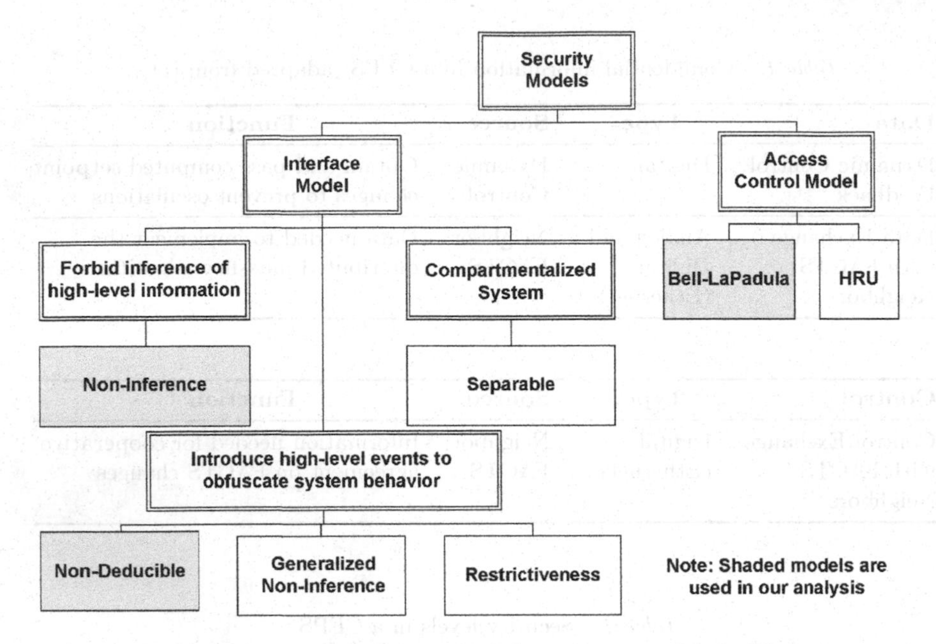

Figure 3. Partial taxonomy of the security models in [8].

- **Assumption 2:** The communications network used by the LTC subsystems to exchange max-flow algorithm messages is secure. In other words, communications between LTCs is secure.

- **Assumption 3:** The power flow information of the entire power network is secure, although some power lines can be measured and local topologies are observable.

Assumptions 1 and 2 define the scope of the problem addressed in this paper, which is to investigate the security of information flow in a CFPS. Assumption 3 provides the basis for our analysis, which is to determine the information that can be obtained through observation.

3.2 Methodology

The inference of confidential information from observable information flow raises serious security issues. Consequently, the information flow in a CFPS needs to be carefully analyzed.

Several security models have been proposed for analyzing the behavior of multi-level security systems from the access control or execution sequence perspectives [6–9, 14]. Figure 3 presents a taxonomy of security models. The models in the shaded boxes are considered in our work.

- **Non-Inference Model:** A system is considered secure if and only if for any legal trace of system events, the trace resulting from a legal trace that is purged of all high-level events is still a legal trace [8].

- **Non-Deducible Model:** A system is considered secure if it is impossible for a low-level user who observes visible events to deduce anything about the sequence of inputs made by a high-level user. In other words, a system is non-deducible if a low-level observation is not consistent with any of the high-level inputs [6, 8]. The term "consistent" means that low-level outputs could result from a high-level input.
- **Bell-LaPadula Model:** This access control model [2] specifies security rules that can be enforced during execution. All entities are either subjects or objects. Subjects are active entities and objects are passive containers of information. The model specifies the following rules for untrusted subjects:
  - Subjects may only read from objects with lower or equal security levels.
  - Subjects may only write to objects with greater or equal security levels.

A CFPS conforms with this multi-level security structure. The non-inference model applies to a CFPS because no low-level input results in high-level outputs. Similarly, the non-deducible model applies because high-level outputs are observable. If a system [6] is non-deducible, then a low-level user of the system will not learn any high-level information through the system. The Bell-LaPadula model is used to illustrate how breaches of confidentiality can occur using a perspective that is different from that employed by the two inference-based models.

4. CFPS Analysis

Security models can be used to identify where a CFPS may divulge information to a lower-level security domain. In our approach, information flow is first analyzed at the component level. Next, the components are combined to build a UPFC device, and information flow at the UPFC device level is analyzed to assess the security of the system.

4.1 Information Flow in UPFC Components

The principal components of a UPFC device include the LTC, dynamic control, digital signal processing (DSP) and power electronics subsystems (Figure 2). The information flow in a UPFC device is shown in Figure 4, where each component is considered to be a security entity. Figure 5 illustrates the information flow in the principal UPFC components using the pictorial notation for traces introduced in [6]. In the figure, the horizontal vectors represent system inputs and outputs. The broken lines and solid lines represent higher-level and lower-level events, respectively.

We now prove three lemmas regarding the components of a UPFC device. These lemmas are used to prove theorems about non-inference and other security properties of the composed system.

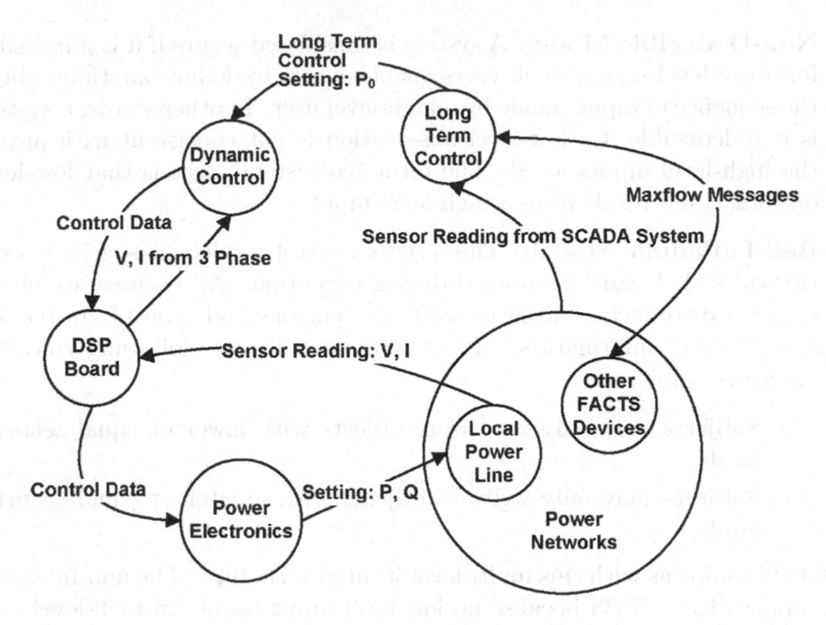

Figure 4. Information flow in a UPFC device.

Lemma 1: The DSP operation is non-inference secure.
Proof: As shown in Figure 5(a), the DSP board is a non-deterministic system, which is built up from traces of the form: $\{\{\}, e_1, e_3, e_4, e_1e_2, e_1e_3, e_1e_4, e_3e_4, e_1e_2e_3, e_1e_2e_4, e_1e_3e_4, e_1e_2e_3e_4, \ldots\}$, where e_1 is a low-level input (LI) event, e_2 is a high-level output (HO) event, e_3 is a high-level input (HI) event and e_4 is an HO event. Note that ... denotes interleavings of listed traces in the system. This system satisfies the definition of non-inference [8, 14] because by purging any legal trace of events not in the low-level security domain, the result is either e_1 or $\{\}$, which are both legal traces of the system. Thus, the DSP board itself is non-inference secure as information flow from the high-level security domain does not interfere with the low-level security domain.

Lemma 2: The dynamic control operation is non-inference secure.
Proof: The dynamic control subsystem is a non-deterministic system (see Figure 5(b)), which contains traces of the form: $\{\{\}, e_1, e_2, e_1e_3, e_1e_2, e_2e_3, e_1e_2e_3, \ldots\}$, where e_1 is an LI event, e_2 is an HI event and e_3 is an HO event. When a legal trace is projected to the low-level security domain or events that are not in the low-level security domain are purged, the result is either e_1 or $\{\}$, which are also legal traces. Therefore, the dynamic control subsystem satisfies the non-inference security model.

The LTC subsystem (see Figure 5(c)) is a non-deterministic system with only high-level events. It is obvious that there is no interference between the high-level security domain and the low-level security domain for the LTC. In other words, there is no information flow out of the high-level security domain.

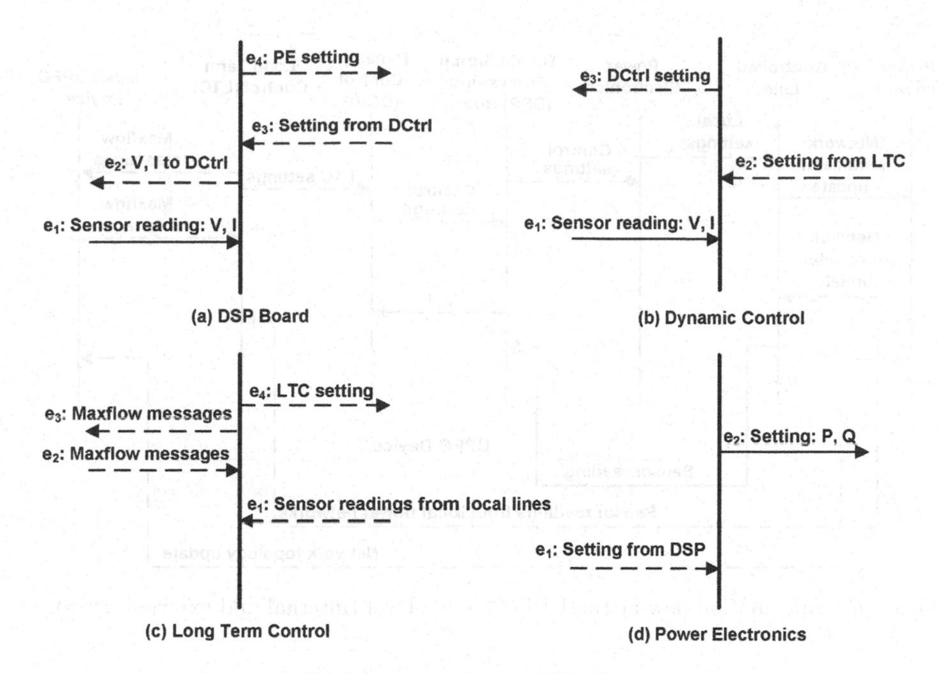

Figure 5. Information flow in UPFC components.

Lemma 3: The power electronics operation is not non-inference secure.
Proof: The power electronics system (see Figure 5(d)) contains the traces: $\{\{\}, e_1, e_1e_2, \ldots\}$. When any legal trace is projected to the low-level security domain, the result is either e_2 or $\{\}$, where e_2 is not a legal trace. Thus, the power electronics system is not non-inference secure. In this system, e_1 (HI) infers e_2 (LO), which means if e_2 occurs, e_1 must occur before e_2.

As a result of the causal relationship between e_1 and e_2, high-level information is downgraded and passed to the low-level security domain. The power electronics system is also not secure from the perspective of the Bell-LaPadula model [2] because high-level information is written to the low-level domain.

4.2 Information Flow in Composed Devices

This section analyzes information flow in a composed UPFC device. After the individual UPFC components are composed, information flows at the UPFC device level are either internal and external flows (Figure 6) or external flows only (Figure 7).

Theorem 1: The composition of the DSP, dynamic control, LTC and power electronics subsystems in a UPFC device is non-inference secure based on external events only.
Proof: From Lemmas 1 and 2, the DSP and dynamic control subsystems are non-inference secure. Connecting DSP and dynamic control subsystems to an

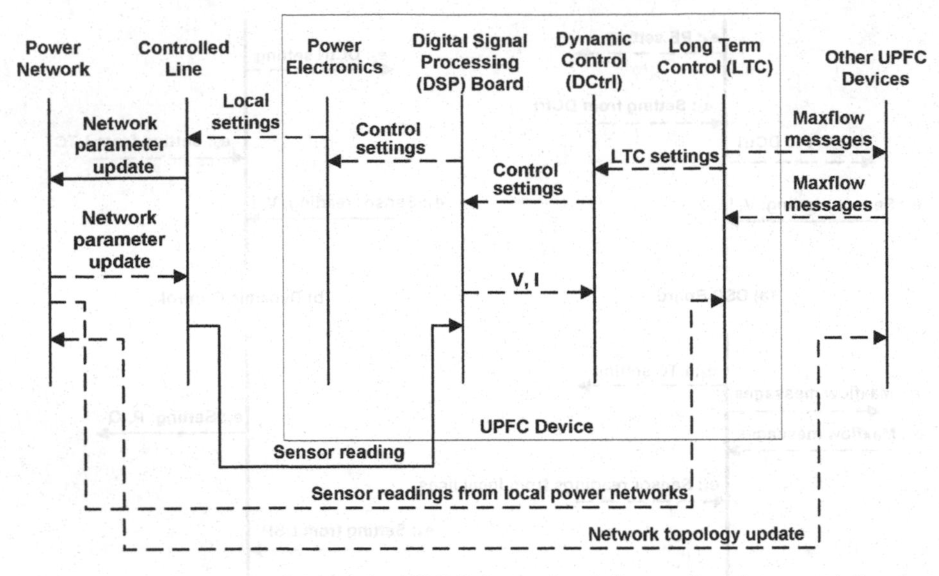

Figure 6. Information flow at the UPFC device level (internal and external flows).

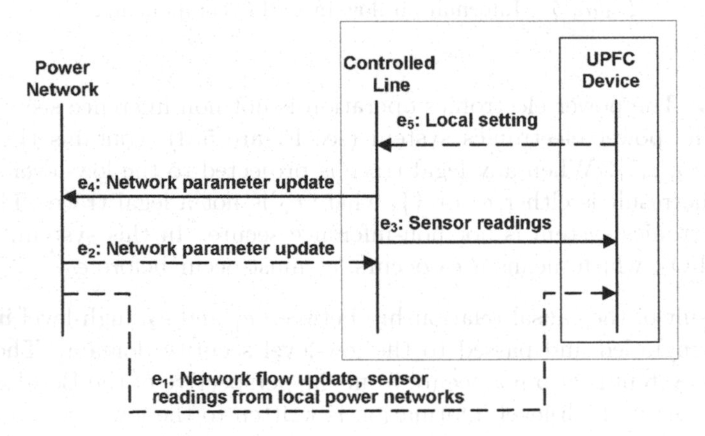

Figure 7. Information flow at the UPFC device level (external flow only).

LTC preserves the non-inference property. Upon examining Figure 7, we see that a UPFC device (considering only its external events) is a non-deterministic system containing the traces: $\{\{\}, e_1, e_3, e_5, e_1e_3, e_1e_5, e_3e_5, e_1e_3e_5, \ldots\}$. (Note that the composed system's boundary is at the UPFC device as shown in Figure 7.) The projection of these external event traces for a UPFC to the low-level domain is either $\{\}$ or e_3, which are both legal traces. This means that a UPFC device, considering only external events, is a non-inference secure system. Because a UPFC device is non-inference secure, an attacker cannot infer higher-level behavior simply by observing low-level events.

The non-inference property proved in Theorem 1 holds for a UPFC device itself but not when a controlled line is linked to a UPFC device. Since a UPFC device has physical protection as stipulated by Standard CIP-006-1 [10], the system boundary is forced to stop at the controlled line.

Theorem 2: The system consisting of a UPFC device connected to a controlled line is non-deducible secure.
Proof: Upon examining the events in the controlled line in Figure 6, we see that the system contains the traces: $\{\{\}, e_1e_4, e_2e_4, e_1e_2e_4, \ldots\}$, where e_4 is an LO event, and e_1 and e_2 are HI events. This system is not non-inference secure because the projection of a legal trace to the low-level domain ($\{e_4\}$) is not a legal trace. However, a system with a boundary at the controlled line is non-deducible secure [6, 8, 14] because every high-level input (either e_1 or e_2 or both) is compatible with the low-level output (e_4).

As shown in Figure 6, changes to a controlled line can be affected by: (i) local settings of the dynamic control subsystem, or (ii) other LTC settings that propagate through the power network, or (iii) topology changes of power lines (e.g., line trips), which trigger the redistribution of power flow in the system. Therefore, it is not possible to determine the source of the information only by observing events interfering with a controlled line.

The fact that a UPFC device (with a boundary at the controlled line) satisfies the non-deducible property is a very favorable result. Even when a UPFC device is constructed from components that are not secure (e.g., a power electronics device according to Lemma 3), the UPFC is still secure based on external information flow. In a real system, however, the controlled line is observable, and this introduces a new vulnerability.

4.3 Observation of Controlled Lines

Given the results of the previous section, the question is whether or not a UPFC device is really secure considering other types of inference. For example, can the UPFC settings be deduced by measuring the power flow in or out of the device? This is an important issue because many electric power network components are exposed and, therefore, can be physically accessed by an attacker. Consider a passive attack involving the use of meters to measure line voltages and current parameters. In such a situation, it is important to determine if the measured data could be used to compute control device settings in the bulk power grid, which could then be used to infer information about control operations. We use the computation model in Figure 8 to show that a passive attack using meters attached to a controlled line can be used to compute UPFC device settings.

Theorem 3: UPFC settings can be deduced by computation along with low-level observations.
Proof: In Figure 8, if two measurements of the three-phase instantaneous voltage and current information are taken at both sides of a UPFC device ($V_t\angle\theta_t$

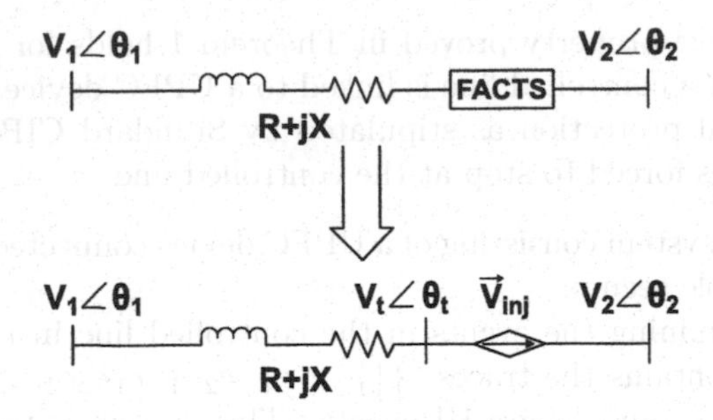

Figure 8. Computational model of a controlled line and FACTS devices.

and $V_2\angle\theta_2$) using Kirchhoff's law, the injected voltage V_{inj} can be computed. Since V_{inj} is known, the UPFC settings can be computed from the dynamic control subsystem. This means the local settings of the UPFC can be observed and high-level information is compromised despite the fact that the system satisfies the security properties related to information flow described in the previous sections.

5. Results

The analysis in Section 4 shows that the principal components of a UPFC device (DSP board, LTC and dynamic control subsystems) individually satisfy the non-inference property (Lemmas 1 and 2). However, according to Lemma 3, the power electronics subsystem permits the flow of information from a higher level to a lower level, which violates confidentiality from the perspective of the interface models. The power electronics subsystem also does not satisfy the "no write down" rule of the Bell-LaPadula model; therefore, the power electronics subsystem is not secure from the access control perspective as well.

The analysis also shows that, in terms of UPFC control operations, information flow is non-inference secure at the boundary of a UPFC device (Theorem 1) and non-deducible secure at the boundary of the controlled line considering only external events of a UPFC device (Theorem 2). This means a low-level observer can neither infer nor deduce any high-level or medium-level control messages by only observing the controlled line. Also, when a component that is not secure (e.g., power electronics subsystem) is composed with secure components (DSP board, LTC and dynamic control subsystems), the addition of other information flows yields a secure system. The events introduced by other secure components or by other systems that have the same or higher security levels obfuscate the system's behavior so that no high-level information can be inferred by observing only low-level information. In a CFPS, this obfuscation arises from the inherent physical characteristics of the power grid. In another words, a malicious attacker attempting to observe the changes to a controlled line cannot infer if the changes are caused by a new setting from the connected UPFC device or by neighboring UPFC devices or by the dynamics of the power network. However, Theorem 3 shows that UPFC settings could nevertheless be deduced using mathematical computations along with low-level observations of the electric power grid.

6. Conclusions

The analysis of information flow in a CFPS from the component level to the UPFC device level verifies that UPFC control operations cannot be inferred by observing low-level CFPS behavior. However, UPFC settings can be deduced using mathematical computations along with low-level observations of a CFPS.

A CFPS with UPFC devices is a typical advanced distributed control system where the computations of the control devices are assumed to be protected. However, the actions of these devices on observable physical systems inherently expose their behavior at the lowest security level. This is a significant issue that should be considered when designing modern distributed control systems used in critical infrastructure components such as the power grid, oil and gas pipelines, vehicular transportation and air traffic control systems.

Our analysis of information flow assumes a non-deterministic system and ignores temporal considerations. However, timing issues such as those involved in interactions between the dynamic control and LTC subsystems can affect the information flow analysis. Although some research has been undertaken in this area (see. e.g., [13]), much more work needs to be done to analyze information flow in a CFPS based on temporal constraints.

Acknowledgements

This research was supported in part by the National Science Foundation under Grants CNS–0420869 and CCF–0614633, and by the Intelligent Systems Center at the University of Missouri at Rolla.

References

[1] A. Armbruster, M. Gosnell, B. McMillin and M. Crow, Power transmission control using distributed max-flow, *Proceedings of the Twenty-Ninth International Conference on Computer Software and Applications*, vol. 1, pp. 256–263, 2005.

[2] D. Bell and L. LaPadula, Secure Computer Systems: Mathematical Foundations, MITRE Technical Report 2547, Volume I, The MITRE Corporation, Bedford, Massachusetts, 1973.

[3] B. Chowdhury and S. Baravc, Creating cascading failure scenarios in interconnected power systems, *Proceedings of the IEEE Power Engineering Society General Meeting*, 2006.

[4] M. Crow, B. McMillin and S. Atcitty, An approach to improving the physical and cyber security of a bulk power system with FACTS, *Proceedings of the Electrical Energy Storage Applications and Technologies Conference*, 2005.

[5] E. Lee, Cyber-physical systems: Are computing foundations adequate? presented at the *NSF Workshop on Cyber-Physical Systems: Research Motivation, Techniques and Roadmap*, 2006.

[6] D. McCullough, Hookup theorem for multilevel security, *IEEE Transactions on Software Engineering*, vol. 16(6), pp. 563–568, 1990.

[7] J. McLean, Security models and information flow, *Proceedings of the IEEE Symposium on Security and Privacy*, pp. 180–189, 1990.

[8] J. McLean, Security models, in *Encyclopedia of Software Engineering*, J. Marciniak (Ed.), John Wiley, New York, pp. 1136–1144, 1994.

[9] J. McLean, A general theory of composition for a class of "possibilistic" properties, *IEEE Transactions on Software Engineering*, vol. 22(1), pp. 53–67, 1996.

[10] North American Electric Reliability Corporation, Reliability standards (Standard CIP-002-1 through Standard CIP-009-1), Princeton, New Jersey (www.nerc.com/~filez/standards/Reliability_Standards.html#Critical_Infrastructure_Protection), 2007.

[11] L. Phillips, M. Baca, J. Hills, J. Margulies, B. Tejani, B. Richardson and L. Weiland, Analysis of Operations and Cyber Security Policies for a System of Cooperating Flexible Alternating Current Transmission System (FACTS) Devices, Technical Report SAND2005-730, Sandia National Laboratories, Albuquerque, New Mexico, 2005.

[12] M. Ryan, S. Markose, X. Liu, B. McMillin and Y. Cheng, Structured object-oriented co-analysis/co-design of hardware/software for the FACTS power system, *Proceedings of the Twenty-Ninth International Conference on Computer Software and Applications*, vol. 2, pp. 396–402, 2005.

[13] Y. Sun, X. Liu and B. McMillin, A methodology for structured object-oriented elicitation and analysis of temporal constraints in hardware/software co-analysis and co-design of real-time systems, *Proceedings of the Thirtieth International Conference on Computer Software and Applications*, pp. 281-290, 2006.

[14] A. Zakinthinos and E. Lee, A general theory of security properties, *Proceedings of the IEEE Symposium on Security and Privacy*, pp. 94–102, 1997.

Chapter 5

SECURING POSITIVE TRAIN CONTROL SYSTEMS

Mark Hartong, Rajni Goel and Duminda Wijesekera

Abstract Positive train control (PTC) systems are distributed interoperable systems that control the movement of passenger and freight trains, providing significant safety enhancements over traditional methods of operating railroads. Due to their reliance on wireless communications, PTC systems are vulnerable to attacks that can compromise safety and potentially cause serious accidents. Designing PTC systems that can mitigate the negative effects of wireless-based exploits are mandatory to ensuring railroad safety. This paper employs use cases and misuse cases to analyze the effects of exploiting vulnerabilities in PTC systems. Use cases specify operational interactions and requirements, while misuse cases specify potential misuse or abuse scenarios. A distributed trust management system is proposed to enable PTC use cases and eliminate identified misuse cases.

Keywords: Railroad security, positive train control, use cases, misuse cases

1. Introduction

Railroads are a critical component of the U.S. transportation and distribution system. The rail infrastructure consists of approximately 141,000 miles of track used by 549 freight railroads to move 25% of all intercity freight by tonnage and 41% of all freight by ton-miles [2, 34].

Positive train control (PTC) systems are used to control the movement of passenger and freight trains, providing significant safety enhancements over traditional methods of operating railroads. Less than 5% of route-miles in the U.S. [3] currently use PTC systems for positive train separation, speed enforcement and roadway worker protection. However, the implementation of PTC systems in the railroad infrastructure is expected to increase over the next decade.

PTC systems use wireless networks to distribute train position data, signals and switch position monitor data, and movement authorities generated by a

Hartong, M., Goel, R. and Wijesekera, D., 2008, in IFIP International Federation for Information Processing, Volume 253, Critical Infrastructure Protection, eds. E. Goetz and S. Shenoi; (Boston: Springer), pp. 57–72.

central office for controlling railroad operations. However, their reliance on wireless networks exposes PTC systems to a slew of attacks that can significantly impact the safety of railroad operations.

This paper employs use cases and misuse cases to analyze the effects of exploiting vulnerabilities in PTC systems. Use cases specify operational interactions and requirements, whereas misuse cases specify potential misuse or abuse scenarios. A distributed trust management system is proposed to enable PTC use cases and eliminate identified misuse cases.

2. Business Context of Railroads

Railroads in the United States are categorized as Class I, Class II or Class III based on their annual revenue. Currently, there are six Class I freight railroads, with the remainder being Class II and Class III railroads.

In 2000, Class I railroads invested 17.8% of their revenues in capital improvements, compared with an average of 3.7% for all manufacturing industries. Between 1991 and 2000, railroad re-investments totaled $54 billion: 67% for roadways and structures, and 33% for equipment. Unfortunately, the total stock market value of railroads is one-fifth of its 1980 value. This has reduced the amount of capital available for improvements and maintenance. The difference between capital expenditures and the amount railroads can invest from their own revenues is about $2 billion annually. As private corporations, it is difficult for railroads to justify spending on new technological initiatives that do not directly support recapitalization requirements.

Domestic policy initiatives do not favor public investment in railroads. In 1998, for example, federal and state expenditures on highway improvements were 33 times greater than the expenditures on passenger rail and freight rail combined. The public sector invested $108 billion in highways, $11 billion in transit, $9 billion in airways and airports, but just $3 billion in railroads [1].

Public sector investment in railroad security is even worse. In 2006, only 2% of all critical infrastructure protection grants from the Department of Homeland Security were designated for railroad security; all of these grants were earmarked for enhancing passenger rail security [9].

3. Consequences of Disrupting Rail Operations

The Congressional Research Service of the Library of Congress [29] and the President's National Security Telecommunications Advisory Committee [26] have identified hacker attacks as a serious threat to wireless networks such as those used in PTC systems. Although no attacks are known to have occurred on the railroad control infrastructure, the General Accountability Office reports that successful attacks have been launched against industrial control systems in other sectors [13].

Disruptions to railway networks can have a significant negative impact on the U.S. economy. Service problems resulting from Union Pacific's inability to position and move their equipment (although not the result of a deliberate

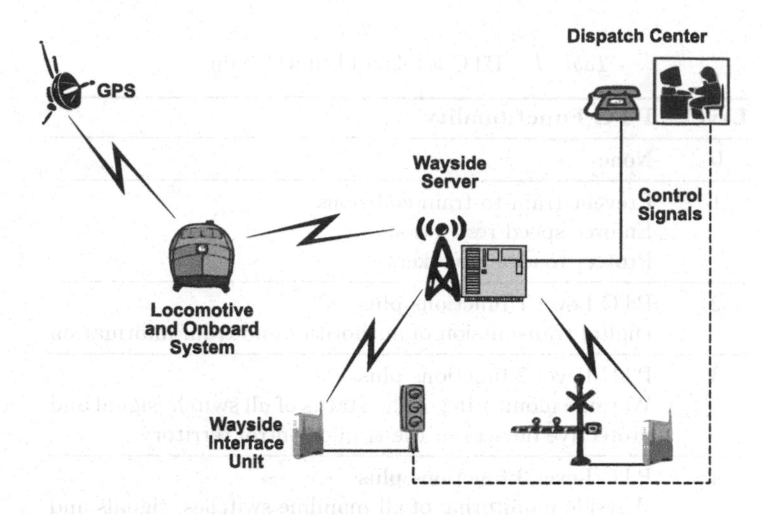

Figure 1. Generic PTC architecture.

attack) resulted in direct costs of $1.093 billion and an additional $643 million in costs to consumers [37]. More recently, commuter and CSX freight rail service on the East Coast experienced cancellations and delays of up to 48 hours because of the accidental introduction of a virus that disabled the computer systems at the CSX headquarters [28].

Vulnerabilities in the rail control infrastructure have been highlighted in several reports (see, e.g., [6, 24]). While these studies were unable to reach conclusions about the threat level and degree of risk, they uniformly emphasize the possibility of serious accidents. For example, a single successful attack on a PTC system can re-position a switch from a mainline to an occupied siding, which would almost certainly result in a collision.

4. PTC Systems

The generic PTC functional architecture (Figure 1) has three major functional subsystems: wayside units, mobile units and a dispatch/control unit. The wayside units include highway grade crossing signals, switches and interlocks; mobile units include locomotives and other equipment that travels on rail along with their onboard controllers; the dispatch/control unit is the central office that runs the railroad. Each major functional subsystem consists of a collection of physical components (information processing equipment and databases) linked via wireless networks.

Table 1 summarizes the five PTC levels and their functionality [10, 11]. Each higher PTC level includes all the functions of the lower levels along with additional functionality. Note that each level maps to multiple security requirements.

The complexity of analyzing security needs increases with the level of PTC functionality. We employ misuse cases to determine potential threat profiles

Table 1. PTC levels and functionality.

Level	PTC Functionality
0	None
1	Prevent train-to-train collisions Enforce speed restrictions Protect roadway workers
2	PTC Level 1 functions plus Digital transmission of authorities and train information
3	PTC Level 2 functions plus Wayside monitoring of the status of all switch, signal and protective devices in the traffic control territory
4	PTC Level 3 functions plus Wayside monitoring of all mainline switches, signals and protective devices Additional protective devices such as slide detectors, high water and bridge interlocks Advanced broken rail detection Roadway worker terminals for dispatcher and train communications

and their effects on railroad safety. Previous work on PTC security has considered possible problems in the rail infrastructure [4], examined communications systems [7, 8], and discussed potential threats [15]. However, security requirements for operating PTC systems without disruption have not been specified as yet. Before we can derive these security requirements, it is necessary to discuss sample misuse cases and show how they can impact PTC functionality.

5. Analyzing Railroad Safety and Security

Recent regulatory initiatives [36] and industry efforts [14] at deploying wireless PTC systems have significantly increased the level of risk. Several techniques have been proposed to analyze non-security related risks. They include:

- Soft systems methodology (SSM) [5]
- Quality function deployment (QFD) [27]
- Controlled requirements expression (CORE) [23, 35]
- Issue-based information systems (IBIS) [21]
- Joint application development (JAD) [38]

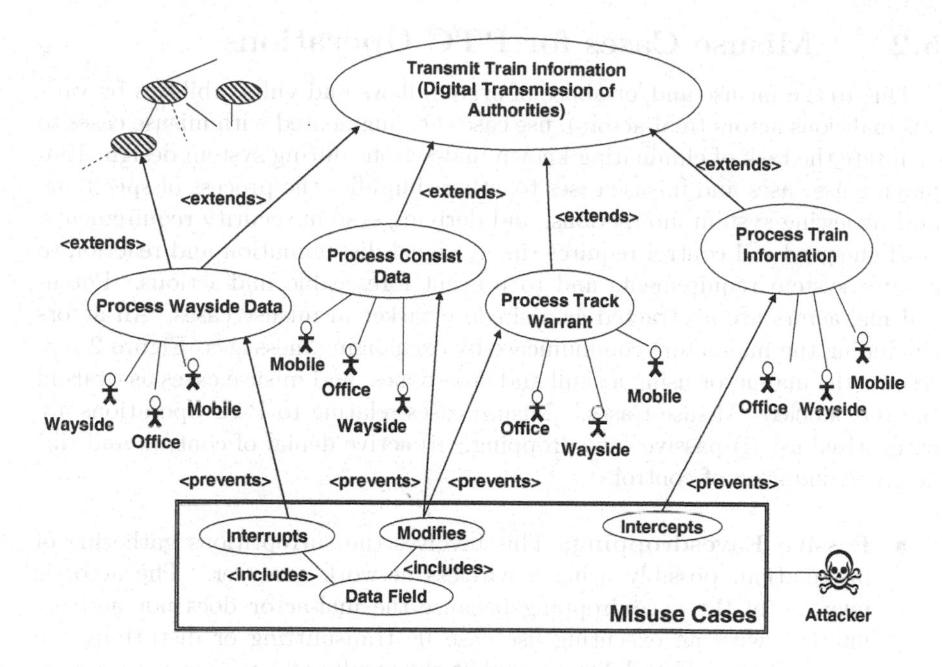

Figure 2. PTC use cases, misuse cases and their relationships.

- Feature-oriented domain analysis (FODA) [20]
- Accelerated requirements method (ARM) [18]
- Use/misuse case analysis [31, 32]

We employ use/misuse cases to analyze the effects of exploiting vulnerabilities in PTC systems. Use cases specify operational interactions and requirements. On the other hand, misuse cases specify potential misuse or abuse scenarios.

5.1 Use Cases for PTC Operations

Use cases are widely employed for capturing functional requirements [19, 30]. They define the set of interactions between actors (users) and a system. Constructs such as <includes> and <extends> may be used to create complex use cases from simple ones. The <includes> relationship is analogous to a use case subroutine, while <extends> specifies an enhancement of the basic interaction pattern.

Figure 2 presents PTC use cases, misuse cases and their relationships. Use cases are represented as ovals, actors as traditional stick figures, and relationships as single lines connecting actors to use cases or intra use case relationships. The shaded ovals in the top left-hand corner of Figure 2 denote additional use cases that have not been fully defined in this example.

5.2 Misuse Cases for PTC Operations

Due to the misuse and/or abuse of system flaws and vulnerabilities by various malicious actors (mal-actors), use cases are augmented with misuse cases to facilitate the task of eliminating known mal-actions during system design. Employing use cases and misuse cases together simplifies the process of specifying and reviewing system interactions, and deriving system security requirements.

High-speed rail control requires timely signal dissemination and reaction to enforce system requirements and to prevent foreseeable mal-actions. Potential mal-actors are abstracted as a single attacker in misuse cases. All actors (including the mal-actor) communicate by exchanging messages. Figure 2 represents the mal-actor using a skull and crossbones, and misuse cases as ovals in the box labeled "Misuse Cases." Misuse cases relating to PTC operations are categorized as: (i) passive eavesdropping, (ii) active denial of control, and (iii) active assumption of control.

- **Passive Eavesdropping:** This involves the surreptitious gathering of information, possibly using a wireless network analyzer. The actor is unaware of the eavesdropping because the mal-actor does not actively interfere with an executing use case by transmitting or disturbing the actor's signal. The ability to exploit the results of a passive misuse case depends on the attacker's technical sophistication (e.g., ability to bypass or overcome protection mechanisms).

- **Active Denial of Control:** This involves a technique such as broadband jamming of the frequency spectrum to disable communications between an actor and the PTC system. This misuse case prevents the actor from issuing commands to the PTC system. Note that the mal-actor does not need to have any knowledge about the parameters in the messages sent by the actor to the PTC system. The Interrupts misuse case in Figure 2 is an example of active denial of control.

  More sophisticated forms of active denial of control such as denial of service (DoS) and distributed denial of service (DDoS) attacks require knowledge of the message parameters. A more specialized misuse case is Power Exhaustion, in which a mal-actor prevents a wayside device from communicating by draining its power.

- **Active Assumption of Control:** This involves a mal-actor who impersonates an actor and gains active control of the PTC system or system component. An example misuse case is a mal-actor spoofing a dispatch center and requesting a locomotive to stop.

6. Deriving Security Requirements

We use a four-step process to derive security requirements from use cases and misuse cases.

- **Step 1:** Specify detailed use cases and misuse cases along with the relationships between them.
- **Step 2:** Specify operational and environmental constraints.
- **Step 3:** Derive system requirements.
- **Step 4:** Infer security objectives.

The following sections describe the four steps in detail.

6.1 Specifying Use Cases and Misuse Cases

As mentioned above, use cases specify functional requirements while misuse cases specify the abuses to be avoided or eliminated in a system being designed. Analyzing the effects that stated misuse cases have on the stated use cases is one of the principal security objectives. Graphical and textual representations such as those in Figure 2 and Tables 2 and 3 facilitate this activity.

Returning to our example, consider the impact of the misuse case Modifies on the use case, Transmit Train Information (Digital Transmission of Authorities) (Level 2). Figure 2 shows that this use case is extended into four use cases: Process Wayside Data, Process Consist Data, Process Track Warrant and Process Train Information by the actors: Office, Wayside and Mobile. The Prevents relationship existing between the Process Track Warrant use case and the Modifies misuse case shows which use cases executed by the actors are affected by misuse cases executed by the mal-actor. Tables 2 and 3 provide a detailed description of the Modify Track Warrant misuse case along with all its relationships.

6.2 Specifying Constraints

Constraints are obtained from the textual descriptions of use cases and misuse cases by employing the "noun-verb" extraction technique [25]. In noun-verb extraction, actions and elements correspond to (ad)verbs and (pro)nouns, respectively, in the text. This process may be performed manually or using automated tools [22]. After the actions and elements have been determined, they become system constraints from the point of view of the actors.

For example, applying the noun-verb extraction technique to the first sentence in the Summary section of the misuse case in Table 2 yields "Text carrying specific authorizations for a mobile unit to occupy a particular section of track," which appears in the first row of the first column of Table 4. Repeating this process for the text in Tables 2 and 3 yields the constraints in Tables 4 and 5.

6.3 Deriving System Requirements

The system requirements follow from the definitions of the constraints. The extracted nouns and verbs that make up the constraints are examined and recast into positive assertions regarding required system behavior. For example,

Table 2. Use/misuse case for Modify Track Warrant.

Number	Description
1	**Summary:** Text carrying specific authorization for a mobile unit to occupy a particular section of track is modified. This track warrant text provides information that prevents train-to-train, train-to-on-track-equipment, on-track-equipment-to-on-track-equipment and train-to-roadway-worker collisions.
2	**Basic Path:** The track warrant text is transmitted from the office/dispatch system to a mobile unit. The CRC is modified while the message is en route, rendering the track warrant text invalid and preventing the mobile unit from receiving a valid track warrant. Mobile units acting on invalid warrants collide with other trains, track vehicles or roadway workers.
3	**Alternate Paths:** The message is relayed through the wayside subsystem and the CRC is modified during transmission between: (i) the office/dispatch subsystem and the wayside subsystem, or (ii) the wayside subsystem and the mobile unit.
4	**Capture Points:** The track warrant message is invalid because one or more of the following message fields are modified: (i) source, (ii) type, (iii) message payload, (iv) message identifier.
5	**Triggers:** A transmitter is placed within range of the defender's receiver and/or transmitter.
6	**Attacker Profile:** The originator's message is captured, read and interpreted, bits in the message are substituted, and the message is retransmitted.

the constraint "Text carrying specific authorizations for a mobile unit to occupy a particular section of track" from the first row and first column in Table 4 is recast to the positive assertion "Authorization to occupy a specific section of track shall be in text." This assertion becomes the requirement in the second column of the first row in Table 4. This process is repeated for each constraint in the first column of Tables 4 and 5 to produce the corresponding requirement in the second column of the two tables.

6.4 Inferring Security Objectives

The first step is to decide which traditional security objectives (confidentiality, integrity, availability, authenticity, accountability and identification) must be enforced to ensure that each specific requirement defined above is met. This step is typically performed by an experienced security engineer. Formally, this involves specifying use cases that mitigate or prevent the stated misuse cases from being executed.

Table 3. Use/misuse case for Modify Track Warrant (continued).

Number	Description
7	**Preconditions:** (i) The office/dispatch subsystem is transmitting a track warrant message to a mobile unit, (ii) the office/dispatch subsystem and the mobile unit are operating normally.
8	**Postconditions (Worst Case):** (i) The mobile unit receives an invalid track warrant, which causes a train-to-train, train-to-on-track-equipment, on-track-equipment-to-on-track-equipment or train-to-roadway-worker collision, (ii) unauthorized modifications of track warrants disable accountability and non-repudiation of specific operational restrictions and authorizations for potentially high hazard events such as commingling of roadway workers and trains, (iii) an invalid warrant halts mobile units at the limits of its current authority, producing a significant operational (if not safety) impact.
9	**Postconditions (Best Case):** (i) Integrity (specifically data origin authentication and data integrity) is maintained, (ii) track warrant modification is identified and isolated, (iii) two entities do not commingle despite operating on altered track warrants.
10	**Business Rules:** (i) Only the office/dispatch subsystem may originate valid track warrant text, (ii) office/dispatch subsystem may push valid track warrant text to a mobile unit or wayside subsystem, (iii) mobile unit may pull or request pulling a valid track warrant text from the wayside subsystem or the office/dispatch subsystem, (iv) wayside subsystem may pull valid track warrant text from the office/dispatch subsystem only after the receipt of a request to pull track warrant text from a mobile unit.

For example, to satisfy the requirement in the second column of the first row in Table 4, namely "Authorization to occupy a specific section of track shall be in text," it is necessary to protect the "integrity" of transmitted track authorities between authenticated senders and receivers. This yields the security objective "Integrity of text" in the third column of the first row of Table 4. This process is repeated for each requirement in the second column of Tables 4 and 5 to produce the corresponding security objective in the third column of the two tables.

In some instances a constraint does not translate to a specific security objective because the requirement generated from the constraint is actually the specification of a higher level use case. For example the constraint "Mobile unit collides with another train, track vehicle or roadway workers" in the fourth row of Table 4 generates the requirement "Mobile unit shall be prevented from colliding with another train, track vehicle and roadway workers." This requirement is, in fact, one of the core use cases that defines a PTC system. Consequently the level of granularity of the requirement will directly impact the

Table 4. Constraints, requirements and security objectives.

Constraint	Requirement	Security Objective
Text carrying specific authorization for a mobile unit to occupy a particular section of track	Authorization to occupy a specific section of track shall be in text	Integrity of text
Track warrant transmitted from office/dispatch subsystem to mobile unit	Track warrant shall be transmitted from office/ dispatch subsystem to mobile unit	Authenticity of sender and receiver
Track warrant invalid as CRC is modified en route	CRC shall be applied to track warrant to detect changes that would render track warrant invalid	Integrity of track warrant
Mobile unit collides with another train, track vehicle or roadway workers	Mobile unit shall be prevented from colliding with another train, track vehicle and roadway workers	
Message relayed to wayside subsystem	Message shall be relayed to wayside unit	Authenticity of receiver
Track warrant invalid as one or more message fields are modified: (i) source, (ii) type, (iii) message payload, (iv) message identifier	Track warrant shall be protected from modification	Integrity of track warrant
Transmitter within range of defender's receiver and/or transmitter	System shall operate when defender is within range of attacker's transmitter	Availability of communications
Attacker captures the originator's message, reads and interprets message, substitutes bits and retransmits the message	System shall operate in environment where originator's message is captured, read and interpreted, message bits are substituted and message is transmitted	Identity of originator; authenticity of sender and receiver; integrity of message

ability of a security engineer to devise mitigating use cases (and subsequently define the required security objectives). Increased granularity of the requirements is, therefore, critical to defining essential security-related use cases.

Table 5. Constraints, requirements and security objectives (continued).

Constraint	Requirement	Security Objective
Office/dispatch subsystem transmits track warrant to mobile unit	Track warrant shall be transmitted from the office/dispatch subsystem to mobile unit	Authenticity of sender and receiver
Office/dispatch subsystem and mobile unit operate normally	Track warrant shall be transmitted from the office/dispatch subsystem to mobile unit when system is operating normally	Authenticity of sender and receiver
Office/dispatch subsystem originates track warrant	Office/dispatch subsystem shall originate track warrant	Accountability of originator
Invalid track warrant halts mobile unit at the limit of its current authority	Invalid track warrant shall halt mobile unit at the limit of its current authority	Integrity of track warrant
Unauthorized modification of track warrant disables the accountability and non-repudiation of specific operational restrictions and authorization for a potentially high hazard event such as commingling roadway workers and trains	Unauthorized modification of track warrant shall disable the accountability and non-repudiation of specific operational restrictions and authorization for a potentially high hazard event such as commingling roadway workers and trains	Integrity of track warrant; identity, accountability and authenticity of sender
Train-to-train, train-to-on-track-equipment, on-track-equipment to on-track-equipment or train to roadway-worker collision	System shall prevent train-to-train, train-to-on-track-equipment, on-track equipment to on-track equipment and train to roadway worker collision	

6.5 Drawbacks of the Process

A major drawback of our four-step process is the high degree of human involvement and skill required to infer the security objectives. As discussed in [33], employing a standard format for use cases and misuse cases simplifies

Table 6. Summary PTC requirements by functional capabilities.

	Confid.	Integ.	Avail.	Auth.	Account.	Ident.
Prevent train-to-train collisions	No	Yes	No	Yes	No	Yes
Enforce speed restrictions	No	Yes	No	Yes	No	Yes
Protect roadway workers	No	Yes	No	Yes	Yes	Yes
Wayside monitoring of traffic control territory	No	Yes	No	Yes	No	Yes
Wayside monitoring of all mainline switches	No	Yes	No	Yes	No	Yes
Additional wayside protection and detection devices	No	Yes	No	Yes	No	Yes
Advanced broken rail detection	No	Yes	No	Yes	No	Yes
Roadway worker terminals	Yes	Yes	No	Yes	Yes	Yes

the task, but does not automate it. Furthermore, it reduces but does not eliminate the need for extensive security engineering domain knowledge.

Consequently, we have pursued the translation of use cases and misuse cases to functional fault trees as an alternative to deriving system requirements and inferring security objectives [17]. This approach combines the user friendliness of graphical and textual specifications with the rigorous analysis provided by functional fault tree based tools.

7. Distributed Trust Management

We have designed a distributed trust management system to help mitigate stated misuse cases [16]. The system provides the use cases described in Figure 2 and includes the misuse case described in Tables 2 and 3 as well as other misuse cases related to communications and identity management. Upon analyzing these use cases and misuse cases, new requirements were generated and additional security objectives were inferred. Table 6 summarizes the security objectives. Each entry in the table indicates the necessity of a specific security objective (confidentiality, integrity, availability, authenticity, accountability and identity).

Interoperability and network management aspects have a significant impact on the security requirements. This is because locomotives are often exchanged between railroads; therefore, onboard PTC subsystems must be compatible with various wayside and dispatch subsystems. Similarly, the logical and physical architectures of PTC systems, security policy issues, labor agreements, budgetary and schedule restrictions along with the skill level and availability of technical resources to manage a secure PTC system are important. The result is that no single optimal solution exists. Consequently, PTC security solutions should be tailored to address the specific railroad environment.

8. Conclusions

PTC systems can significantly enhance railroad safety by maintaining inter-train distances, enforcing speed restrictions and preventing train-to-wayside-worker accidents. Although they have been extensively analyzed for operational safety, PTC security issues have not been fully addressed. Due to their reliance on wireless networks, PTC systems are vulnerable to attacks that target wireless communications. Use/misuse case analysis is a systematic methodology for identifying how a mal-actor can negatively impact the functional objectives of a PTC system. The negative impacts on PTC use cases can be employed to design PTC systems that are resistant and resilient to misuse cases. Addressing these issues at the design stage rather than after deployment is an important security engineering practice.

PTC systems are currently not economically viable from the point of view of their safety business case alone [10, 11]. However, when combined with other advanced technologies, PTC systems can offer significant economic and safety benefits [12]. This will, however, depend on the ability to ensure that PTC systems are both resistant and resilient to attacks.

Note that the views and opinions expressed in this paper are those of the authors. They do not reflect any official policy or position of the Federal Railroad Administration, U.S. Department of Transportation or the U.S. Government, and shall not be used for advertising or product endorsement purposes.

References

[1] American Association of State Highway and Transportation Officials, Transportation: Invest in America – Freight-Rail Bottom Line Report, Washington, DC (freight.transportation.org/doc/FreightRailReport.pdf), 2002.

[2] Association of American Railroads, U.S. Freight Railroad Statistics, Washington, DC, 2004.

[3] Bureau of Transportation Statistics, Federal Railroad Administration National Rail Network 1:100,000 (Line), National Transportation Atlas Database 2003, Department of Transportation, Washington, DC, 2003.

[4] A. Carlson, D. Frincke and M. Laude, Railway security issues: A survey of developing railway technology, *Proceedings of the International Conference on Computer, Communications and Control Technologies*, vol. 1, pp. 1–6, 2003.

[5] P. Checkland and J. Scholes, *Soft Systems Methodology in Action*, John Wiley, Chichester, United Kingdom, 1999.

[6] C. Chittester and Y. Haimes, Risks of terrorism to information technology and to critical interdependent infrastructures, *Journal of Homeland Security and Emergency Management*, vol. 1(4), 2004.

[7] P. Craven, A brief look at railroad communication vulnerabilities, *Proceedings of the Seventh IEEE International Conference on Intelligent Transportation Systems*, pp. 345–349, 2004.

[8] P. Craven and A. Craven, Security of ATCS wireless railway communications, *Proceedings of the IEEE/ASME Joint Rail Conference*, pp. 227–238, 2005.

[9] Department of Homeland Security, FY 2006 Infrastructure Protection Program: Intercity Passenger Rail Security Program Guidelines and Application Kit, Washington, DC, 2006.

[10] Federal Railroad Administration, Railroad Communications and Train Control, Technical Report, Department of Transportation, Washington, DC, 1994.

[11] Federal Railroad Administration, Implementation of Positive Train Control Systems, Technical Report, Department of Transportation, Washington, DC, 1999.

[12] Federal Railroad Administration, Benefits and Costs of Positive Train Control, Report in Response to the Request of the Appropriations Committees, Department of Transportation, Washington, DC, 2004.

[13] General Accounting Office, Critical Infrastructure Protection: Challenges and Efforts to Secure Control Systems, Report to Congressional Requesters, GAO-04-354, Washington, DC, 2004.

[14] M. Hartong, R. Goel and D. Wijesekera, Communications-based positive train control systems architecture in the USA, *Proceedings of the Sixty-Third IEEE Vehicular Technology Conference*, vol. 6, pp. 2987–2991, 2006.

[15] M. Hartong, R. Goel and D. Wijesekera, Communications security concerns in communications-based train control, *Proceedings of the Tenth International Conference on Computer System Design and Operation in the Railway and Other Transit Systems*, 2006.

[16] M. Hartong, R. Goel and D. Wijesekera, Key management requirements for positive train control communications security, *Proceedings of the IEEE/ASME Joint Rail Conference*, pp. 253–262, 2006.

[17] M. Hartong, R. Goel and D. Wijesekera, Mapping misuse cases to functional fault trees in order to secure positive train control systems, *Proceedings of the Ninth International Conference on Applications of Advanced Technology in Transportation Engineering*, pp. 394–399, 2006.

[18] R. Hubbard, N. Mead and C. Schroeder, An assessment of the relative efficiency of a facilitator-driven requirements collection process with respect to the conventional interview method, *Proceedings of the Fourth International Conference on Requirements Engineering*, pp. 178–186, 2000.

[19] I. Jacobson, *Object-Oriented Software Engineering: A Use Case Driven Approach*, Addison-Wesley, Boston, Massachusetts, 1992.

[20] K. Kang, S. Cohen, J. Hess, W. Novack and A. Peterson, Feature-Oriented Domain Analysis Feasibility Study, Technical Report CMU/SEI-90-TR-021, Software Engineering Institute, Carnegie Mellon University, Pittsburgh, Pennsylvania, 1990.

[21] W. Kunz and H. Rittel, Issues as elements of information systems, Working Paper WP-131, Berkeley Institute of Urban and Regional Development, University of California, Berkeley, California, 1970.

[22] C. Lerman, *Applying UML and Patterns: An Introduction to Object-Oriented Analysis and Design and the Unified Process*, Prentice Hall, Upper Saddle River, New Jersey, 1998.

[23] G. Mullery, CORE: A method for controlled requirements specification, *Proceedings of the Fourth International Conference on Software Engineering*, pp. 126–135, 1979.

[24] National Research Council, *Cybersecurity of Freight Information Systems: A Scoping Study*, Transportation Research Board, National Academy of Sciences, Washington, DC, 2003.

[25] S. Overmyer, L. Benoit and R. Owen, Conceptual modeling through linguistic analysis using LIDA, *Proceedings of the Twenty-Third International Conference on Software Engineering*, pp. 401–410, 2001.

[26] President's National Security Telecommunications Advisory Committee (NSTAC), Wireless Security Report, Wireless Task Force Report, National Communications System, Arlington, Virginia (www.ncs.gov/nstac/reports/2003/WTF%20Wireless%20Security%20Report.pdf), 2003.

[27] QFD Institute, Frequently asked questions about QFD (www.qfdi.org/what_is_qfd/faqs_about_qfd.htm).

[28] W. Rash, Engaging in worm warfare, *InfoWorld*, January 9, 2004.

[29] J. Rollins and C. Wilson, Terrorist Capabilities for Cyberattack: Overview and Policy Issues, Report RL33123, Congressional Research Service, Library of Congress, Washington, DC, 2007.

[30] J. Rumbaugh, Getting started: Using use cases to capture requirements, *Journal of Object-Oriented Programming*, vol. 7(5), pp. 8–12, 1994.

[31] G. Sindre and A. Opdahl, Eliciting security requirements by misuse cases, *Proceedings of the Thirty-Seventh International Conference on Technology of Object-Oriented Languages and Systems*, pp. 120–131, 2000.

[32] G. Sindre and A. Opdahl, Capturing security requirements through misuse cases, *Proceedings of the Fourteenth Norwegian Informatics Conference*, 2001.

[33] G. Sindre and A. Opdahl, Templates for misuse case description, *Proceedings of the Seventh International Workshop on Requirements Engineering*, 2001.

[34] Surface Transportation Board, 2003 Statistics of Class I Freight Railroads in the United States, Department of Transportation, Washington, DC, 2003.

[35] Systems Designers Scientific, *CORE – The Method: User Manual*, SD-Scicon, London, United Kingdom, 1986.

[36] U.S. Government, Standards for the development and use of processor based signal and train control systems, *Federal Register*, vol. 70(232), pp. 72382–72385, 2005.

[37] B. Weinstein and T. Clower, The Impacts of the Union Pacific Service Disruptions on the Texas and National Economies: An Unfinished Story, Center for Economic Development and Research, University of North Texas, Denton, Texas, 1998.

[38] J. Wood and D. Silver, *Joint Application Development*, John Wiley, New York, 1995.

Chapter 6

LESSONS LEARNED FROM THE MAROOCHY WATER BREACH

Jill Slay and Michael Miller

Abstract Supervisory control and data acquisition (SCADA) systems are widely used to monitor and control operations in electrical power distribution facilities, oil and gas pipelines, water distribution systems and sewage treatment plants. Technological advances over the past decade have seen these traditionally closed systems become open and Internet-connected, which puts the service infrastructures at risk. This paper examines the response to the 2000 SCADA security incident at Maroochy Water Services in Queensland, Australia. The lessons learned from this incident are useful for establishing academic and industry-based research agendas in SCADA security as well as for safeguarding critical infrastructure components.

Keywords: SCADA security, Maroochy Water Services breach

1. Introduction

Great concern has been expressed regarding the security of supervisory control and data acquisition (SCADA) systems in the light of the breach that occurred in 2000 at Maroochy Water Services in Queensland, Australia [6, 13]. This paper discusses the Maroochy Water incident and the response to the incident. Lessons learned from the incident, which have not been widely reported, are discussed in this paper. These lessons are useful for establishing academic and industry-based research agendas in SCADA security as well as for safeguarding critical infrastructure components.

2. SCADA Systems

SCADA systems are used for gathering real-time data, monitoring equipment and controlling processes in industrial facilities and public utilities, including chemical plants and refineries, electrical power generation and transmission systems, oil and gas pipelines, and water and sewage treatment plants [9]. Servers,

Slay, J. and Miller, M., 2008, in IFIP International Federation for Information Processing, Volume 253, Critical Infrastructure Protection, eds. E. Goetz and S. Shenoi; (Boston: Springer), pp. 73–82.

which are generally located in the main plant, communicate with sensors and control devices, which may be inside the plant or at remote locations. Sensors and control devices are placed wherever equipment needs to be monitored or controlled. A SCADA network can cover large geographical areas, especially in the case of public utilities.

A SCADA system generally has three types of components:

- **Field Devices:** These devices include sensors and controllers, e.g., remote telemetry units (RTUs) and programmable logic controllers (PLCs). Sensors collect data from various sources. Controllers perform actions (e.g. starting a pump or closing a valve) based on sensor data and control algorithms. RTUs and PLCs are small dedicated devices, which are hardened for outdoor use and industrial environments. They may be interfaced using serial connections or Ethernet. In this paper, field devices are generally referred to as PLCs. However, a field device could be a PLC, an RTU or a combination (as in some plants).
- **Servers:** Servers are responsible for collecting and analyzing various field inputs. They are responsible for raising alarms, starting and stopping processes, and implementing the logic required to automate processes.
- **Clients:** Client machines interact with servers via terminals. Clients are used to monitor the state of a SCADA network. They also have the ability to start and stop processes running within the network.

Australian SCADA systems are often very complex because of the vastness of the country and the remoteness of many of the utility plants and field stations. For example, the networked SCADA system at the ETSA electric utility company in South Australia covers more than 70,000 square miles of terrain. It incorporates 25,000 physical I/O points and in excess of 100,000 tags. The system monitors daily data for current, temperature, power variables, load shedding systems and fire alarms, reducing the response time for dealing with anomalies and faults.

3. The Maroochy Water Services Case

One of the most celebrated SCADA system breaches occurred at Maroochy Water Services on Queensland's Sunshine Coast in Australia [6, 13]. In March 2000, Maroochy Shire Council experienced problems with its new wastewater system. Communications sent by radio links to wastewater pumping stations were being lost, pumps were not working properly, and alarms put in place to alert staff to faults were not going off.

It was initially thought there were teething problems with the new system. Some time later, an engineer who was monitoring every signal passing through the system, discovered that someone was hacking into the system and deliberately causing the problems. In time, the perpetrator, Vitek Boden, a former contractor, was arrested and eventually jailed.

Mr. Boden used a laptop computer and a radio transmitter to take control of 150 sewage pumping stations. Over a three-month period, he released one million liters of untreated sewage into a stormwater drain from where it flowed to local waterways. The attack was motivated by revenge on the part of Mr. Boden after he failed to secure a job with the Maroochy Shire Council.

The Maroochy Water Services case has been cited around the world as an example of the damage that could occur if SCADA systems are not secured. The incident was mentioned in a recent report on IT security by the U.S. President's Information Technology Advisory Committee [13].

This SCADA security incident also has to be viewed in the context of Australian data on cyber crime, particularly network security breaches. Electronic attacks on 127 Australian companies surveyed in 2003 [1] resulted in increases in financial losses of 20% over 2002, bringing the average loss to approximately $116,000 per company. The survey also revealed that organizations that were part of Australia's critical information infrastructure reported greater losses (50%) compared with organizations that were not part of the infrastructure (42%). Other key findings were that more organizations experienced attacks on the confidentiality, availability and integrity of computer systems and data in 2004 than did in 2003. The percentage of organizations affected was up from 42% in 2003 to 49% of those surveyed in 2004. Most attacks were sourced externally (88%), but fewer organizations experienced external attacks than in 2003 (91%). Infections due to viruses, worms and Trojans were most common, accounting for 45% of total losses in 2004. Other prevalent forms of electronic crime were fraud, followed by abuse and misuse of computer network access or resources.

4. SCADA Security

SCADA systems are used by 270 utilities in the United States [4]. Since this amounts to roughly eighty percent of U.S. power facilities, the risk of system-wide failure and the resulting economic loss are very high. For example, during the August 25, 2003 power outage in North America, more than 100 power plants were shut down, affecting 50 million people in the U.S. and Canada. Also, it led to the closure of ten major airports and the New York City subway system. This emphasizes the need to protect SCADA systems, especially from targeted cyber attacks.

Oman and co-workers [11] stress the importance of securing SCADA systems at a time when the terrorist threat level is high. A major concern is malicious actors gaining remote access to substations at various points in power grid, and then launching large-scale attacks throughout the infrastructure. Oman and colleagues also discuss how an "open" SCADA network can be penetrated in a relatively easy manner.

SCADA security has been highlighted in a recent report by the U.S. President's Information Technology Advisory Committee [13]. The FBI has also reinforced the need to secure SCADA networks, especially as several nation states and other actors are attempting to develop information warfare capabilities.

Utilities are prime targets for attackers because shutting them down can have a large-scale societal impact. Since SCADA systems are vital to plant operations, it is crucial to secure them to the extent possible [5].

The U.S. National Communication System [9] has identified that interconnections between SCADA networks and corporate networks increases the risk and the consequences of attack. There is a false impression that a SCADA system is safe because it is in a separate closed network. As networks become interconnected for convenience and for business reasons, an attacker who enters a corporate network can tunnel into a SCADA system, and potentially target any device.

Byres [3] has emphasized that increased interconnectivity means that hacker attacks are not the only threat. In January 2003, the Slammer worm infiltrated an Ohio nuclear power plant and several other power utilities. Byres identified four relatively innocuous entry points used by the worm:

- Contractor's T1 line (affected a power plant computer)
- Virtual private network (affected a power company SCADA system)
- Laptop (affected a petroleum plant control system)
- Dial-up modem (affected a paper plant human-machine interface (HMI)).

These infiltration points demonstrate that many SCADA systems are being connected to the Internet without consideration of security. Once it is connected to a corporate network, a SCADA network becomes vulnerable to worms and viruses originating from the Internet.

The U.S. Department of Energy's Office of Energy Assurance [10] lists several strategies for improving the security of SCADA systems. It recommends the use of evaluations, audits and surveys to identify weak points, which must then be strengthened to protect against intrusions. Many security problems can be reduced, if not eliminated, using administrative approaches, e.g., developing documentation about the SCADA system, specifying policies and procedures, and conducting periodic assessments. Similar approaches have been proposed by Sandia researchers [16]. They maintain that identifying security problems and performing a risk assessment should be the first step in securing a SCADA system. Moreover, before implementing any security controls, it is important to have a clear understanding of the architecture and configuration of the SCADA system.

Riptech [14], the security services firm, which was acquired by Symantec in 2002, identified three major misconceptions about SCADA security: (i) SCADA systems reside on physically-separate, stand-alone networks; (ii) SCADA systems are protected from corporate networks using strong access controls; and (iii) SCADA systems require specialized knowledge, which makes them difficult for intruders to access and exploit. The Riptech document asserts that these statements applied when SCADA systems, with their proprietary hardware, software and protocols, were located in isolated networks. The statements do not hold at present, especially as corporate networks are often connected to SCADA systems.

Symantec [17] has specified a network architecture that incorporates various security controls, including firewalls to protect corporate and SCADA-client terminals from attacks originating from the Internet. Of course, due to network connectivity, it is usually the case that multiple entry points exist into SCADA systems; therefore, it is important that all entering traffic be screened.

In general, there is heightened awareness about SCADA systems and the need to secure them from attacks from insiders as well as external entities. Numerous research and development efforts have been initiated on SCADA security. Comprehensive solutions are needed that can address security in SCADA systems that comprise legacy components, proprietary hardware and software, as well as commodity computing and network equipment. Because of the scale of SCADA systems, the solutions should be relatively inexpensive. Moreover, they must not adversely impact plant operations.

5. Australian Efforts

The Australian Department of Communications, Information Technology and the Arts (DCITA) [7] has launched an effort to convince senior management of the potential risks to their SCADA systems and has recommended various physical, logical and administrative controls for managing risk. DCITA has also held a series of workshops across the country targeting SCADA owners and operators as well as academic researchers to spur research and developments focused on SCADA security. The Australian government recently initiated an effort through the Attorney General's Department called the Trusted Information Sharing Network for Critical Infrastructure Protection, which has a major focus on SCADA security.

We have worked with an Australian SCADA integrator to develop a security architecture for SCADA systems with modern and legacy components [15]. The goals of the security architecture (Figure 1) are to prevent or minimize system attacks while reducing overhead that could impact control functions. The architecture is inspired by the defense-in-depth philosophy. It incorporates security mechanisms and the application of policies and procedures to create a secure SCADA environment.

Security mechanisms consume network resources and add communications overhead. Therefore, it is important to ensure that they do not affect the real-time performance of the SCADA system.

The principal security controls are implemented at the boundary of the network. The security gateway situated at the network boundary includes a firewall, intrusion detection system and anti-virus software. The three mechanisms provide distinct layers of security that screen suspicious network traffic. In particular, incoming traffic must satisfy the firewall rules, not raise any alarms in the intrusion detection system, and pass the anti-virus checker.

A demilitarized zone (DMZ) separates the SCADA system from the corporate network. Shared resources are placed in the DMZ; for example, corporate

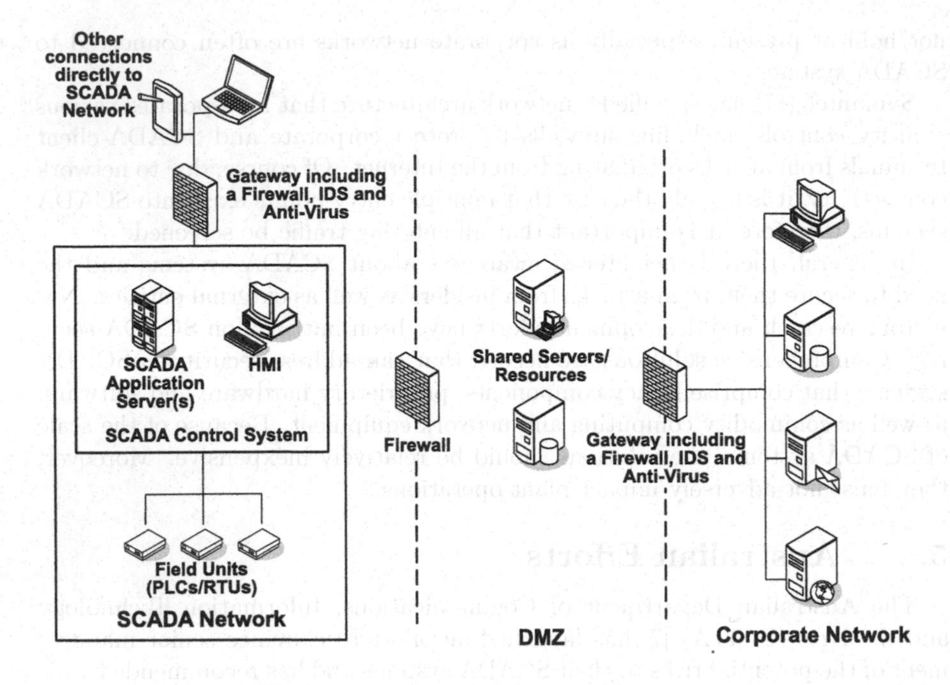

Figure 1. Proposed security architecture.

network users can obtain plant and control data by querying a DMZ historian without having to access the SCADA system.

A second firewall is located between the SCADA system and DMZ. Since entering traffic has already been screened at the gateway, this firewall can be relatively simple. However, if a corporate partner has direct access to the DMZ, then a gateway with substantial security functionality should be implemented at the boundary of the SCADA system and DMZ.

Firewalls screen all traffic entering and leaving the SCADA network, and are an inexpensive but effective security solution [2]. They eliminate direct connections from the Internet, restrict access from the corporate network, control traffic entering from wireless access points, and screen access in the case of remote connections (e.g., those used by maintenance personnel). Other important security solutions include network management and administration (e.g., managing user accounts and passwords) and addressing protocol-level vulnerabilities.

6. Lessons Learned

As we reflected on our work [15], we were challenged to consider if our solution – had it been implemented at Maroochy Water Services – would have prevented or deterred Vitek Boden from attacking the SCADA system.

Robert Stringfellow, who was the civil engineer in charge of the water supply and sewage systems at Maroochy Water Services during the time of the breach, has presented his analysis in closed forums. The best open source discussion of Mr. Stringfellow's views is provided by Mustard [8], which we consider in our analysis.

The Maroochy SCADA system employed two monitoring stations and three radio frequencies to control the operations of 142 sewage pumping stations. The faults that occurred when the system was being investigated (prior to the discovery of the hacking attacks) included:

- Unexplained pump station alarms
- Increased radio traffic that caused communication failures
- Modified configuration settings for pump station software
- Pumps running continually or turned off unexpectedly
- Pump station lockups and pumps turned off without any alarms
- Computer communication lockups and no alarm monitoring

Stringfellow commented that at first it was easier to blame installation errors for the problems. However, upon reinstalling all the software and checking the system, he noticed that pump station settings kept changing beyond the ability of the system to do this automatically. He, therefore, concluded that an external malicious entity was responsible. With the help of advanced monitoring tools, Stringfellow determined that a hacker was using wireless equipment to access the SCADA system. At one point, Stringfellow actually "dueled" with the attacker as he was connecting to pump stations from his laptop.

Stringfellow's analysis of the incident made several important points. First, it is very difficult to protect against insider attacks. Second, radio communications commonly used in SCADA systems are generally insecure or are improperly configured. Third, SCADA devices and software should be secured to the extent possible using physical and logical controls; but it is often that case that security controls are not implemented or are not used properly. Finally, SCADA systems must record all device accesses and commands, especially those involving connections to or from remote sites; this requires fairly sophisticated logging mechanisms.

Stringfellow also recommended the use of anti-virus and firewall protection along with appropriate use of encryption. He emphasized a need for upgradeable SCADA systems (from a security perspective), proper staff training, and security auditing and control.

Our research [15] indicates that several technical solutions are already available for securing SCADA systems. The solutions vary in their coverage and may not be very robust; nevertheless, they are good starting points for implementing security in SCADA systems.

Due to their specialized architecture, protocols and security goals, it is not appropriate to simply apply IT security techniques and tools to SCADA systems. Instead, it is important to design security solutions catered specifically to

SCADA systems. For example, tools that understand SCADA protocols and are designed to operate in industrial environments would be able to identify and block suspicious traffic in a more efficient and reliable manner.

Peterson [12] discusses the need for specialized intrusion detection systems for SCADA networks. Most existing systems only pick up traditional attacks, e.g., an attacker attempting to gain control of a server by exploiting a Windows vulnerability; effective intrusion detection systems must also incorporate SCADA attack signatures. Likewise, SCADA-aware firewalls must also be developed; their specialized SCADA rule sets would greatly enhance the blocking and filtering of suspicious packets.

Peterson [12] also emphasizes the need for logging activities and events in SCADA systems. Logs can provide valuable information pertaining to attacks. This includes information about the escalation of user privileges in SCADA applications, failed login attempts, and disabled alarms and changed displays, which could fool operators into believing that a system is running normally.

In addition to investing in security techniques, mechanisms and tools, it is imperative to focus on the human aspects of SCADA security. Staff must be well-trained and should be kept abreast of the latest security practices, exploits and countermeasures. Security policies and procedures should be developed, refined periodically, and applied consistently. Only the combination of technological solutions and human best practices can ensure that SCADA systems are secure and reliable.

7. Conclusions

SCADA systems control vital assets in practically every critical infrastructure sector. Given the ubiquity of SCADA systems and their inherent vulnerabilities, strong efforts should be taken by asset owners and operators to secure SCADA systems, especially those comprising legacy components, proprietary hardware and software, and commodity computing and network equipment, which expose the entire system to external attacks. Since the Maroochy Water Services breach, numerous research and development efforts have been initiated on SCADA security. Some of the most successful efforts have involved significant collaboration between academic researchers, vendors, owners and operators, and government agencies. But these efforts should be broader and more sustained. Moreover, security solutions should be effective, reliable and economically viable, and should not adversely impact operations.

The incident at Maroochy Water Services is a prime example of the kind of attack that can be launched on SCADA systems. The incident was serious, but it was caused by a lone hacker who attacked just one system in a single infrastructure. One can only imagine – at a time when terrorist threat levels are high – how much devastation could result from large-scale coordinated attacks on SCADA systems throughout the interconnected critical infrastructure sectors.

References

[1] Australian Computer Emergency Response Team, 2004 Australian Computer Crime and Security Survey (www.auscert.org.au/render.html?it=2001), 2005.

[2] British Columbia Institute of Technology, Good Practice Guide on Firewall Deployment for SCADA and Process Control Networks, National Infrastructure Security Co-ordination Centre, London, United Kingdom, 2005.

[3] E. Byres and J. Lowe, The myths and facts behind cyber security risks for industrial control systems, presented at the *VDE Congress*, 2004.

[4] J. Fernandez and A. Fernandez, SCADA systems: Vulnerabilities and remediation, *Journal of Computing Sciences in Colleges*, vol. 20(4), pp. 160–168, 2005.

[5] General Accounting Office, Critical Infrastructure Protection: Challenges and Efforts to Secure Control Systems, Report to Congressional Requesters, GAO-04-354, Washington, DC, 2004.

[6] G. Hughes, The cyberspace invaders, *The Age*, June 22, 2003.

[7] IT Security Advisory Group, SCADA security: Advice for CEOs, Department of Communications, Information Technology and the Arts, Canberra, Australia (www.dcita.gov.au/communications_for_business/security/critical_infrastructure_security/key_documents), 2005.

[8] S. Mustard, Security of distributed control systems: The concern increases, *Computing and Control Engineering Journal*, vol. 16(6), pp. 19–25, 2005.

[9] National Communications System, Supervisory Control and Data Acquisition (SCADA) Systems, Technical Information Bulletin NCS TIB 04-1, Arlington, Virginia, 2004.

[10] Office of Energy Assurance, 21 Steps to Improve Cyber Security of SCADA Networks, U.S. Department of Energy, Washington, DC, 2002.

[11] P. Oman, E. Schweitzer and D. Frincke, Concerns about intrusions into remotely accessible substation controllers and SCADA systems, *Proceedings of the Twenty-Seventh Annual Western Protective Relay Conference*, 2000.

[12] D. Peterson, Intrusion detection and cyber security, *InTech*, May 2004.

[13] President's Information Technology Advisory Committee, Cyber Security: A Crisis of Prioritization, Report to the President, National Coordination Office for Information Technology Research and Development, Arlington, Virginia, 2005.

[14] Riptech, Understanding SCADA system security vulnerabilities (www.iwar.org.uk/cip/resources/utilities/SCADAWhitepaperfinal1.pdf), 2001.

[15] J. Slay and M. Miller, A security architecture for SCADA networks, *Proceedings of the Seventeenth Australasian Conference on Information Systems*, 2006.

[16] J. Stamp, P. Campbell, J. DePoy, J. Dillinger and W. Young, Sustainable security for infrastructure SCADA, Sandia National Laboratories, Albuquerque, New Mexico (www.sandia.gov/scada/documents/SustainableSecurity.pdf), 2003.

[17] Symantec, Understanding SCADA system security vulnerabilities (www4.symantec.com/Vrt/offer?a_id=20249), 2004.

Chapter 7

REDUCING RISK IN OIL AND GAS PRODUCTION OPERATIONS

Stig Johnsen, Rune Ask and Randi Roisli

Abstract Remote operations are commonly employed in oil and gas installations in the North Sea and elsewhere. The use of information and communications technologies (ICT) has resulted in process control systems being connected to corporate networks as well as the Internet. In addition, multiple companies, functioning as a virtual organization, are involved in operations and management. The increased connectivity and human collaboration in remote operations have significantly enhanced the risks to safety and security.

This paper discusses methods and guidelines for addressing different types of risks posed by remote operations: technical ICT-based risks, organizational risks and risks related to human factors. Three techniques are described: (i) ISO 27001 based information security requirements for process control, safety and support ICT systems; (ii) CRIOP, an ISO 11064 based methodology that provides a checklist and scenario analysis for remote operations centers; and (iii) CheckIT, a method for improving an organization's safety and security culture.

Keywords: Oil and gas production, remote operations, information security, human factors

1. Introduction

Remote operations of offshore oil and gas installations are increasing in the North Sea and elsewhere [12]. The main motivations for remote operations are the potential for cost reduction, higher yields from fields, improved collaboration and increased safety. However, projects focused on implementing remote operations (especially moving personnel onshore) have often been scaled back or delayed due to higher degrees of complexity than originally anticipated.

The technologies used in remote operations are changing from proprietary stand-alone systems to standardized PC-based IT systems and networks, which, in turn, may be connected to the Internet. The reliance on commercial

Johnsen, S., Ask, R. and Roisli, R., 2008, in IFIP International Federation for Information Processing, Volume 253, Critical Infrastructure Protection, eds. E. Goetz and S. Shenoi; (Boston: Springer), pp. 83–95.

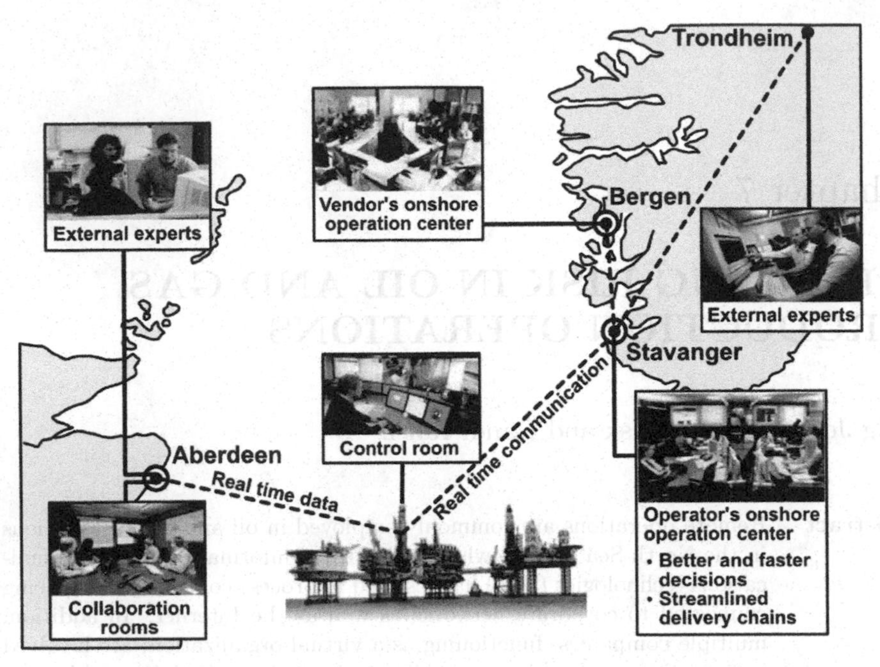

Figure 1. Key actors involved in remote operations [12].

off-the-shelf (COTS) operating systems increases the connectivity between process control systems (or supervisory control and data acquisition (SCADA)) systems and the general information technology and telecommunications (ICT) infrastructure. (Note that we refer to process control systems as SCADA systems in this paper.) This also increases the overall vulnerability. SCADA systems are fundamentally different from ICT systems. Several challenges are introduced when ICT and SCADA systems are integrated, including the need for anti-virus solutions, patches and enhanced information security.

There has been an increase in security incidents related to SCADA systems, some of which have significantly impacted operations [15]. However, security breaches are seldom reported and detailed information is almost never shared. The traditional view in North Sea operations was that SCADA systems were sheltered from threats emerging from public networks. This perception still seems to be widespread in the automation profession, which raises serious questions about the safety and security of remote operations [15].

The operating environment has changed. Remote operations involve the collaboration of experts at different geographical locations. Operations and maintenance tasks are being outsourced to suppliers and vendors, a trend that will likely increase. This situation coupled with enhanced connectivity increases the likelihood of accidents and malicious incidents, which can result in significant economic losses and, in the worst case, loss of lives. Figure 1 illustrates the scale of remote operations and identifies the key actors and their roles.

Security incidents and accidents can lead to costly production stoppages. The costs of a stoppage on the Norwegian Continental Shelf are usually in the two or three million dollar range, but can be much higher if a key production facility is affected [13]. It is widely acknowledged that human errors contribute significantly to accidents and casualties [4, 11], and must therefore be included when discussing the challenges posed by remote operations. History shows that personnel involved in remote operations have a tendency to focus too much on technology, often at the expense of organizational and cultural issues. Virtual organizations and the increased number of vulnerabilities create the need for a common risk perception and a pervasive safety and security culture to reduce risks. All elements of risk mitigation must be addressed in order to establish the appropriate depth and breadth of defenses.

2. Remote Operations

This paper identifies several key challenges related to remote operations in the oil and gas industry, especially those involving the integration of SCADA and ICT systems. The challenges, which cover technology, organizations and human factors, are listed in Table 1. Major challenges include reducing the new vulnerabilities introduced by organizational changes, integrating SCADA and ICT systems, and addressing human factors issues related to the involvement of actors from multiple organizations, often with different cultural views.

Integrating SCADA and ICT systems is difficult because the two types of systems differ in many respects. Availability is the most important factor for SCADA systems (key processes must be managed in milliseconds), followed by integrity, and then confidentiality. In contrast, confidentiality and integrity are crucial for ICT systems used in business settings. Availability is less important as response times are typically measured in seconds and short delays or outages are generally not critical to business operations.

SCADA systems generally have complex, specially-designed architectures. Anti-virus software is difficult or impossible to deploy and must be manually updated; there are often long delays in patch deployment, requiring complex testing and certification by vendors. Furthermore, SCADA system changes are rare, and are typically local and informal. SCADA systems have long lifecycles of five to twenty-five years. On the other hand, ICT systems are usually standardized and centrally managed in terms of their architecture and deployment of anti-virus software and patches. Also, automated tools are widely used, changes are frequent and centrally managed, and system lifecycles are much shorter at three to five years.

Despite the differences between the SCADA and ICT systems, systematic testing of integrated SCADA-ICT systems is not always performed. This can lead to operational problems – 30% of SCADA components in one facility broke down when exposed to high ICT traffic loads [10]. The scope and inherent complexities of the systems to be integrated and the organizational challenges faced by technical support personnel should not be underestimated.

Table 1. Organizational challenges in remote operations.

Present Status	Local Operations	Changes Related to Remote Operations
Integration	Large degree of segregation of SCADA systems	Increased need to integrate SCADA and ICT systems offshore and onshore
Standardization	Local, complex tailor-made solutions	Increased standardization for cost-effective, secure management of remote installations
Virtual Organizations	Operations are performed locally using local resources	Operations are performed by a virtual organization with geographically distributed entities
Generalization vs. Specialization	General expertise centered at a local installation	Experts available at any time remotely; reduced local expertise
24/7 Responsibility	Local responsibility; actors are available 24/7	Dispersed responsibilities must be defined for actors involved in 24/7 operations
Mode of Operations (Local vs. Remote)	Operations team close to the operational environment	Operations team isolated from the operational environment
Proactive vs. Reactive	Reactive	Focus on planning and proactive management
Culturally Driven	Managed by procedures and work orders; inter-personal trust	Focus on attitudes, knowledge, perceptions and improvisation; distributed competence and technology
Organizational Change Management	Few fundamental changes; focus on safety and costs/benefits	Large changes to organization and work processes (new technology and moving functions onshore); fear of reduced safety

Systematic checklists should be used in addition to thorough risk analysis such as hazard and operability (HAZOP) studies to establish common risk perceptions. Testing should be performed to ensure resilience against denial of service (DoS) attacks, viruses, worms and other malicious code. The probabilities and consequences of likely incidents should be documented in a risk matrix. The risk matrix should be developed in close collaboration between management, ICT personnel, operations personnel and human factors experts to ensure common risk perceptions. A new industry best practice named ISBR (Information Security Baseline Requirements for Process Control, Safety and

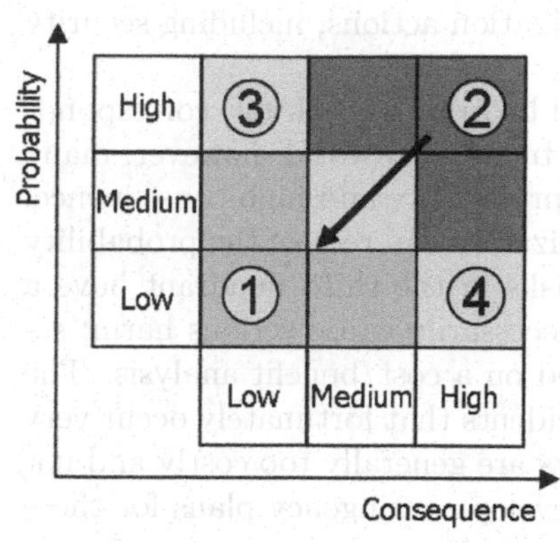

Example (Probability Scale):

- P1–Low: More than 10 years
- P2–Medium: 1 year to 10 years
- P3–High: Several times a year

Example (Consequence Scale):

- C1–Low: Less than $1,000
- C2–Medium: $1,000 to $100,000
- C3–High: More than $100,000

Figure 2. Common risk matrix in the oil and gas industry.

Support ICT Systems) [3] based on ISO/IEC 27001:2005 has been developed by the Norwegian Oil Industry Association (OLF) to aid in this process.

The differences between SCADA and ICT systems based on organizational and human factors are important, but are not considered adequately. For SCADA systems, responsibility and expertise often reside locally and solutions are not well documented. Risk management and hazard analysis are done explicitly and emergency shutdown systems are essential. For SCADA systems, while knowledge about vulnerabilities and threats (and information security skills) is quite poor, the potential risk impact is significant (loss of control, loss of production, loss of life). For ICT systems, responsibility and knowledge are centralized, tasks are outsourced and safety is rarely an issue. Furthermore, knowledge about ICT vulnerabilities and threats is moderate to high, and the potential risk impact is mainly restricted to the loss of data.

Cooperation between SCADA and ICT staff is not well established due to differences in technology and system separation. However, remote operations require integration, which is difficult to implement because of differences in organization, terminology and expertise in addition to the technical differences. Key mitigation factors include cooperation, increased training, establishing common goals and understanding the risks. To this end, a common risk matrix should be established that documents the technical, organizational and human factors issues. This is achieved using the methods and tools described in this paper: ISBR, information security baseline requirements for process control, safety and support ICT systems; CRIOP scenario analysis for remote operations centers; and CheckIT, a questionnaire-based method for improving an organization's safety and security culture.

3. Major Risks

Security incidents should be analyzed and placed in a risk matrix (Figure 2) to help stakeholders focus on the major risks. A risk matrix creates a foundation for the development and prioritization of mitigation actions, including security guidelines and procedures.

Ideally, all the risks in a risk matrix should be in first quadrant, corresponding to low probability and low consequence. In the real world, however, many of the risks are in the second quadrant, high probability and high consequence. By implementing security controls, the organization can reduce the probability or the consequence or, better still, both. Risks in the third quadrant have a high probability of occurrence, but do not necessarily cause serious harm; security measures should be implemented based on a cost/benefit analysis. The fourth quadrant corresponds to unwanted incidents that fortunately occur very rarely; mitigation measures for these incidents are generally too costly and not worthwhile. Instead, organizations should develop contingency plans for these eventualities.

Based on interviews and discussions with oil and gas industry experts, we have documented common risks and security incidents related to remote operations in oil and gas facilities. Some of the risks lie in the high probability/high consequence quadrant of the risk matrix:

- **Poor Situational Awareness:** A remote operations system does not give a comprehensive overview of the situation, resulting in poor situational awareness. This can lead to communication problems, misunderstanding and, ultimately, serious safety or security incidents.

- **ICT Traffic Impact:** A SCADA system crashes due to unexpected or unauthorized traffic from ICT systems. This could be caused by excessive ICT traffic affecting a key communication component between onshore and offshore systems, resulting in a shutdown of remote operations. Tests at CERN have demonstrated that 30% of SCADA components crashed when they were subjected to large volumes of ICT traffic or erroneous ICT traffic [10].

- **Virus/Worm Attacks:** A virus or worm causes unpredictable behavior or shuts down key SCADA components, disrupting production processes. This can occur if a PC or other IT equipment is connected to a network without screening it for malware. In mid August 2005, the Zotob.E worm attacked a major Norwegian oil and gas company. By September 15, 2005, 157 computers were infected, many of which were located in offshore facilities. The ICT staff had to explain the consequences to operations personnel at some length before adequate mitigative actions (patching computer systems used for safety-critical operations) could be implemented. Fortunately no accidents occurred as a result of the worm infection [14].

As described above, the major risks to remote operations at oil and gas facilities are poor situational awareness, denial of service and virus/worm attacks. A human factors approach to mitigating these risks involves working with technology, organizations and humans. The following three sections describe strategies for addressing technical ICT-based risks, organizational risks and risks related to human factors.

4. Information Security Baseline Requirements

Legislation and business practices related to health, safety and the environment for offshore operations have existed for decades, but information security issues have been largely ignored until very recently. As increasing numbers of companies set up remote operations and interconnect with vendors and suppliers, a need for a common information security baseline has emerged. Responding to this need, the Norwegian Oil Industry Association (OLF) has developed ISBR – information security baseline requirements for process control, safety and support ICT systems [3]. The guidelines, which came into force in July 2007, include the following sixteen requirements:

- An information security policy for process control, safety and support ICT systems shall be documented.
- Risk assessments shall be performed for process control, safety and support ICT systems and networks.
- Process control, safety and support ICT systems shall have designated system and data owners.
- The infrastructure shall provide network segregation and all communication paths shall be controlled.
- Users of process control, safety and support ICT systems shall be knowledgeable about information security requirements and acceptable use of ICT systems.
- Process control, safety and support ICT systems shall be used for designated purposes only.
- Disaster recovery plans shall be documented and tested for critical process control, safety and support ICT systems.
- Information security requirements for ICT components shall be integrated in engineering, procurement and commissioning processes.
- Critical process control, safety and support ICT systems shall have defined and documented service and support levels.
- Change management and work permit procedures shall be followed for all connections and changes to process control, safety and support ICT systems and networks.
- Updated network topology diagrams that include all system components and interfaces shall be available.

- ICT systems shall be kept updated and patched when connected to process control, safety and support networks.
- Process control, safety and support ICT systems shall have adequate, updated and active protection against malicious software.
- All access rights shall be denied unless explicitly granted.
- Required operational and maintenance procedures shall be documented and kept current.
- Procedures for reporting security events and incidents shall be documented and implemented.

The baseline requirements represent information security best practices that have been adapted to the oil and gas sector from the ISO/IEC 27001:2005 (formerly BS7799-2) specifications. The requirements are supposed to be implemented over and above a company's information security policies subject to national legislation; consequently, the requirements are neither pre-emptive nor exhaustive. Implementation guidance for requirements is available, and a self-assessment tool for companies to verify compliance has also been developed [3].

5. CRIOP Methodology

CRIOP [6] is a methodology for verifying and validating the ability of a control center to safely and efficiently handle all modes of operations. It can be applied to central control rooms; drillers' cabins, cranes and other types of cabins; and onshore, offshore and emergency control rooms. CRIOP has been used with much success in the Norwegian oil and gas sector since 1990 to provide situational awareness, clarify responsibilities in distributed teams and mitigate risk in cooperating organizations.

A CRIOP analysis takes between two and five days. The methodology was improved in 2003 to support and validate the ISO 11064 standard (Ergonomic Design of Control Centers). CRIOP was further enhanced in 2004 to assess the influence of remote operations and integrated operations. These changes have been tested and are scheduled to be fully implemented in 2007.

The key elements of CRIOP are:

- A learning arena where operators, designers, management and other actors can meet and evaluate the optimal control center during design, construction and operations
- Checklists covering relevant areas in the design of a control center
- Analysis of key scenarios

The CRIOP methodology attempts to ensure that human factors issues are emphasized in all aspects of remote operations. The primary human-factors-based principles are to: form interdisciplinary teams, ensure systematic end-user participation, conduct human factors analyses (e.g., function and task

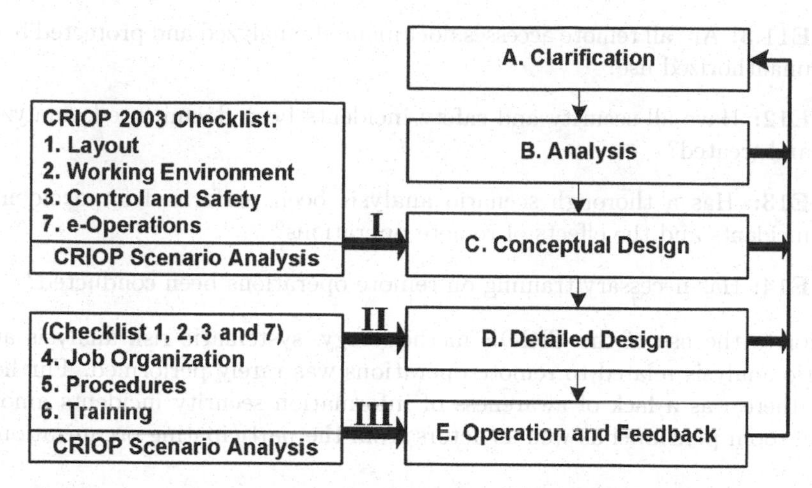

Figure 3. Suggested use of CRIOP based on the ISO 11064 phases.

analyses), and improve design through iteration and documentation of the process.

Figure 3 presents the suggested use of CRIOP based on the ISO 11064 phases. Several Norwegian oil and gas companies use CRIOP on a regular basis. In particular, they recommend using CRIOP in three stages (I, II and III) in design and operations processes.

CRIOP's scenario analysis is a dynamic approach that helps assess control room actions in response to possible critical scenarios. An example scenario is exception handling involving offshore and onshore control centers during remote operations. The main steps in scenario analysis are: (i) selection of a realistic scenario; (ii) description of the scenario using a sequential time event plotting (STEP) diagram [6]; (iii) identification of critical decisions and analysis of the decisions; and (iv) evaluation of possible barriers. Scenario analysis is typically performed by a group of participants from the control center or central control room along with key personnel from offshore operations centers.

The CRIOP methodology uses a checklist to identify relevant scenarios related to remote operations [8]. The principal elements of the checklist are:

- **E1:** Is the term "remote operations" defined precisely?
- **E5:** Are the major stakeholders identified, analyzed and involved in the change project?
- **E8:** Are the requirements for establishing common situational knowledge for participants in remote operations established?
- **E10:** Are all interfaces and organizational areas of responsibility clearly defined?
- **E11:** Has a risk assessment been performed prior to and after the implementation of remote operations?

- **E11.3:** Are all remote accesses documented, analyzed and protected from unauthorized use?
- **E12:** Have all security and safety incidents been documented, analyzed and treated?
- **E13:** Has a thorough scenario analysis been performed for accidents, incidents and the effects of remote operations?
- **E14:** Has necessary training on remote operations been conducted?

Prior to the use of the CRIOP methodology, systematic risk analysis and scenario analysis related to remote operations was rarely performed. Furthermore, there was a lack of awareness of information security incidents among control room personnel as well as actors from the participating organizations.

6. CheckIT Tool

Personnel involved in remote operations have a tendency to focus on technology, often at the expense of organizational and cultural issues [2]. The reliance on virtual organizations and the presence of vulnerabilities create the need for common risk perceptions and a safety and security culture [1] in the involved organizations in order to reduce risk.

The CheckIT [7] tool was developed to help organizations improve their safety and security cultures. The CheckIT questionnaire has 31 questions, each of which has three alternative answers corresponding to distinct cultural levels:

- **Level 1:** Denial culture
- **Level 3:** Rule-based culture
- **Level 5:** Learning/generative culture (application of best practices)

The goal is to rate an organization on a five-point numerical scale. The scale provides a normalized score for the organization, which makes it possible to compare results over time or between organizations.

Using CheckIT could be a challenge in a technology-driven industry; therefore, organizations should attempt to build support for the process among stakeholders and document short-term improvements along the way [9].

The first step in the CheckIT process is to identify key indicators and goals to be improved (e.g., number of security incidents). The next step is to perform an assessment of the safety and security culture using the CheckIT questionnaire to identify challenges. The challenges and areas for possible improvement should then be discussed by a group of stakeholders. Finally, the stakeholder group should agree on and implement the actions needed to achieve the goals.

The structure and layout of the questionnaire is inspired by the work of Hudson and van der Graaf from BP [5]. An example question is: "To what extent is experience used as feedback in the organization?" The following responses were provided to this question at each of the three major cultural levels:

- **Denial Culture (Level 1):** A large number of incidents are not reported. A database of serious incident reports exists, but it is incomplete and not useful. The system does not have open access. Management is not informed about serious incidents.

- **Rule-Based Culture (Level 3):** A database with detailed descriptions of incidents and near incidents exists and is used internally. Efforts are made to use the database actively, but it is not fully established as a useful tool.

- **Proactive/Generative Culture (Level 5):** A company's experiences and other companies' experiences are used to continuously improve the safety and security performance, as well as the performance of the industry as a whole. Interfaces are seen as an important learning arena. Simulators are used as a training tool to gain experience across interfaces and create understanding.

Some of the other CheckIT questions are:

- To what extent is senior management involved and committed to information security?

- To what extent are employees and suppliers involved in developing information security?

- To what extent are training and sharing of common stories appreciated?

- To what extent are information security incidents analyzed and used as learning experiences for all actors?

- To what extent is reporting of unwanted incidents appreciated?

- To what extent are incidents and accidents used to improve operations rather than blaming individuals?

- To what extent are rules and procedures continuously adjusted to reduce the risks related to ICT?

- To what extent are key personnel given extensive system insight?

- To what extent is there precise and good communication related to situational awareness?

Use of the CheckIT tool has demonstrated that vendors, suppliers and other members of virtual organizations must be more involved in information security. Furthermore, information security is often problematic in large-scale projects because of the tendency to incorporate security as an add-on. CheckIT has also shown that risk analyses of individual systems and integrated SCADA/ICT systems have not been performed. Finally, the use of the tool has highlighted the fact that information sharing of incidents and best practices is poor both within and outside organizations. A CheckIT analysis can be completed in one to two days. However, improvements to the safety and security culture must be treated as an ongoing process.

7. Conclusions

Remote operations in oil and gas facilities increase system vulnerabilities and the likelihood of safety and security incidents. Oil and gas industry experts have identified three main challenges that impact safety and security: poor situational awareness, negative interactions caused by ICT traffic on SCADA systems, and virus/worm attacks.

Mitigating these risks requires a holistic approach that addresses technical ICT-based risks, organizational risks and risks related to human factors. Specifying baseline information security requirements and applying the CRIOP and CheckIT methodologies are promising approaches for addressing these different types of risks. These methods and guidelines are currently being implemented in the oil and gas sector with much success. Our future research will focus on obtaining quantitative evaluations of the impact of these strategies on the safety and security of remote operations in oil and gas facilities.

Acknowledgements

This research was supported by the Center for E-Field and Integrated Operations for the Petroleum Industry at the Norwegian University of Science and Technology (NTNU). We also acknowledge the participation of the Norwegian National Security Authority (NNSA) in the development of CheckIT.

References

[1] Advisory Committee on the Safety of Nuclear Installations, *Third Report of the Advisory Committee on the Safety of Nuclear Installations: Organizing for Safety*, Health and Safety Commission Books, Norwich, United Kingdom, 1993.

[2] S. Andersen, Improving Safety Through Integrated Operations, Master's Thesis, Department of Industrial Economics and Technology Management, Norwegian University of Science and Technology, Trondheim, Norway, 2006.

[3] R. Ask, R. Roisli, S. Johnsen, M. Line, T. Ellefsen, A. Ueland, B. Hovland, L. Groteide, B. Birkeland, A. Steinbakk, A. Pettersen, E. Hagelsteen, O. Longva and T. Losnedahl, Information security baseline requirements for process control, safety and support ICT systems, OLF Guideline No. 104, Norwegian Oil Industry Association (OLF), Stavanger, Norway, 2006.

[4] G. Chadwell, F. Leverenz and S. Rose, Contribution of human factors to incidents in the petroleum refining industry, *Process Safety Progress*, vol. 18(4), pp. 206–210, 1999.

[5] P. Hudson and G. van der Graaf, Hearts and minds: The status after 15 years research, *Proceedings of the SPE International Conference on Health, Safety and Environment in Oil and Gas Exploration and Production (SPE 73941)*, 2002.

[6] S. Johnsen, C. Bjorkli, T. Steiro, H. Fartum, H. Haukenes, J. Ramberg and J. Skriver, CRIOP: A scenario method for crisis intervention and operability analysis (www.criop.sintef.no/The%20CRIOP%20report/CRIOP Report.pdf), 2006.

[7] S. Johnsen, C. Hansen, Y. Nordby and M. Line, CheckIT: Measurement and improvement of information security and safety culture, *Proceedings of the International Conference on Probabilistic Safety Assessment and Management*, 2006.

[8] S. Johnsen, M. Lundteigen, H. Fartum and J. Monsen, Identification and reduction of risks in remote operations of offshore oil and gas installations, in *Advances in Safety and Reliability (Volume 1)*, K. Kolowrocki (Ed.), Taylor and Francis/Balkema, Leiden, The Netherlands, pp. 957–964, 2005.

[9] P. Kotter, *Leading Change*, Harvard Business School Press, Boston, Massachusetts, 1996.

[10] S. Luders, CERN tests reveal security flaws with industrial networked devices, *The Industrial Ethernet Book*, GGH Marketing Communications, Titchfield, United Kingdom, pp. 12–23, November 2006.

[11] D. McCafferty and C. Baker, Human error and marine systems: Current trends, *Proceedings of the Second Annual IBC Conference on Human Error*, 2002.

[12] Norwegian Oil Industry Association (OLF), Integrated operations on the Norwegian Continental Shelf, Stavanger, Norway (www.olf.no/?22894.pdf), 2004.

[13] Norwegian Petroleum Directorate (NPD), The NPD's fact pages, Stavanger, Norway (www.npd.no/engelsk/cwi/pbl/en/index.htm).

[14] Petroleum Safety Authority (www.ptil.no/English/Frontpage.htm).

[15] K. Stouffer, J. Falco and K. Kent, Guide to Supervisory Control and Data Acquisition (SCADA) and Industrial Control Systems Security – Initial Public Draft, National Institute of Standards and Technology, Gaithersburg, Maryland, 2006.

III

CONTROL SYSTEMS SECURITY

Chapter 8

SECURING CURRENT AND FUTURE PROCESS CONTROL SYSTEMS

Robert Cunningham, Steven Cheung, Martin Fong, Ulf Lindqvist, David Nicol, Ronald Pawlowski, Eric Robinson, William Sanders, Sankalp Singh, Alfonso Valdes, Bradley Woodworth and Michael Zhivich

Abstract Process control systems (PCSs) are instrumental to the safe, reliable and efficient operation of many critical infrastructure components. However, PCSs increasingly employ commodity information technology (IT) elements and are being connected to the Internet. As a result, they have inherited IT cyber risks, threats and attacks that could affect the safe and reliable operation of infrastructure components, adversely affecting human safety and the economy.

This paper focuses on the problem of securing current and future PCSs, and describes tools that automate the task. For current systems, we advocate specifying a policy that restricts control network access and verifying its implementation. We further advocate monitoring the control network to ensure policy implementation and verify that network use matches the design specifications. For future process control networks, we advocate hosting critical PCS software on platforms that tolerate malicious activity and protect PCS processes, and testing software with specialized tools to ensure that certain classes of vulnerabilities are absent prior to shipping.

Keywords: Process control systems, access control, intrusion detection, secure platforms, vulnerability testing

1. Introduction

Process control systems (PCSs) are used in a variety of critical infrastructures, including chemical plants, electrical power generation, transmission and distribution systems, water distribution networks, and waste water treatment plants [3]. Until recently, PCSs were isolated, purpose-built systems that used specialized hardware and proprietary protocols; communications was provided by radio and/or direct serial modem connections without regard to security.

Cunningham, R., Cheung, S., Fong, M., Lindqvist, U., Nicol, D., Pawlowski, R., Robinson, E., Sanders, W., Singh, S., Valdes, A., Woodworth, B. and Zhivich, M., 2008, in IFIP International Federation for Information Processing, Volume 253, Critical Infrastructure Protection, eds. E. Goetz and S. Shenoi; (Boston: Springer), pp. 99–115.

However, current PCSs are increasingly adopting standard computer platforms and networking protocols, often encapsulating legacy protocols in Internet protocols (e.g., Modbus encapsulated in TCP running on Windows, Unix or real-time embedded platforms using IP networks with conventional switches and routers) [4]. The change is driven by the improved functionality and lower cost offered by these technologies and the demand for data to travel over existing corporate networks to provide information to engineers, suppliers, business managers and maintenance personnel [2]. Unfortunately, enterprise IT systems based on conventional hardware, software and networking technologies are vulnerable to myriad attacks. In some cases, PCSs are built using commodity components that are known to have vulnerabilities (e.g., WinCE [16] and QNX [17]) and, unless the vulnerabilities are eliminated or mitigated, the long life of PCS components means that these vulnerabilities will persist in industrial control environments [10].

The Energy Sector Roadmap [10] envisions that within ten years, "control systems ... will be designed, installed, operated and maintained to survive an intentional cyber assault with no loss of critical function." Achieving this goal will be difficult, so concrete steps must be taken now to improve the security of current and future control systems.

This paper focuses on the problem of securing current and future PCSs, and describes tools that automate the task. For current systems, we advocate adopting techniques from enterprise IT: developing a security policy, limiting access to and from selected hosts, verifying the security policy implementation, and monitoring network use to ensure the policy is met. In particular, we describe two tools. The first tool, APT, verifies that firewall configurations match the specified security policy. The second tool, EMERALD, ensures that network traffic matches policy.

For future control systems, we advocate using secure platforms and automated testing for vulnerabilities in PCS applications. We describe two tools to achieve these goals. The first tool, SHARP, monitors applications and restricts privileges. The second, DEADBOLT, automates testing for buffer overflows in applications software.

Security in enterprise systems places a higher value on confidentiality and integrity than availability. Frequent patching and system reboots are standard practice. Also, there is typically a fairly low suspicion threshold before administrators take a system offline for forensic examination and remediation. In control systems, on the other hand, availability is the primary security goal. As a result, security components that sacrifice availability will be adopted more cautiously in industrial control environments. We therefore advocate intrusion detection systems rather than intrusion prevention systems for process control networks, and implementation-time testing to prevent certain classes of vulnerabilities instead of employing *post hoc* techniques that sacrifice availability for integrity (e.g., stack canaries [7]). Moreover, it is important to ensure that the defensive mechanisms used in industrial control systems and networks do not themselves become attack vectors.

2. Securing Current Systems

This section describes two strategies for securing current PCSs. The first involves the verification of security policy implementations in PCSs (using APT). The second strategy involves model-based intrusion detection (using EMERALD), which is very effective in control systems because of their regular topologies and connectivity patterns.

2.1 Verifying Access Policy Implementations

The management of the defense of a PCS against cyber attacks is driven by a set of objectives; specifically, what activities the system should or should not allow. For a control network built using current communications technologies such as Ethernet and TCP/IP, the objectives might involve accepting or rejecting traffic at the network layer; accepting or rejecting protocol sessions at the transport layer; and ensuring that application layer resources are used securely. System-wide security objectives are ultimately implemented and enforced by mechanisms that form the first line of defense against an adversary by restricting host and user access to devices, services and files. These access control mechanisms include, but are not limited to:

- Router-based dedicated firewalls (e.g., Cisco PIX series).
- Host-based firewalls, which could be based in software (e.g., iptables [20] in Linux, in-built firewalls in Windows XP, and various products from Symantec and McAfee for Windows) or hardware (e.g., 3Com Embedded Firewall NICs [1]).
- Operating-system-based mechanisms (e.g., discretionary access control in Linux and Windows, and mandatory access control in SELinux [19] or similar functionality provided for Windows systems by the Cisco Security Agent [6]).
- Middleware-based mechanisms (e.g., Java Security Manager) that provide for the specification and enforcement of fine granularity access control policies for Java programs.

The rules imposed by these distributed and layered mechanisms are complex with hard-to-anticipate interactions; thus, the true security posture of a PCS relative to a global policy is difficult to discern. Therefore, it is not surprising that misconfigurations of these mechanisms are a major source of security vulnerabilities. In fact, a recent study suggests that most deployed firewalls suffer from misconfigurations [31].

In an industrial environment it is important to isolate the process control network to ensure proper functioning and system security. Conflicts in the implementation of policy objectives due to the configuration of myriad access control elements can lead to access being denied or traffic being dropped in situations where the opposite would be preferred. Improper configurations can

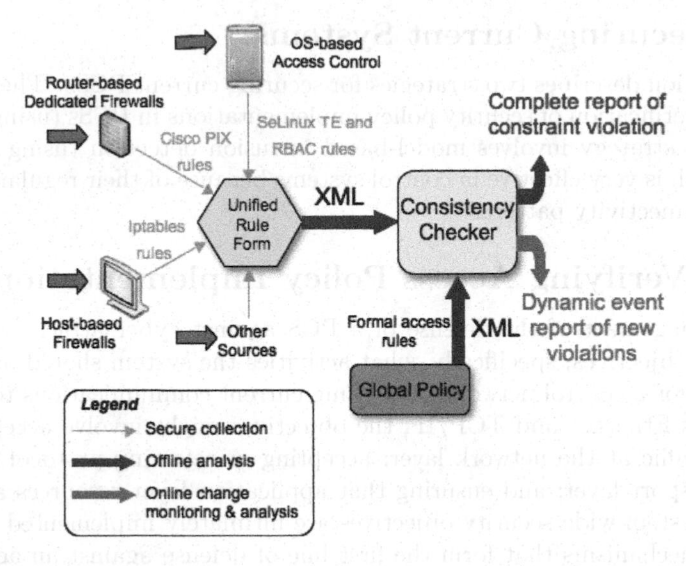

Figure 1. Operational overview of APT.

also lead to access being granted or traffic being accepted in contexts where this is not intended. This type of vulnerability may arise because a network administrator tried to "fix" a conflict that denied desired or convenient access, and by doing so created a hole. It can also arise more subtly from interactions between routing and firewall functions, or routing and operating system functions, among other interactions. Therefore, it is important for security administrators to ensure that high-level specifications of system access constraints are reflected in the configurations of access control mechanisms that are distributed throughout the network, and that changes to the configurations adhere to the global security objectives. In addition to discovering (and possibly quantifying) the deviations between configurations and policy objectives, an accurate and precise diagnosis of the root causes of the deviations would be of great utility.

We have developed the Access Policy Tool (APT) to address the needs described above. APT analyzes the security policy implementation for conformance with the global security policy specification (Figure 1). It captures configuration information from a variety of sources typically found in control networks and conducts a comprehensive offline analysis as well as dynamic online analysis of compliance to ensure that all access control elements work in harmony. The tool includes a graphical front-end to increase usability and provide ease of information management. It complements and supplements other tools and technologies used to secure PCSs. It can ensure the proper configuration of COTS and proprietary components by verification against a specification of intended functionality. In the online mode, APT provides an immediate analysis of configuration changes, and generates alerts for an intrusion

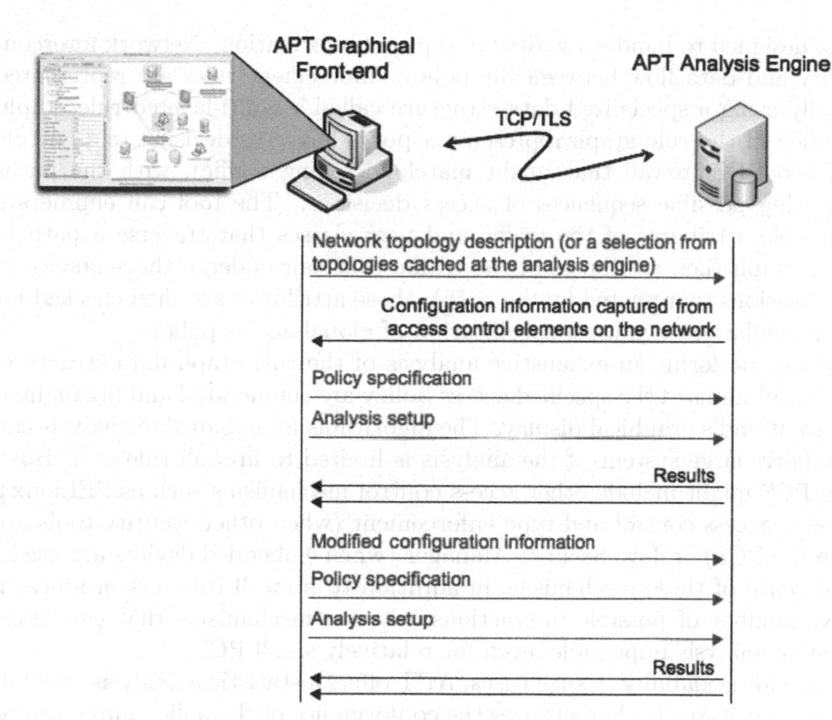

Figure 2. APT architecture.

detection or anomaly detection system if any policy holes are detected during system operation.

APT has two components: a graphical front-end written in Java Swing, and the analysis engine written in C++ (Figure 2). The two components can run on separate machines in a network, communicating with each other securely via TCP/TLS. The analysis engine needs to automatically and securely capture the configuration information of various network devices, and hence it should be deployed at a strategic location in the network. The separation of the two components allows for such a deployment, while enabling systems administrators to use the front-end as a management console run from their workstations. Using the front-end, the analysis engine can be configured with basic information about network topology and parameters for secure access to the various constituent devices. Thus, APT can obtain a snapshot of the overall configuration in a secure manner.

The access control mechanisms that APT considers for analysis include, but are not limited to: router-based dedicated firewalls (e.g., Cisco's PIX firewalls); host-based firewalls implemented in software (e.g., iptables in Linux) or hardware (e.g., 3Com's Embedded Firewall NICs); OS-based mechanisms (e.g., NSA's SELinux); and middleware-based mechanisms (e.g., Java Security Manager). The configuration information obtained is translated to an XML schema designed to handle a variety of types of information. Network interconnectivity and data flow between the policy enforcement rules are represented internally using a specialized data structure called a multi-layered rule graph. Each node in the rule graph represents a possible access decision (e.g., a rule in a Cisco PIX firewall that might match incoming traffic), with the paths representing possible sequences of access decisions. The tool can enumerate the possible attributes of the traffic and user classes that traverse a path in the rule graph (i.e., attributes of the traffic that can undergo the sequence of access decisions represented by the path); these attributes are then checked for potential violations against a specification of global access policy.

The tool performs an exhaustive analysis of the rule graph data structure. Possible violations of the specified access policy are enumerated and highlighted in the front-end's graphical display. The algorithms for exhaustive analysis can handle fairly large systems if the analysis is limited to firewall rule sets. However, a PCS might include other access control mechanisms such as SELinux's role-based access control and type enforcement (when other security tools are used in the PCS) or Java Security Manager (when embedded devices are used). The presence of these mechanisms in addition to firewall rule sets produces a massive number of possible interactions between mechanisms that can make exhaustive analysis impossible, even for relatively small PCSs.

To provide scalability in such cases, APT offers a statistical analysis capability that quantitatively characterizes the conformance of the policy implementation to the specification of the global access policy. This is accomplished using a statistical technique known as importance sampling backed by appropriate mathematical constructs for variance reduction [12, 26]. Thus, a fairly accurate estimation of the security posture can be obtained with a limited (and hence, rapid) exploration of the rule graph data structure. The statistical analysis produces a (likely incomplete) sample set of policy violations and quantitative estimates of the remaining violations. The latter includes the total number of violations, average number of rules (or other access decisions) involved in a violation, and the probability that there are no violations given that none were discovered after the analysis was performed for a specified amount of time.

Efficient data structures and algorithms are used to represent and manipulate the traffic attribute sets. These include multi-dimensional interval trees for representing the network traffic component of the attribute sets and custom data structures for efficiently representing the discrete components of attribute sets (e.g., security contexts and object permissions). Intelligent caching of the results of sub-path analysis helps minimize repeated computations.

We have used APT to analyze a variety of PCS configurations, including those for the Sandia testbed (Figure 3), which represents a typical process control network used in the oil and gas sector. The testbed has two dedicated Cisco PIX firewalls with about 15 rules each, which we augmented with host-based firewalls (iptables) for five (of 17) hosts. All the hosts run stock versions of Windows or Linux. The global access constraints were defined using the tool's graphical front-end and were set to emphasize the tightly controlled isolation

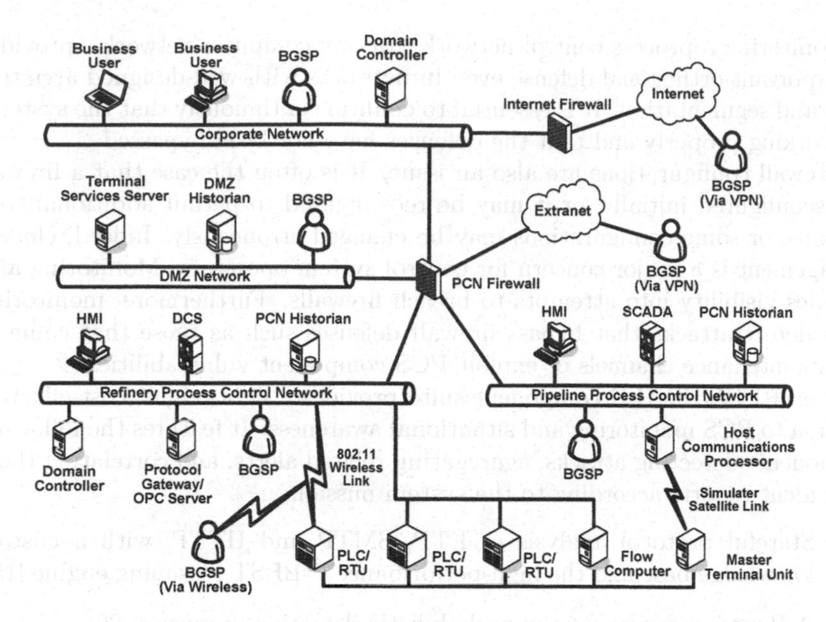

Figure 3. Representative testbed (courtesy Sandia National Laboratories).

of the process control network from the corporate network. In particular, hosts in the process control network could access each other, but only the historian could be accessed from outside the control network. Furthermore, the historian could be accessed by (and only by) a user belonging to the "sysadmin" class via the DMZ historian and by a "manager" class user from a host in the corporate network.

APT discovered more than 80 policy violations in under 10 seconds. Its post-analysis evaluation identified two rules, one in each of the two Cisco firewalls, as the root cause of the problems. The tool generated alert messages indicating the identified rules and suggestions for modification. The indicated rules were then modified or deleted using APT's user interface to quickly produce a configuration that did not result in any violations. Our experimental results indicate that the tool's exhaustive analysis functionality is very useful for analyzing network layer concerns, allowing operators to gain confidence in the implementation and configuration of their control networks.

2.2 Monitoring Process Control Systems

Intrusion detection and prevention are still relatively new to control system applications. Early implementations typically build on the signature-based intrusion detection technologies developed for enterprise systems. We believe that model-based detection, which includes specification-based detection and learning-based anomaly detection, would be very effective in process control networks because they have more regular topologies and connectivity patterns than enterprise networks.

Monitoring a process control network—or any computer network—provides an important orthogonal defense even in networks with well-designed architectures and segmentation. It is essential to confirm continuously that the systems are working properly and that the defenses have not been bypassed.

Firewall configurations are also an issue. It is often the case that a firewall is misconfigured initially, or it may be reconfigured to permit additional connections, or some configurations may be changed erroneously. Indeed, change management is a major concern for control system operators. Monitoring also provides visibility into attempts to breach firewalls. Furthermore, monitoring helps detect attacks that bypass firewall defenses such as those that come in over maintenance channels or exploit PCS component vulnerabilities.

The SRI EMERALD component suite provides a lightweight, cost-effective solution to PCS monitoring and situational awareness. It features the following components detecting attacks, aggregating related alerts, and correlating them in incident reports according to the system mission:

- Stateful protocol analysis of FTP, SMTP and HTTP, with a custom knowledge base and the high-performance P-BEST reasoning engine [15].
- A Bayesian sensor for the probabilistic detection of misuse [29].
- A service discovery and monitoring component coupled to the Bayesian sensor discovers new TCP services (new services in a stable system may be suspicious) and monitors the status of learned services [29].
- A version of the popular Snort IDS [24] with signature set tuned to complement the above, as well as to provide a unique model-based detection capability [5].
- A high-performance, near-sensor alert aggregator combines alerts from heterogeneous sensors based on probabilistic sensor fusion [30].
- Mission-aware correlation (MCORR) that correlates alerts from EMERALD components and other sensors (via an API), and prioritizes security incidents according to user-specified asset/mission criticality [23].

The knowledge base incorporates the Digital Bond SCADA rule set [8] as well as methods developed for Modbus service discovery and model-based detection [5]. Our protocol-based models use the specification of the Modbus protocol, and detect unacceptable Modbus messages by considering, for example, deviations in single-field and dependent-field values and ranges. The model-based approach also detects deviations from expected communication patterns and roles in the control network. This approach is based on the hypothesis that specification-based—or more generally model-based—detection, which is difficult in enterprise networks due to the cost and complexity of encoding accurate models, can be effective in control networks because of their relatively static topology, small number of simple protocols and regular communication patterns. Moreover, model-based detection can detect new (zero day) attacks because it does not depend on attack signatures.

The EMERALD intrusion detection appliance uses a passive monitoring interface, which is connected to a span port of a switch or router; its reporting interface is ideally connected to a private network dedicated to security functions. As such, the appliance itself is invisible on the monitored network. Depending on performance requirements, the recommended deployment is to house the detection components on multiple platforms and MCORR on another, with the detection platforms reporting to the MCORR platform. If network traffic is light, all the components can be installed on one platform.

Users of this or any other integrated PCS security monitoring system benefit from the ability to detect a variety of attacks and suspicious events. The system alerts users to probes crossing network boundaries (e.g., DMZ and control system probes from the Internet by way of the corporate network or control system probes from a compromised node on the DMZ), known exploits against commodity platforms and operating systems, appearance of new Modbus function codes in a stable system, and unexpected communication patterns.

The performance of the system was validated via experiments on Sandia's PCS testbed (Figure 3). Also, Sandia developed a multi-step attack scenario in which an adversary first compromised a system on the corporate network. From there, the attacker gained access to the DMZ historian server and subsequently accessed a historian in the process control network. The attacker then performed reconnaissance before attacking Modbus servers and other hosts in the process control network. During an attack run, `tcpdump` traces were collected, which were later used to validate the sensors.

The experimental results provide evidence that the model-based intrusion detection approach is effective for monitoring process control networks, and that it complements the signature-based approach. Different sensors detected different aspects of the multi-step attack scenario. Specifically, Snort and EMERALD's Bayesian sensor detected network scans. The signature-based rules developed by Digital Bond detected events involving an unauthorized host sending read and write attempts to a Modbus server. The system also generated Modbus server/service discovery messages during a Modbus attack. The protocol-level rules detected invalid Modbus requests (e.g., Modbus requests containing unsupported function codes). Finally, the communication pattern rules generated alerts for attack steps that violated the expected communication patterns.

3. Securing Future Systems

This section describes two strategies for securing PCSs of the future. The first, involving SHARP, provides security for PCS platforms. The second, involving DEADBOLT, is intended to assist vendors in eliminating buffer overflows in PCS software.

3.1 Securing Control System Platforms

PCSs often run on commodity computers that are susceptible to attack by malicious insiders and outsiders. None of the common operating systems were

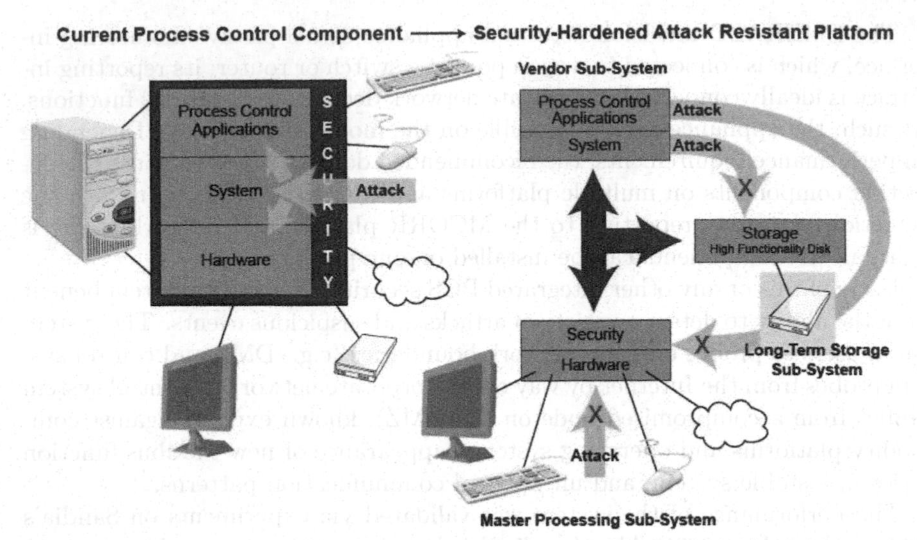

Figure 4. Vulnerable PCS system (left); SHARP platform (right).

designed with security as a primary requirement [28]. Experience has shown that securing such operating systems requires high levels of skill and is a never-ending process involving configuration changes, software patches and new layers of security software. The result is uncertain and fragile security coupled with higher costs and reduced productivity. Furthermore, security is commonly achieved by limiting network connections and restricting applications to a minimal audited set of services. These security measures result in limited functionality that can inhibit or compromise the primary function of a PCS. The Security-Hardened Attack-Resistant Platform (SHARP) concept was created to address this issue: it provides increased security for PCSs without limiting the functionality of PCS software.

SHARP is a hardware and software architecture designed to reliably detect and respond to unauthorized physical and/or network access by malicious users and software. By design, SHARP employs publicly available or commercial computing platforms that use proven security methodologies. For example, SHARP uses minimized hardened operating systems [21] to reduce the number of attack vectors and separation of duty via different roles to mitigate risk. Additionally, it uses an independent security supervisor that runs on separate hardware [27]. This supervisor constantly assesses the security state of the PCS, monitors network traffic and data access, and constrains user activities. SHARP also uses system partitioning to better secure the PCS. It places high-value, harder-to-secure systems behind a high-performance security system that provides better protection and monitoring capabilities (Figure 4).

SHARP partitions a PCS system into three parts: vendor subsystem (VSS), long-term storage subsystem (LSS) and master processing subsystem (MPS).

VSSs are high-value legacy master terminal units, human machine interfaces and other systems that are needed for operations. As the left-hand side of Figure 4 illustrates, an adversary who gains access to a classical PCS can obtain control of the entire system. However, as shown in the right-hand side of Figure 4, an adversary who successfully attacks a VSS will have difficulty accessing the other partitions used by the PCS application. All VSS inputs and outputs are proxied and monitored by the MPS (discussed below).

However, the VSS also provides some security services, including authentication, authorization and integrity checking as dictated by the underlying software and associated policies. These measures are independent of the security services provided by the MPS.

The LSS partitions and secures all SHARP data that requires persistence. It runs separately from other system components and is secured by permitting access only through special protocols. Also, it can provide encrypted storage of persistent data to reduce insider threats.

The MPS is the core of SHARP, serving as an intelligent, high-security data traffic controller. It mitigates vulnerabilities and protects against internal and external threats without user interaction. The MPS also provides validation of itself and other system components; this enhances attack detection. It boots only from read-only media so that any detected coercion is remedied by a restart from a known good state. Furthermore, it initializes cryptographic functions and communications to combat insider threats.

The MPS uses three major technologies to provide security services:

- **File Monitor:** This detector monitors all proxied data I/O between a VSS and LSS. It looks for policy violations and responds by interrupting or reversing the activity, alerting operators or implementing other appropriate responses according to policy.

- **Network Monitor:** This detector monitors the ingress and egress sides of the MPS network stack. It adaptively responds to network-based denial of service attacks using a decision engine that implements a security policy.

- **Memory Monitor:** This detector monitors process images in memory for unexpected changes. The system can respond to these changes by restarting the process from a CD-ROM image.

The use of these technologies enhances PCS security and, therefore, availability by detecting specific malicious activities and responding to them based on preset policies. For example, if a denial of service attack on a vendor-provided PCS platform is perpetrated by flooding the network interface, the network monitor on the MPS will give priority to known communications and block other (lower priority) packets that are received in high volume.

SHARP is very successful at limiting unauthorized changes to PCS settings, which can occur after a successful attack on a VSS. It continues to protect the PCS even when other measures to control unauthorized access to the VSS have failed; this increases system availability. The physical partitioning of computing resources within SHARP provides these security services with minimal impact to PCS applications. This enhances the availability of existing systems that would otherwise only be achieved by investing in new platforms to support the functional PCS infrastructure.

The risk to plant operations increases when a physical failure is coupled with a simultaneous control system failure [22]. SHARP is designed to increase the availability of the control system in the face of deliberate attacks and unanticipated failures without the additional cost of a major upgrade to the process control infrastructure. Moreover, the additional effort required to attack SHARP would produce a stronger attack signature that could be detected more easily by other network security mechanisms. Our future work will focus on developing a memory monitor for the MPS, and implementing SHARP as a plug-in appliance for existing PCSs.

3.2 Securing Control System Applications

Buffer overflows are among the most common errors that affect the security of open source and commercial software. According to the National Vulnerability Database, buffer overflows constituted 22% of "high-severity" vulnerabilities in 2005 [18]. Techniques to prevent attackers from exploiting these errors can be divided into those that discover the vulnerability before software is deployed (and thus enable the developer to fix the core problem) and others that make the successful exploitation of deployed vulnerabilities more difficult by creating additional barriers at runtime.

Current manual techniques for finding errors in software (e.g., code review by expert programmers) are expensive, slow and error-prone. Automated review by static analysis systems is also prone to very high false negative and false positive rates [33]. Code instrumentation (e.g., fine-grained bounds checking [25] or program shepherding [13]) can detect runtime problems when they occur, but it usually slows execution, sometimes significantly. Faster techniques that catch fewer attacks (e.g., address space layout randomization and using canaries to detect overflows [7]) can be implemented and supported by the operating system; in fact, both of these methods are used in modern enterprise operating systems (e.g., Microsoft Vista and Linux). All these techniques raise exceptions that translate programming errors into denials of service, which is an acceptable strategy for many enterprise systems and applications. However, such a defensive response is unsuitable for PCSs, where data must be reliably collected and control must be maintained.

A better solution would be to discover and fix errors before deployment; this eliminates the vulnerability entirely and prevents denials of service due to foiled attacks. Such an approach is also cheaper: it costs thirteen times less to fix software during development than after deployment [14]. Furthermore, if vulnerabilities can be reliably fixed at implementation time, solutions that require even modest amounts of additional memory (e.g., [7]) or hardware support (e.g., the per-page no-execute bit) would not be required. Even these modest

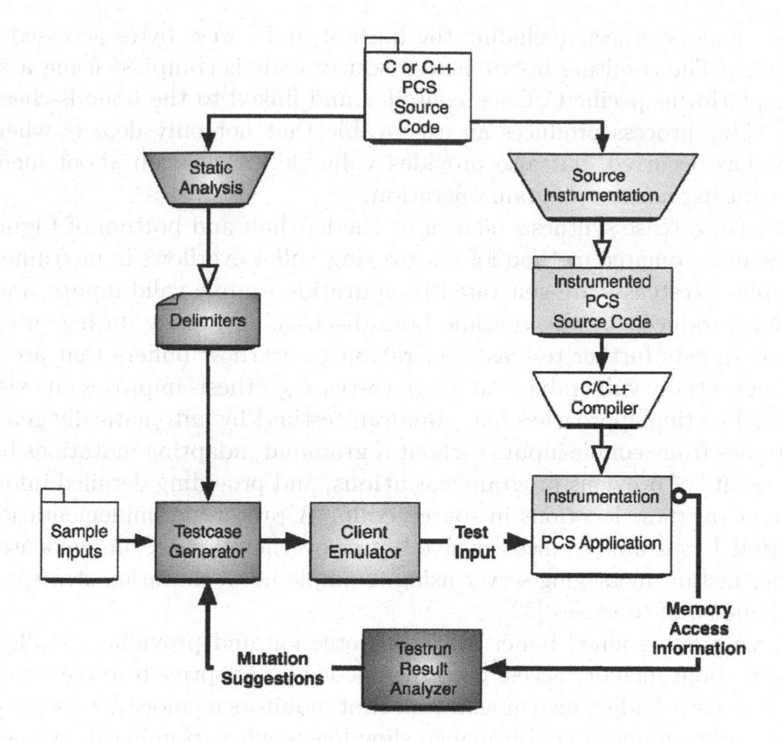

Figure 5. DEADBOLT architecture.

gains are important in embedded systems, where memory is at a premium and hardware support is limited.

To accomplish these objectives, we have developed DEADBOLT, a developer environment for automated buffer overflow testing (Figure 5). DEADBOLT uses source code instrumentation and adaptive testcase synthesis to discover buffer overflows automatically. Code instrumentation in the form of a bounds-checking runtime library enables detection of overflows as small as one byte beyond an allocated buffer [25]. However, fine-grained buffer overflow detection alone is insufficient to identify buffer overflows—a way to trigger the overflow is also required. This task is performed by adaptive testcase synthesis that mutates sample valid inputs into ones that cause buffer overflows.

Code instrumentation (shown in the right half of Figure 5) is implemented using a source-to-source translator that parses the original C++ code and inserts calls to a library that monitors memory accesses at runtime. The library keeps track of all allocated memory objects (regardless of whether they were explicitly allocated by the programmer) in a splay tree that enables determination of a "referent object" (memory object referenced by a pointer) whenever a pointer operation is performed. Thus, all memory operations using a pointer can be checked against the size of "referent object" and violations reported as errors. In addition, the bounds-checking library keeps track of memory access statistics for each memory object, including the highest and lowest bytes accessed over its lifetime. The resulting instrumented source code is compiled using a standard or platform-specific C/C++ compiler and linked to the bounds-checking library. This process produces an executable that not only detects when an overflow has occurred, but also provides valuable information about memory accesses during normal program operation.

Adaptive testcase synthesis (shown in the left half and bottom of Figure 5) provides an automated method for discovering buffer overflows in instrumented executables. Testcases are generated by mutating sample valid inputs, and information produced by the runtime bounds-checking library during program execution directs further testcase generation to overflow buffers that are considered potentially vulnerable. Adaptive testcase synthesis improves on existing automated testing approaches (e.g., random testing) by automatically generating testcases from sample inputs without a grammar, adapting mutations based on the results of previous program executions, and providing detailed information about overflow locations in source code. A prototype implementation of DEADBOLT was able to discover five buffer overflows in a C implementation of Jabber instant messaging server using a simple input mutation strategy and only a handful of testcases [32].

Achieving fine-grained buffer overflow detection and providing detailed information about memory access patterns needed for adaptive testcase synthesis comes at a cost. Adding instrumentation that monitors memory accesses results in potentially significant performance slowdowns when running instrumented executables; this is because all pointer operations are converted to calls to the bounds-checking library, and additional calls are inserted to keep track of memory object creation and deletion. This additional code also increases the memory footprint of the instrumented executable, which may become too large to run on an embedded device with limited memory. In such cases, testing can be conducted using an emulator on the developer's desktop that has sufficient memory and computing power. We believe that these tradeoffs are acceptable, as the application performance and memory footprint are only affected during testing—once errors are found and fixed, the application may be compiled and shipped without any instrumentation.

We anticipated that the relatively small scale of PCS firmware and software would facilitate the reliable detection of vulnerabilities at implementation time. After discussions with several vendors, we discovered that many PCSs are implemented using the entire C++ language, not the simplified Embedded C++ [11]. Therefore, our solution developed for software written in C (which includes only a subset of C++ features) would not protect a significant portion of PCS software.

To extend DEADBOLT to support applications that use advanced C++ features such as templates and exception handling, we are employing a C++ front-end from Edison Design Group [9] to translate C++ constructs to a functionally equivalent C implementation. This transformation enables the use of simpler instrumentation while retaining information about the original source code that is necessary for accurate and meaningful error messages. We are also focusing on input mutation strategies and test framework modifications that will enable DEADBOLT to provide effective buffer overflow discovery for PCS applications. Once modifications and further testing are complete, we hope to make the tool available to PCS vendors to assist them in eliminating buffer overflows when developing process control applications.

4. Conclusions

Unlike their enterprise network counterparts, industrial control networks emphasize availability over confidentiality and integrity. This requires techniques and tools designed for enterprise networks to be adapted for use in industrial control environments. Alternatively, new techniques and tools must be developed specifically for control environments. Our strategy for securing current and future process control systems and networks is to leverage existing enterprise security solutions as well as research results from the broader discipline of information assurance. This strategy has led to the development of an innovative suite of tools: APT, a tool for verifying access policy implementations; EMERALD, an intrusion detection system for identifying security policy violations; SHARP, a tool that mitigates risk by partitioning security services on tightly controlled hardware platforms; and DEADBOLT, a tool for eliminating buffer overflows during software development. The security requirements for industrial control environments differ from those for enterprise networks. Nevertheless, effective security solutions can be developed for process control networks by considering the special security requirements of industrial control environments, and carefully selecting, adapting and integrating appropriate enterprise security techniques and tools.

Acknowledgements

This work was partially supported by the Institute for Information Infrastructure Protection (I3P) under Award 2003-TK-TX-0003 from the Science and Technology Directorate of the U.S. Department of Homeland Security, and by Air Force Contract FA8721-05-C-0002.

References

[1] 3Com Corporation, 3Com embedded firewall solution (www.3com.com/other/pdfs/products/en_US/400741.pdf), 2006.

[2] T. Aubuchon, I. Susanto and B. Peterson, Oil and gas industry partnership with government to improve cyber security, presented at the *SPE International Oil and Gas Conference*, 2006.

[3] S. Boyer, *SCADA: Supervisory Control and Data Acquisition*, Instrumentation, Systems and Automation Society, Research Triangle Park, North Carolina, 2004.

[4] E. Byres, J. Carter, A. Elramly and D. Hoffman, Worlds in collision: Ethernet on the plant floor, *Proceedings of the ISA Emerging Technologies Conference*, 2002.

[5] S. Cheung, B. Dutertre, M. Fong, U. Lindqvist, K. Skinner and A. Valdes, Using model-based intrusion detection for SCADA networks, presented at the *SCADA Security Scientific Syposium*, 2007.

[6] Cisco Systems, Cisco security agent (www.cisco.com/en/US/products/sw/secursw/ps5057/index.html), 2006.

[7] C. Cowan, C. Pu, D. Maier, H. Hinton, J. Walpole, P. Bakke, S. Beattie, A. Grier, P. Wagle and Q. Zhang, StackGuard: Automatic adaptive detection and prevention of buffer overflow attacks, *Proceedings of the Seventh USENIX Security Symposium*, pp. 63–78, 1998.

[8] Digital Bond, SCADA IDS signatures (digitalbond.com/index.php/category/scada-ids), 2005.

[9] Edison Design Group, C++ front end (www.edg.com/index.php?location=c_frontend), 2006.

[10] J. Eisenhauer, P. Donnelly, M. Elllis and M. O'Brien, Roadmap to Secure Control Systems in the Energy Sector, Energetics, Columbia, Maryland, 2006.

[11] Embedded C++ Technical Committee, The embedded C++ specification (www.caravan.net/ec2plus/spec.html), 2006.

[12] P. Heidelberger, Fast simulation of rare events in queueing and reliability models, *ACM Transactions on Modeling and Computer Simulations*, vol. 5(1), pp. 43–85, 1995.

[13] V. Kiriansky, D. Bruening and S. Amarasinghe, Secure execution via program shepherding, *Proceedings of the Eleventh USENIX Security Symposium*, pp. 191–206, 2002.

[14] R. Lindner, Software development at a Baldridge winner: IBM Rochester, presented at the *Total Quality Management for Software Conference*, 1991.

[15] U. Lindqvist and P. Porras, Detecting computer and network misuse through the production-based expert system toolset (P-BEST), *Proceedings of the IEEE Symposium on Security and Privacy*, pp. 146–161, 1999.

[16] National Institute of Standards and Technology, CVE-2004-0775: Buffer overflow in WIDCOMM Bluetooth Connectivity Software (nvd.nist.gov/nvd.cfm?cvename=CVE-2004-0775), 2005.

[17] National Institute of Standards and Technology, CVE-2004-1390: Multiple buffer overflows in the PPPoE daemon (nvd.nist.gov/nvd.cfm?cvename=CVE-2004-1390), 2005.

[18] National Institute of Standards and Technology, National Vulnerability Database Version 2.0 (nvd.nist.gov), 2007.

[19] National Security Agency, Security-enhanced Linux (www.nsa.gov/selinux/index.cfm).

[20] netfilter.org, The netfilter.org iptables project (www.netfilter.org/projects/iptables/index.html).

[21] P. Neumann and R. Feiertag, PSOS revisited, *Proceedings of the Nineteenth Annual Computer Security Applications Conference*, pp. 208–216, 2003.

[22] C. Piller, Hackers target energy industry, *Los Angeles Times*, July 8, 2002.

[23] P. Porras, M. Fong and A. Valdes, A mission-impact-based approach to INFOSEC alarm correlation, in *Recent Advances in Intrusion Detection (LNCS 2516)*, A. Wespi, G. Vigna and L. Deri (Eds.), Springer, Berlin-Heilderberg, pp. 95–114, 2002.

[24] M. Roesch, Snort: Lightweight intrusion detection for networks, presented at the *Thirteenth USENIX Systems Administration Conference*, 1999.

[25] O. Ruwase and M. Lam, A practical dynamic buffer overflow detector, *Proceedings of the Network and Distributed System Security Symposium*, pp. 159–169, 2004.

[26] S. Singh, J. Lyons and D. Nicol, Fast model-based penetration testing, *Proceedings of the 2004 Winter Simulation Conference*, pp. 309–317, 2004.

[27] S. Smith, *Trusted Computing Platforms: Design and Applications*, Springer, New York, 2005.

[28] K. Stouffer, J. Falco and K. Kent, Guide to Supervisory Control and Data Acquisition (SCADA) and Industrial Control Systems Security – Initial Public Draft, National Institute of Standards and Technology, Gaithersburg, Maryland, 2006.

[29] A. Valdes and K. Skinner, Adaptive model-based monitoring for cyber attack detection, in *Recent Advances in Intrusion Detection (LNCS 1907)*, H. Debar, L. Me and S. Wu (Eds.), Springer, Berlin-Heilderberg, pp. 80–92, 2000.

[30] A. Valdes and K. Skinner, Probabilistic alert correlation, in *Recent Advances in Intrusion Detection (LNCS 2212)*, W. Lee, L. Me and A. Wespi (Eds.), Springer, Berlin-Heidelberg, pp. 54-68, 2001.

[31] A. Wool, A quantitative study of firewall configuration errors, *IEEE Computer*, vol. 37(6), pp. 62–67, 2004.

[32] M. Zhivich, Detecting Buffer Overflows Using Testcase Synthesis and Code Instrumentation, M.S. Thesis, Department of Electrical Engineering and Computer Sciences, Massachusetts Institute of Technology, Cambridge, Massachusetts, 2005.

[33] M. Zitser, R. Lippmann and T. Leek, Testing static analysis tools using exploitable buffer overflows from open-source code, *Proceedings of the International Symposium on the Foundations of Software Engineering*, pp. 97–106, 2004.

Chapter 9

SECURITY STRATEGIES FOR SCADA NETWORKS

Rodrigo Chandia, Jesus Gonzalez, Tim Kilpatrick, Mauricio Papa and Sujeet Shenoi

Abstract SCADA systems have historically been isolated from other computing resources. However, the use of TCP/IP as a carrier protocol and the trend to interconnect SCADA systems with enterprise networks introduce serious security threats. This paper describes two strategies for securing SCADA networks, both of which have been implemented in a laboratory-scale Modbus network. The first utilizes a security services suite that minimizes the impact on time-critical industrial process systems while adhering to industry standards. The second engages a sophisticated forensic system for SCADA network traffic collection and analysis. The forensic system supports the *post mortem* analysis of security breaches and the monitoring of process behavior to optimize plant performance.

Keywords: SCADA networks, security services, forensics

1. Introduction

Industrial control systems, also known as SCADA systems, typically incorporate sensors, actuators and control software that are deployed in widely dispersed locations. SCADA systems originally employed relatively primitive serial protocols and communications infrastructures to link SCADA components and to transport control and data messages. Also, they favored operational requirements over security because SCADA equipment was physically and logically isolated from other networks.

To increase efficiency, enhance interconnectivity, and leverage COTS (commercial off-the-shelf) hardware and software, most major industrial control protocols now include standards for transporting SCADA messages using TCP/IP. The Modbus-TCP and DNP3-over-LAN/WAN specifications are a clear indication that TCP/IP is becoming the predominant carrier protocol in modern SCADA networks. Meanwhile, TCP/IP is also facilitating interconnections

Chandia, R., Gonzalez, J., Kilpatrick, T., Papa, M. and Shenoi, S., 2008, in IFIP International Federation for Information Processing, Volume 253, Critical Infrastructure Protection, eds. E. Goetz and S. Shenoi; (Boston: Springer), pp. 117–131.

between previously isolated SCADA networks and corporate information technology and communications infrastructures.

This trend raises serious security issues. Most SCADA protocols were designed without any security mechanisms. Therefore, an attack on the TCP/IP carrier can severely expose the unprotected SCADA protocol. Furthermore, attacks on an interconnected corporate network could tunnel into a SCADA network and wreak havoc on the industrial process [4, 6].

The SCADA community has created standards that adapt information technology security solutions to mitigate risk in industrial control environments. The ISA-SP99 Committee on Manufacturing and Control Systems Security has produced two technical reports [11, 12] and is currently developing an ANSI/ISA standard. The American Petroleum Institute has released a pipeline SCADA security standard API-1164 [3], and the American Gas Association has proposed the AGA-12 [1, 2] standard for cryptographic protection of SCADA communications. The United Kingdom's National Infrastructure Security Co-ordination Centre (NISCC) has released a good practice guide on firewall deployment for SCADA systems and process control networks [5]. Meanwhile, NIST has produced two documents, a system protection profile for industrial control systems [17] and a guide for securing control systems [21].

When SCADA systems are used in critical infrastructure installations, it is important to consider security requirements and to develop security mechanisms and strategies that conform with industry initiatives and standards [7, 10, 13]. This paper discusses two such strategies for securing SCADA networks, both of which have minimal impact on real-time plant operations. The first involves the deployment of a security services suite for serial and multipoint network links that provides risk mitigation facilities in response to identified risk factors and known protocol vulnerabilities. The second strategy engages a forensic system for the capture, storage and analysis of SCADA network traffic. This system supports the investigation of security incidents and assists in monitoring process behavior and examining trends to optimize plant performance.

2. SCADA Network Architecture

SCADA networks range from small home automation systems to vast, distributed networks used in oil and gas pipelines and electric power distribution. Figure 1 presents a reference SCADA network architecture, which we use to discuss the functional design and interconnectivity aspects of SCADA networks.

A SCADA network comprises two major components, a control center and the plant it controls (Sites A through F in Figure 1). The control center and the plant are connected via a SCADA server to sites that are co-located with the control center or are within a short distance of the control center (Sites A, B and C). Remote sites are often connected to the control center by radio or satellite links, leased telephone lines or even the Internet (Sites D, E and F).

The control center is the hub of SCADA network operations. Its components include human machine interfaces (HMIs), engineering workstations, plant data historians, databases and various shared resources. Control center components

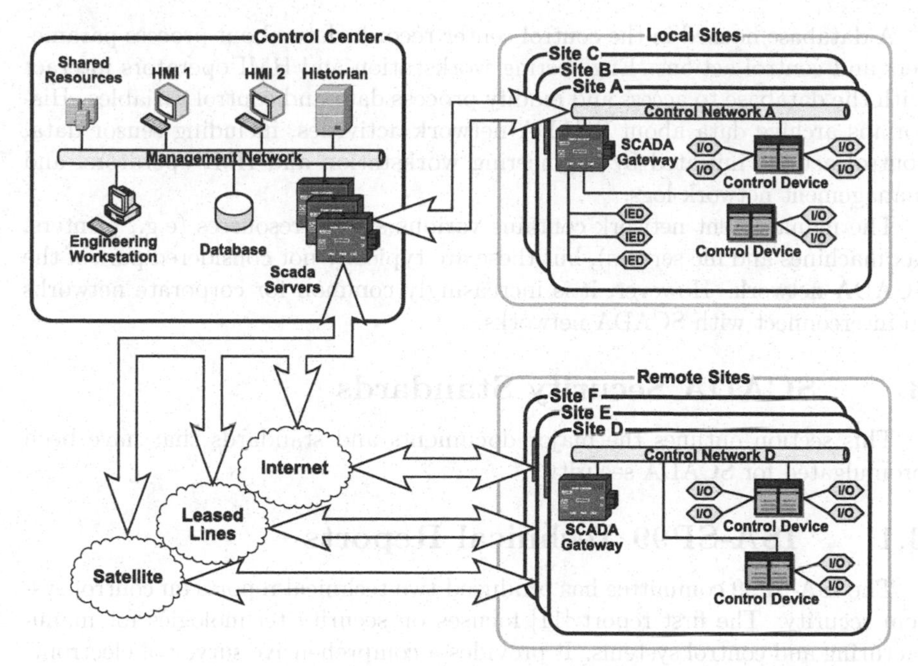

Figure 1. Generic SCADA network architecture.

communicate with each other using the management network, and with the plant (Sites A to F) and other SCADA networks using SCADA servers. Depending on their lower-level protocols, SCADA servers are usually implemented with vendor-specific software and their services are often based on the OPC standard [8].

A control network (e.g., Control Network A) has three types of components: control devices, I/O devices and a SCADA gateway. Control devices, which include programmable logic controllers (PLCs), remote terminal units (RTUs), input/output controllers (IOCs) and intelligent electronic devices (IEDs), implement the process control logic. These devices interface with and manipulate I/O devices (sensors and actuators). Sensors measure specific process parameters (e.g., temperature or pressure). Actuators perform control actions (e.g., open or close a valve) to effect the desired changes to the process parameters.

A SCADA gateway interfaces control network components that cannot communicate directly with the SCADA server. Depending on its functionality, any control device can serve as a SCADA gateway. Special units called front-end processors (FEPs) are commonly used as SCADA gateways in industrial control environments.

Human operators in the control center use human machine interfaces (HMIs) to interact with industrial process systems. Engineering workstation operators, on the other hand, have more authority over the SCADA network; they can reconfigure HMIs and control devices, and modify control algorithms (e.g., ladder logic).

A database housed in the control center records data about process parameters and control actions. Engineering workstation and HMI operators interact with the database to access and modify process data and control variables. Historians archive data about SCADA network activities, including sensor data, control actions initiated by engineering workstation and HMI operators, and management network logs.

The management network contains various shared resources (e.g., printers, fax machines and file servers), but these are typically not considered part of the SCADA network. However, it is increasingly common for corporate networks to interconnect with SCADA networks.

3. SCADA Security Standards

This section outlines the major documents and standards that have been promulgated for SCADA security.

3.1 ISA-SP99 Technical Reports

The ISA-SP99 committee has produced two technical reports on control system security. The first report [11] focuses on security technologies for manufacturing and control systems. It provides a comprehensive survey of electronic security technologies, complemented by usage guidance and security assessments. The second report [12] addresses the integration of security components in manufacturing and control system environments. Elements identified by the first report are used to integrate security in industrial environments using well-defined plans that include requirements, policies, procedures and best practices. The main goal of the report is to provide effective security implementation guidelines for control systems.

3.2 NIST System Protection Profile

In October 2004, NIST released a system protection profile (SPP) for industrial control systems [17], which provides guidance for developing formal statements of functional and security assurance requirements for industrial systems. The NIST document adopts protection profiles as defined by the Common Criteria.

The SPP core specifies functional requirements (login control, role-based access control, data authentication, etc.) and assurance requirements (configuration management, delivery and operation, vulnerability assessment, assurance maintenance, etc.). The NIST SPP also provides guidelines for developing focused protection profiles for various classes of industrial control systems.

3.3 API-1164 Security Standard

The API-1164 Pipeline SCADA Security Standard [3] was released in September 2004. This standard provides guidelines, operator checklists and a security plan template for system integrity and security. The API-1164 standard provides operators with a description of industry practices in SCADA security along with a framework for developing and implementing sound security practices.

API-1164 guidelines also address access control, communication, information distribution and classification, physical security, data flow, network design, and a management system for personnel. The API-1164 operator checklist is a comprehensive list of measures for evaluating the security status of SCADA systems. Each measure is classified as being required, in-place or not needed. The standard also contains a security plan template that adheres to API-1164 best practices and can be used with minimal modifications.

3.4 AGA-12 Documents

Three weeks after September 11, 2001, the American Gas Association established a working group to recommend protocols and mechanisms for securing industrial control systems from cyber attacks. The working group has produced two documents. The first document, AGA-12 Part 1 [1], addresses policies, assessment and audits. Also, it describes cryptographic system requirements and test planning for security devices. AGA-12 Part 1 requires security devices to comply with NIST FIPS 140-2 (Security Requirements for Cryptographic Modules).

The second document, AGA-12 Part 2 [2], discusses retrofitting serial communications and encapsulation/encryption of serial communication channels. The document describes a session-based protocol with authentication services using symmetric keys (AES and SHA1 are used to implement confidentiality and integrity, respectively). The simple design has minimal impact on latency and jitter and uses sequence numbers to protect against replay attacks. Also, it can encapsulate and transport other protocols, e.g., Modbus and DNP3.

AGA is currently developing Parts 3 and 4 of the AGA-12 documents, which will address the protection of networked systems and the embedding of security in SCADA components.

3.5 NISCC Firewall Deployment Guide

The NISCC Good Practice Guide on Firewall Deployment for SCADA and Process Control Networks [5] was developed by the British Columbia Institute of Technology for the U.K.'s National Infrastructure Security Co-ordination Centre (NISCC) in February 2005. It provides guidelines for firewall configuration and deployment in industrial environments. In particular, it describes and evaluates eight segregation architectures from dual-homed computers to VLAN-based network separation. Each architecture is evaluated on the basis of manageability, scalability and security.

The NISCC guide also discusses the implementation, configuration and management of firewalls and other architectural components. Its discussion of future technologies to be used in industrial networks highlights the importance of quality of service, and the need for devices to be aware of industrial protocols.

3.6 NIST SP 800-82 Document

In September 2006, NIST released the first public draft of a guide for SCADA and industrial control systems security (NIST SP 800-82 Document [21]). The NIST document presents a comprehensive treatment of security aspects. In particular, it discusses common system topologies, threats and vulnerabilities, and suggests security countermeasures to be used in mitigating risk. Also, it re-targets management, operational and technical security controls, which were originally specified in the context of federal information systems, for industrial control environments. In addition, the SP 800-82 document discusses other initiatives and efforts focused on developing security best practices for SCADA and industrial control systems.

4. Security Services Suite

We have designed the security services suite as a technical solution for securing industrial networks in accordance with the industry/government standards described in Section 3. The security suite has been implemented in a laboratory-scale Modbus network. It incorporates five approaches that provide security functionality at different levels of the network infrastructure: message monitoring, protocol-based solutions, tunneling services, middleware components and cryptographic key management. The suite also provides security mechanisms compatible with legacy systems, permitting the establishment of trusted and secure communication paths without the need to replace existing equipment.

The five approaches are presented in order of increasing complexity and implementation effort.

4.1 Message Monitoring

The ability to interpret and filter SCADA protocol messages can enhance security while conforming with security standards. The design involves message parsers and a grammar that defines filtering rules and actions to be taken when a SCADA message matches one or more rules in a detection profile.

Message monitoring, which can be implemented in inexpensive field devices, is intended to control traffic directed at specific network components and segments. The monitoring functionality may also be incorporated within RTUs to implement host-based filtering. However, it important to ensure that message monitoring does not impact system performance.

4.2 Protocol-Based Solutions

Security solutions for legacy SCADA systems must conform with protocol specifications and standards. Protocol-based security solutions make this possible by employing standard protocol messages with special codes in unused function fields as the enabling mechanism.

In our prototype implementation, user-defined function codes in Modbus and special data objects in DNP3 are used to convey security-related messages. This is accomplished by: (i) implementing security functionality via user-defined codes (Modbus [16]) and data objects reserved for future expansion (DNP3 [20]), or (ii) using a subset of the functions currently implemented in field devices.

Regardless of the protocol in use, the two options listed above are abstracted into a security service module placed in the application layer (option (i)) or in the user application layer (option (ii)). Protocol-based solutions allow the implementation of session management, integrity and confidentiality services.

Most industrial control protocols rely on a request/reply mechanism for communication and plant operations. Protocol-based messages extend this mode of operation as the enabling mechanism for implementing challenge-response exchanges and other security primitives. These security primitives serve as building blocks for more sophisticated security services.

Integrity and confidentiality services may be implemented using protocol frames with special fields. These fields contain signatures and, in the case of confidential information, plaintext headers for decrypting data.

The impact on system performance must be considered for both alternatives. For systems where the security module resides in the application layer, incompatibility could occur at the message level if vendors do not use the same semantics for user-defined codes. On the other hand, placing a security module in the application layer only requires field devices to be reprogrammed.

4.3 Tunneling Services

This solution employs simple communication tunnels as wrappers around SCADA protocols to add security functionality in a transparent manner. Note that this approach conforms with methodologies suggested in AGA-12 Part 2 [2] involving secure tunnels with authentication and encryption services over serial links.

Message encapsulation is the primary mechanism for constructing protected tunnels for communicating entities. These tunnels can provide a range of services, including message integrity and confidentiality. Tunneling enables these services to be inserted transparently as an independent layer in field devices or within specialized embedded devices offering services typically associated with gateways.

4.4 Middleware Components

Middleware components provide sophisticated security services in heterogeneous environments. The use of middleware components, which are implemented as protocol sub-layers, differs from the protocol-based and tunneling solutions in that it supports the integration of system components across different networks.

Our approach seeks to develop solutions similar to those provided by IPSec in IP networks. These solutions are integrated at different levels within an existing SCADA network infrastructure to provide various security services, including authentication, integrity and confidentiality.

The following areas are ideal for applying middleware components as they require sophisticated services in part provided by protocol-based solutions:

- Network access control for SCADA network perimeter defense
- Protocol translation to facilitate device interoperation in heterogeneous environments
- Memory address space mapping to hide internal device memory structure
- Transport and routing of SCADA network packets
- Integration and use of existing information technology security solutions in SCADA networks
- Security, transport and routing for Layer 2 services

4.5 Cryptographic Key Management

Several security services that involve cryptography require efficient key management solutions. Many of the SCADA security standards [1, 12] recognize the importance of key management, but more research is necessary to develop practical solutions.

Creating, distributing, storing and destroying keys without compromising security are challenging tasks. To reduce the risk of key compromise, it is necessary to change keys periodically and to revoke access privileges associated with old keys, which are also difficult tasks.

Consider a fully-connected network of n nodes where a secret key is maintained for each link. As the number of nodes n grows in the fully-connected network, the number of links (and secret keys) increases as n^2. Solutions proposed for addressing this problem include public key cryptography, certificate-based trust chains and special cryptographic protocols that tie the complexity to the number of nodes instead of the number of links. Fortunately, SCADA networks are not fully connected and, in most cases, only the communications between the control center and field devices must be secured (field devices rarely, if ever, communicate with each other). Thus, SCADA network topologies require much smaller numbers of keys and, consequently, involve simpler key management solutions.

We propose three key management solutions for SCADA networks:

- **Hash-Based Key Management:** This solution uses hashing operations for key generation, certification and verification. For example, key generation is performed by hashing the master key specific to a device with other information such as the device ID, timestamp or nonce. In cases where confidentiality is not required, hash values provide integrity guarantees with less processing requirements than other cryptographic primitives.

- **PKI-Based Key Management:** This solution uses a standard PKI that takes into account the unique features of SCADA systems for key lifetimes, and certification revocation list (CRL) verification and distribution procedures. Some of these modifications include making certification lifetimes match the physical maintenance cycles, performing CRL verification sporadically when there is connectivity with the control center, and using normal maintenance operations as opportunities to install new private keys and root certificates.

- **Symmetric Key Distribution:** This solution provides services similar to PKI, except that symmetric key cryptography is used. The prototype implementation uses the Davis-Swick protocol [9] that engages symmetric encryption and symmetric key certificates.

Extending established SCADA protocols (e.g., Modbus) to support the secure transmission and management of keys should be considered as a first approach to minimize system impact. For example, user-defined Modbus function codes could be used to initiate a master secret key exchange protocol to convey cryptographic parameters and handle key expiration and revocation.

5. SCADA Network Forensics

Forensics becomes relevant after a security incident is detected [15]. The goal is to discover the cause of the incident. If the incident is an attack, forensic analysis also seeks to determine the *modus operandi* and identities of the attackers, as well as what went wrong so that the computing system or network can be hardened to prevent future incidents. The following sections describe a forensic architecture for SCADA network traffic collection and analysis [14]. This architecture, which conforms with SCADA security standards, has been implemented in a laboratory-scale Modbus network.

5.1 Role of Forensics

A network forensic system captures and stores network traffic during enterprise operations, and provides data querying and analysis functionality to support post-incident investigations, including incident reconstruction [18, 19]. However, a SCADA network forensics system can also enhance industrial operations [14]. In the context of a SCADA network, the capture and analysis of sensor data and control actions assists in monitoring process behavior and examining trends for the purpose of optimizing plant performance.

Forensics in large-scale information technology (IT) networks is extremely complicated and expensive [18, 19]. On the other hand, SCADA network forensics can be relatively simple. SCADA traffic is routine and predictable, unlike traffic in IT networks, which transport user-generated traffic with complex communication patterns. Traffic uniformity and low traffic volumes in SCADA networks make it possible to log relevant process/control data associated with every message and to subsequently analyze the data in forensic investigations

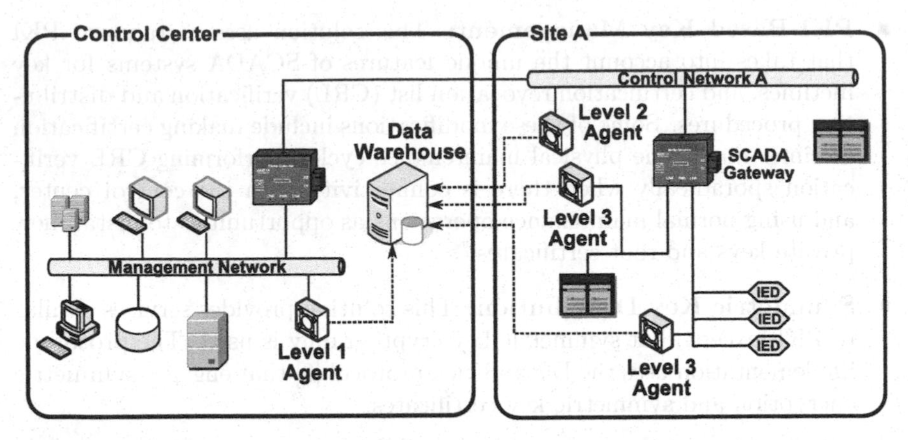

Figure 2. SCADA network with forensic capabilities.

and plant performance evaluations. In fact, our architecture makes use of the regularity of traffic in SCADA networks to minimize the volume of data collected for forensic analysis and incident response.

5.2 Forensic Architecture

Figure 2 presents a forensic architecture that supports the capture, storage and analysis of SCADA network traffic. The architecture employs "forensic agents" at strategic locations within a SCADA network to systematically capture state information and network traffic [14]. These agents forward relevant portions of network packets ("synopses") to a central location for storage and subsequent retrieval. A complete history of SCADA operations may be obtained by the stateful analysis and reconstruction of network events from the stored synopses.

The forensic architecture incorporates multiple agents and a data warehouse. An agent captures SCADA traffic in its local network segment and forwards a synopsis of each packet [18, 19] to the data warehouse. The data warehouse analyzes each packet synopsis and creates a data signature, which it stores along with the synopsis in a storage area designated for the sending agent. The data warehouse also supports queries on the stored data. An isolated network is used for all communications between agents and the data warehouse.

A SCADA network typically has several types of agents. A Level 1 agent is connected directly to the management network. Level 2 agents are located on the control networks. Level 3 agents are positioned downstream from SCADA gateways.

Industrial operations often involve multiple interconnected SCADA networks, which makes it necessary to log traffic across different SCADA networks. This is accomplished by positioning Level 0 agents between SCADA networks and employing a Level 0 data warehouses (not shown in Figure 2). To facili-

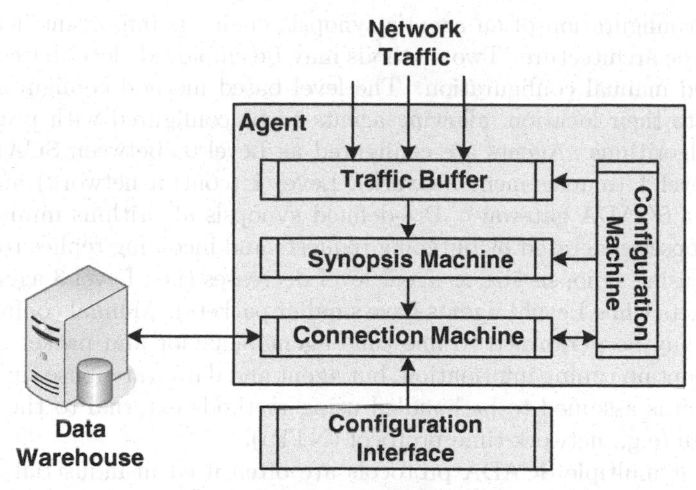

Figure 3. Synopsis generation.

tate robust querying, a Level 0 data warehouse must be connected to the data warehouses of the individual SCADA networks using an isolated network.

5.3 Forensic Agents

Forensic agents capture SCADA traffic and create synopses of network packets that contain information relevant to forensic analysis [18, 19]. An agent incorporates a network traffic buffer, synopsis machine, connection machine and configuration machine (Figure 3).

The traffic buffer stores unprocessed network traffic. It employs a multithreaded implementation of the standard producer/consumer algorithm and a bounded buffer.

The synopsis machine is the core of a forensic agent. It examines packets in the traffic buffer and generates packet synopses according to its configuration rules. Partial synopses are produced for each encapsulating protocol, e.g., agents configured for the OSI model might produce Layer 3 (network) and Layer 4 (transport) synopses. The partial synopses are combined with location information and timestamps to produce synopsis objects that are forwarded to the data warehouse.

The connection machine facilitates communication between agents and a data warehouse. Secure communication is achieved by requiring architectural components to register with an authentication engine. Access control lists (ACLs) are used to implement mutual authentication.

The configuration machine provides mechanisms for regulating agent operation. External devices attempting to configure an agent must be registered with the authentication engine and must use a common configuration interface. Some security settings are similar to those employed in IT networks; others, such as synopsis settings, are unique to this architecture.

Proper configuration of an agent's synopsis engine is important because of its role in the architecture. Two methods may be employed: level-based configuration and manual configuration. The level-based method configures agents according to their location, allowing agents to be configured with pre-defined synopsis algorithms. Agents are configured as Level 0 (between SCADA networks), Level 1 (management network), Level 2 (control network) and Level 3 (behind a SCADA gateway). Pre-defined synopsis algorithms minimize the size of synopses generated by outgoing requests and incoming replies to agents, while increasing synopsis size as agent level decreases (i.e., Level 3 agents have larger packets while Level 1 agents have smaller packets). Manual configuration of agents may be performed to fine tune agent behavior and packet analysis. Synopses contain timing information, but agent and data warehouse timing synchronization is assumed to be handled using methods external to the forensic architecture (e.g., network time protocol (NTP)).

Note that multiple SCADA protocols are often used in industrial environments. Moreover, in addition to standard protocols, e.g., Modbus and DNP3, some environments implement variations of standard protocols or proprietary protocols. The requirement to deal with diverse SCADA protocols has motivated the design of modular agents with configurable synopsis engines.

5.4 Traffic Storage and Querying

Forensic agents submit their SCADA traffic synopses to a designated data repository for storage. The design uses a relational database and query mechanisms to support forensic investigations. The traffic storage and querying facility incorporates a connection machine, data buffer, analysis machine, storage machine, query interface, query processor and agent configuration interface (Figure 4).

The connection machine supports communications between data warehouses and registered agents. Connections between a data warehouse and registered agents are used to receive synopses and configure agents. Connections to other data warehouses facilitate the processing of queries that span multiple SCADA networks.

Synopses submitted by agents for storage are placed in the data buffer and passed to the analysis machine using a producer/consumer algorithm. The analysis machine creates signatures associated with synopses that are used for event reconstruction and for analyzing and correlating SCADA traffic patterns. Signatures reduce storage requirements while maintaining forensic capabilities. For example, if a PLC communicates with certain field devices, only those device addresses must be stored and associated with the PLC. The corresponding device-based signature is generated by correlating synopses from all the agents that observe traffic associated with the PLC.

Pattern analysis capabilities may be developed for the forensic architecture. For example, PLCs often execute repetitive control loops with well-defined communication patterns. These patterns can be analyzed to produce network-based signatures for forensic investigations and anomaly detection.

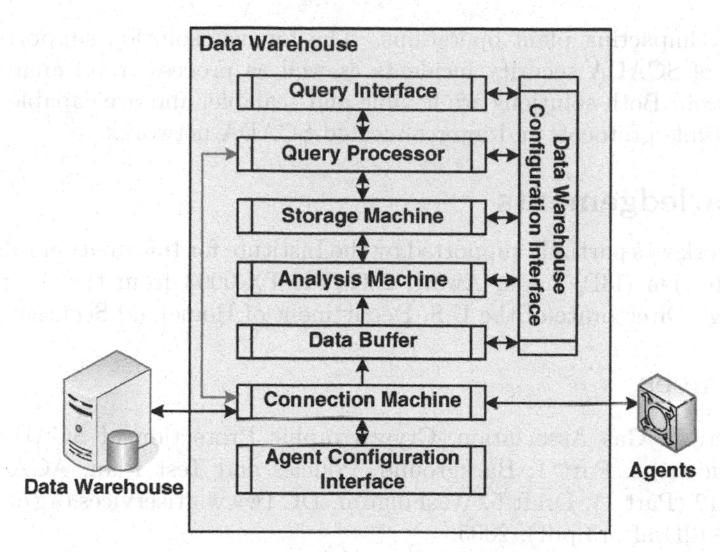

Figure 4. Traffic storage and querying.

The storage machine uses hash tables and a relational database. Each registered agent has a set of hash tables, which are used to index repetitive signature data associated with an agent. For example, partial synopses generated during communications between two devices with largely static-address-oriented data need not be stored more than once. Instead, a pointer to the entry is used as the signature (stored in the database) for identifying the communication. The number of tables associated with an agent depends on the types and quantity of synopses generated by the agent.

The query interface supports incident reconstruction, system checking and process trend analysis. The interface provides two SQL-based querying mechanisms. One uses a GUI and pre-defined options for routine analysis. The other provides a console that gives analysts more freedom to specify queries. Results are presented in reports augmented with graphical information about the SCADA network, including its component systems, devices and agents.

The query processor fields queries received from a local query interface or from another SCADA network via the connection machine. The processor determines whether or not the resolution of the query involves information from another SCADA network. If this is the case, a query is sent to the appropriate data warehouse, which in turn dynamically generates and processes a query whose response is returned to the sender.

6. Conclusions

The security strategies discussed in this paper are promising because they balance assurance and performance while adhering to SCADA protocols and standards. The security services solution can be systematically integrated into process control networks as part of a risk management process without negatively impacting plant operations. The forensic solution supports investigations of SCADA security incidents as well as process trend analysis and optimization. Both solutions are flexible and scalable, and are capable of handling multiple protocols and interconnected SCADA networks.

Acknowledgements

This work was partially supported by the Institute for Information Infrastructure Protection (I3P) under Award 2003-TK-TX-0003 from the Science and Technology Directorate of the U.S. Department of Homeland Security.

References

[1] American Gas Association, Cryptographic Protection of SCADA Communications; Part 1: Background, Policies and Test Plan, AGA Report No. 12 (Part 1), Draft 5, Washington, DC (www.gtiservices.org/security/AGA12Draft5r3.pdf), 2005.

[2] American Gas Association, Cryptographic Protection of SCADA Communications; Part 2: Retrofit Link Encryption for Asynchronous Serial Communications, AGA Report No. 12 (Part 2), Draft, Washington, DC (www.gtiservices.org/security/aga-12p2-draft-0512.pdf), 2005.

[3] American Petroleum Institute, API 1164: SCADA Security, Washington, DC, 2004.

[4] M. Berg and J. Stamp, A reference model for control and automation systems in electric power, Technical Report SAND2005-1000C, Sandia National Laboratories, Albuquerque, New Mexico, 2005.

[5] British Columbia Institute of Technology, Good Practice Guide on Firewall Deployment for SCADA and Process Control Networks, National Infrastructure Security Co-ordination Centre, London, United Kingdom, 2005.

[6] E. Byres, J. Carter, A. Elramly and D. Hoffman, Worlds in collision: Ethernet on the plant floor, *Proceedings of the ISA Emerging Technologies Conference*, 2002.

[7] E. Byres, M. Franz and D. Miller, The use of attack trees in assessing vulnerabilities in SCADA systems, *Proceedings of the International Infrastructure Survivability Workshop*, 2004.

[8] E. Byres and T. Nguyen, Using OPC to integrate control systems from competing vendors, *Proceedings of the Canadian Pulp and Paper Association Technical Conference*, 2000.

[9] D. Davis and R. Swick, Network security via private key certificates, *Operating Systems Review*, vol. 24, pp. 64–67, 1990.

[10] J. Graham and S. Patel, Security considerations in SCADA communication protocols, Technical Report TR-ISRL-04-01, Intelligent System Research Laboratory, Department of Computer Engineering and Computer Science, University of Louisville, Louisville, Kentucky, 2004.

[11] Instrumentation Systems and Automation Society, Security Technologies for Manufacturing and Control Systems (ANSI/ISA-TR99.00.01-2004), Research Triangle Park, North Carolina, 2004.

[12] Instrumentation Systems and Automation Society, Integrating Electronic Security into the Manufacturing and Control Systems Environment (ANSI/ISA-TR99.00.02-2004), Research Triangle Park, North Carolina, 2004.

[13] D. Kilman and J. Stamp, Framework for SCADA security policy, Technical Report SAND2005-1002C, Sandia National Laboratories, Albuquerque, New Mexico, 2005.

[14] T. Kilpatrick, J. Gonzalez, R. Chandia, M. Papa and S. Shenoi, An architecture for SCADA network forensics, in *Advances in Digital Forensics II*, M. Olivier and S. Shenoi (Eds.), Springer, New York, pp. 273–285, 2006.

[15] K. Mandia, C. Prosise and M. Pepe, *Incident Response and Computer Forensics*, McGraw-Hill/Osborne, Emeryville, California, 2003.

[16] Modbus IDA, MODBUS Application Protocol Specification v1.1a, North Grafton, Massachusetts (www.modbus.org/specs.php), 2004.

[17] National Institute of Standards and Technology, System Protection Profile – Industrial Control Systems v1.0, Gaithersburg, Maryland, 2004.

[18] K. Shanmugasundaram, H. Bronnimann and N. Memon, Integrating digital forensics in network architectures, in *Advances in Digital Forensics*, M. Pollitt and S. Shenoi (Eds.), Springer, New York, pp. 127–140, 2005.

[19] K. Shanmugasundaram, N. Memon, A. Savant and H. Bronnimann, Fornet: A distributed forensics system, *Proceedings of the Second International Workshop on Mathematical Methods, Models and Architectures for Computer Network Security*, 2003.

[20] M. Smith and M. Copps, DNP3 V3.00 Data Object Library Version 0.02, DNP Users Group, Pasadena, California, 1993.

[21] K. Stouffer, J. Falco and K. Kent, Guide to Supervisory Control and Data Acquisition (SCADA) and Industrial Control Systems Security – Initial Public Draft, National Institute of Standards and Technology, Gaithersburg, Maryland, 2006.

Chapter 10

SECURITY ENHANCEMENTS FOR DISTRIBUTED CONTROL SYSTEMS

Jeffrey Hieb, James Graham and Sandip Patel

Abstract Security enhancements for distributed control systems (DCSs) must be sensitive to operational issues, especially availability. This paper presents three security enhancements for DCSs that satisfy this requirement: end-to-end security for DCS protocol communications, role-based authorization to control access to devices and prevent unauthorized changes to operational parameters, and reduced operating system kernels for enhanced device security. The security enhancements have been implemented on a laboratory-scale testbed utilizing the DNP3 protocol, which is widely used in electrical power distribution systems. The test results show that the performance penalty for implementing the security enhancements is modest, and that the implemented mechanisms do not interfere with plant operations.

Keywords: DNP3, secure communication, role-based authorization, RTU security

1. Introduction

Distributed control systems (DCSs) are networks of computer systems used for measurement and control of physical systems. They play a vital role in the operation of geographically-distributed critical infrastructures such as gas, water and electrical power distribution and the railroad transportation system. DCSs are also integral to chemical plants, refineries and water treatment facilities. The 1997 report of the President's Commission on Critical Infrastructure Protection [30] and the 1998 Presidential Decision Directive 63 [9] stressed the vulnerabilities of DCSs to cyber attacks. For years, DCSs have been relatively secure because of their isolation and obscurity, but recent data indicates that cyber attacks against these systems are on the rise [8].

Industrial control systems present unique security challenges. DCSs are widely-dispersed, complex, real-time systems that provide instrumentation and telemetry for real-world processes. Delays or lack of availability that might be acceptable in traditional information technology environments are unacceptable

Hieb, J., Graham, J. and Patel, S., 2008, in IFIP International Federation for Information Processing, Volume 253, Critical Infrastructure Protection, eds. E. Goetz and S. Shenoi; (Boston: Springer), pp. 133–146.

in DCSs. Consequently, securing DCSs requires the design and implementation of real-time, high-speed and low-overhead solutions that do not interfere with industrial plant operations.

This paper presents three security enhancements to DCSs that satisfy these requirements: end-to-end security for DCS protocol communications, role-based authorization to control access to devices and prevent unauthorized changes to operational parameters, and reduced operating system kernels for enhanced device security. The security enhancements have been implemented and evaluated on a laboratory-scale testbed utilizing the DNP3 protocol, which is widely used in electrical power distribution systems.

2. DCS Security

Early control systems used a combination of knobs, dials and lights mounted on custom-built control panels. Communication with process machinery and field equipment was achieved using analog control signals carried by dedicated cables that connected the process control panels to field equipment [7]. Securing these systems was simply a matter of locking the door to the control room. Eventually, control systems began to use digital signals on serial lines based on the RS-232, RS-422 and RS-485 standards. This meant that, while networks were still relatively isolated, there was a consolidation of communication channels and communication standards. Distributed control systems (DCSs) of this era were still special-purpose stand-alone systems that were not intended to be connected to other systems [22]. They used vendor-developed proprietary protocols for communications between master terminal units (MTUs) and remote terminal units (RTUs). Due to the low fidelity and limited channel capacity of early serial communications, these protocols supported only the minimal functionality needed to achieve reliable scanning and control of remote devices [25].

Modern DCSs have been influenced by the successful use of open standards and commodity systems in information technology that have realized significant cost reductions through competition and economies of scale. This has led to the creation of modern DCS networks that are characterized by open architectures and open communication standards such as DNP3, MODBUS and IEC 60870. But the resulting network convergence has exposed DCSs to significant security threats [11, 27, 28]. The lack of authentication in DCS protocols makes communications vulnerable to spoofing, modification and replay attacks. Furthermore, the use of commercial off-the-shelf (COTS) hardware and software, especially commercial operating systems, in DCS devices makes them vulnerable to common cyber attacks. Attacks on DCSs can have serious consequences, including loss of service to utility customers, financial loss to service providers due to damaged equipment and corruption of metering information, environmental damage, even the loss of human life.

Mitigation of the risks posed by cyber attacks on DCSs has received increasing attention over the past few years. Several articles in the literature describe best practices for securing control networks [1, 11, 26, 28]. In general, security vulnerabilities are mitigated using well-established network security techniques (e.g., network segmentation, access control, VPNs and firewalls) along with standard IT security policies and practices (e.g., strong passwords). Formal standards and guidelines for control network security can be found in documents from NIST [33] and ISA [17, 18].

There has been some work on developing DCS-specific security solutions. The American Gas Association (AGA) has been working to develop a "bump in the wire" (in-line) cryptographic solution for securing point-to-point serial communications in DCS networks [4, 5, 36]. Another bump in the wire solution using COTS equipment is described in [31]. Other efforts have produced a process-control-specific intrusion detection system [24], a DoS-deterrent technique for IP-based DCS devices [6], and an improved authentication and authorization technique for maintaining port access to field devices [35].

3. DCS Security Enhancements

This section discusses three DCS security enhancements that go beyond network perimeter defenses. The enhancements are: (i) securing DCS communications, (ii) restricting operations on RTUs, and (iii) hardening RTU operating systems. In addition, a security architecture for RTUs is described.

3.1 Security-Enhanced DNP3 Communications

Two techniques for enhancing security in DNP3 communications were presented in [15]. The first uses digital signatures to verify sender identity and message integrity. The second uses a challenge-response approach to allow either party to spontaneously authenticate the sender and verify the integrity of the most recently received message. The enhancements were formally verified using OFMC and SPEAR II, and were found not to contain flaws [29].

Authentication using Digital Signatures Authentication via digital signatures is implemented by appending an authentication fragment (AF) to each DNP3 message. The AF contains an encrypted hash digest of the message concatenated with a timestamp and nonce. The timestamp is used by the receiver to verify that the time of reception does not vary from the time of transmission by a pre-specified amount. The digest is encrypted using the sender's private key, but the message itself is not encrypted to reduce processing time. The receiver decrypts the hash digest using the sender's public key and compares it with the hash digest it calculates independently. If the decrypted AF matches the computed hash digest of the received message (excluding the AF), the receiver concludes that the message is unaltered and comes from an authentic source.

Authentication via Challenge-Response Authentication using challenge-response permits the verification of the identity of the communicating party and the integrity of the most recent message. The challenge-response mechanism requires that all parties possess a shared secret. Either device (master or field unit) can initiate the challenge. The mechanism involves the following steps:

1. After the link is established, the authenticating device sends a random "challenge" message to the other device.
2. The other device responds with a value calculated using a one-way hash function. The hash stream contains the shared secret so that only a valid device can compute the correct hash value.
3. The challenger checks the response against the hash value it computes. If the values match, the DNP3 operation proceeds; otherwise the connection is terminated.
4. The authenticator sends new challenges to the other device at random intervals and repeats Steps 1–3 above.

Typically, a device would issue a challenge when an initial connection is created to prevent any further communication until the other device is authenticated. However, it is important that devices also issue challenges periodically to protect against man-in-the-middle attacks. For example, a device should issue a challenge immediately upon receiving a request to perform a critical operation, but before taking any action. To protect against replay attacks, the challenge message should contain data that changes randomly each time a challenge is issued. As usual, the responder must perform the cryptographic algorithm specified in the challenge message to produce the correct response.

3.2 RTU Authorization Model

In addition to external attacks, RTUs also face insider threats. While insider threats can never be completely mitigated, restricting users to authorized operations can limit the threat and constrain potential damage. This section describes an authorization model for controlling operations in a security-hardened RTU.

RTUs are typically connected to sensors and actuators. Central to RTU operation is a set of data values referred to as "points." These data values are digital representations of the telemetry and control provided by an RTU. "Status points" represent values read from a sensor (e.g., temperature); "command points" dictate the behavior of connected actuators; and "set points" influence local control algorithms. A security-hardened RTU should limit an individual user of a DCS to a set of authorized points and operations on those points. The possible operations on points for standard DCS communications (read, select and operate) are described in [13].

Access control to RTU points employs a role-based access control (RBAC) model [12] with an added constraint for expressing restrictions on permissions granted to roles based on the type of point. The subjects of the model are DCS users. Table 1 presents the access control model, including its key elements and functions.

Table 1. RTU access control model.

Function	**Arguments**	**Preconditions**	**Postconditions**
create_session	user, session	user $\in SU$; session $\notin S$	session $\in S$; session_role(session) = r | r $\in SR \wedge$ (user, r) $\in SUA$; user_session(session) = user
delete_session	session	session $\in S$	session $\notin S$; session_role(session) = null; user_session(session) = null
check_access	session, op, p, result	session $\in S$; op $\in SOP$; p $\in P$	result = (op, p, session_role(session)) $\in PA$
add_user	user	user $\notin SU$	user $\in SU$; $\neg\exists r \in SR$| (user, r) $\in SUA$
delete_user	user	user $\in SU$	user $\notin SU$; $\neg\exists r \in SR$| (user, r) $\in SUA$
assign_user	user, role	user $\in SU$; role $\in SR$; $\neg\exists$ r $\in SR$| (user, r) $\in SUA$	(user, role) $\in SUA$
deassign_user	user, role	user $\in SU$; role $\in SR$; (user, role) $\in SUA$	(user, role) $\notin SUA$
assign_role	role, op, obj	role $\in SR$; (op, obj) $\in PER$; (role, type(op)) $\in RT$	((op, obj), role) $\in PA$
deassign_role	role, op, obj	role $\in SR$; (op, obj) $\in PER$; ((ob, obj), role) $\in PA$	((op, obj), role) $\notin PA$

SU: Set of DCS users; SR: Set of DCS roles; S: Set of sessions;
SUA: Many to one mapping of users to roles ($SU \times SR$);
SOP: Set of DCS operations and administrative operations;
P: Set of RTU points; PER: Set of permissions ($SOP \times P$); PT: Set of point types;
PA: Many to many mapping of permissions to roles ($PER \times SR$);
PTA: Many to one mapping of points to point types ($P \times PT$);
RT: Set of tuples $SR \times PT$ indicating which point types a role may operate;
user_session(s:S) $\rightarrow$ u:SU: Function mapping each session s_i to a single user;
session_role(s:S) $\rightarrow$ r:SR: Function mapping each session s_i to a role;
type(p:P) $\rightarrow$ pt:PT: Function mapping each point to a type.

The access control model includes both DAC and MAC components. Dynamic modifications are limited to the addition and deletion of users, assignment and de-assignment of users to roles, and assignment of permissions to roles. These operations are subject to some MAC constraints, which are defined by the relations *SUA*, *RT* and *PA*. *SUA* enforces the constraint that every user can be assigned only one role. *RT* defines the point types a particular role may act upon. *PA* enforces constraints related to permissions and roles, e.g., an administrator cannot perform any operation other than administrative tasks and no user can obtain all permissions. Other elements of the model are considered to be fixed for a particular RTU and are set when the RTU is configured.

3.3 Reduced Kernels for RTUs

System vulnerabilities introduced by COTS components, such as commercial operating systems, expose RTUs to common attacks that circumvent protocol and application layer security controls and allow attackers access to critical RTU resources. This section describes two reduced kernel approaches for providing a hardened operating system base for RTUs; in addition, it presents a high-level security architecture for RTUs.

Operating systems play a central role in security because they mediate all access to shared physical resources. The operating system kernel provides the lowest level of abstraction between the hardware and the rest of the system through the system call interface, and implements access control mechanisms to protect system objects and processes. In the case of RTUs, flaws and vulnerabilities in the operating system kernel and misconfigured security settings can allow malicious code to modify or interfere with other running applications (e.g., local control algorithms and DCS applications) or bypass security mechanisms and directly access the I/O ports that operate field equipment. In the following, we describe two minimal kernel approaches for creating a hardened RTU kernel.

As mentioned previously, clear economic advantages exist to using COTS operating systems in RTUs and other field devices. But today's commodity operating systems have large monolithic kernels and contain numerous known and unknown vulnerabilities that are inherited by RTUs. A simple and straightforward approach to address this problem is to minimize the COTS operating system to include only the components needed for RTU operations. Enhanced RTU security is achieved through reduced complexity and the elimination of vulnerabilities due to the exclusion of non-essential components.

The second approach involves the use of a microkernel architecture [20], i.e., a minimal kernel that implements only those services that cannot be implemented in user space. Microkernels have three minimal requirements: address space, inter-process communication and unique identifiers. The virtues of a microkernel include greater stability, reduced TCB and less time spent in kernel mode. The MILS initiative has developed a high-assurance, real-time architecture for embedded systems [3, 16]. The core of the MILS architecture is a

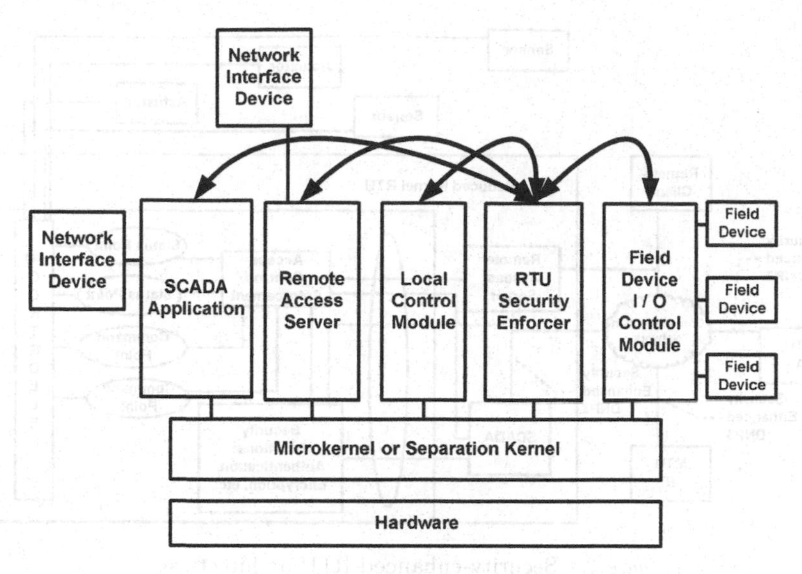

Figure 1. Microkernel-based RTU.

separation kernel, which is small enough (approximately 4,000 lines of code) to be formally verified. The separation kernel isolates processes and their resources into partitions. Processes running in different partitions can neither communicate nor interfere with processes in other partitions unless explicitly allowed by the kernel. MILS leverages the partitioning to allow security functions traditionally implemented in the operating system kernel to be moved into their own isolated partitions. These modules, which are part of the MILS middleware, are also small enough to be formally verified.

A hardened RTU can be created using a separation kernel or similar microkernel. The design places various RTU functional components in their own partitions or address spaces with well-defined communication paths (Figure 1). Digital and analog I/O modules can be placed in separate partitions and given exclusive access to the appropriate hardware. RTU applications that provide network services are placed in their own partitions as well. Finally, a security enforcement module is positioned between the partitions to provide mandatory enforcement of the RTU security policy.

3.4 Security Architecture for RTUs

The proposed security-enhanced RTU architecture builds on the microkernel concept of isolating system components and security functions in their own partitions. Figure 2 presents a high-level description of the security-enhanced RTU architecture. In the model, only an I/O controller has access to analog and digital I/O ports. Access to status points and command points is restricted by the access control enforcement and security functions modules, which provide a public interface for RTU services and share a private (trusted)

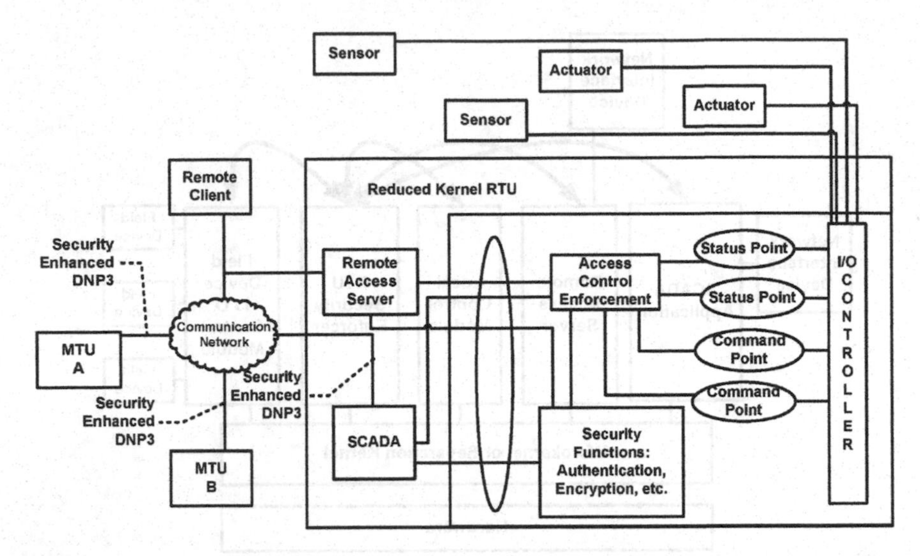

Figure 2. Security-enhanced RTU architecture.

communication interface for security-relevant information. All access to RTU points is via the access control enforcement module, where access control decisions are influenced by the access control policy and trusted security attributes obtained from protected and verified security functions.

4. Experimental Results

In our preliminary experiments, standard PCs were used to emulate RTUs and tests were conducted to measure the relative performance of the security enhancements. A more elaborate testbed is currently under development. The testbed incorporates a binary distillation column and a water-level control system. This testbed will also incorporate a hardened RTU prototype developed by modifying a commercially-available SIXNET RTU.

The DNP3 security enhancements involving authentication fragments and challenge-response authentication were tested in a simulated DCS environment. A minimal kernel RTU was created using LynxOS from LynuxWorks [21] that ran on a standard PC; this prototype also provided role-based access control to simulated device points. A MILS system or separation kernel was not available for testing.

4.1 Security-Enhanced DNP3 Communications

The authentication fragment (AF) and challenge-response enhancements were implemented on a DCS testbed [29] that simulated a subset of DNP3 MTU–RTU communications. SHA-256 was used as the hash function for the AF implementation. In the preliminary experiments, the hash was encrypted

Table 2. Performance of security-enhanced DNP3 communications.

	Total Time (ms)	MTU (ms)	RTU) (ms)
DNP3	325	4	66
DNP3 with AF and software encryption	2,146	340	1,168
DNP3 with AF and hardware encryption (est.)	764	22	104
DNP3 with challenge response	446	25	32

using AES-128; note, however, that an asymmetric cryptographic algorithm and PKI would be required for the complete implementation.

The challenge-response algorithm used a four-byte shared secret. The SHA-256 hashing algorithm was used by the MTU and RTU. The MTU was a 1.0 GHz Intel Pentium IV PC running Windows XP and web server software to provide an HMI. The RTU was a Windows-2000-based 350 MHz PC with 256 MB of RAM, which was connected to the DCS hardware.

The goal of the performance analysis was to assess the relative impact of the enhancements on communication latency. Table 2 shows the time requirements in milliseconds (ms) for processing an entire message, along with the time required by the MTU and RTU to process a message before sending a reply. The baseline values were provided by an implemented subset of DNP3 without security enhancements. As expected, encryption comes at a cost (Row 2 in Table 2). However, the performance can be improved significantly using hardware encryption (Row 3). A field-programmable gate array (FPGA) provides a low-cost, practical solution to the encryption/decryption needs of the authentication fragment model and provides throughput up to 18 Gbps [34]. Note that a conservative throughput of 10 Mbps was used to calculate the values in Table 2, assuming that a DCS network uses an in-line encryption device, which is considerably slower than other encryption devices.

4.2 RTU Authorization

Access control on the RTU was implemented as a middleware layer that had access to all the simulated device points and that provided an external interface for applications using IPC `msgsend` and `msgrecv` calls. Applications such as the DNP3 module retrieve points through IPC and use authentication credentials (initially userid and password) to establish a session for reading and writing points. The access control policy was stored in files accessible only to the enforcement module. The operation `check_permission(session, permission)` was used to apply the policy by searching for a matching permission assigned to the role associated with the session. A DNP3 module was implemented to provide a DNP3 interface to the RTU. DNP3 over TCP/IP was used on the laboratory LAN. The RTU was configured with three users, each assigned a different role (`engineer`, `operator`, `monitor`). An MTU was implemented to interrogate the RTU by polling the RTU for each point and then writing the command points back to the RTU. Three timing measurements were collected while the MTU interrogated the RTU using different users: (i) time elapsed while the MTU waited on an RTU response, (ii) time elapsed between the DNP3 module receiving a message and sending a response, and (ii) time the DNP3 module spent blocked on IPC `msgrecv`, i.e., waiting on the access control module.

The interrogation of the MTU was initially performed with the access control call `check_permission()` disabled; the call was subsequently enabled to determine the relative performance impact. Without the RTU's role-based access control feature, the MTU experienced a mean response time of 0.45 ms and a worst case response time of 0.70 ms. The mean time taken by the RTU to process a DNP3 message was 71 μs and the DNP3 module spent 32 μs blocked waiting on the IPC. With role-based access control enforced, the mean response time experienced by the MTU was 0.70 ms, with a worst case response time of 1.56 ms. On the RTU, the mean time to process a DNP3 request was 198 μs, with 146 μs spent blocked waiting on the IPC. As expected, there is some performance impact, but the impact is small, an increase of just 0.25 ms on the average. Since most continuous polling techniques have built-in delays [32], a small increase in response time does not impact system stability and throughput. However, the addition of many users and permissions, manifested by a large number of points on the RTU, would lead to performance degradation; therefore, suitable modeling and optimization techniques will have to be investigated. Furthermore, actual DCS traffic is needed to conduct a more thorough analysis of the performance impact of the access control implementation.

4.3 Reduced Kernel RTU

A prototype reduced kernel RTU was developed on a standard PC using the real-time OS (RTOS) LynxOS from LynuxWorks [21]. The RTU had a total of ten simulated points, and the access control model described in Section 3.2 was also integrated into the prototype. The DNP3 security enhancements were developed in parallel so that authentication used a username and password with the assumption that future prototypes would use authentication schemes compatible with protocol enhancements. A subset of DNP3 was used for RTU–MTU communications, and was extended to include an authentication credentials request function `0xF7`, an authentication object (group `0x20`) comprising a username and password, and an internal indicator status flag to indicate if authentication failed or a session timed out. The MTU was implemented to interrogate the RTU by polling each device point then writing back to each device output point.

To create a reduced kernel RTU, all unnecessary device drivers (SCSI, IDE, USB, etc.) and support for NFS and IPv6 were removed from the kernel. The size of the standard kernel was approximately 1.4 MB; the reduced kernel was 906 KB, a reduction of approximately 36%. We believe that significant additional reductions can be achieved by conducting a fine-grained (and tedious) examination of kernel components to identify unused kernel libraries and routines and by modifying kernel parameters that affect kernel data structures. System binaries and libraries, which also make up the operating system, were reduced as well. This involved excluding binaries and libraries that were not needed for RTU operation. Of particular relevance are unneeded network services such as `finger` and RPC, which could be initiated inadvertently or maliciously to provide an attacker with additional vectors. The kernel and the system binaries together make up the boot image, which was reduced from 4.7 MB to 2.5 MB. We expect to reduce the boot image even further through reductions in kernel size and by conducting a detailed analysis of library dependencies.

5. Conclusions

DCSs are large distributed networks with a variety of architectural components; consequently, securing these systems requires security mechanisms to be embedded throughout their different components and layers. However, most DCS security strategies have focused on applying standard IT security technologies. In contrast, the security enhancements presented in this paper are designed specifically for DCSs. The enhancements, which include end-to-end security for DCS protocol communications, role-based authorization to control access to devices and prevent unauthorized changes to operational parameters, and reduced operating system kernels for enhanced device security, balance security and availability. The performance penalty for implementing the security enhancements is modest; simulation results demonstrate that they do not interfere with plant operations. Future research will concentrate on extending and refining the secure communication and access control strategies for use in large-scale industrial environments. Efforts will also be undertaken to harden RTU operating systems by reducing kernel size while embedding security within the kernel.

References

[1] J. Abshier, Ten principles for securing control systems, *Control*, vol. 18(10), pp. 77–81, 2005.

[2] J. Abshier and J. Weiss, Securing control systems: What you need to know, *Control*, vol. 17(2), pp. 43–48, 2004.

[3] J. Alves-Foss, C. Taylor and P. Oman, A multi-layered approach to security in high assurance systems, *Proceedings of the Thirty-Seventh Annual Hawaii International Conference on System Sciences*, 2004.

[4] American Gas Association, Cryptographic Protection of SCADA Communications; Part 1: Background, Policies and Test Plan, AGA Report No. 12 (Part 1), Draft 5, Washington, DC (www.gtiservices.org/security/AGA12Draft5r3.pdf), 2005.

[5] American Gas Association, Cryptographic Protection of SCADA Communications; Part 2: Retrofit Link Encryption for Asynchronous Serial Communications, AGA Report No. 12 (Part 2), Draft, Washington, DC (www.gtiservices.org/security/aga-12p2-draft-0512.pdf), 2005.

[6] C. Bowen III, T. Buennemeyer and R. Thomas, Next generation SCADA security: Best practices and client puzzles, *Proceedings of the Sixth Annual IEEE Systems, Man and Cybernetics Information Assurance Workshop*, pp. 426–427, 2005.

[7] T. Brown, Security in SCADA systems: How to handle the growing menace to process automation, *Computing and Control Engineering Journal*, vol. 16(3), pp. 42–47, 2005.

[8] E. Byres and J. Lowe, The myths and facts behind cyber security risks for industrial control systems, presented at the *VDE Congress*, 2004.

[9] W. Clinton, Presidential Decision Directive 63, The White House, Washington, DC (www.fas.org/irp/offdocs/pdd/pdd-63.htm), 1998.

[10] A. Creery and E. Byres, Industrial cyber security for power system and SCADA networks, *Proceedings of the Fifty-Second Annual Petroleum and Chemical Industry Conference*, pp. 303–309, 2005.

[11] J. Fernandez and A. Fernandez, SCADA systems: Vulnerabilities and remediation, *Journal of Computing Sciences in Colleges*, vol. 20(4), pp. 160–168, 2005.

[12] D. Ferraiolo, R. Sandhu, S. Gavrila, D. Kuhn and R. Chandramouli, Proposed NIST standard for role-based access control, *ACM Transactions on Information and System Security*, vol. 4(3), pp. 224–274, 2001.

[13] D. Gaushell and W. Block, SCADA communication techniques and standards, *Computer Applications in Power*, vol. 6(3), pp. 45–50, 1993.

[14] D. Geer, Security of critical control systems sparks concern, *IEEE Computer*, vol. 39(1), pp. 20–23, 2006.

[15] J. Graham and S. Patel, Correctness proofs for SCADA communications protocols, *Proceedings of the Ninth World Multi-Conference on Systemics, Cybernetics and Informatics*, pp. 392–397, 2005.

[16] W. Harrison, N. Hanebutte, P. Oman and J. Alves-Foss, The MILS architecture for a secure global information grid, *CrossTalk: The Journal of Defense Software Engineering*, vol. 18(10), pp. 20–24, 2005.

[17] Instrumentation Systems and Automation Society, Security Technologies for Manufacturing and Control Systems (ANSI/ISA-TR99.00.01-2004), Research Triangle Park, North Carolina, 2004.

[18] Instrumentation Systems and Automation Society, Integrating Electronic Security into the Manufacturing and Control Systems Environment (ANSI/ISA-TR99.00.02-2004), Research Triangle Park, North Carolina, 2004.

[19] T. Kropp, System threats and vulnerabilities (power system protection), *IEEE Power and Energy*, vol. 4(2), pp. 46–50, 2006.

[20] J. Liedtke, On micro-kernel construction, *Proceedings of the Fifteenth ACM Symposium on Operating Systems Principles*, pp. 237–250, 1995.

[21] LynuxWorks (www.lynuxworks.com).

[22] R. McClanahan, SCADA and IP: Is network convergence really here? *IEEE Industry Applications*, vol. 9(2), pp. 29–36, 2003.

[23] A. Miller, Trends in process control systems security, *IEEE Security and Privacy*, vol. 3(5), pp. 57–60, 2005.

[24] M. Naedele and O. Biderbost, Human-assisted intrusion detection for process control systems, *Proceedings of the Second International Conference on Applied Cryptography and Network Security*, 2004.

[25] National Communications System, Supervisory Control and Data Acquisition (SCADA) Systems, Technical Bulletin 04-1, Arlington, Virginia, 2004.

[26] Office of Energy Assurance, 21 Steps to Improve Cyber Security of SCADA Networks, U.S. Department of Energy, Washington, DC, 2002.

[27] P. Oman, E. Schweitzer and D. Frincke, Concerns about intrusions into remotely accessible substation controllers and SCADA systems, *Proceedings of the Twenty-Seventh Annual Western Protective Relay Conference*, 2000.

[28] P. Oman, E. Schweitzer and J. Roberts, Safeguarding IEDs, substations and SCADA systems against electronic intrusions, *Proceedings of the Western Power Delivery Automation Conference*, 2001.

[29] S. Patel, Secure Internet-Based Communication Protocol for SCADA Networks, Ph.D. Dissertation, Department of Computer Engineering and Computer Science, University of Louisville, Louisville, Kentucky, 2006.

[30] President's Commission on Critical Infrastructure Protection, Critical Foundations: Protecting America's Infrastructures, Report Number 040-000-00699-1, United States Government Printing Office, Washington, DC, 1997.

[31] A. Risely, J. Roberts and P. LaDow, Electronic security of real-time protection and SCADA communications, *Proceedings of the Fifth Annual Western Power Delivery Automation Conference*, 2003.

[32] W. Rush and A. Shah, Impact of Information Security Systems on Real-Time Process Control, Final Report, NIST Project SB1341-02-C-081, Gas Technology Institute, Des Plaines, Illinois (www.isd.mel.nist.gov/projects/processcontrol/testbed/GTI_Final_April2005.pdf), 2005.

[33] K. Stouffer, J. Falco and K. Kent, Guide to Supervisory Control and Data Acquisition (SCADA) and Industrial Control Systems Security – Initial Public Draft, National Institute of Standards and Technology, Gaithersburg, Maryland, 2006.

[34] E. Swankoski, N. Vijaykrishnan, M. Kandemir and M. Irwin, A parallel architecture for secure FPGA symmetric encryption, *Proceedings of the Eighteenth International Parallel and Distributed Processing Symposium*, 2004.

[35] A. Wright, Proposal on secure authentication and authorization for remote access to SCADA field equipment, presented at the *Instrumentation Systems and Automation (ISA) Society EXPO*, 2005.

[36] A. Wright, J. Kinast and J. McCarty, Low-latency cryptographic protection for SCADA communications, in *Applied Cryptography and Network Security (LNCS 3089)*, M. Jakobsson, M. Yung and J. Zhou (Eds.), Springer, Berlin-Heidelberg, Germany, pp. 263–277, 2004.

Chapter 11

SECURITY CHALLENGES OF RECONFIGURABLE DEVICES IN THE POWER GRID

Suvda Myagmar, Roy Campbell and Marianne Winslett

Abstract Control systems used in the electrical power grid cover large geographic areas with hundreds or thousands of remote sensors and actuators. Software defined radios (SDRs) are a popular wireless alternative for replacing legacy communication devices in power grid control systems. The advantages include a low-cost, extensible communications infrastructure and the ability to reconfigure devices over-the-air, enabling the rapid implementation and upgrade of control networks.

This paper focuses on the security issues related to deploying reconfigurable SDR devices as communication platforms for substations and field instruments in the power grid. The security goals are to prevent the installation and execution of unauthorized software, ensure that devices operate within the allowed frequency bands and power levels, and prevent devices from operating in a malicious manner. The main challenges are to dynamically and securely configure software components supplied by different vendors, and to validate device configurations. This paper analyzes the security goals and challenges, and formulates security requirements for a trusted SDR device configuration framework.

Keywords: Power grid, reconfigurable devices, software defined radios, security

1. Introduction

Critical infrastructures are systems whose failure or destruction could have a debilitating impact on a nation's economy [2]. One of the largest critical infrastructure systems is the electrical power grid. The North American power grid involves nearly 3,500 utilities delivering electricity to 300 million people over more than 200,000 miles of transmission lines. Yet, this critical infrastructure is susceptible to grid-wide phenomena such as the 2003 blackout that affected

Myagmar, S., Campbell, R. and Winslett, M., 2008, in IFIP International Federation for Information Processing, Volume 253, Critical Infrastructure Protection, eds. E. Goetz and S. Shenoi; (Boston: Springer), pp. 147–160.

50 million people in the northeastern United States and Canada, and caused financial losses of approximately $6 billion.

As was highlighted in the aftermath of the 2003 blackout, the power grid has an antiquated communications infrastructure. The architecture often limits the deployment of control and protection schemes involved in managing power generation, transmission and distribution. Ideally, grid companies desire fine-grained monitoring and control of their distribution networks, even down to the last transformer. Supervisory control and data acquisition (SCADA) systems are being used to monitor and control substations and field instruments. However, many distribution substations do not have SCADA systems and require manual monitoring and control. For example, one Illinois power company has only 200 of its 550 substations equipped with SCADA systems.

A SCADA system gathers information (e.g., about voltage spikes) from field instruments, and transfers the information back to the substation and control center. It alerts the control center of alarm conditions (e.g., voltages above or below critical levels), and allows the control center to take the appropriate control actions on the distribution system. Implementing SCADA systems on power grid substations requires the installation of a communications infrastructure that connects the control center to legacy field devices such as remote terminal units (RTUs) as well as modern equipment such as intelligent electronic devices (IEDs) and synchronous phaser measurement units (PMUs) that give insights into grid dynamics and system operations [4]. However, this data cannot easily be utilized beyond the substation when the power grid has a limited communications infrastructure.

There is also a need for point-to-point communications between substations to implement special protection schemes (SPSs). SPSs address some of the wide-area control issues where the occurrence of events at one point in the grid trigger actions (e.g., tripping breakers) at another. Current communication architectures do not link substations directly. A communications network is needed to connect SCADA control centers with substations and field instruments, and to link substations. Such a network can be very expensive to build and maintain.

Most companies rely on leased lines from telecom providers, which have very high installation and maintenance costs. Leased telephone channels also provide limited reliability and sometimes may not even be available at substation sites. In fact, one company recently disclosed to us that the local phone company would no longer provide dedicated copper lines for their substations.

Power line carrier (PLC), which uses power lines to transmit radio frequency signals in the 30–500 kHz range [6], is more reliable than leased telephone lines. However, power lines are a hostile environment for signal propagation with excessive noise levels and cable attenuation. Also, PLC is not independent of the power distribution system, which makes it unsuitable in emergency situations as communication lines must operate even when power lines are not in service.

Wireless technologies are an attractive option because they offer lower installation and maintenance costs than fixed lines, and provide more flexibility in network configurations. The possibilities include satellites, very high frequency radio, ultra high frequency radio and microwave radio. Advantages of satellite systems are wide coverage, easy access to remote sites and low error rates; the disadvantages include transmission time delay and leasing costs incurred on a time-of-use basis.

Very high frequency (VHF) radio operates in the 30–300 MHz band and is mostly reserved for mobile services. On the other hand, ultra high frequency (UHF) systems operate in the 300–3,000 MHz band, and are available in point-to-point (PTP), point-to-multipoint (PTM), trunked mobile radio (TPR) and spread spectrum systems. VHF radios and UHF radios (PTP and PTM) can propagate over non-line-of-sight paths and are low-cost systems, but they have low channel capacity and digital data bit rates. Spread spectrum systems are the basis for many wireless applications, including 802.11 networks, and can operate with low power radios without licenses. However, these radios are subject to interference from co-channel transmitters and have limited path lengths because of restrictions on RF power output.

Microwave radio is a UHF scheme that operates at frequencies above 1 GHz. These systems have high channel capacities and data rates. However, microwave radios require line of sight clearance, are more expensive than VHF and UHF, and the appropriate frequency assignments may not be available in urban areas.

A SCADA radio device can be implemented using any of the technologies mentioned above. Figure 1 illustrates how wireless communications could be deployed in the power grid. Researchers have conducted evaluations of radio technologies, especially 802.11, GPRS and 900 MHz [8, 9]. Each technology has one or more disadvantages, and may become outdated in the long term. More importantly, it is costly and time consuming to upgrade thousands of devices. This is the reason why power grid communications lines and equipment that were installed decades ago are still in place.

An ideal radio platform for the power grid would accommodate future wireless communication needs, have low installation and maintenance costs, and support reconfiguration and updates of its operation and software. These considerations favor the use of software defined radio (SDR) as a platform for the power grid. SDR implements radio device functions such as modulation, signal generation, coding and link-layer protocols as software modules running on generic hardware platforms. Traditional radios are built for particular frequency ranges, modulation types and output power. On the other hand, SDR radio frequency (RF) parameters can be configured while a device is in use. This enables highly flexible radios that can switch from one communications technology to another to suit specific applications and environments. Furthermore, the protocols that implement various radio technologies and services can be downloaded over-the-air onto SDR devices.

Software radio is a suitable wireless media to replace legacy communications devices in the power grid. The reconfigurability of SDR supports the integration and co-existence of multiple radio access technologies on general-purpose

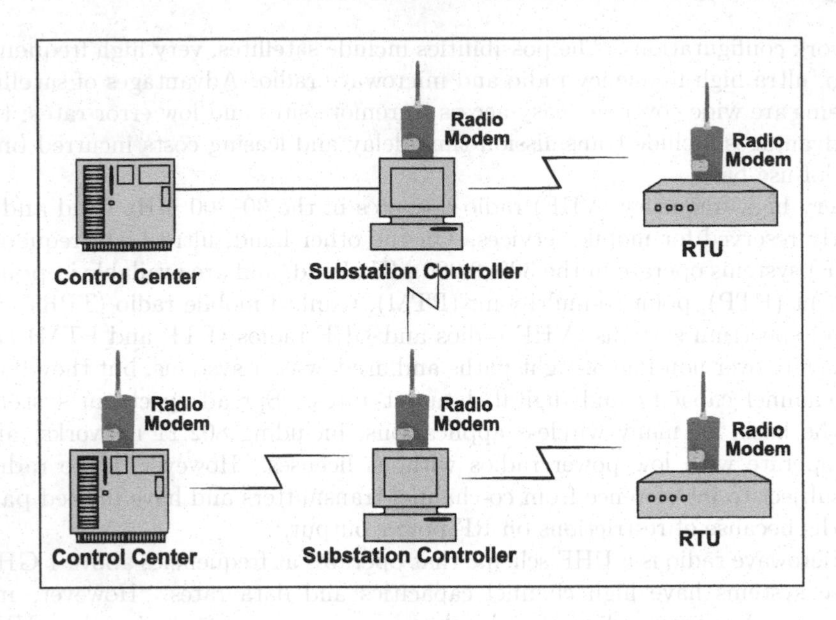

Figure 1. Wireless communications in the power grid.

radio equipment, facilitating the implementation of powerful SCADA networks. At the same time, the wireless and reconfigurable nature of SDR introduces potentially serious security problems such as unauthorized access, spoofing or suppression of utility alarms, and the configuration of malfunctioning or malicious radio equipment.

This paper examines the security issues involved in deploying SDR devices in the power grid. The security goals are to prevent the installation and execution of unauthorized software, ensure that devices operate in the allowed frequency bands and power levels, and prevent devices from operating in a malicious manner. The main challenges are to dynamically and securely configure software components on radio devices that possibly originate from different vendors, and to attest the validity of radio device configurations to a master node. This paper analyzes the security challenges in detail, and formulates security requirements and a trusted configuration framework for SDR devices in the power grid.

2. Software Defined Radios

The Federal Communications Commission (FCC) has adopted the following regulatory definition for a software defined radio (SDR) [3]:

> A radio that includes a transmitter in which the operating parameters of frequency range, modulation type or maximum output power (either radiated or conducted) can be altered by making a change in software without making any changes to hardware components that affect the radio frequency emissions.

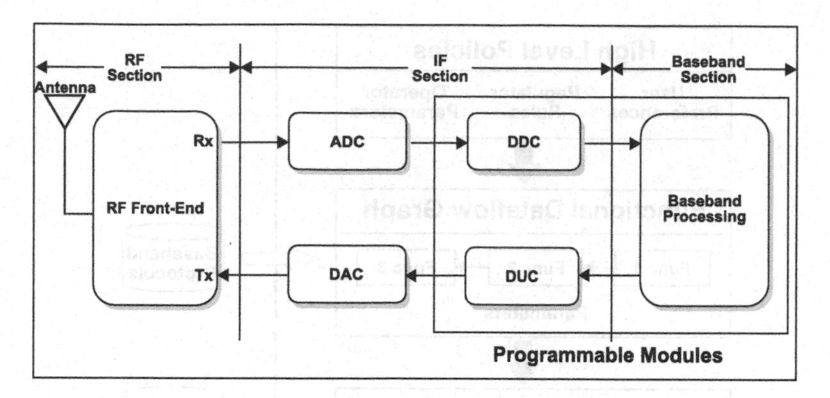

Figure 2. Digital radio transceiver.

We begin by examining how a software radio differs from a regular digital radio. Figure 2 shows the block diagram of a digital radio transceiver consisting of a radio frequency (RF) front-end, intermediate frequency (IF) section and baseband section. The RF front-end serves as the transmitter and receiver of RF signals transmitted/received via the antenna. It "down-converts" an RF signal to an IF signal or "up-converts" an IF signal to an RF signal. The IF section is responsible for analog-to-digital conversion (ADC) and digital-to-analog conversion (DAC). The digital down converter (DDC) and digital up-converter (DUC) jointly assume the functions of a modem.

The baseband section performs operations such as connection setup, equalization, frequency hopping, timing recovery and correlation. In SDR, baseband processing and the DDC and DUC modules (highlighted in Figure 2) are designed to be programmable via software [10]. The link layer protocols, modulation and demodulation operations are implemented in software.

In an electric utility environment, system upgrades and bug fixes are easier with reconfigurable devices than fixed devices. SDR enables the rapid introduction of new applications in a SCADA system. However, SDR technology has several technical challenges that need to be resolved before it can be successfully deployed. The challenges include advanced spectrum management for dynamic allocation of spectrum according to traffic needs, robust security measures for terminal configuration, secure software downloads, prevention of system misuse, and open software architectures with well-defined interfaces.

To successfully deploy SDR devices in the electrical power grid, it is important to address the problems of secure configuration of radios and the attestation of radio configurations to a master node in the grid. Before examining the security issues, we briefly discuss SDR configuration and attestation.

2.1 Radio Configuration

The primary challenge in SDR configuration is to compose radio software components according to certain constraints (e.g., regulatory requirements,

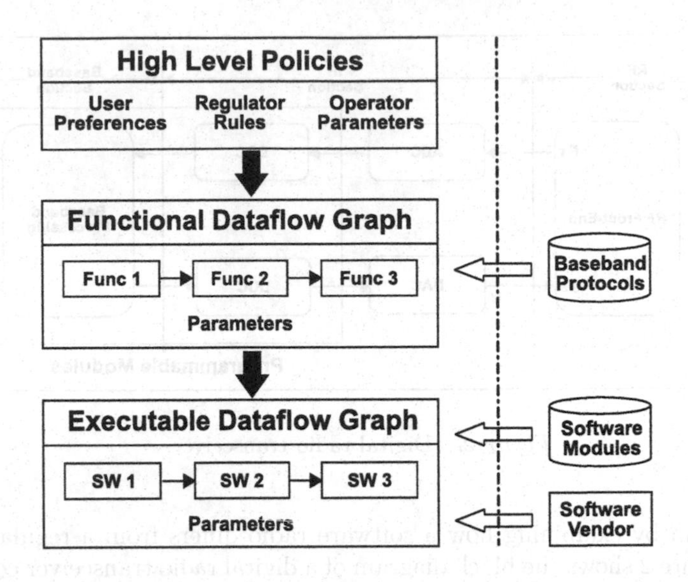

Figure 3. Composition model.

wireless communication requirements for the power grid and device hardware specifications). These constraints are provided in the form of machine-readable policies, which specify the radio access technology (e.g., GSM, UMTS), allocated frequency band (e.g., 806–902 MHz), and hardware parameters (e.g., IF, power, interfaces). The difficulty lies in mapping the configuration policies into a "functional dataflow graph" and, then, into an "executable dataflow graph." The executable dataflow graph specifies the software modules that implement various functional blocks; it is used to activate new radio modes.

The configuration process involves a sequence of steps. First, the utility application or SCADA master node requests a new configuration of the terminal. Next, rules and policies specifying regulatory and power grid communication requirements are downloaded to the terminal. Then, the requester sends its specifications for a new configuration along with the request if the specific configuration has not been activated previously on the terminal.

At the heart of configuration composition is the problem of mapping high-level policies into the executable dataflow graph. High-level policies are a collection of regulatory rules and wireless communication parameters for the power grid. First, these policies are mapped into an intermediate graph that we call a "functional dataflow graph." The functional graph is constructed according to a baseband protocol specified in the high-level policies, and it consists of functional blocks and their parameters. Then, the functional graph is mapped into the executable dataflow graph consisting of software modules and their associated parameters. If suitable software modules are not available in the local repository, they may be downloaded from a software vendor via the SCADA control center. Figure 3 presents a high-level view of the composition model.

A baseband protocol specifies the order and type of the mathematical functions used to process the signal stream. For example, if the radio access technology is GSM, the baseband protocol specifies the types and order of the modulators, encoders and filters used for processing signals.

2.2 Remote Radio Attestation

The substation or control center may request a proof of conformity with the standards before allowing a field instrument or substation to participate in utility operations. The challenge in remote attestation is to enable the terminal to prove to its master node that its configuration is in compliance with standards and regulations, and it is not a rogue or malfunctioning device. Should the configuration be found as non-conforming at any point, the terminal rolls back to a previously-validated configuration.

The remote attestation process starts with a request from the master node to attest the configuration of the remote device before it participates in utility communications. This is done to ensure that the terminal is configured correctly to fully benefit from the service, and also to prevent a misconfigured terminal from interfering with other communications. Normally, the master node validates the remote device once in the beginning; it subsequently verifies that the device configuration has not been modified.

3. Security Challenges

The *IEEE Guide for Electric Power Substation Physical and Electronic Security* [5] cautions that the increased use of computers to remotely access substations may be exposing control and protection devices to the same vulnerabilities as traditional IT systems. Indeed, serious concerns have been raised about cyber threats to critical infrastructure components such as the power grid. The President's Commission on Critical Infrastructure Protection (PCCIP) [2] and IEEE [5] have issued reports that highlight the threats to utilities. Categories of threats that are specific to SCADA systems, substation controllers and field instruments are [7]:

- Blunders, errors and omissions
- Fraud, theft and criminal activity
- Disgruntled employees and insiders
- Recreational and malicious hackers
- Malicious code
- Industrial espionage
- Foreign espionage and information warfare

Security issues relating to general RTUs, substations and wireless devices are discussed elsewhere (see, e.g., [7]). This paper focuses on security issues

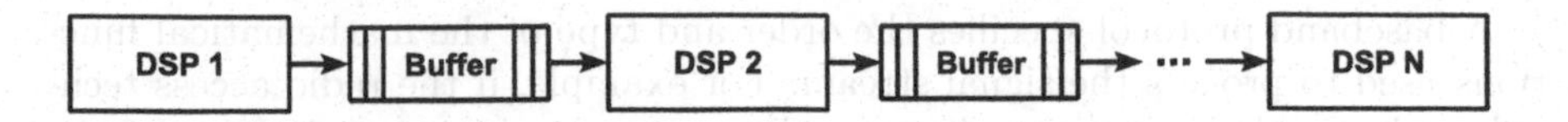

Figure 4. Generic flow graph of DSP modules.

that are unique to software radios. Since the distinguishing characteristic of a software radio is its reconfigurability, the primary issue is configuration security.

Before designing protection mechanisms for SDRs in the power grid, it is necessary to conduct a detailed security analysis of the system. For this purpose, we utilize a three-step threat modeling technique:

- **System Characterization:** This step focuses on understanding system components and their interconnections, and creating a system model that captures its main characteristics.

- **Asset and Access Point Identification:** This step involves the identification of the abstract and concrete system resources that must be protected from misuse by an adversary, and the identification of the points of access to these resources.

- **Threat Identification:** This step involves an examination of the identified security-critical assets, a review of the attack goals for each asset that violate confidentiality, integrity or availability, and the creation of a threat profile of the system describing the potential attacks that must be mitigated.

First, we clarify some important concepts of the SDR architecture. In the previous section, we discussed the steps involved in the configuration process, but did not explain how a radio configuration is represented in the system.

An SDR configuration describes the waveform and digital signal processing (DSP) modules that define the radio operating mode, the interconnections between the modules, and the input parameters for the modules. At the core of a radio configuration is a set of pipelines, each containing several DSP modules in a row. A pipeline is also referred to as a "flow graph" because it depicts the flow of transmitted/received data as it is processed by one DSP module after another. Figure 4 shows a generic flow graph characterizing the configuration of an SDR terminal. The vertices of the graph are DSP modules that perform various mathematical manipulations (e.g., modulation, filtering or mixing) of the input signal stream. The edges of the graph indicate the direction of data flow and the connections to adjacent DSP modules via memory buffers, which temporarily store the signal stream being processed.

SDR threats may result from deliberate overt or covert actions of third parties (e.g., hackers and viruses), or through human error (e.g., software bugs). The points of attack are the communications infrastructure and end terminals.

3.1 Security Threats

The following security threats relating to SDR configuration were identified by the threat modeling effort. We provide the classification of each threat (in parentheses), and describe its effects and consequences.

- **Configuration of a Malicious Device (DoS, Disclosure)** A malicious user may configure a SDR terminal so that it becomes an eavesdropping or jamming device. A malicious device with sufficiently high power could force other devices in the communications network to operate at higher power levels, causing them to drain their batteries. If the network devices do not change their power levels, their communications are disrupted.

- **Violation of Regulatory Constraints (DoS):** A device may be configured so that it does not adhere to regional regulations and equipment specifications (e.g., EMC emission requirements). This may render the device inoperable. Also, the device may unintentionally operate in unauthorized bands (e.g., military use bands).

- **Invalid Configuration (DoS):** A device could be configured so that it does not work or it works incorrectly. The received and transmitted signal streams may be processed incorrectly, resulting in garbled messages. The wireless protocol specified by the master node or the utility provider could be disregarded.

- **Insecure Software Download (Tampering):** Configuration and other system software may be illegally modified en route, or an adversary may supply malicious software. This enables the launching of other attacks such as the configuration of a malicious device or exhaustion of system resources.

- **Exhaustion of System Resources (DoS):** Malicious or buggy software may launch DoS attacks against legitimate processes by consuming system resources such as memory.

- **Improper Software Functionality (Tampering):** Even software supplied by a certified vendor or downloaded from a trusted master node could be buggy. It might not work properly or implement the expected functionality. Such software can accidentally modify process parameters or garble a signal stream (e.g., via a buffer overflow).

- **Unauthorized Access to Private Data (Information Disclosure):** Sensitive information is involved in the configuration process. Access to information about communication specifications and configuration data must be protected.

The threats identified above serve as the basis for deriving the security objectives and requirements of the configuration framework. Note that other threats (e.g., unauthorized use of network services and unauthorized login into radio devices) also concern SDR devices, but they are outside the scope of this work.

3.2 Security Requirements

To mitigate the above security threats, we specify the following security requirements for the SDR configuration framework:

- It shall prevent the loading, installation and instantiation of unauthorized or unproven software.
- It shall ensure the secrecy and integrity of over-the-air software downloads.
- It shall verify that downloaded software is supplied by a certified vendor.
- It shall ensure that SDR terminal operations are limited to frequency bands and power levels authorized by regulatory bodies and power grid operators.
- It shall implement a trusted configuration module responsible for flow graph construction.
- It shall provide fault domain isolation for reconfigurable modules so that each module has access only to its own memory area.
- It shall ensure that software installed on terminals is not modified or tampered with when the terminals are in a powered down condition.
- It shall ensure confidentiality, integrity and authenticity of information used in the configuration process.
- It shall provide trusted configuration information to other nodes in the power grid on request.

4. Configuration Framework

The SDR configuration framework presented in Figure 5 is designed to support trusted radio platforms for field instruments and substations in the electrical power grid. The framework consists of the following components:

- **Execution Environment:** This environment provides a platform for executing all equipment functions, including configuration management and control. The challenge for SDRs is to ensure that applications cannot access information or interfere with the flow of information at a higher security classification (e.g., during device configuration). A secure partitioning method is needed to support multiple levels of security on a single processor. A secure memory management unit (MMU) with hardware-enforced memory protection can be used to isolate data in different partitions.

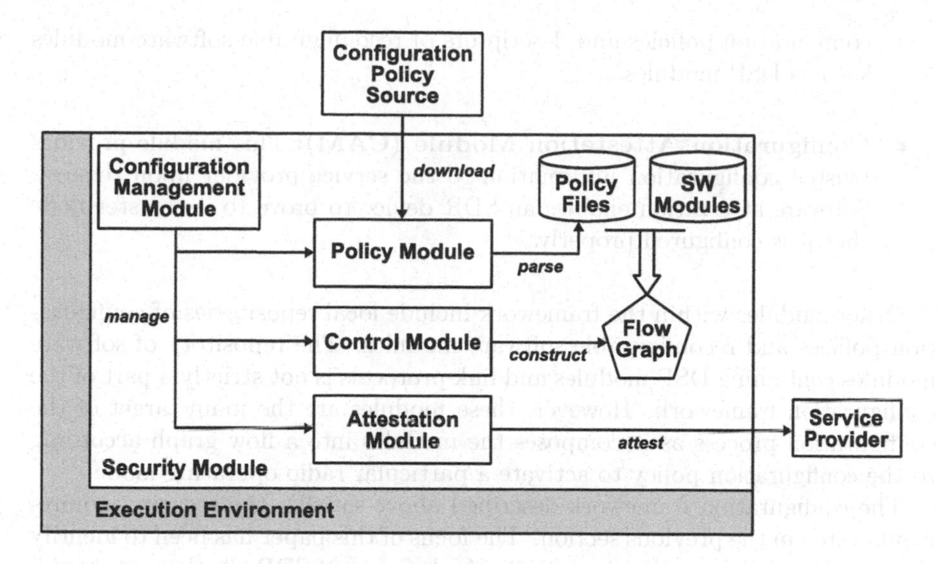

Figure 5. Configuration framework.

- **Security Module:** This module ensures that all the security requirements specified for the configuration process are satisfied. It provides the basic security functions to all other configuration modules. For example, it provides authentication functionality to the MMU when a DSP module attempts to access the shared memory buffer of a flow graph.

- **Configuration Management Module (CMM):** This module is responsible for managing all configuration activities. It initiates, coordinates and performs configuration functions, and manages communications between all configuration-related components. The module also supports tasks such as mode selection, download of configuration policies and software modules, and approval of new radio configurations.

- **Configuration Control Module (CCM):** This module is designed to support the CMM by controlling and supervising reconfigurations. The selected and verified configuration policy is passed to the CCM for construction of a flow graph composed of DSP modules specified in the policy. The flow graph is then executed by the runtime environment, which activates the requested radio operating mode. The module also ensures that the new configuration is in compliance with regulatory requirements before executing the configuration.

- **Policy Management Module (PMM):** This module provisions a configuration policy for a new configuration approved by the CMM. It parses and verifies downloaded configuration policies, and manages the update and versioning of the local policy repository. XML is used to specify configuration policies and descriptors of reconfigurable software modules such as DSP modules.

- **Configuration Attestation Module (CAM):** This module provides trusted configuration information to the service provider upon request. Software attestation enables an SDR device to prove to its master node that it is configured properly.

Other modules within the framework include local repositories of configuration policies and reconfigurable software modules. The repository of software modules containing DSP modules and link protocols is not strictly a part of the configuration framework. However, these modules are the main target of the configuration process as it composes the modules into a flow graph according to the configuration policy to activate a particular radio operating mode.

The configuration framework described above satisfies the security requirements listed in the previous section. The focus of this paper has been to identify the security challenges that impact the deployment of SDRs in the power grid. Implementation details and proofs of security properties for the configuration framework will be provided in a future publication.

5. Related Work

Several researchers have investigated the use of wireless protocols in the electrical power grid, but SDR applications have been largely ignored. Shea [9] has described the deployment of 900/928/952 MHz radios by the Houston Lighting and Power Company in its SCADA systems for power distribution. The deployment of these radios for master-RTU communications resulted in lower installation and maintenance costs, while providing higher reliability than leased phone lines. Problems included occasional interference from systems operating in neighboring bands, and regulatory constraints regarding frequency licensing and the maximum distance between master units and RTUs.

Eichelburg [1] has presented a wireless communication architecture that uses GPRS modems to connect medium-voltage substations in a German municipal utility; GRPS modems combined with VPN routers enable substations to communicate with the SCADA control center through the public Internet. Risley and Roberts [8] have analyzed the security risks associated with the use of 802.11 radios in the electrical power grid. Also, they have identified security flaws inherent in the WEP encryption of the 802.11 protocol.

6. Conclusions

The existing communications infrastructure for controlling the electrical power grid is inadequate. The installation of fixed communications lines is expensive. Wireless technologies such as VHF, UHF and microwave radios are reliable, low-cost alternatives, but they have some disadvantages that make it difficult for utility companies to incorporate them in long-term solutions.

Software defined radio (SDR) appears to be an ideal technology to accommodate current and future wireless communication needs. Like all radio solutions, it has low installation and maintenance costs. Furthermore, new wireless protocols may be downloaded and configured to activate new radio modes. This ability to reconfigure devices over-the-air facilitates the rapid implementation and upgrade of power grid control networks.

Our investigation of security issues specific to deploying SDRs in the power grid has identified several challenges. They include the configuration of malicious devices, insecure software downloads, and violations of regulatory constraints. These challenges can be addressed by dynamically and securely configuring SDR devices, and by validating device configurations. The configuration framework presented in this paper is an attractive solution because it supports secure radio configuration and remote attestation of SDRs.

Acknowledgements

This research was undertaken under the TCIP Project: Trustworthy Infrastructure for the Power Grid, which was supported by National Science Foundation Grant CNS–0524695.

References

[1] W. Eichelburg, Using GPRS to connect outlying distribution substations, *Proceedings of the Eighteenth International Conference and Exhibition on Electricity Distribution*, vol. 3, p. 54, 2005.

[2] J. Ellis, D. Fisher, T. Longstaff, L. Pesante and R. Pethia, Report to the President's Commission on Critical Infrastructure Protection, Special Report CMU/SEI-97 SR-003, Software Engineering Institute, Carnegie Mellon University, Pittsburgh, Pennsylvania, 1997.

[3] Federal Communications Commission, In the Matter of Authorization and Use of Software Defined Radios, First Report and Order (FCC 01-264), Washington, DC (www.fcc.gov/Bureaus/Engineering_Technology/Orders/2001/fcc01264.pdf), 2001.

[4] C. Hauser, D. Bakken and A. Bose, A failure to communicate, *IEEE Power and Energy*, vol. 3(2), pp. 47–55, 2005.

[5] Institute of Electrical and Electronics Engineers, IEEE 1402 Guide for Electric Power Substation Physical and Electronic Security, Document IEEE 1402, Piscataway, New Jersey, 2000.

[6] National Communications System, Supervisory Control and Data Acquisition (SCADA) Systems, Technical Information Bulletin NCS TIB 04-1, Arlington, Virginia, 2004.

[7] P. Oman, E. Schweitzer and D. Frincke, Concerns about intrusions into remotely accessible substation controllers and SCADA systems, *Proceedings of the Twenty-Seventh Annual Western Protective Relay Conference*, 2000.

[8] A. Risley and J. Roberts, Electronic security risks associated with the use of wireless point-to-point communications in the electric power industry, presented at the *DistribuTECH Conference and Exhibition*, 2003.

[9] M. Shea, 900 MHz radio signals operational control, *IEEE Computer Applications in Power*, vol. 5(4), pp. 29–32, 1992.

[10] Wipro Technologies, Software defined radio, White Paper (www.wipro.com/webpages/insights/softwareradio.htm), 2002.

Chapter 12

INTRUSION DETECTION AND EVENT MONITORING IN SCADA NETWORKS

Paul Oman and Matthew Phillips

Abstract This paper describes the implementation of a customized intrusion detection and event monitoring system for a SCADA/sensor testbed. The system raises alerts upon detecting potential unauthorized access and changes in device settings. By markedly increasing the logging of critical network events, the system shows dramatic improvements in both the security and overall auditing capabilities. In addition to its role in securing SCADA networks, the system assists operators in identifying common configuration errors.

Keywords: Intrusion detection, real-time monitoring, SCADA networks

1. Introduction

Power system control was once a laborious process. Prior to the use of digital control equipment and communications networks, engineers had to travel to each substation to view system conditions and make changes. Technological advances enabled engineers to monitor their systems from a central location, controlling dozens of substations from a single terminal [8]. Further advances now permit engineers to control their systems – even from home – using the Internet, telephone system and wireless networks [2].

When control systems were stand-alone, devices were required to meet strict standards on operating temperatures, electrical disturbances and other environmental concerns. The operating environment has changed. In addition to meeting the harsh realities of an industrial environment, engineers must now account for new "disturbances" – electronic attacks.

Process control systems are very heterogeneous environments. A power substation may have devices from a dozen different manufacturers. Some devices may communicate serially or via proprietary protocols on proprietary cabling, others may use Ethernet, and still others tunneling protocols over Ethernet. Some devices may be 20 years old, while others are brand new.

Oman, P. and Phillips, M., 2008, in IFIP International Federation for Information Processing, Volume 253, Critical Infrastructure Protection, eds. E. Goetz and S. Shenoi; (Boston: Springer), pp. 161–173.

Process control systems are built to operate in high stress, time-sensitive environments. The devices are simple and dedicated to performing their limited tasks well. Therefore, most devices do not have the memory, processing power and bandwidth required to perform security functions. Real-time control systems have several additional limitations, including:

- Weak authentication mechanisms that do not differentiate between human users.
- No privilege separation or user account management to control access (e.g., one account, one password).
- Most devices do not record login attempts (e.g., success, failure and number of attempts).
- Most devices cannot run user programs; they can only perform simple logic operations.
- Many users do not change the factory default settings of devices.
- Many control networks are not designed with cyber security in mind.
- Proprietary protocols slow the integration of security tools in control networks.
- Overall lack of monitoring and auditing (e.g., tracking changes to settings and firmware upgrades).
- Devices are notoriously difficult to set up and are typically configured once and left alone.
- Heterogeneous control networks with components varying in age and capabilities require singular attention to secure, making broad adoption unaffordable.

These factors severely hamper efforts to secure control systems [1, 9]. Fortunately, the solutions are well-known in the information technology field [5]. Indeed, many security solutions can be realized using existing technology at a reasonable cost.

We have identified common security weaknesses in automated process control systems, with particular attention to remotely-accessible power substations [3, 4], and have created a model SCADA/sensor testbed for experimentation. This paper describes the implementation of a customized intrusion detection and event monitoring system for the testbed. The system raises alerts upon detecting potential unauthorized access and changes in device settings. It is useful for securing SCADA networks as well as assisting operators in identifying erroneous or malicious settings on SCADA devices.

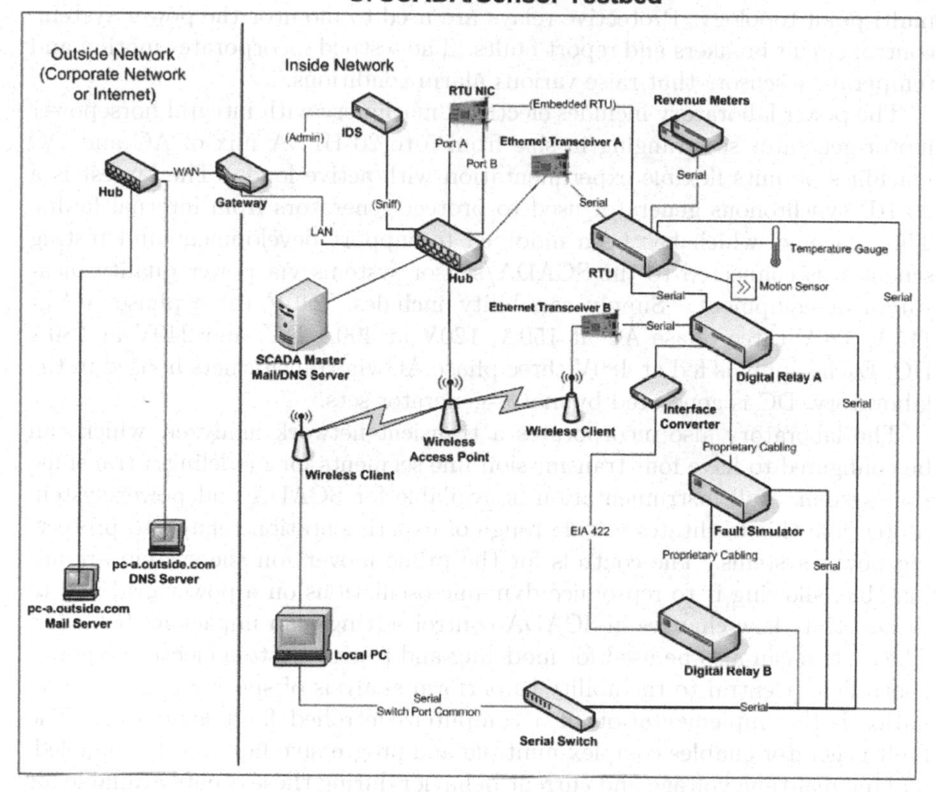

Figure 1. SCADA/sensor system testbed.

2. SCADA/Sensor System Testbed

Our SCADA/sensor system testbed was created to provide a learning and research environment for efforts related to SCADA security and survivability. The testbed leverages facilities at the University of Idaho's Electrical Engineering Power Laboratory, a fully functioning high-voltage facility [10, 11].

A schematic diagram of the testbed is presented in Figure 1. The testbed incorporates a communications system, sensor system, digital fault simulator and a priority messaging system. The communication system includes a wired Ethernet network, which simulates Internet or corporate LAN traffic, and an 802.11b wireless network. These networks connect a substation communications processor to the SCADA master unit and other computers to enable remote access. The communications processor is a microprocessor-based device that replaces the traditional (and archaic) remote terminal unit (RTU) still found in many SCADA systems. It is logically programmable and serves as a data collection and communications hub with connections to the sensor system and protective relay equipment. The wireless component of the communications system consists of two wireless bridges configured to communicate via a point to multi-point topology. Protective relays are used to monitor the power system, control circuit breakers and report faults. The testbed incorporates motion and temperature sensors that raise various alarm conditions.

The power laboratory includes electrical machinery with integral horsepower motor-generator sets ranging in size from 5 to 20 HP. A mix of AC and DC machines permits flexible experimentation with active loads. The largest is a 20 HP synchronous generator used to protect generators from internal faults. This machine, which has been modified to support development and testing schemes, is connected to the SCADA/sensor systems via power quality measurement equipment. Supply capability includes: 240V three phase AC at 115A, 120V three phase AC at 150A, 120V at 400A DC, and 240V at 180A DC. Each supply is fed at 480V three phase AC via transformers housed in the laboratory. DC is generated by motor-generator sets.

The laboratory also incorporates a transient network analyzer, which can be configured to have four transmission line segments for modeling a transmission system. Full instrumentation is available for SCADA and power system protection; this facilitates a wide range of experimentation related to protecting power systems. The controls for the prime movers on the system are adjustable, allowing it to reproduce dynamic oscillations on a power grid and to demonstrate how changes in SCADA control settings can impact its behavior. The system can also be used for modeling and testing custom electronic power controllers. Central to the ability to perform analysis of specific transient scenarios is the implementation of a computer-controlled fault generator. The fault generator enables complex multiple and progressive faults to be modeled, making real-time voltage and current behavior during these events available for analysis. The laboratory incorporates mechanical circuit breakers controlled by commercial protective relays.

3. Research Objectives

A network intrusion detection system acts as an eavesdropping tool, listening on a network for different types of traffic and payload data. Such a tool could noticeably improve security in a SCADA network. SCADA networks also need tools that remotely track changes to device configurations and settings. Monitoring network traffic and auditing network device settings provide the basis for intrusion detection in IT networks; they are just as effective in SCADA networks [6, 10, 11].

Our research had three objectives. First, we wanted to better secure the communication systems of SCADA networks by monitoring for commands that could adversely impact the reliable operation of these networks. Second, we wanted to better monitor the settings on SCADA devices by using an automated technique for gathering settings and comparing them with known (working) values. Third, we wanted to use existing technologies in an extensible, cost-effective approach to improving intrusion detection and event monitoring in SCADA networks.

Industrial control networks severely underreport many important details regarding system access. Therefore, any effort to detect intrusions must involve the observation and recording of important network events. These events include:

- Login attempts on a network device, including:
  - Time of day
  - Origin and destination IP addresses of the attempt
  - Whether the attempt succeeds or fails
  - Frequency of attempts over a given time interval
- Major SCADA-specific commands, including:
  - Commands to view or set passwords
  - Commands to upload new firmware
  - Commands to show or change settings
  - Attempts to upgrade user privileges

Our intent was to incorporate intrusion detection and event monitoring in the testbed. Due to the critical nature of the work performed by SCADA devices, it is important to record even legitimate access attempts. Moreover, research shows that many errors can be attributed to mistakes made by SCADA operators; it is logical to provide services to reduce human error and mitigate any adverse effects.

4. Prototype System

The automated gathering and comparison of device settings over time can be very useful to SCADA operators, who typically rely on personal notes and reminders about which settings were changed and when. Because `telnet` is the most common means for connecting to SCADA devices, we chose to automate this process using the Perl programming language and its Expect module that automates interactions with other programs. This combination has simplified the automation of terminal connections with various SCADA devices. Moreover, it readily supports secure connection protocols like SSL and `ssh`.

Figure 2 presents a logical diagram of the intrusion detection and event monitoring system. To complement settings gathering and command logging, we added a customized uptime measurement component to the testbed. Using `ping`, `telnet`, Expect and a database backend, we were able to graphically represent the uptimes of each SCADA device over day-, fortnight- and month-long periods. This proved to be very effective in identifying faulty devices and network paths, especially involving devices that are seldom used but that are expected to be reliable. Network connectivity was tested for all SCADA devices and the mean time to repair (MTTR) was computed for each device.

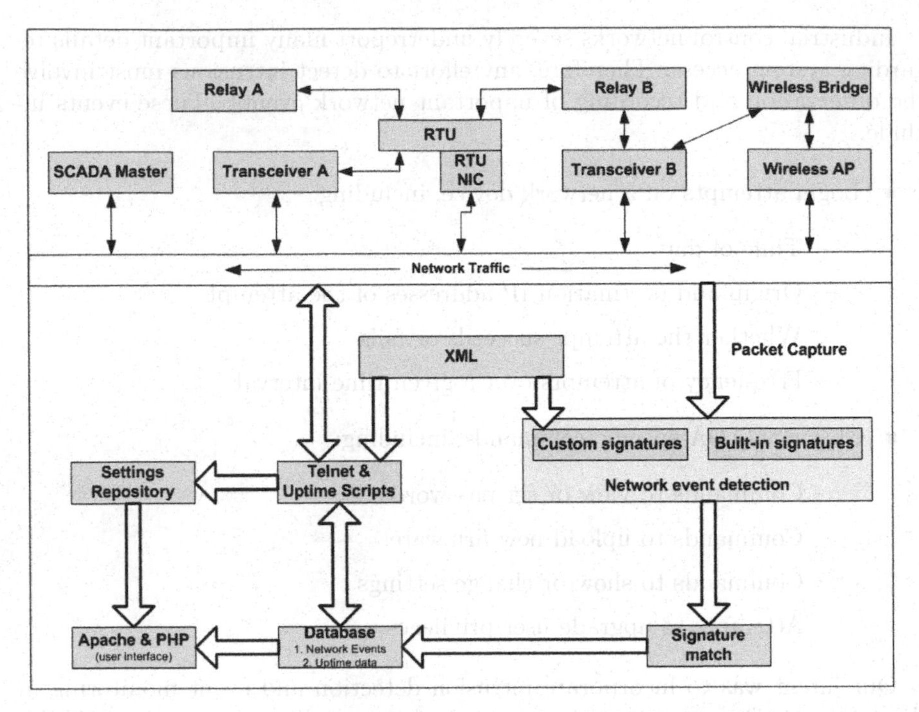

Figure 2. Logical diagram of event monitoring flow and SCADA testbed components.

4.1 Intrusion Signature Generation

Details about each SCADA device in the testbed are expressed using XML. XML provides a standard way to describe diverse SCADA devices. Moreover, the XML format is very expressive and highly extensible.

Details stored about each device include its IP address, `telnet` port, legal commands for the device, whether or not to create intrusion signatures for specific commands, and whether or not to issue a certain command during the automated process of retrieving settings. Table 1 shows a portion of the XML profile for the RTU.

Table 2 lists many of the legal commands available on the RTU. Each command has an entry in the RTU's XML profile. A Perl program parses the XML profile and creates a Snort IDS signature [7] for legal commands on the RTU in order to monitor normal operations. Two automatically-generated signatures are shown in Table 3.

Since there well over 100 signatures, it is beneficial to have a mechanism that can automatically generate IDS signatures. However, not all signatures can be created in this manner. Failed password attempts, for example, require pattern matching on the RTU's failed response to a bad login attempt. In this case, a packet sniffer is used to determine the response and a customized signature is created to detect login failures, which are then graphed over various

Table 1. XML profile for the RTU.

```
<?xml version="1.0"?>
<device>
    <device_name>Remote Terminal Unit</device_name>
    <ip>192.168.0.17</ip>
    <telnet_port>23</telnet_port>
    <admin_port>1024</admin_port>
    <description>This device serves as the communications
    processor in the testbed.</description>
    <level1_user>ACCESS1</level1_user>
    <level1_pass>PASS_1</level1_pass>
    <level2_user>ACCESS2</level2_user>
    <level2_pass>PASS_2</level2_pass>
    <cmd>
        <name>ID</name>
        <description>SETTINGS -- Show port settings for info
        on connected devices.</description>
        <automate>no</automate>
    </cmd> . . . . . . . .
```

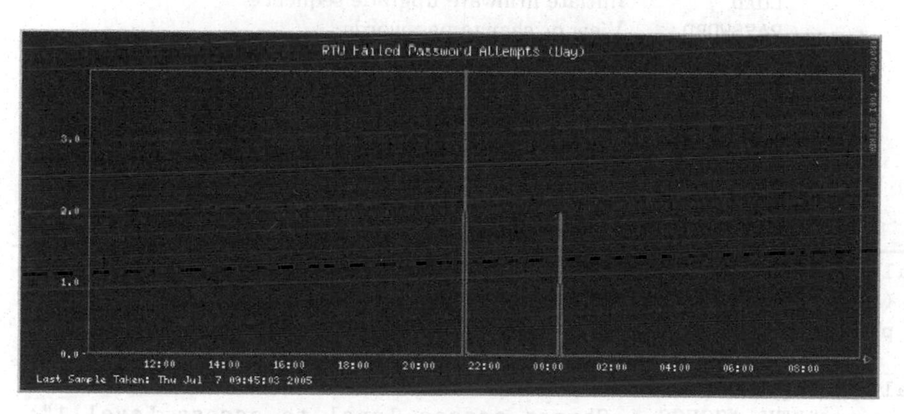

Figure 3. Graph of failed login attempts over a 24-hour period.

time periods (Figure 3). Thus, network events are detected (and subsequently graphed) using automatically-generated signatures or customized signatures for failed login attempts and other complex events. In the near future, signatures will be generated for all the devices listed in Table 4.

4.2 Monitoring Settings

The second component of our system involves monitoring changes to device settings, including changes made at the local terminal and those performed

Table 2. Common commands used in the testbed.

Command	Description
BROADCAST	Communicate with all IEDs
CLEAR	Clear information from a memory area
DNP	View DNP data and settings
MODBUS	View MODBUS data and settings
DATE	View or change the date
HELP	Provide information on available commands
ID	Display device identification information
CLOCK	Force time update using IRIG output
PORT	Provide direct access to a port
ACCESS	Change access level to Level 1
2ACCESS	Change access level to Level 2
QUIT	Revert to access Level 0
SETTINGS	Show all device settings
STATUS	Display status and configuration information
TIME	View or change the time
VIEW	View information from the database
WHO	Show directly connected devices
COPY	Copy settings between ports
LOAD	Initiate firmware upgrade sequence
PASSWORD	View or change passwords
PING	Ping a network device
FTP	FTP metering data from a device

Table 3. Signatures for ACCESS and 2ACCESS commands.

```
alert tcp $HOME_NET any -> $RTU $RTU_PORT
 (msg:"RTU 2ACCESS - Change access level to access Level 2";
 pcre:"/\b2AC/i"; session: printable sid:1200014 rev: 10;)

alert tcp $HOME_NET any -> $RTU $RTU_PORT
 (msg:"RTU ACCESS - Change access level to access Level 1";
 pcre:"/\bACC/i"; session: printable sid:1200015 rev: 10;)
```

over the network. To implement this functionality, a single settings repository is maintained for the SCADA testbed; each device has one or more baseline settings files in the repository. Successive settings are compared against the baseline settings to determine what changes have been made. It is important to know when the settings are changed because a network monitoring device cannot detect changes made from the local terminal. Monitoring settings in this manner implies that the baseline is known to be correct. Therefore, the baseline should be created before the system is brought online. Also, baseline

Table 4. Testbed devices.

Device	IP Address
RTU Network Card	192.168.0.17
Transceiver A	192.168.0.11
Transceiver B	192.168.0.12
Digital Relay A	Accessible via RTU
Digital Relay B	Accessible via RTU
Wireless AP	192.168.0.227
Wireless Bridge	192.168.0.225
Wireless Client	192.168.0.14
SCADA-MASTER	192.168.0.140
Gateway	192.168.0.1

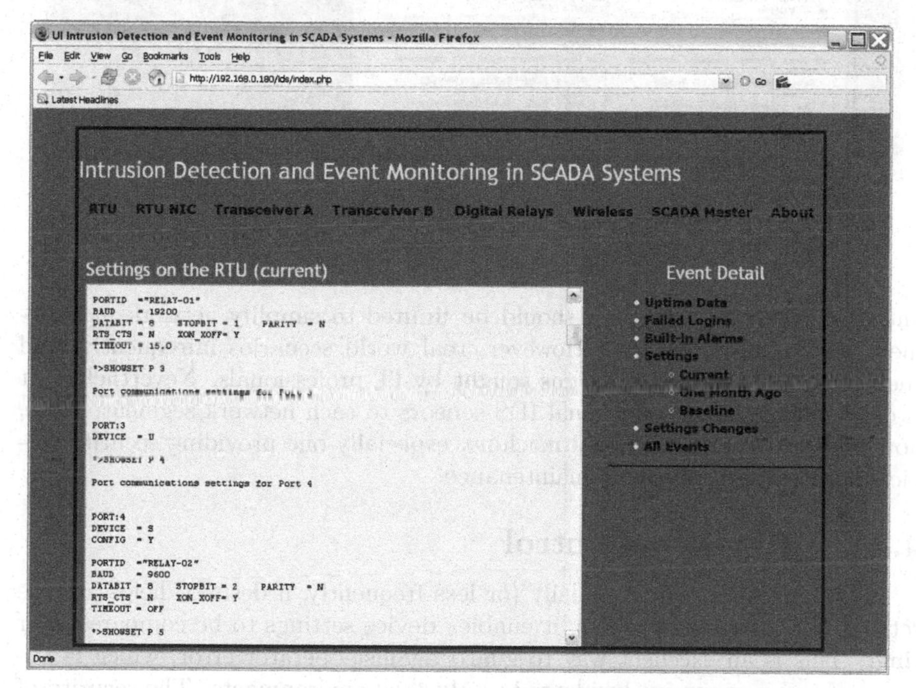

Figure 4. Screenshot of RTU settings after automated retrieval.

data should be protected from unauthorized access and modification. Figure 4 shows a screenshot of the settings recovered from the RTU.

Note that it may be infeasible to monitor every segment of a SCADA network, which is often the case when a wireless network is used to connect remote devices and/or substations. Fortunately, proper network design at the outset can alleviate problems due to a missed network segment. For example, entry

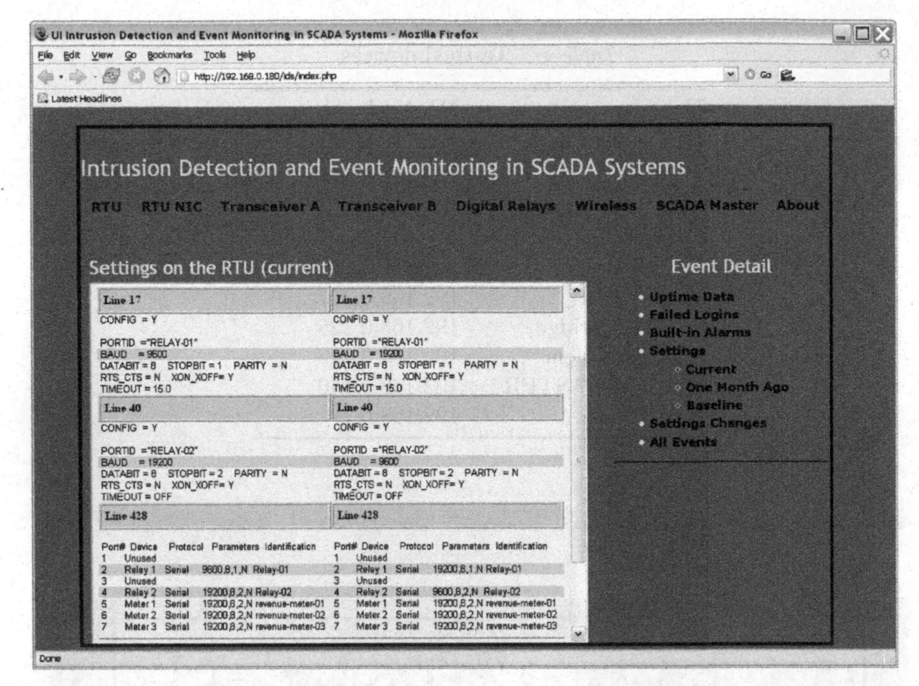

Figure 5. Screenshot of changed RTU settings.

and exit points to a network should be limited to simplify network management and reduce exposure. However, real world scenarios infrequently lend themselves to the elegant designs sought by IT professionals. Nevertheless, it is easy enough to add additional IDS sensors to each network segment. Note, however, that every additional machine, especially one providing security services, will require additional maintenance.

4.3 Revision Control

Retrieving device settings daily (or less frequently, if desired) helps archive settings for later review. Also, it enables device settings to be compared over time. This is an excellent way to guard against operator error, which is the cause of many expensive incidents in industrial environments. The security of the system is also enhanced because it is possible to determine if the settings have been changed by unauthorized parties. Most SCADA systems either do not provide this functionality or it is too difficult to implement because of the limited capabilities of SCADA devices.

Figure 5 shows a screenshot of the RTU's settings, where the baud rates for Port 2 and Port 4 have been interchanged. The two ports are directly connected to digital relays. Consequently, swapping the settings would immediately disable all communications to the relays, a very serious condition in a power substation. Subtle changes like this are often the most difficult to

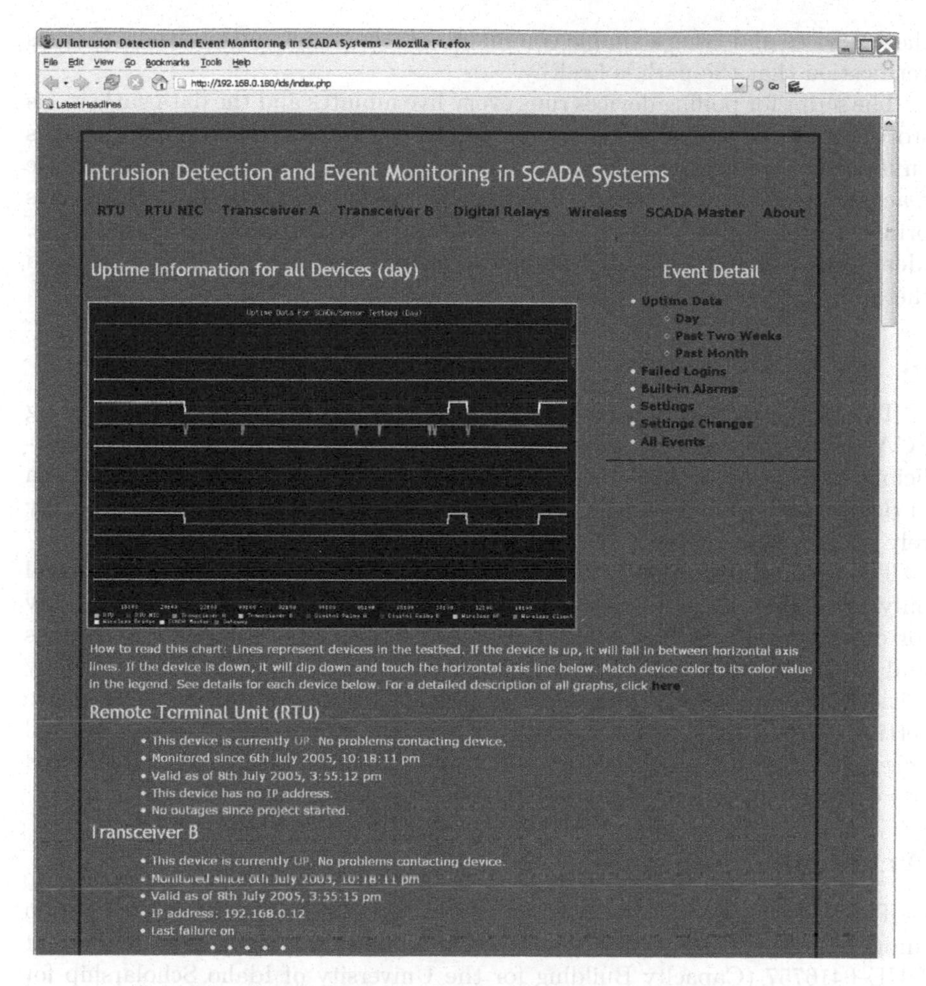

Figure 6. Screenshot of device uptimes over a 24-hour period.

detect, especially when there are dozens of relays and other devices in a network. When troubleshooting such problems, engineers usually rely on handwritten notes that may or may not be accurate. It is sometimes the case that this information was provided by another individual (or contractor) who no longer works at the facility.

4.4 Uptime Monitoring

As with most IT networks, connectivity to all SCADA network devices is essential to knowing that the communications system is healthy. Our solution provides day-, fortnight- and month-long intervals of uptime data for each device (Figure 6). Not all devices have IP addresses, so pinging some devices is not an option. However, using a Perl/Expect script, it is possible to log onto these devices and issue a simple command – if the command succeeds, there is verification that the path is healthy.

The script for polling devices runs every five minutes and the data gathered is stored in a database. A second script graphs the data. Such graphing provides an immediate indication when a device is unreachable; even for devices that are reachable only through others. Figure 6, for example, shows that the wireless bridge is probably down, which results in transceiver B becoming unreachable. Mean time to repair (MTTR) can be calculated based on how long it takes on the average to re-establish contact.

5. Conclusions

The intrusion detection and event monitoring system is useful for securing SCADA networks as well as assisting operators in identifying erroneous or malicious settings on SCADA devices. The automated gathering and comparison of device settings over time is very useful to SCADA operators, who typically rely on personal notes and reminders about device settings.

The current prototype automates intrusion detection and settings retrieval only for RTUs. It is currently being extended to provide this functionality for other SCADA devices. Special attention will be paid to retrieving settings and detecting events involving digital relays, which are the backbone of many critical infrastructures. Our longer term goals are to place all SCADA device settings under revision control and to generate signatures for unauthorized access to other devices. Once this is accomplished, the system will be adapted to vendor-specific needs and other SCADA configurations.

Acknowledgements

This research was partially supported by the National Science Foundation under Grant DUE–0114016 (Cyber Service Training and Education) and Grant DUE–0416757 (Capacity Building for the University of Idaho Scholarship for Service Program).

References

[1] Office of Energy Assurance, 21 Steps to Improve Cyber Security of SCADA Networks, U.S. Department of Energy, Washington, DC, 2002.

[2] P. Oman, A. Krings, D. Conte de Leon and J. Alves-Foss, Analyzing the security and survivability of real-time control systems, *Proceedings of the Fifth Annual IEEE Systems, Man and Cybernetics Information Assurance Workshop*, pp. 342–349, 2004.

[3] P. Oman, E. Schweitzer and D. Frincke, Concerns about intrusions into remotely accessible substation controllers and SCADA systems, *Proceedings of the Twenty-Seventh Annual Western Protective Relay Conference*, 2000.

[4] P. Oman, E. Schweitzer and J. Roberts, Protecting the grid from cyber attack – Part 1: Recognizing our vulnerabilities, *Utility Automation & Enginering T&D*, vol. 6(7), pp. 16–22, 2001.

[5] P. Oman, E. Schweitzer and J. Roberts, Protecting the grid from cyber attack – Part 2: Safeguarding IEDs, substations and SCADA systems, *Utility Automation & Enginering T&D*, vol. 7(1), pp. 25–32, 2002.

[6] M. Phillips, Event Monitoring and Intrusion Detection in SCADA Systems, M.S. Thesis, Department of Computer Science, University of Idaho, Moscow, Idaho, 2005.

[7] M. Roesch, Snort (www.snort.org).

[8] F. Sheldon, T. Potok, A. Krings and P. Oman, Critical energy infrastructure survivability: Inherent limitations, obstacles and mitigation strategies, *International Journal of Power and Energy Systems*, pp. 86–92, 2004.

[9] U.S. House of Representatives (Committee on Government Reform), Telecommunications and SCADA: Secure links or open portals to the security of our nation's critical infrastructure, Serial No. 108–196, U.S. Government Printing Office, Washington, DC, March 30, 2004.

[10] J. Waite, A Testbed for SCADA Security and Survivability Research and Instruction, M.S. Thesis, Department of Computer Science, University of Idaho, Moscow, Idaho, 2004.

[11] J. Waite, J. Oman, M. Phillips, S. Melton and V. Nair, A SCADA testbed for teaching and learning, *Proceedings of the Thirty-Sixth Annual North American Power Symposium*, pp. 447–451, 2004.

Chapter 13

PASSIVE SCANNING IN MODBUS NETWORKS

Jesus Gonzalez and Mauricio Papa

Abstract This paper describes the design and implementation of a passive scanner for Modbus networks. The tool integrates packet parsing and passive scanning functionality to interpret Modbus transactions and provide accurate network representations. In particular, the scanner monitors Modbus messages to maintain and update state table entries associated with field devices. Entries in the state tables record important information including function codes, transaction state, memory access and memory contents. The performance and reporting capabilities of the passive scanner make it an attractive network troubleshooting and security tool for process control environments.

Keywords: Process control systems, Modbus protocol, passive network scanning

1. Introduction

Industrial processes are increasingly relying on sophisticated process control systems (PCSs) – also known as SCADA systems – for supervisory control and data acquisition. PCSs control industrial processes using networks of sensors and actuators. Sensors provide data about process variables as input to the PCS. Actuators make adjustments to the process variables based on output signals received from the PCS. The PCS control algorithm defines how PCS inputs are used to compute the output signals that drive the industrial process to the desired state.

In many industrial environments, sensors, actuators and controllers are deployed in widely dispersed locations, requiring a communication infrastructure and protocols to support supervisory control and data acquisition. The communication protocols have traditionally favored operational requirements over security because the field equipment and communications infrastructure were physically and logically isolated from other networks. However, the specifications for most major industrial protocols, e.g., Modbus [7, 8] and DNP3 [15, 16],

Gonzalez, J. and Papa, M., 2008, in IFIP International Federation for Information Processing, Volume 253, Critical Infrastructure Protection, eds. E. Goetz and S. Shenoi; (Boston: Springer), pp. 175–187.

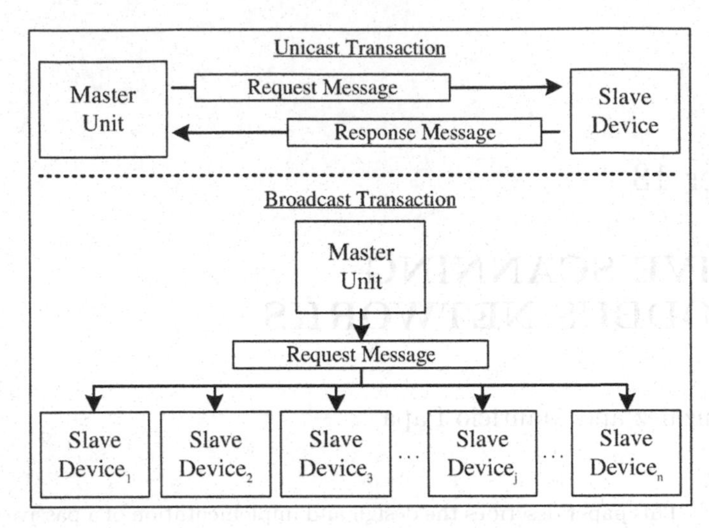

Figure 1. Master-slave transaction.

now include mechanisms to transport control data using TCP/IP stacks. The use of TCP/IP as a transport mechanism in industrial control networks raises serious issues, largely because it promotes the trend to interconnect with corporate IT networks. It is, therefore, extremely important to deploy security tools that are designed specifically for industrial control networks that use TCP/IP stacks [1, 3–5, 12].

This paper describes the design and implementation of a passive scanning tool for Modbus networks, which are commonly used for pipeline operations in the oil and gas sector. The scanning tool monitors Modbus protocol communications to obtain detailed information about network topology and control device configurations and status. As such, the tool is valuable to security administrators for event logging, troubleshooting, intrusion detection and forensic investigations [6, 13, 14].

2. Modbus Protocol

Modbus is a communication protocol for industrial control systems. Developed by Modicon (now Schneider Automation) in 1979, the Modbus protocol specifications and standards are currently maintained by the independent group Modbus IDA. Three documents are at the core of the Modbus standard: the protocol specification [7] and implementation guides for use in serial lines [10] and TCP/IP networks [8].

2.1 Function Codes

The Modbus protocol was designed as a simple request/reply communication mechanism between a master unit and slave devices. Figure 1 illustrates a Modbus transaction. Communication may occur over serial lines or, more recently,

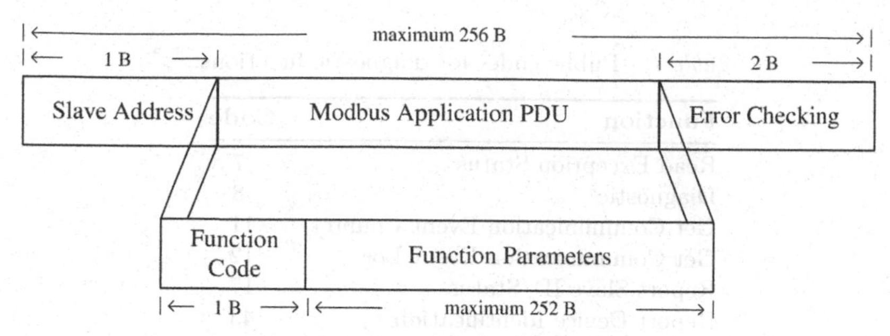

Figure 2. Modbus serial message.

using TCP/IP as a transport mechanism for Modbus messages. A function code included in a Modbus message describes the purpose of the message.

The simple, yet functional, structure of the Modbus protocol has contributed to its implementation by several vendors, enabling seamless interconnection of devices in multiplatform environments. The open nature of the Modbus specifications has led to its current standing as the *de facto* industry standard for process control system communications in the oil and gas sector.

Modbus messages have two major parts, a header with address and control information (possibly spanning multiple network layers) and a protocol data unit (PDU) specifying application-level operations. When the protocol is used in serial lines, messages also include error checking data as a trailer (Figure 2). PDUs comprise two fields [7]: (i) a function code part describing the purpose of the message, and (ii) a function parameters part associated with function invocation (for a request message) or function results (for a reply message). The function code is important because it specifies the operation requested by the master unit; also, it conveys error information in cases where an exception has occurred in a slave device.

The Modbus function code length is 8 bits and the maximum length of the PDU is 253 bytes, providing a maximum of 252 bytes for use as function parameters (Figure 2). The limit on PDU length originates from legacy implementations of Modbus on serial lines.

Modbus has three types of function codes: (i) public codes, (ii) user-defined codes, and (iii) reserved codes. Public codes correspond to functions whose semantics are completely defined or will be defined in the standard. Public code values fall in the non-contiguous ranges {1–64, 73–99, 111–127}. User-defined codes in the ranges {65–72, 100–110} support functions that are not considered in the standard. The implementation of user-defined codes is left to the vendor and there are no guarantees of functional compatibility in heterogeneous environments. Reserved function codes overlap with the space assigned to public codes; they correspond to public codes that are not available for public use to ensure compatibility with legacy systems [7]. Function codes in the range {128–255} are used to denote error conditions. If an error condition occurs for a function code $x \in \{1\text{–}127\}$ in a request from a master to a slave, the error

Table 1. Public codes for diagnostic functions.

Function	**Code**
Read Exception Status	7
Diagnostic	8
Get Communication Event Counter	11
Get Communication Event Log	12
Report Slave ID/Status	17
Report Device Identification	43

situation is indicated by the function code $x + 128$ in the reply message from the slave to the master.

Public function codes are used for diagnostics, and for data access and manipulation in slave devices. Most diagnostic codes are defined for obtaining status information from slave devices in serial lines (Table 1).

Data access functions are designed to read/write data objects from/to primary tables. Modbus defines four types of primary tables: discrete inputs, coils, input registers and holding registers. The first two types of tables contain single-bit objects that are read-only and read-write, respectively. The other two types of tables contain 16-bit objects that are read-only and read-write, respectively. Table 2 summarizes the public codes corresponding to data access functions for the four types of primary tables.

Single-bit discrete inputs and coils are normally associated with discrete I/O systems. On the other hand, input registers and holding registers are generally associated with analog systems, i.e., analog inputs and outputs, respectively. Any of the four primary data objects may also be used as program variables for implementing control logic.

The Modbus standard also permits files to be used to read and write device data (process-related data and configuration data). In this case, the data objects are called "records" and each file contains 10,000 records. The length of a record is file-dependent and is specified using a 16-bit word. It is important to note that the Modbus standard allows memory allocations for primary tables and files to overlap.

2.2 Transactions

A Modbus transaction involves the exchange of a request message from a master and a reply message from the addressed slave (except for broadcast messages, which have no reply messages). The master communicates using the unicast address associated with the slave device (i.e., its network ID) as the destination address of the request, or by sending a request message to the broadcast address [10, 11]. Note that if the broadcast address is used by the master, the request is received and processed by all listening slaves, but no response messages are provided by the slaves. When the unicast address of a

Table 2. Public codes for data access functions.

Function	Code	Type	Size (Bits)
Read Discrete Inputs	2	Read Only	1
Read Coils	1	Read/Write	1
Write Single Coil	5	Read/Write	1
Write Multiple Coils	15	Read/Write	1
Read Input Registers	4	Read Only	16
Write Single Register	6	Read/Write	16
Read Holding Registers	3	Read/Write	16
Write Multiple Registers	16	Read/Write	16
Read File Records	20	Read/Write	16
Write File Records	21	Read/Write	16
Mask Write Register	22	Read/Write	16
Read/Write Multiple Registers	23	Read/Write	16
Read FIFO Queue	24	Read/Write	16

slave is used, the addressed slave is required to send a response message back to the master.

Frame headers for Modbus messages in serial lines (Figure 2) only include the address of the intended slave recipient (for requests and replies). In a request message, this address identifies the recipient; in a response message, the address is used by the master to identify the responding slave. The address field is 8 bits long. The broadcast address is 0 (zero); values in the range {1–247} are used for individual slave addresses and values in the range {248–255} are reserved. Note that the maximum size of a Modbus frame in serial line is 256 bytes (including two trailer bytes used for error detection).

As described above, an error condition is indicated by sending a different function code in the reply message. Also, an exception code is included in the function parameter section of the PDU.

2.3 TCP/IP Services

Modbus TCP transactions are functionally equivalent to those specified in the serial version, i.e., master and slave devices exchange PDUs, except that transactions are encapsulated in TCP messages. Modbus TCP extends the functionality offered by the serial version by enabling slave devices to engage in concurrent communications with more than one master. Also, the master can have multiple outstanding transactions.

The implementation guide for Modbus messaging over TCP/IP [8] specifies that slave devices must listen for incoming TCP connections on port 502 (IANA assigned port) and may optionally listen on additional ports. The slave device that performs the passive open operation on TCP is designated as the "server." On the other hand, the master device that performs the active open operation on TCP is designated as the "client." Note that Modbus roles cannot

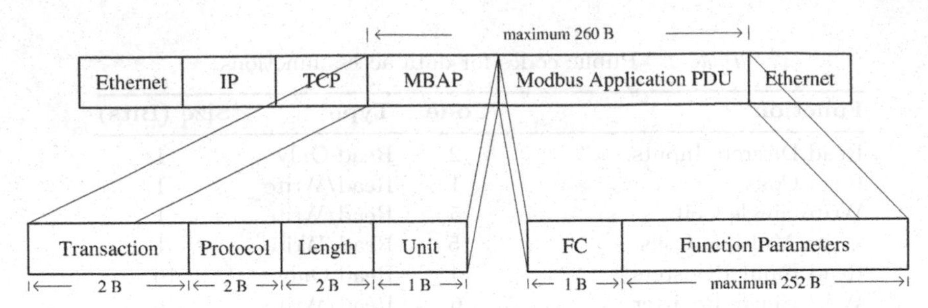

Figure 3. Modbus TCP message.

be changed on a TCP communication channel once it is established; however, multiple outstanding transactions may exist on the channel. A new communication channel is established when a device needs to assume a different role.

A Modbus TCP PDU includes an extra header to handle the additional capabilities. This Modbus Application Protocol (MBAP) header has four fields (Figure 3): (i) transaction identifier, (ii) protocol identifier, (iii) length, and (iv) unit identifier. The transaction identifier enables a device to pair matching requests and replies belonging to the same transaction. The protocol identifier indicates what application protocol is encapsulated by the MBAP header (zero for Modbus). The length field indicates the length in bytes of the remaining fields (unit identifier and PDU). Finally, the unit identifier indicates the slave device associated with the transaction.

The Modbus TCP specification requires that only one application PDU be transported in the payload of a TCP packet [8]. Since application PDUs have a maximum size of 253 bytes (see Figure 2) and the length of the MBAP is fixed at seven bytes, the maximum length of a Modbus TCP data unit is 260 bytes.

3. Architecture

This section describes the architecture of the passive Modbus scanner that monitors Modbus messages to identify and extract information about master and slave devices in an industrial control network. The information is useful for monitoring network status and troubleshooting device configurations and connections. Given an appropriate amount of time, the tool can discover each communicating Modbus device and the set of function codes used on the device. Also, the tool can monitor the status of Modbus transactions, i.e., whether they result in positive or negative responses.

To support security evaluations, the passive scanner can be used to detect and log the presence of rogue devices, monitor memory transfer operations and detect variations in network use in real time. Note that the monitoring and logging of memory transfer operations help detect anomalous activity and support forensic investigations.

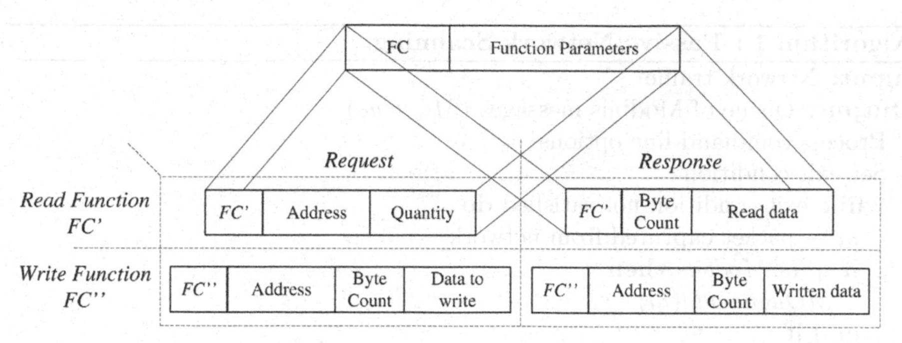

Figure 4. Modbus message structure for memory access operations.

3.1 Design and Features

The passive scanning tool has three main components: (i) a network scanner, (ii) a Modbus transaction checker, and (iii) an incremental network mapper. The network scanner passively captures and parses Modbus messages. Information captured by the scanner is passed to the transaction checker to pair matching sets of messages. The incremental network mapper uses the collected information to populate dynamic data structures that store network topology and status information.

Messages in a SCADA network tend to follow repetitive, often predictable communication patterns. Based on this assumption, we use an incremental network mapping algorithm that only updates its data structures when a new pattern, feature or device is identified. In most cases, the rate at which new information is added decreases over time; depending on the network traffic, no new information may be added for a relatively long period of time. Abrupt changes to the expected trend may indicate anomalous activity and could be used as a metric for anomaly detection.

Data access messages (Figure 4) provide valuable information associated with a slave device such as memory addresses, types and contents. Furthermore, since function parameters in Modbus messages always contain slave device information, i.e., a message is a request directed at a slave or a response from a slave, Modbus communications tend to reveal more information about slave devices than the master unit. Consequently, the reports produced by the passive scanner concentrate mainly on slave devices.

Whenever a Modbus message captured by the scanner is matched by the transaction checker, the network mapper inspects the transaction and updates the state of the data structure. The following information is extracted and stored: master id, slave id, function code and transaction status. In addition, for each operation that involves memory manipulation, the data type associated with the operation, access type (read/write), memory contents (accessed from or written to the slave device), and memory addresses associated with the data transfer are recorded.

Algorithm 1 : Passive Network Scanning.

Input: Network traffic
Output: Queue of Modbus messages (*MQueue*)

```
Process command line options
Set exit condition
while exit condition not satisfied do
  m ← packet captured from network
  if m is Modbus then
    MQueue.add(m)
  end if
end while
```

3.2 Algorithms

This section describes the algorithms used for passive scanning of Modbus networks. Data input is provided by a simple packet capture utility that parses and filters Modbus messages (Algorithm 1). The algorithms use three key data structures:

- *MQueue*: This FIFO queue stores unprocessed Modbus messages. The network scanner inserts elements in the queue and the transaction checker removes elements from the queue during processing.

- *MTReq*: This hash table stores pending Modbus requests. Hash value i for $MTReq[i]$ is computed from Modbus message fields, i.e., $i = hash(x_1, x_2, \cdots, x_n)$. For example, a hash value could be computed using $x_1 = slaveIP$, $x_2 = masterIP$, $x_3 = slavePort$, $x_4 = masterPort$, and $x_5 = TransactionID$. Note that slave devices listen on TCP port 502 by default, thus, $x_3 = 502$ in most cases. The hash table is primarily used by the transaction checker to generate matching request and reply messages for Modbus transactions, which enable the incremental network mapper to collect device information.

- *MDev*: This hash table stores objects associated with a specific Modbus device. Hash value j for $MDev[j]$ is computed from Modbus message fields, i.e., $j = hash(y_1, y_2, \cdots, y_m)$. In this case, the set of fields uniquely identify a Modbus device on the network, i.e., $y_1 = slaveIP$, $y_2 = slave\ MAC\ address$, $y_3 = unitID$. Individual entries in the table store device-specific information such as the addresses associated with the slave device, addresses of master devices that communicated with the slave device, and the function codes and parameters seen in transactions associated with the device.

The transaction checker is responsible for matching request and reply Modbus messages that belong to the same transaction, i.e., it is a stateful transaction monitor (Algorithm 2). Note that only request messages are stored in

Algorithm 2 : Modbus Transaction Checking.

```
Input: Queue of unprocessed Modbus messages (MQueue)
Output: Queue of Modbus transactions (TQueue)
  while exit condition not satisfied do
    m ← MQueue.next()
    i ← hash(x_1, x_2, ··· , x_n)
    if m is a request then
      if MTReq[i] ≠ ∅ then
        log("Multiple identical requests")
      end if
      MTReq[i] ← m
    else // Message m is a response
      if MTReq[i] = ∅ then
        log("No matching request found")
      else
        valid_transaction = check_transaction(MTReq[i], m)
        if valid_transaction = false then
          log("Invalid transaction - (invalid request/reply parameters)")
        else // MTReq[i] and m constitute a valid transaction
          TQueue.add({MTReq[i], m})
          MTReq[i] ← ∅
        end if
      end if
    end if
  end while
```

MTReq. Reply messages for which there are no matching requests are immediately logged to indicate the anomaly and *MTReq* remains unchanged. If a matching reply is received and validated, an entry is added to the transaction queue *TQueue* (an auxiliary data structure) and the request is removed from *MTReq*. On the other hand, if a matching reply is not validated, a log entry is produced and the request message remains in *MTReq* in case a matching reply is received later.

Transactions in *TQueue* are the input for the incremental network mapping algorithm (Algorithm 3). This algorithm records information about all Modbus devices *MDev* detected in network communications. First, the algorithm determines whether a transaction involves a new Modbus device; if this is the case, an entry associated with the new device is added to *MDev*. Next, the algorithm stores relevant transaction information, including the master ID, function codes and function parameters. Note that transaction information is considered relevant (and logged) only if it provides new information about the network.

Modbus transactions may involve memory access/updates on the remote devices as well as diagnostic operations. When operations manipulate device

Algorithm 3 : Incremental Network Mapping.

Input: Queue of Modbus transactions ($TQueue$)
Output: Hash table of Modbus device objects ($MDev$)
 while exit condition not satisfied **do**
  $trans \leftarrow TQueue.next()$
  $j \leftarrow hash(y_1, y_2, \cdots, y_m)$
  if $MDev[j] = \emptyset$ **then** // Handle new observed devices
   $MDev[j] \leftarrow newMDev(trans.slave)$
  end if
  if $trans.master \notin MDev[j]$ **then** // Process master information
   $MDev[j] \leftarrow MDev[j] \bigcup trans.master$
  end if
  if $trans.fcode \notin MDev[j]$ **then** // Process function code
   $MDev[j] \leftarrow MDev[j] \bigcup trans.fcode$
  end if
  if $trans.fparameters \notin MDev[j]$ **then** // Process function parameters
   $MDev[j] \leftarrow MDev[j] \bigcup trans.fparameters$
  end if
 end while

memory, each operation and the corresponding memory contents are logged. These logs are useful for system monitoring, troubleshooting problems with devices, detecting system anomalies and reconstructing network events.

4. Experimental Results

A prototype implementation of the passive Modbus scanner was tested in a laboratory environment using two programmable logic controllers (PLCs), one master and one slave, in an Ethernet segment. Two experiments were conducted. The first experiment involved normal Modbus TCP communications between both devices. The second involved a rogue master. Modbus traffic was generated by having the master read two coils (associated with two PLC inputs) and then write a coil (associated with a PLC output) in a continuous loop.

The two input coils were located at memory addresses 3088 and 3152; the output coil was located at address 3104. The slave device was assigned the IP address `192.168.37.12` and was configured to respond to `192.168.37.11`, the IP address of a master.

In the first experiment, Modbus traffic was captured over a sufficiently long period of time to obtain most of the descriptive features of the network. The passive scanner then created a report based on the captured traffic (Figure 5a).

The report describing the network has four sections (for each slave device). The first section provides slave device ID information, i.e., the unit identifier, MAC address and IP address. The second section provides information about the master devices (IP and MAC addresses) that communicated with

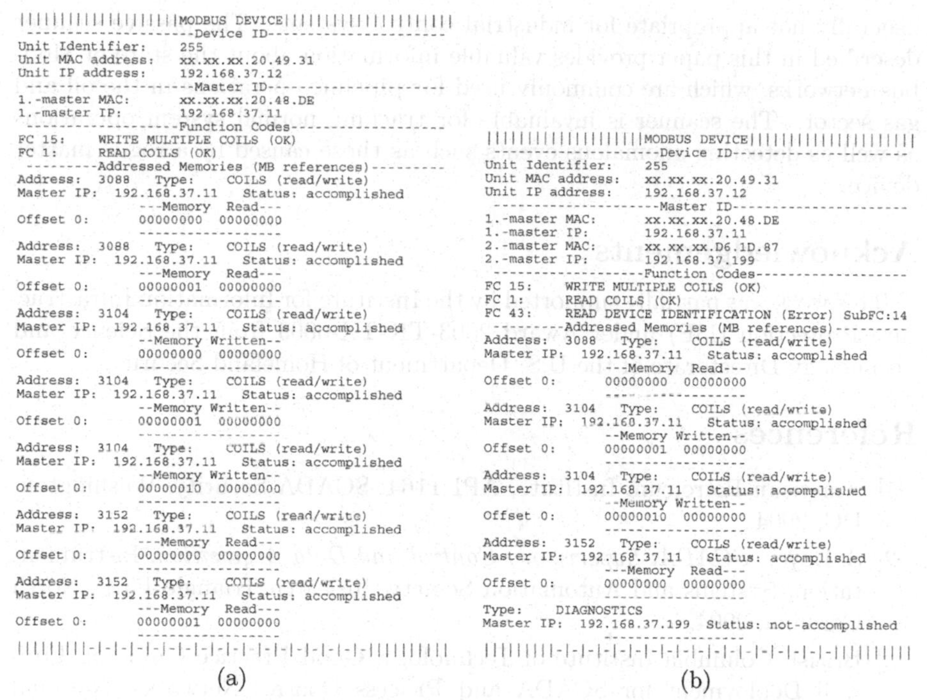

Figure 5. Experimental results: (a) Normal operation; (b) Rogue master.

the slave device. The third section describes all the function codes associated with requests sent to the slave device and whether or not the associated replies indicated error conditions. The fourth section provides detailed information associated with memory access/update operations and diagnostics. For example, in Figure 5a, the report lists the values read from input coils at addresses 3088 and 3152, and the values written to output coil at address 3104.

The second experiment involved a rogue master unit, which was assigned the IP address `192.168.37.199`. Network traffic was captured for a shorter period of time than in the first experiment (resulting in a shorter report) but long enough to reveal the existence of the second master. The report in Figure 5b shows the presence of two masters. The report also shows that the rogue master attempted to execute function code 43 (encapsulated interface transport) with sub-code 14, a diagnostic function used to obtain (read) slave device identification information. Note that a negative response was obtained, i.e., the operation could not be completed.

5. Conclusions

The use of TCP/IP as a carrier protocol for SCADA systems and the interconnection of SCADA networks with IT networks opens pathways for remote access to industrial control systems. Security tools specifically designed for the SCADA networks are required because traditional IT security tools are generally not appropriate for industrial control systems. The passive scanner described in this paper provides valuable information about the state of Modbus networks, which are commonly used for pipeline operations in the oil and gas sector. The scanner is invaluable for tracking normal system operations as well as detecting anomalous events such as those caused by a rogue master device.

Acknowledgements

This work was partially supported by the Institute for Information Infrastructure Protection (I3P) under Award 2003-TK-TX-0003 from the Science and Technology Directorate of the U.S. Department of Homeland Security.

References

[1] American Petroleum Institute, API 1164: SCADA Security, Washington, DC, 2004.

[2] S. Boyer, *SCADA: Supervisory Control and Data Acquisition*, Instrumentation, Systems and Automation Society, Research Triangle Park, North Carolina, 2004.

[3] British Columbia Institute of Technology, Good Practice Guide on Firewall Deployment for SCADA and Process Control Networks, National Infrastructure Security Co-ordination Centre, London, United Kingdom, 2005.

[4] E. Byres, J. Carter, A. Elramly and D. Hoffman, Worlds in collision: Ethernet on the plant floor, *Proceedings of the ISA Emerging Technologies Conference*, 2002.

[5] Instrumentation Systems and Automation Society, Security Technologies for Manufacturing and Control Systems (ANSI/ISA-TR99.00.01-2004), Research Triangle Park, North Carolina, 2004.

[6] K. Mandia, C. Prosise and M. Pepe, *Incident Response and Computer Forensics*, McGraw-Hill/Osborne, Emeryville, California, 2003.

[7] Modbus IDA, MODBUS Application Protocol Specification v1.1a, North Grafton, Massachusetts (www.modbus.org/specs.php), June 4, 2004.

[8] Modbus IDA, MODBUS Messaging on TCP/IP Implementation Guide v1.0a, North Grafton, Massachusetts (www.modbus.org/specs.php), June 4, 2004.

[9] Modbus IDA, Modbus TCP is world leader in new ARC study, North Grafton, Massachusetts, (www.modbus.org/docs/Modbus_ARC_study-May2005.pdf), 2005.

[10] Modbus.org, MODBUS over Serial Line Specification and Implementation Guide v1.0, North Grafton, Massachusetts (www. modbus.org/specs.php), February 12, 2002.

[11] Modicon, Inc., MODBUS Protocol Reference Guide, Document PI-MBUS-300 Rev. J, North Andover, Massachusetts, 1996.

[12] National Institute of Standards and Technology, System Protection Profile – Industrial Control Systems v1.0, Gaithersburg, Maryland, 2004.

[13] S. Northcutt and J. Novak, *Network Intrusion Detection: An Analyst's Handbook*, New Riders, Indianapolis, Indiana, 2002.

[14] S. Northcutt, L. Zeltser, S. Winters, K. Frederick and R. Ritchey, *Inside Network Perimeter Security: The Definitive Guide to Firewalls, VPNs, Routers and Intrusion Detection Systems*, New Riders, Indiana, 2002.

[15] M. Smith and M. Copps, DNP3 V3.00 Data Object Library Version 0.02, DNP Users Group, Pasadena, California, 1993.

[16] M. Smith and J. McFadyen, DNP V3.00 Data Link Layer Protocol Description, DNP Users Group, Pasadena, California, 2000.

Chapter 14

FORMAL MODELING AND ANALYSIS OF THE MODBUS PROTOCOL

Bruno Dutertre

Abstract Modbus is a communication protocol that is widely used in SCADA systems and distributed control applications. This paper presents formal specifications of Modbus developed using PVS, a generic theorem prover; and SAL, a toolset for the automatic analysis of state-transition systems. Both formalizations are based on the Modbus Application Protocol, which specifies the format of Modbus request and response messages. This formal modeling effort is the first step in the development of automated methods for systematic and extensive testing of Modbus devices.

Keywords: Modbus, formal methods, modeling, test-case generation

1. Introduction

A distributed control system—sometimes called a SCADA system—is a network of devices and computers for monitoring and controlling industrial processes such as oil production and refining, electric power distribution, and manufacturing plants. The network requirements for these applications include real-time constraints, resilience to electromagnetic noise, and reliability that are different from those of traditional communication networks. Historically, the manufacturers of control systems have developed specialized, often proprietary networks and protocols, and have kept them isolated from enterprise networks and the Internet.

This historical trend is now being reversed. Distributed control applications are migrating to networking standards such as TCP/IP and Ethernet. This migration is enabled by the increased sophistication of control devices. Also, the migration provides increased bandwidth and functionality, and economic benefits. Control systems are now using the same technologies and protocols as communication networks, and the separation that existed between control networks and other networks is disappearing. SCADA systems are now often

Dutertre, B., 2008, in IFIP International Federation for Information Processing, Volume 253, Critical Infrastructure Protection, eds. E. Goetz and S. Shenoi; (Boston: Springer), pp. 189–204.

connected to conventional enterprise networks, which are often linked to the Internet.

This interconnection increases the risk of remote attacks on industrial control systems, which could have devastating consequences. Intrusion detection systems and firewalls may provide some protection, but it is important that the control devices are reliable and resilient to attacks. Detecting and eliminating vulnerabilities in these devices is essential to ensuring that industrial control networks are secure.

Extensive testing is a useful approach to detecting vulnerabilities in software. It has the advantage of being applicable without access to the source code. As is well known, security vulnerabilities often reside in parts of the software that are rarely exercised under normal conditions. Traditional testing methods, which attempt to check proper functionality under reasonable inputs, can fail to detect such vulnerabilities. To be effective, security testing requires wide coverage. The set of test-cases must cover not only normal conditions, but also inputs that are not likely to be observed in normal device use. Indeed, flaws in handling malformed and unexpected inputs have been exploited by many attacks on computer systems, including the ubiquitous buffer-overflow attacks.

A major challenge to exhaustive testing is the generation of relevant test-cases. It is difficult and expensive to manually generate large numbers of test-cases to achieve adequate coverage. An attractive alternative is to generate test-cases automatically using formal methods. This is accomplished by constructing test-cases mechanically from a specification of the system under test and a set of testing goals called "test purposes." The concept has been successfully applied to hardware, networking and software systems [1, 5–7, 12, 13]. This paper explores the application of similar ideas to SCADA devices. More precisely, we focus on devices that support the Modbus Application Protocol [8], a protocol widely used in distributed control systems.

Automated test-case generation for Modbus devices requires formal models of the protocol that serve as a reference, and algorithms for automatically generating test-cases from such models. We present two formal models that satisfy these goals. The first model is developed using the PVS specification and verification system [11]. This model captures the Modbus specifications as defined in the Modbus standard [8]: it includes a precise definition of valid Modbus requests and, for each request class, the specification of acceptable responses. The PVS model is executable and can be used as a reference for validating responses from a device under test. Given a test request r and an observed response m, it is possible to determine whether the device passes or fails the test by executing the PVS model with input r and m.

The second model is designed for automated test generation, i.e., for constructing Modbus requests that satisfy a test purpose. This model is developed using the SAL environment for modeling and verifying state transition systems [2, 3]. In this approach, test-case generation is translated to a state-reachability problem that can be solved using SAL's model checking tools. This approach is more efficient and more powerful than attempting to generate test-cases directly from PVS specifications.

The Modbus standard is very flexible, and devices are highly configurable. Modbus-compliant devices may support only a subset of the defined functions, and, for each function, devices may support a subset of the possible parameters. Several functions are left open as "user definable." To be effective, a testing strategy must be tailored to the device of interest and specialized to the functions and parameters supported by the device. Special care has been taken to address this need for flexibility. The formal models presented in this paper are easily customized to accommodate the different features and configurations of Modbus devices.

2. Modbus Protocol Overview

Modbus is a communication protocol widely used in distributed control applications. Modbus was introduced in 1979 as a serial-line protocol for communication between "intelligent" control devices. It has become a *de facto* standard implemented by many manufacturers and used in a variety of industries.

The Modbus serial-line specifications describe the physical and link-layer protocols for exchanging data [10]. Two main variants of the link-layer protocol are defined and two types of serial lines are supported. In addition, the specifications define an application-layer protocol, called the Modbus Application Protocol, for controlling and querying SCADA devices [8].

Modbus was subsequently extended to support other types of buses and networks. The Modbus Application Protocol assumes an abstract communication layer that allows devices to exchange small packets. Serial-line Modbus remains an option for implementing this communication layer, but other networks and protocols may be used. Many modern SCADA systems implement the communication layer using TCP, as described in the Modbus over TCP/IP specifications [9].

2.1 Modbus Serial Protocol

Figure 1 presents a typical architecture employing the Modbus serial protocol. Several devices are connected to a single bus (serial line) and communicate with a central controller. Modbus uses a master-slave approach to control access to the shared communication line and prevent message collisions. Communication is initiated by the controller (master device), which issues commands (requests) on the bus, usually destined for a single device (slave). This slave device may then access the bus and transmit the response to the master. Slave devices do not communicate directly with each other, nor do they transmit data without a request from the master device. Modbus also permits multicast messages from a master to several slave devices, but these transactions have no response messages.

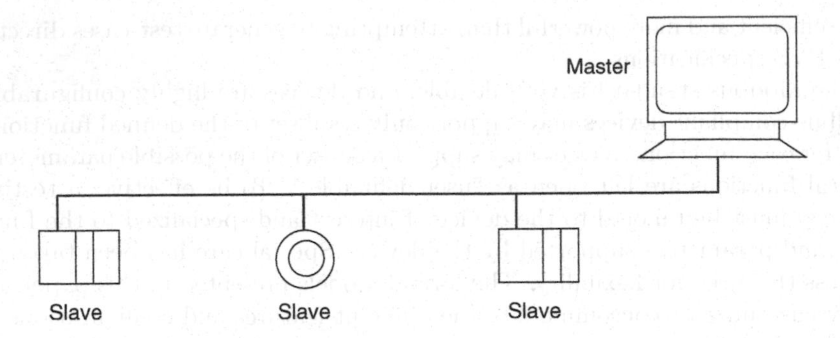

Figure 1. Modbus serial-line architecture.

The Modbus specification defines a physical layer and describes packet formatting, device addressing, error checking and timing constraints. Several design decisions have an impact on the Modbus Application Protocol and on Modbus over TCP/IP.

- The application protocol follows the same master-slave design as the serial line protocol. Each transaction in the application layer is a simple request-response exchange initiated by the master and addressed to a single slave device.
- Modbus requests and responses are required to fit in a single serial-line frame. The maximum length of a Modbus frame is 256 bytes. One byte is reserved for the device address and two bytes for CRC error checking. Therefore, the maximum length of a request or response is 253 bytes.

2.2 Modbus TCP Protocol

The Modbus TCP protocol uses TCP as the communication layer, but attempts to remain compatible with the Modbus serial protocol. The specification defines an embedding of Modbus packets into TCP frames and assigns a specific IP port number (502) for Modbus TCP. The frame includes the usual IP and TCP headers, followed by a Modbus-specific header and the payload. The payload is limited to 253 bytes to maintain compatibility with the Modbus serial protocol. Several fields in the Modbus TCP header are also inherited from the serial protocol [9].

Modbus TCP has economic advantages because of the wide availability of TCP- and TCP/IP-compatible networks. It is also more flexible. However, from a security perspective, migrating to TCP/IP introduces vulnerabilities and adds considerable complexity. The master-slave architecture presented in Figure 1 can be implemented using relatively simple devices since most of the protocol control and functionality are incorporated in the master device. The situation is reversed in Modbus TCP: the master is a "TCP client" and the slave devices are "TCP servers." As far as networking is concerned, devices that support Modbus TCP must implement all (or a significant subset) of the features of a TCP/IP server. The TCP client/server semantics is also more general than the simple master-slave model. For example, multiple Modbus transactions can be sent concurrently to a single device and a device may accept connections from different clients. Interested readers are referred to [9] for additional details and guidance on Modbus TCP implementations.

2.3 Modbus Application Protocol

The application protocol is common to all variants of Modbus. As mentioned earlier, this protocol is very simple as it was originally intended for the Modbus master-slave protocol on serial lines. Almost all transactions consist of a request sent by the master to a single slave, followed by a response from the slave device. The few exceptions are transactions involving requests sent by the master that require no response messages on the part of the slave devices.

The majority of Modbus requests are commands to read or write registers in slave devices. The Modbus standard defines four main classes of registers:

- **Coils:** Single-bit, readable and writable registers
- **Discrete Inputs:** Single-bit, read-only registers
- **Holding Registers:** 16-bit, readable and writable registers
- **Input Registers:** 16-bit, read-only registers

Individual registers in each category are identified by a 16-bit address. There is no requirement for a Modbus device to support the full range of addresses or the four types of registers. The four address spaces are allowed to overlap. For example, a single control bit may have its own address as a coil and be part of a 16-bit holding register.

Table 1 shows the format of a Modbus command and the associated responses. The first byte of the request identifies a specific command, in this example, function code 0x02 corresponding to *Read Discrete Inputs*. The rest of the request contains parameters. The example command has two parameters: a start address between 0x0000 and 0xFFFF (in hexadecimal) and the number of discrete inputs to read expressed as a 16-bit integer. The device may either reject the request and send an error packet or return the requested data in a single packet. The format of a valid response is also indicated in Table 1: the first byte is a copy of the function code in the request, the second byte contains the size of the response (if n bits are requested, this byte is $\lceil n/8 \rceil$), and the rest of the packet is the data itself. An error packet contains a copy of the function code of the request with the high-order bit flipped and an exception code that indicates the reason for the failure. Figure 2 summarizes how the request should be processed and how the exception code should be set in case of failure.

Read and write commands are all similar to the example in Table 1. Other commands in the Modbus Application Protocol are related to device identification and diagnostics. Every command starts with a one-byte function code,

Table 1. Example Modbus command and associated responses.

Request		
Function Code	1 byte	0x02
Start Address	2 bytes	0x0000 to 0xFFFF
Quantity	2 bytes	1 to 2000

Response		
Function Code	1 byte	0x02
Byte Count	1 byte	N
Data	N bytes	

Error		
Error Code	1 byte	0x82
Exception Code	1 byte	01 to 04

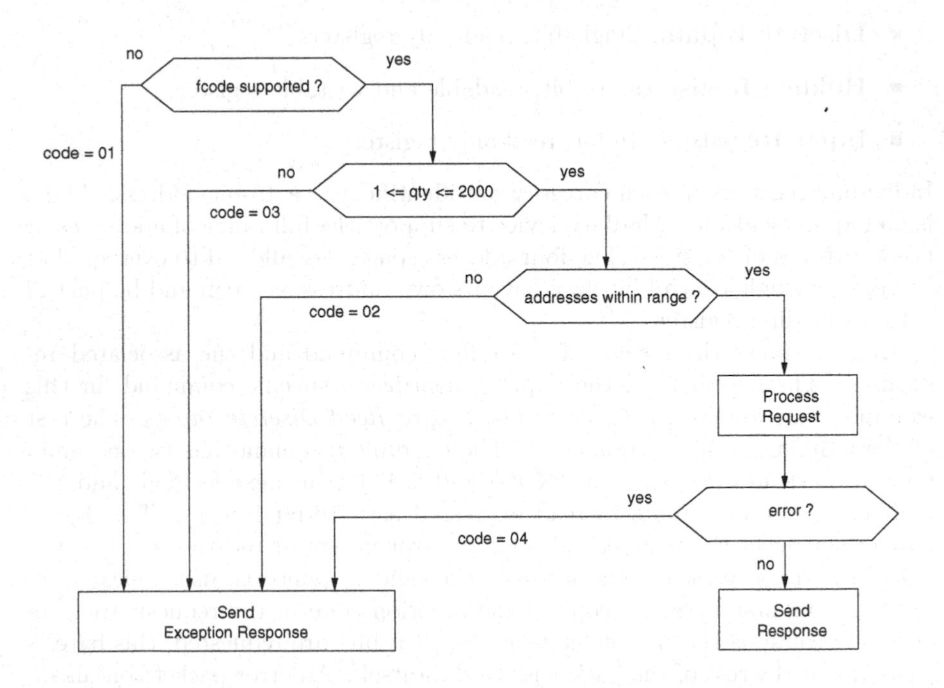

Figure 2. Example command (processing and error reporting).

a value between 1 and 127. Following the function code are parameters that are specific to the function code (e.g., register addresses and quantity) and optionally other data (e.g., values to write in registers). Correct execution is indicated by sending back a response packet whose first byte (function code) is the same as the command, and other data (e.g., response to a read command). A failure to execute the command is indicated by responding with a two-byte error packet.

The Modbus standard defines the meaning of nineteen of the 127 possible function codes. The other function codes are either unassigned and reserved for future use, or they are reserved for legacy implementations and are not available, or they are user defined. A device is allowed to support only a subset of the public functions, and within each function code to support only a subset of the parameters. The only requirement is for the device to return an appropriate error packet to signal that a function is not supported or that an address is out of range.

The protocol standard is loose and flexible. Modbus-compliant devices may vary widely in the functions, number of registers and address spaces they support. The interpretation of user-defined function codes is not specified by the standard and different devices may assign different interpretations to the same user-defined code.

3. Formal Specification

The formal models discussed in this paper deal with the Modbus Application Protocol. As summarized previously, the transactions in this protocol consist of a single request followed by a single response. Both requests and responses are small packets of at most 253 bytes in length. Because it is so simple, the Modbus Application Protocol is not a good candidate for traditional formal verification, whose goal is typically to prove some non obvious but critical property. Instead, our formal modeling and analysis efforts are geared to support extensive, automated testing of Modbus devices.

Given a formal model, we show how to automatically derive test scenarios, i.e., specific Modbus requests, and check whether the device issues correct responses. Because test-cases can be generated automatically and the model can be specialized for a given device, this approach enables extensive testing, beyond checking for compliance with the Modbus standard. For example, the method enables tests of how a device responds to a variety of malformed requests that it would not receive during normal operation (e.g., requests that are too long or too short, and requests containing bad function codes or unsupported addresses). Our goal is to help detect vulnerabilities in Modbus devices, including buffer overflows and other flaws.

3.1 PVS Model

Our first formal model of Modbus was developed using the PVS specification and verification system [11]. PVS is a general-purpose interactive theorem prover based on higher-order logic. Details on the PVS specification language, theorem prover and other features may be found on the PVS website (pvs.csl.sri.com). Our full PVS specification of the Modbus Application Protocol is available in an extended version of this paper [4]. The specification is a straightforward formalization of the Modbus Application Protocol standard [8]. The PVS model defines the exact format of the Modbus requests and, for each request type, it specifies the format of the valid responses and possible error messages.

The definition of well-formed requests is summarized as follows:

- The type `raw_msg` represents arbitrary packets (raw messages), which are modeled as byte arrays of length from 1 to 253.

- Correct formatting of requests is defined by a succession of predicates and subtypes of `raw_msg`:

  – Given a raw message `m`, `standard_fcode(m)` holds if the function code of `m` is one of the nineteen assigned codes. A `pre_request` is a raw message that satisfies the predicate `standard_fcode`.

  – Given a prerequest `sr`, `acceptable_length(sr)` holds if the length of `sr` is within the bounds specified by Modbus for the function code of `sr`. A `request` is a prerequest that satisfies `acceptable_length`.

  – Given a request `r`, `valid_data(r)` holds if `r` is well formed. This predicate captures constraints on the number and ranges of request parameters that depend on the function code.

In summary, a valid request is a raw message that satisfies the three predicates `standard_fcode`, `acceptable_length` and `valid_data`.

The definition of acceptable responses to a given request follows the same general scheme and involves a series of PVS predicates. The main predicate `acceptable_response(v, r)` is `true` whenever `r` is a possible response to a valid request `v`. The definition takes into account the function code and parameters of `v` and checks that the response `r` (raw message) has the appropriate format.

The predicates and types summarized so far are device neutral. They capture the general formatting requirements of Modbus [8]. Since devices are not required to implement all the functions and since different devices may support different address ranges, it is useful to specialize the PVS specifications to device characteristics and configurations. For this purpose, the PVS model is parameterized and includes device-specific properties such as supported function codes and valid address ranges for coils, discrete inputs, holding registers and input registers. Once these are specified, the final PVS definition is the predicate `modbus_response(m, r)` that captures formatting and device-specific constraints. The predicate holds when `r` is a response for the given device to a properly-formatted request `m`. Constraints on error reporting are included in this definition.

3.2 Applications

The PVS formalization is as an unambiguous and precise specification of the Modbus Application Protocol. The specification is executable, so it can be used as a reference implementation. For example, it is possible to check that the responses to the bad requests [|0|] and [|1|] are as specified in the standard:

```
modbus_resp([| 0 |], illegal_function(0));
==>  TRUE

modbus_resp([| 1 |], illegal_function(1));
==>  FALSE

modbus_resp([| 1 |], illegal_data_value(1));
==>  TRUE
```

Request [|0|] is a packet containing the single byte 0, i.e., a packet of length 1 with invalid function code 0. The corresponding response must be the packet illegal_function(0). For packet [|1|], the function code is valid and supported by the device, but the format is incorrect. The error code in such a case is required to be illegal_data_value(1). The following examples illustrate the responses to a read command:

```
modbus((: READ_COILS, 0, 10, 0, 8 :), (: READ_COILS, 1, 165 :));
==>  TRUE

modbus((: READ_COILS, 0, 10, 0, 8 :), (: READ_COILS, 10, 165 :));
==> FALSE

modbus((: READ_COILS, 0, 10, 0, 8 :), (: READ_COILS, 2, 165, 182 :));
==> FALSE
```

The read command above is a request for the values of 8 coils starting at address 10. A valid response must consist of a copy of the function code READ_COILS, followed by a byte count of 1, followed by an arbitrary 8-bit value (first line above). The second line shows a badly-formatted response with an incorrect byte count of 10. In the third line, the response has the correct format, but it does not match the request because it returns the values of 16 instead of 8 coils.

4. Automated Test-Case Generation

Traditional software testing typically relies on exercising a piece of software using hand-crafted inputs. This method does not scale well for moderately complex software, as the cost of generating interesting test-cases by hand is prohibitive. In many cases, it is possible to automate the generation of test-cases from formal specifications. This section outlines such an approach, which is developed to test devices that run the Modbus Application Protocol.

Most test-case generation tools require a model of the expected behavior (such as the PVS specifications of Modbus presented in the previous section). The goal is to generate input data for the system under test and check whether the system's behavior in response to the input data satisfies the specifications. To guide the search, additional constraints may be specified on the input data so that particular aspects of the system under test are exercised. The extra constraints are often called "test purposes" or "test goals." For example, one may want to test the response of a device to a specific class of commands by giving an adequate test purpose.

To some extent, PVS and the formal specifications presented previously can be used for test-case generation. This is accomplished by using PVS's built-in mechanisms to find counterexamples to postulated properties. This method is explained in detail in [4]. However, a test-case generation procedure using PVS is limited because it relies exclusively on random search. Specifically, the PVS procedure randomly generates arrays of bytes of different lengths, and checks these byte arrays until one is found that satisfies the test purpose. For many test purposes, such a naïve random search has a low probability of success.

To address this issue, we have constructed a new model of Modbus, which is specifically intended for test-case generation. This model was developed using the SAL toolkit. SAL provides many more tools for exploring models and searching for counterexamples than PVS, and is, thus, better suited for test-case generation. In particular, a test purpose can be encoded as a Boolean satisfiability problem and test-cases can be generated using efficient satisfiability solvers.

4.1 SAL Model

SAL, the Symbolic Analysis Laboratory, is a framework for the specification and analysis of concurrent systems modeled as state transition systems. SAL is less general than PVS, but it provides more automated forms of analysis, including several symbolic model checkers, a bounded model checker based on SAT solving for finite systems, and a more general bounded model checker for infinite systems. Descriptions of these tools and the SAL specification language can be found in [2, 3]. Additional details are available at the SAL website (sal.csl.sri.com).

The SAL model is presented in [4]. The model is intended to support automated test-case generation by constructing Modbus requests that satisfy given constraints (test purposes). For this reason, and unlike the PVS formalization discussed previously, the SAL model covers only half of the Modbus Application Protocol, namely, the formatting of Modbus requests.

The SAL model relies on the observation that the set of well-formatted Modbus requests is a regular language; such a language can be recognized by a finite-state automaton. In fact, the SAL model is essentially a finite-state automaton written in SAL notation. This automaton is defined as module `modbus` whose state variables are shown in Figure 3 (in SAL, "module" is a synonym for state-transition system). The `modbus` module has a single one-byte input variable `b`. Its internal state consists of the ten local variables listed in Figure 3. All these variables have a finite type, so the module is a finite state machine.

```
INPUT
   b: byte
LOCAL
   aux: byte,
   stat: status,
   pc: state,
   len: byte,
   fcode: byte,
   byte_count: byte,
   first_word: word,
   second_word: word,
   third_word: word,
   fourth_word: word
```

Figure 3. Interface of the modbus module in SAL.

The main state variables are pc and stat, which record the current control state of the module and a status flag. Informally, the SAL module reads a Modbus request as a sequence of bytes on input variable b. Each input byte is processed and checked according to the current control state pc. The check depends on the position of the byte in the input sequence and on the preceding bytes. If an error is detected, a diagnostic code is stored in the stat variable; otherwise, the control variable pc is updated and the module proceeds to read the next byte. Processing of a single packet terminates when a state with pc = done is reached. At this point, stat = valid_request if the packet is well formed or stat has a diagnostic value that indicates why the packet is not well formed. For example, the diagnostic value may be length_too_short, fcode_is_invalid, invalid_address, and so on. In addition to computing the status variable, the SAL module extracts and stores important attributes of the input packet such as function code and packet length.

Figure 4 shows a fragment of the SAL specifications that extracts the first word of a packet (16-bit number that follows the function code). The specification uses guarded commands, written condition --> assignment. The condition refers to the current state and the assignment defines the values of the variables in the next state. The identifier X refers to the current value of a variable X, and X' refers to the value of X in the next state.

Default processing of the first word is straightforward: when control variable pc is equal to read_first_word_byte1, the first byte of the word is read from input b and stored in an auxiliary variable aux. Then, pc is updated to read_first_word_byte2. On the next state transition, the full word is computed from aux and b, and stored in variable first_word. Special checking is required if fcode is either DIAGNOSTIC or READ_FIFO_QUEUE. Otherwise, control variable pc is updated to read the second word of the packet. If the function code is DIAGNOSTIC, additional checks are performed on the first word and state variable stat is updated. An invalid word is indicated by setting stat to diagnostic_subcode_is_reserved. Otherwise, stat is set either to valid_request (to indicate that a full packet was read with no errors) or to

```
[] pc = read_first_word_byte1 -->
        aux' = b;
        pc' = read_first_word_byte2

[] pc = read_first_word_byte2 AND fcode = DIAGNOSTIC -->
        first_word' = 256 * aux + b;
        stat' = IF reserved_diagnostic_subcode(first_word')
                THEN diagnostic_subcode_is_reserved
                ELSIF first_word' = RETURN_QUERY_DATA
                THEN valid_request
                ELSE unknown
                ENDIF;

        aux' = len - 3;
        %% aux' = number of extra bytes for RETURN_QUERY_DATA

        pc' = IF reserved_diagnostic_subcode(first_word')
              THEN done
              ELSIF first_word' = RETURN_QUERY_DATA
              THEN read_rest
              ELSE read_second_word_byte1
              ENDIF

[] pc = read_first_word_byte2 AND fcode = READ_FIFO_QUEUE -->
        first_word' = 256 * aux + b;
        stat' = valid_request;
        pc' = done

[] pc = read_first_word_byte2 AND fcode /= DIAGNOSTIC AND
        fcode /= READ_FIFO_QUEUE -->
        first_word' = 256 * aux + b;
        pc' = read_second_word_byte1
```

Figure 4. SAL Fragment: Reading the first word of a packet.

`unknown` (to indicate that more input must be read and more checking must be performed).

Just like the PVS model discussed previously, the SAL model can be specialized to the features of a given Modbus device. For example, one may specify the exact set of function codes supported by the device and the valid address ranges for each function.

4.2 Test-Case Generation Using SAL

By using a state-machine model to specify the format of Modbus requests, the problem of test-case generation is transformed into a state-reachability problem. Given an input sequence of n bytes $b_1, \ldots, b_n$, the SAL `modbus` machine performs n state transitions and reaches a state s_n. We determine whether $b_1, \ldots, b_n$ is a well-formed Modbus request by examining the values of variables `pc` and `status` in state s_n:

- if `pc` = `done` and `stat` = `valid_request` then $b_1, \ldots, b_n$ is a well-formatted request;

- if pc = done and stat $\neq$ valid_request then $b_1, \ldots, b_n$ is an invalid request;
- if pc $\neq$ done then the status of $b_1, \ldots, b_n$ is not known yet (this means that $b_1, \ldots, b_n$ is an incomplete packet that may extend to a valid request).

To generate an invalid Modbus request of length n, we search for a sequence $b_1, \ldots, b_n$ that satisfies the second condition. This problem is solved using SAL's bounded model checker. In general, a bounded model checker searches for counterexamples to a property P that have a fixed length n. In SAL, given a state machine M, a counterexample is a finite sequence of n state transitions:

$$s_0 \rightarrow s_1 \rightarrow \ldots \rightarrow s_n$$

such that s_0 is an initial state of M and one of the states s_i violates P. The property must be negated to use bounded model checking for test-case generation. For example, to obtain an invalid packet, we search for a counterexample to the following property:

```
test18: LEMMA modbus |- G(pc = done => stat /= invalid_data);
```

This lemma states that property pc = done $\Rightarrow$ stat $\neq$ invalid_data is an invariant of module modbus. In other words, it postulates that in all reachable states of modbus, either pc $\neq$ done or stat $\neq$ invalid_data. This property is not true, and a counterexample is exactly what is needed: a sequence of bytes that reaches a state where pc = done and stat = invalid_data. Counterexamples to this property can be obtained by invoking SAL's bounded model checker as follows:

```
sal-bmc flat_modbus test18 -d 20
```

This searches for a counterexample to lemma test18 defined in input file flat_modbus.sal. The option -d 20 specifies a search depth of 20 steps. The resulting counterexample, if any, will be of length 20 or less. The counterexample produced is the sequence of bytes [4, 128, 0, 254, 64]. The state reached after this byte sequence is:

```
stat = invalid_data
pc = done
len = 5
fcode = 4
byte_count = 0
first_word = 32768
second_word = 65088
```

The values of pc and stat are as required; the other variables give more information about the packet generated: its length is 5 bytes and the function code is 4 (*Read Input Register*). For this command, the first word is interpreted as the address of a register and the second word as the number of registers to read. The second word is incorrect because the maximum number of registers allowed in the command is 125. As defined in the Modbus standard, the answer to this command must be an error packet with a code corresponding to "invalid data." Property `test18` is a test purpose designed to construct such an invalid request. By modifying the property, it is possible to search for test cases that satisfy other constraints. For example, the lemma:

```
test20: LEMMA modbus |-
        G(pc = done AND stat = valid_request => len < 200);
```

is a test purpose for a valid request of at least 200 bytes. More complex variants are possible. A variety of scenarios are discussed in [4].

The search algorithm employed by the finite-state bounded model checker is based on converting the problem into a Boolean satisfiability (SAT) problem and using a SAT solver. Any solution to the resulting SAT problem is then converted back to a sequence of transitions, which forms a counterexample or test-case. Although SAT solving is NP-complete, modern SAT solvers can routinely handle problems with millions of clauses and hundreds of thousands of variables. This approach to test-case generation is much more efficient than the random search used with PVS. In SAL, test-case generation is guided by the test purpose. Because the SAT solver used by SAL is complete, the method finds a solution whenever one exists. Given any satisfiable test purpose, `sal-bmc` will generate a test-case. For example, `sal-bmc` can easily construct valid requests, which have a very low probability of being generated by the PVS random search.

The time required for generating test-cases is short, usually a few seconds when running `sal-bmc` on a 3 GHz Intel PC. However, the cost of the search grows as the search depth increases, since the number of variables and clauses in the translation to SAT grows linearly with the depth. Longer test-cases are more expensive to construct; still, the time required is acceptable in most cases. For example, any counterexample to `test20` must be at least 200 bytes long. Finding such a counterexample requires a search depth at least as high; `sal-bmc -d 204` finds such a solution in 80 seconds by solving a SAT problem with more than 500,000 Boolean variables and 2,000,000 clauses. Thus, a large set of test-cases can be generated for many scenarios at little cost. This enables extensive testing of device compliance with Modbus specifications as well as testing for device vulnerabilities by generating a variety of malformed requests. It is also possible to target a specific model or device configuration by modifying the device-specific features of the SAL model. A large number of device-specific test-cases can be generated automatically within a few minutes.

5. Conclusions

The framework presented in this paper supports the systematic and extensive testing of control devices that implement the Modbus Application Protocol. It helps increase the robustness and security of Modbus devices by detecting vulnerabilities that conventional testing methods may easily miss. The framework relies on two main components. The first is a formal PVS specification of the Modbus protocol, which serves as a reference when checking whether or not device responses to test requests satisfy the standard. The second component is a state-machine model of Modbus requests, which functions as an automated test-case generator. Both the models accommodate the variability in Modbus functions and parameters. Furthermore, they are parameterized and can be rapidly specialized to the features of the Modbus device being tested.

Our future research will adapt the formal models to facilitate online monitoring of Modbus devices; by monitoring Modbus requests and responses, it should be possible achieve accurate, high-coverage intrusion detection. Another research objective is to automatically derive intrusion detection sensors from formal models of the expected function and behavior of Modbus devices in a test-case environment.

Acknowledgements

This work was partially supported by the Institute for Information Infrastructure Protection (I3P) under Award 2003-TK-TX-0003 from the Science and Technology Directorate of the U.S. Department of Homeland Security.

References

[1] P. Ammann, P. Black and W. Majurski, Using model checking to generate tests from specifications, *Proceedings of the Second IEEE International Conference on Formal Engineering Methods*, pp. 46–54, 1998.

[2] L. de Moura, S. Owre, H. Ruess, J. Rushby, N. Shankar, M. Sorea and A. Tiwari, SAL 2, in *Proceedings of the Sixteenth International Conference on Computer Aided Verification (LNCS 3114)*, R. Alur and D. Peled (Eds.), Springer, Berlin-Heidelberg, Germany, pp. 496–500, 2004.

[3] L. de Moura, S. Owre and N. Shankar, The SAL Language Manual, Technical Report SRI-CSL-01-02, SRI International, Menlo Park, California, 2003.

[4] B. Dutertre, Formal Modeling and Analysis of the Modbus Protocol, Technical Report, SRI International, Menlo Park, California, 2006.

[5] A. Gargantini and C. Heitmeyer, Using model checking to generate tests from requirements specifications, in *Proceedings of the Seventh European Software Engineering Conference (LNCS 1687)*, O. Nierstrasz and M. Lemoine (Eds.), Springer, Berlin-Heidelberg, Germany, pp. 146–162, 1999.

[6] D. Geist, M. Farkas, A. Landver, Y. Lichtenstein, S. Ur and Y. Wolfsthal, Coverage-directed test generation using symbolic techniques, in *Proceedings of the First International Conference on Formal Methods in Computer-Aided Design (LNCS 1166)*, M. Srivas and A. Camilleri (Eds.), Springer, Berlin-Heidelberg, Germany, pp. 143–158, 1996.

[7] G. Hamon, L. de Moura and J. Rushby, Generating efficient test sets with a model checker, *Proceedings of the Second International Conference on Software Engineering and Formal Methods*, pp. 261–270, 2004.

[8] Modbus IDA, MODBUS Application Protocol Specification v1.1a, North Grafton, Massachusetts (www.modbus.org/specs.php), June 4, 2004.

[9] Modbus IDA, MODBUS Messaging on TCP/IP Implementation Guide v1.0a, North Grafton, Massachusetts (www.modbus.org/specs.php), June 4, 2004.

[10] Modbus.org, MODBUS over Serial Line Specification and Implementation Guide v1.0, North Grafton, Massachusetts (www. modbus.org/specs.php), February 12, 2002.

[11] S. Owre, J. Rushby, N. Shankar and F. von Henke, Formal verification for fault-tolerant architectures: Prolegomena to the design of PVS, *IEEE Transactions on Software Engineering*, vol. 21(2), pp. 107–125, 1995.

[12] S. Rayadurgam and M Heimdahl, Coverage based test-case generation using model checkers, *Proceedings of the Eighth Annual IEEE International Conference and Workshop on the Engineering of Computer Based Systems*, pp. 83–91, 2001.

[13] V. Rusu, L. du Bousquet and T. Jéron, An approach to symbolic test generation, in *Proceedings of the Second International Conference on Integrated Formal Methods (LNCS 1945)*, W. Grieskamp, T. Santen and B. Stoddart (Eds.), Springer, Berlin-Heidelberg, Germany, pp. 338–357, 2000.

Chapter 15

SECURITY ANALYSIS OF MULTILAYER SCADA PROTOCOLS: A MODBUS TCP CASE STUDY

Janica Edmonds, Mauricio Papa and Sujeet Shenoi

Abstract The layering of protocols in critical infrastructure networks – exemplified by Modbus TCP in the oil and gas sector and SS7oIP in the telecommunications sector – raises important security issues. The individual protocol stacks, e.g., Modbus and SS7, have certain vulnerabilities, and transporting these protocols using carrier protocols, e.g., TCP/IP, brings into play the vulnerabilities of the carrier protocols. Moreover, the layering produces unintended inter-protocol interactions and, possibly, new vulnerabilities. This paper describes a formal methodology for evaluating the security of multilayer SCADA protocols. The methodology, involving the analysis of peer-to-peer communications and multilayer protocol interactions, is discussed in the context of Modbus TCP, the predominant protocol used for oil and gas pipeline operations.

Keywords: Multilayer protocols, Modbus TCP, security analysis, formal methods

1. Introduction

Critical infrastructure systems, e.g., SCADA and public telephone networks, have traditionally employed specialized equipment and protocol stacks. Moreover, they were usually isolated from TCP/IP networks.

In recent years, however, the proliferation of TCP/IP networks, along with the advanced services they provide and the availability of inexpensive COTS equipment, have caused several critical infrastructure protocol stacks to be re-designed to use TCP/IP as a foundation for transport and network interconnectivity. For example, in the oil and gas sector, the original Modbus Serial protocol [14] is transported by TCP in the Modbus TCP variant [13], which provides increased network connectivity and multiple, concurrent transactions.

Similarly, in the telecommunications sector, the SS7 over IP (SS7oIP) protocol [6, 15] "floats" the top three layers of the SS7 protocol stack on IP using

Edmonds, J., Papa, M., and Shenoi, S., 2008, in IFIP International Federation for Information Processing, Volume 253, Critical Infrastructure Protection, eds. E. Goetz and S. Shenoi; (Boston: Springer), pp. 205–221.

another protocol (RUDP) as "glue." SS7oIP significantly reduces the operating costs of telecommunications carriers by migrating SS7 traffic from dedicated long-haul signaling links to inexpensive WAN backbones. Furthermore, combining cost-effective IP transport equipment and service-rich SS7 applications enables carriers to provide enhanced services (e.g., Short Message Service and Unified Messaging) and pursue new business opportunities.

The layering of protocols raises important security issues. The individual protocols (e.g., Modbus) or protocol stacks (e.g., SS7) have vulnerabilities. Transporting them over TCP/IP and RUDP brings into play the vulnerabilities of the carrier protocols. Meanwhile, layering multiple protocols produces unintended interactions between protocols and, possibly, new vulnerabilities.

This paper describes a methodology for evaluating the security properties of multilayer protocols used in critical infrastructure networks. The security analysis methodology involves the modeling of protocol communications, and the analysis and verification of protocols using formal methods. The methodology analyzes multilayer protocols from the point of view of single-layer protocol (peer-to-peer) communications and multilayer protocol interactions. A case study is discussed in the context of Modbus TCP, the predominant protocol used in the oil and gas sector. In the case study, a vulnerability is identified in the peer-to-peer Modbus protocol, a correction is proposed, and the security of the corrected protocol is verified. Next, a vulnerability involving inter-protocol interactions in the corrected peer-to-peer protocol is identified, and a correction is proposed, which is subsequently verified.

Several techniques have been proposed for modeling, analyzing and verifying the security properties of peer-to-peer protocols [1–4, 8, 11, 16–18]. This paper engages standard cryptographic protocol strategies for modeling and analyzing protocol communications and the knowledge held by communicating entities (principals and intruders). A verification tool, AVISPA [3, 18], is then used to identify violations of desired security properties and, subsequently, to verify the proposed corrections. The principal contribution of this work is the extension of peer-to-peer techniques to address protocol stack interactions, which is vital to securing critical infrastructure networks.

2. Modbus Protocol

Modbus is one of the oldest, but most widely used industrial control protocols [12–14]. Modbus' open specifications and TCP extension have contributed to its popularity, especially in the oil and gas sector, where it is the *de facto* standard for process control networks.

The Modbus protocol establishes the rules and message structure used by programmable logic controllers (PLCs) to communicate amongst themselves and with human machine interfaces (HMIs). The Modbus application layer defines the mechanisms by which devices exchange supervisory, control and data acquisition information for operating and controlling industrial processes.

Modbus engages a simple request/reply communication mechanism between a master unit and slave devices (Figure 1). For example, a control center

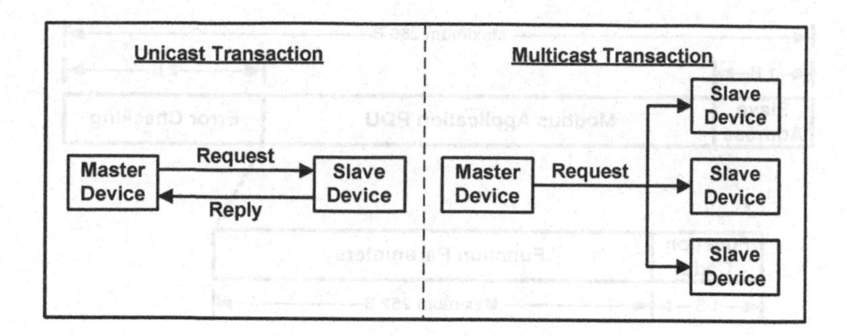

Figure 1. Modbus master-slave communications.

(master) might send a "read" message to a sensor (slave) to obtain the value of a process parameter (e.g., temperature). Alternatively, it might send a "write" message to an actuator (slave) to perform a control action (e.g., open a valve).

A unicast transaction involving the master and an addressed slave comprises two messages, a request message (e.g., for a temperature reading or to open a valve) and the corresponding response message (e.g., the temperature reading or an acknowledgment that the valve was opened). On the other hand, a broadcast transaction involves one request message from the master that is received by all the slaves; the slaves do not send response messages. An example broadcast transaction is a "write" message that resets all sensors and actuators.

Modbus communications occur over serial lines or, more recently, using TCP/IP as a transport mechanism. The following sections describe the serial and TCP variants of the Modbus protocol. For additional details, readers are referred to the protocol specification [12] and the guides for serial [14] and TCP/IP network [13] implementations.

2.1 Modbus Serial Protocol

In the Modbus Serial protocol, messages are transmitted over a serial line using the ASCII or RTU transmission modes. A Modbus Serial message has three components: (i) slave address, (ii) Modbus Application Protocol Data Unit (PDU), and (iii) an error checking field (Figure 2). The slave address in a request message identifies the intended recipient; the corresponding address in a response message is used by the master to identify the responding slave. A broadcast message has an address of 0. A unicast message has an address in the [1,247] range that identifies an individual slave in the network. Values in the [248,255] range are reserved addresses.

The Modbus PDU has two fields, a one-byte function code and function parameters (max 252 bytes). The function code specifies the operation requested by the master; it also conveys error information when an exception occurs in a slave device. The function parameters field contains data pertaining to function invocation (request messages) or function results (reply messages).

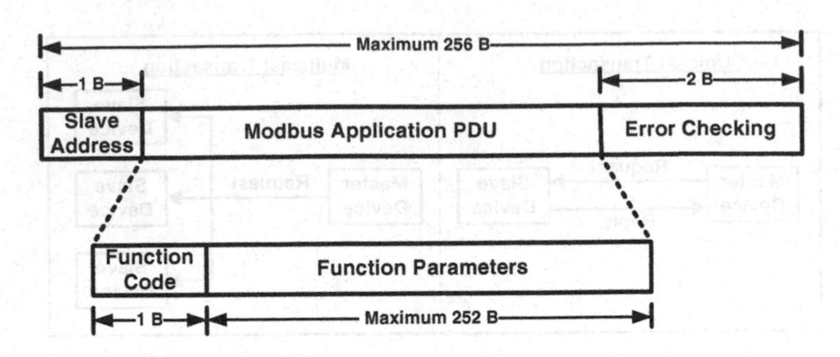

Figure 2. Modbus Serial message.

Modbus function codes specify a variety of read and write operations on slaves, as well as diagnostic functions and error conditions. Public codes correspond to functions whose semantics are completely defined or will be defined in the Modbus standard. Valid public codes fall in the non-contiguous ranges: [1,64], [73,99] and [111,127]. User-defined codes in the [65,72] and [100,110] ranges are not considered by the Modbus standard; their implementations are left to vendors and there are no guarantees regarding their compatibility. Reserved function codes are public codes that are reserved to ensure compatibility with legacy systems. Function code values in the unused range [128,255] are for indicating error conditions in response messages.

Response messages have the same structure as request messages. The Modbus specification defines positive and negative responses to request messages. A positive response informs the master that the slave has successfully performed the requested action; this is indicated by including the request message function code in the response. On the other hand, a negative or exception response notifies the master that the transaction could not be performed by the addressed slave. The function code for a negative response is computed by adding 128 to the function code of the request message; thus, function codes in the [128,255] range denote error conditions. A negative response also includes an exception code in the function parameters part of the response message that provides information about the cause of the error. The Modbus specification defines nine exception responses whose format and content depend on the issuing entity and the type of event producing the exception.

2.2 Modbus TCP Protocol

The Modbus TCP protocol provides connectivity within a Modbus network (a master and its slaves) as well as for TCP/IP interconnected Modbus networks (multiple masters, each with multiple slaves). Modbus TCP enables a master to have multiple outstanding transactions. Moreover, it permits a slave to engage in concurrent communications with multiple masters.

In Modbus TCP, slaves listen for incoming TCP connections on port 502 (IANA assigned port) and may optionally listen on additional ports. The device

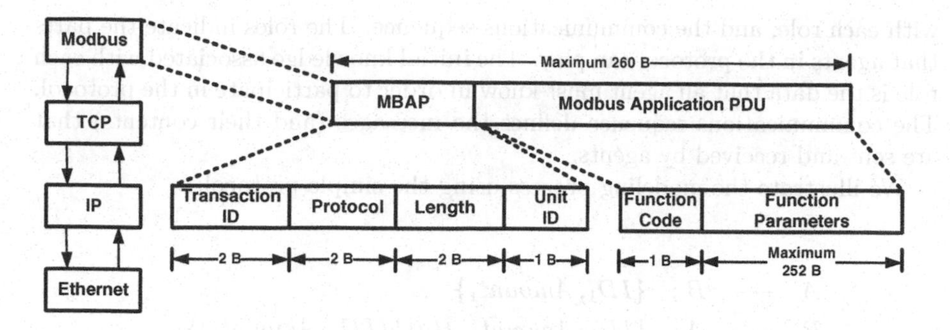

Figure 3. Modbus TCP message.

that performs the passive open operation on TCP (server) assumes the role of a Modbus slave. Similarly, the device performing the active open operation on TCP (client) assumes the role of a Modbus master. Once a TCP communication channel has been established, Modbus roles cannot be changed on that channel; however, multiple outstanding transactions can exist on the channel. Another communication channel must be opened if a device is to assume a different role.

Modbus TCP transactions are functionally equivalent to their serial counterparts: the master and slaves exchange PDUs, except that the transactions are encapsulated in TCP messages (Figure 3). Consequently, a Modbus TCP PDU includes the Modbus Application Protocol (MBAP) in addition to the Modbus Application PDU used in Modbus Serial.

The MBAP header has four fields: (i) transaction identifier, (ii) protocol identifier, (iii) length and (iv) unit identifier. The transaction identifier allows devices to pair transaction requests and replies. The protocol identifier indicates the application protocol encapsulated by the MBAP header (zero for Modbus). The length field indicates the length in bytes of the remaining fields (unit identifier and PDU). The unit identifier indicates the slave associated with the transaction (used only in the case of legacy implementations).

The Modbus TCP specification requires that only one application PDU be transported in the payload of a TCP packet. Since application PDUs have a maximum size of 253 bytes and the length of the MBAP is fixed at seven bytes, the maximum length of a Modbus TCP data unit is 260 bytes.

3. Security Analysis Methodology

This section describes the formalism used to model protocols. In addition, it discusses the technique used to identify violations of security properties and to verify corrections made to protocols.

3.1 Protocol Modeling

The first step in security analysis is to model the protocol. It is necessary to capture the roles of the participating agents, the initial knowledge associated with each role, and the communications sequence. The roles indicate the parts that agents in the protocol can play. The initial knowledge associated with each role is the data that an agent must know in order to participate in the protocol. The communications sequence defines the messages (and their contents) that are sent and received by agents.

We illustrate the modeling process using the simple protocol:

$$A \longrightarrow B: \{ID_1, Amount_1\}$$
$$B \longrightarrow A: \{ID_1, Amount_1, Hash(ID_1, Amount_1)\}_{K_{ab}}$$

The protocol has two agents (A and B) and a two-step communication sequence. Agents A and B assume the roles of initiator and responder, respectively. A knows the values ID_1 and $Amount_1$, which it sends to B. B receives the values from A, computes a hash of the two values, and sends all the information to A encrypted using a symmetric key K_{ab} known only to A and B.

In the following, we describe the modeling of agent communications and intruder attacks in more detail.

3.1.1 Agent Communications.

Agents communicate when a message sent by one agent matches the pattern exposed by another agent. We specify the constructs involved in modeling agent communications, including complex messages, encryption/decryption and pattern matching [16, 17].

Definition 1: A *key* ($key \in KEY$) is a public/private key (K_n/K_n^{-1}), a shared or secret key (K_n^s), or *nil*, for an unencrypted message:

$$key \ ::= \ K_n \mid K_n^{-1} \mid K_n^s \mid nil$$

We assume the existence of a basic type $NAME$ comprising an infinite set of *names*. This basic type is used to create unique keys, and data for messages and patterns. For example, n and m in Definition 1 are of type $NAME$ ($n, m \in NAME$).

A key matching operator is required to determine whether or not a key can be used to decrypt a message. The first two rules in the definition below are for asymmetric and symmetric encryption, respectively. The third rule is used for cleartext messages.

Definition 2: The key matching operator ($\overset{K}{\sim}$) is defined by:

$$K_a \overset{K}{\sim} K_b^{-1} \text{ iff } a = b$$
$$K_a^s \overset{K}{\sim} K_b^s \text{ iff } a = b$$
$$nil \overset{K}{\sim} nil$$

Messages exchanged by agents are nested tuples of values encrypted under a key, where the values can be keys, messages, data, nonces or timestamps.

Definition 3: A *message* is a list of values $\{v_1, v_2, ., v_j\}$ encrypted under *key*, i.e., $\{v_1, v_2, \cdots, v_j\}_{key}$. A value is a key, a message, a name or a fresh name:

$$message = \{v_1, v_2, \cdots, v_j\}_{key}$$

$$value = key|message|n|\#n$$

Note that the names in a message represent message data. Fresh names refer to nonces and timestamps that are generated in a single run of a protocol.

Communication between agents occurs when the sending agent's message matches the receiving agent's pattern. The pattern exposed by the receiving agent reveals the knowledge that it has about the incoming message.

Definition 4: A *pattern* is a list of patterns $\{p_1, p_2, \cdots, p_j\}$ encrypted under *key* and denoted by $\{p_1, p_2, \cdots, p_j\}_{key}$ or a key, a wildcard or placeholder $(n?)$ for capturing values or a name (n):

$$pattern = \{p_1, p_2, \cdots, p_j\}_{key}|key|n?|n$$

Finally, we specify the rules for matching messages and patterns.

Definition 5: The message-pattern matching operator $\sim$ is defined by the following rules ($v, v_i \in VAL$, $p, p_i \in PAT$, $key, key_i \in KEY$, $m \in MSG$ and $n \in NAME$):

$$\begin{aligned}
\{v_1, v_2, ..., v_j\}_{key_1} &\sim \{p_1, p_2, ..., p_j\}_{key_2} \text{ iff} \\
& key_1 \overset{K}{\sim} key_2 \wedge v_i \sim p_i \ \forall i = 1..j \\
m &\sim n? \\
m &\sim key? \\
v &\sim n? \\
v &\sim n \text{ iff } v = n \\
key &\sim key?
\end{aligned}$$

Figure 4 presents a formal model of the two-step communication sequence:

$$\begin{aligned}
A &\longrightarrow B: \ \{ID_1, Amount_1\} \\
B &\longrightarrow A: \ \{ID_1, Amount_1, Hash(ID_1, Amount_1)\}_{K_{ab}}
\end{aligned}$$

The figure formally specifies the agents' roles and initial knowledge. Also, it illustrates the modeling of messages and patterns, and the exchange of information between agents.

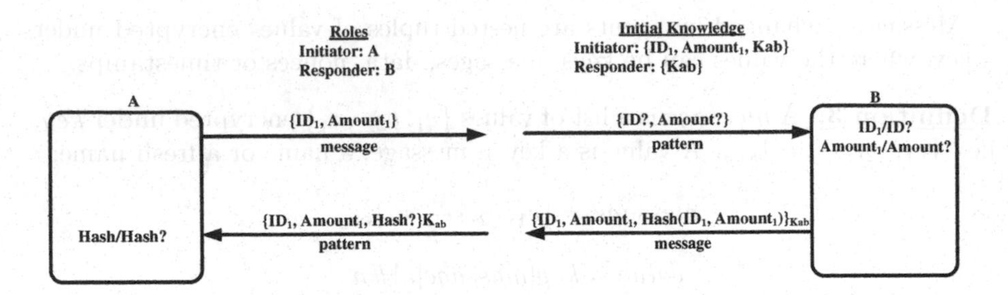

Figure 4. Modeling agent communications.

In the first step, A sends the message $\{ID_1, Amount_1\}$, which is matched by the pattern $\{ID?, Amount?\}$ exposed by B. The match causes the values ID_1 and $Amount_1$ to be bound to B's wildcard variables $ID?$ and $Amount?$, respectively. The binding is denoted by $ID_1/ID?$ and $Amount_1/Amount?$ in B. Thus, B obtains (knows) the values ID_1 and $Amount_1$.

After receiving ID_1 and $Amount_1$, B computes the hash value of ID_1 and $Amount_1$. In the second step, B sends ID_1, $Amount_1$ and the hash value to A in an encrypted message, i.e., $\{ID_1, Amount_1, Hash(ID_1, Amount_1)\}_{K_{ab}}$. Note that the message is encrypted under K_{ab}, a secret key shared by A and B. As shown in Figure 4, the encrypted message is matched by the pattern $\{ID_1, Amount_1, Hash?\}_{Kab}$ exposed by A. Thus, A's wildcard variable $Hash?$ receives the hash value computed by B.

3.1.2 Intruder Attacks.

An intruder I may perpetrate an attack by exposing an appropriate pattern to capture information sent by agent A. Next, it creates a fabricated message, which it sends to B. The corresponding communication sequence involving agents A, I and B is:

$$
\begin{array}{llll}
A & \longrightarrow & I: & \{ID_1, Amount_1\} \\
I & \longrightarrow & B: & \{ID_1, Amount_2\} \\
B & \longrightarrow & I: & \{ID_1, Amount_2, Hash(ID_1, Amount_2)\}_{K_{ab}} \\
I & \longrightarrow & A: & \{ID_1, Amount_2, Hash(ID_1, Amount_2)\}_{K_{ab}}
\end{array}
$$

In the first step, I might expose the pattern $\{ID?, Amount?\}$ to capture both ID_1 and $Amount_1$ in the message sent by A. Alternatively, if I only intends to capture a value for $Amount?$, it might expose the pattern $\{ID_1, Amount?\}$ – this means that I has initial knowledge of ID_1. Of course, this pattern would not work if A were to send the message $\{ID_2, Amount_1\}$ because ID_2 in the message would not match ID_1 in the pattern $\{ID_1, Amount?\}$ exposed by intruder I (according to Definition 5).

In the second step, I sends the message $\{ID_1, Amount_2\}$, which matches B's exposed pattern $\{ID?, Amount?\}$, enabling B to obtain the values ID_1

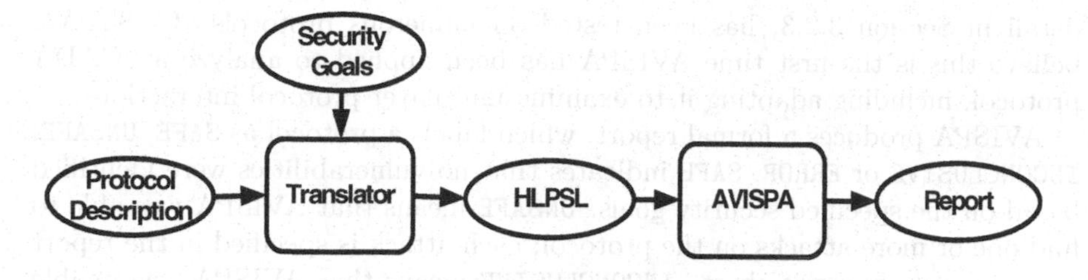

Figure 5. Analysis and verification framework.

and $Amount_2$. B computes the hash value, and sends an encrypted message, which is intercepted by I (Step 3). I obtains the encrypted message by exposing a pattern $\{Message?\}$. However, I is unable to unlock the message because it does not know key K_{ab}, so it can only forward the encrypted message to A (Step 4). Of course, when A unlocks the message and checks the hash, it notices that something is amiss. Thus, I's attack only has nuisance value.

Note that I is only able to change values that are eventually bound to wildcards (variables) in a pattern exposed by a receiver (e.g., *Amount?*, which receives the value $Amount_2$ instead of $Amount_1$ in the attack). The other values in the exposed pattern are determined by the receiver and cannot be changed by I.

3.2 Protocol Analysis and Verification

This section discusses the protocol analysis and verification methodology [7]. In particular, it describes the analysis and verification framework, the specification of security goals, and the application of AVISPA [3, 18], an automated tool for validating Internet security protocols.

3.2.1 Framework. The framework used for protocol analysis and verification is presented in Figure 5. A formal protocol specification (e.g., the example in Section 3.1) and security goals (described in Section 3.2.2 below) are translated into the High Level Protocol Specification Language (HLPSL) for use by the AVISPA tool [3, 18]. AVISPA produces a report that documents whether or not the security goals are satisfied. The report also describes the attacks (if any exist) that may be perpetrated by an intruder.

HLPSL is an expressive, modular role-based formal language that can be used to specify control flow patterns, data structures, alternative intruder models [5] and complex security properties, along with various cryptographic primitives and their algebraic properties. HLPSL models agent communications, including both messages and patterns, and security goals for protocols. Currently, the translation to HLPSL is performed manually. However, it is relatively simple to construct a compiler that automates the translation process.

The HLPSL file with protocol specifications and security goals is submitted to AVISPA for analysis and verification. AVISPA, which is described in more detail in Section 3.2.3, has been tested on numerous protocols [3, 18]. We believe this is the first time AVISPA has been applied to analyze a SCADA protocol, including adapting it to examine multilayer protocol interactions.

AVISPA produces a formal report, which labels a protocol as `SAFE`, `UNSAFE`, `INCONCLUSIVE` or `ERROR`. `SAFE` indicates that no vulnerabilities were identified based on the specified security goals. `UNSAFE` means that AVISPA was able to find one or more attacks on the protocol; each attack is specified in the report as a message sequence chart. `INCONCLUSIVE` means that AVISPA was unable to reach any conclusions in a bounded number of iterations; in other words, the protocol is safe or additional iterations are required to identify an attack. `ERROR` implies that AVISPA was unable to correctly interpret the HLPSL file.

3.2.2 Security Goals.

The security goals are the properties that must be satisfied by a protocol being analyzed by AVISPA, e.g., authentication and secrecy, key agreement properties, anonymity and non-repudiation [3]. Specific security goals that can be evaluated by AVISPA include:

- **Peer Entity Authentication:** Assuring one agent of the identity of a second agent through the presentation of evidence and/or credentials.
- **Data Origin Authentication:** Ensuring confidence that a received message or piece of data was created by a certain agent at some time in the past, and has not been altered or corrupted. This property is also called message authentication.
- **Implicit Destination Authentication:** Ensuring that a message is only readable by agents authorized by the sender.
- **Replay Protection:** Assuring that a previously authenticated message is not reused.
- **Key Authentication:** Ensuring that a particular secret key is limited to specific known and trusted parties.
- **Key Confirmation:** An agent has proof that a second agent has a particular secret key.
- **Fresh Key Derivation:** Dynamic key management is used to derive fresh session keys.
- **Identity Protection Against Eavesdroppers:** An intruder should not be able to establish the real identity of an agent based on communications exchanged by the agent.
- **Proof of Origin:** Undeniable evidence that an agent sent a message.
- **Proof of Delivery:** Undeniable evidence that an agent received a message.

AVISPA can reason about other security goals, but these may involve additional implementation efforts. Security goals are specified by augmenting the transitions of roles (messages and patterns) with *goal-facts*. HLPSL has built-in support for three primitive goals: secrecy, weak authentication and strong authentication. The expression $secrecy\_of\ X$ indicates that if an intruder obtains X, a violation of the specified security requirement has occurred. It is important to note that AVISPA assumes that all protocol roles with access to variable X will keep their respective copies a secret. The weak and strong authentication goals are modeled after Lowe's [10] notions of non-injective and injective agreement, respectively.

A weak authentication of Y by X on variable Z, expressed as X *weakly authenticates* Y *on* Z, is achieved if at the end of a protocol run initiated by X, both X and Y agree on the value Z. This definition does not guarantee a one-to-one relationship between the number of times X has participated in a valid protocol run and the number of times Y has participated, i.e., it is possible for X to believe that it has participated in two valid runs when Y has been taking part on a single run. A strong authentication goal, simply expressed as X *authenticates* Y *on* Z, requires that each protocol run initiated by X corresponds to a unique run of the protocol by Y. The HLPSL goal section is used to describe the combinations of facts that indicate an attack.

The internal representation of attack conditions is in terms of temporal logic [9]; additional properties must be expressed using temporal logic. Of the three main security goals for SCADA protocols, integrity is most easily verified using AVISPA.

In the example in Section 3.1, agent A might wish to ensure the integrity of the message from B. The following three statements would be introduced in the corresponding HLPSL file to check the integrity of the communications. The statement $witness(B, A, hash\_function, hash(ID_1,\ Amount_1))$ in B's role definition states that B has produced a certain hash value for A. The statement $request(A, B, hash\_function, hash?)$ in A's role definition states that A wants the hash value to be verified. The HLPSL goal statement A *authenticates* B *on* $hash\_function$ indicates that A and B must agree on the value of $hash\_function$.

3.2.3 AVISPA. AVISPA [3] was created to analyze Internet protocols and applications. It incorporates four separate backends: OFMC, CL-AtSe, SATMC and TA4SP. AVISPA has been tested on numerous industrial protocols, and has uncovered many known and unknown flaws [18].

To understand how AVISPA works, note that the values that an intruder I can assign to a variable (wildcard) depend on the values in I's knowledge base and the current state of the protocol run. These values must match the receiver's exposed pattern. If the values do not match, the message will be ignored or rejected, and the protocol run will not be completed. Knowledge about the specific values to be given to variables may come from information gathered about messages that are sent/received later in the protocol sequence.

Indeed, I requires knowledge about the protocol communication sequence to perpetrate an attack. AVISPA automates the process of searching for values assigned to variables that satisfy the protocol constraints. If an assignment of values results in a security requirement not being satisfied, AVISPA reports this fact and presents a sequence of communication exchanges as proof.

AVISPA provides a web interface that enables users to edit protocol specifications, and select and configure AVISPA backend tools. One or more backends may be used to evaluate a protocol. Input to all AVISPA backends must be in HLPSL.

AVISPA outputs a vulnerabilities report that lists the attacks that could be perpetrated by an intruder. An attack is detected when a communication sequence is found such that there is a successful protocol run and one or more security requirements are violated. Otherwise, it is assumed that an intruder is unable to generate an attack in the given scenario.

4. Modbus TCP Case Study

This section presents a Modbus TCP case study, which focuses on the authentication of Modbus agents and the origins of messages. The study shows that identifying and correcting flaws at the peer-to-peer (Modbus Serial) level are insufficient. It is imperative that security analyses of multilayer protocols, such as Modbus TCP, also be performed at the inter-protocol level.

4.1 Modbus Serial Analysis

Unicast transactions in the Modbus Serial protocol involve the exchange of request and reply messages. Figure 6(a) models a unicast transaction using the formalism discussed in Section 3. The $Master$ unit sends the message $\{Slave, FC_1, Data_1, CRC_1\}$ to $Slave$ requesting it to perform function FC_1 with parameters $Data_1$; CRC_1 is included to verify the integrity of the message. The $Slave$ listens for messages by exposing the pattern $\{Slave, FC_1?, Data_1?, CRC_1?\}$. The first field (with value $Slave$) indicates that $Slave$ only receives messages addressed to $Slave$ (see Definition 5 in Section 3). The remaining three fields $FC_1?$, $Data_1?$ and $CRC_1?$ are wildcards (variables) that are bound to the data values FC_1, $Data_1$ and CRC_1, respectively.

Upon executing the request, $Slave$ responds with the message $\{Slave, FC_2, Data_2, CRC_2\}$ indicating that it ($Slave$) is responding with status FC_2 ($FC_2 = FC_1$ or $FC_2 = FC_1 + 128$ for positive/negative replies [12]) as described by $Data_2$; CRC_2 is used to establish message integrity. $Master$ exposes the pattern $\{Slave, FC_2?, Data_2?, CRC_2?\}$ to receive this data from $Slave$.

A flaw was discovered after formally modeling $Master$-$Slave$ communications and using the protocol analysis technique described in Section 3. The flaw enables an $Intruder$ to intercept and modify messages sent by the $Master$ and $Slave$ (Figure 6(b)). In this attack, the $Intruder$ intercepts $Master$'s request message $\{Slave, FC_1, Data_1, CRC_1\}$ and sends the fabricated message $\{Slave, FC_2, Data_2, CRC_2\}$ to $Slave$. Upon receiving this message, $Slave$

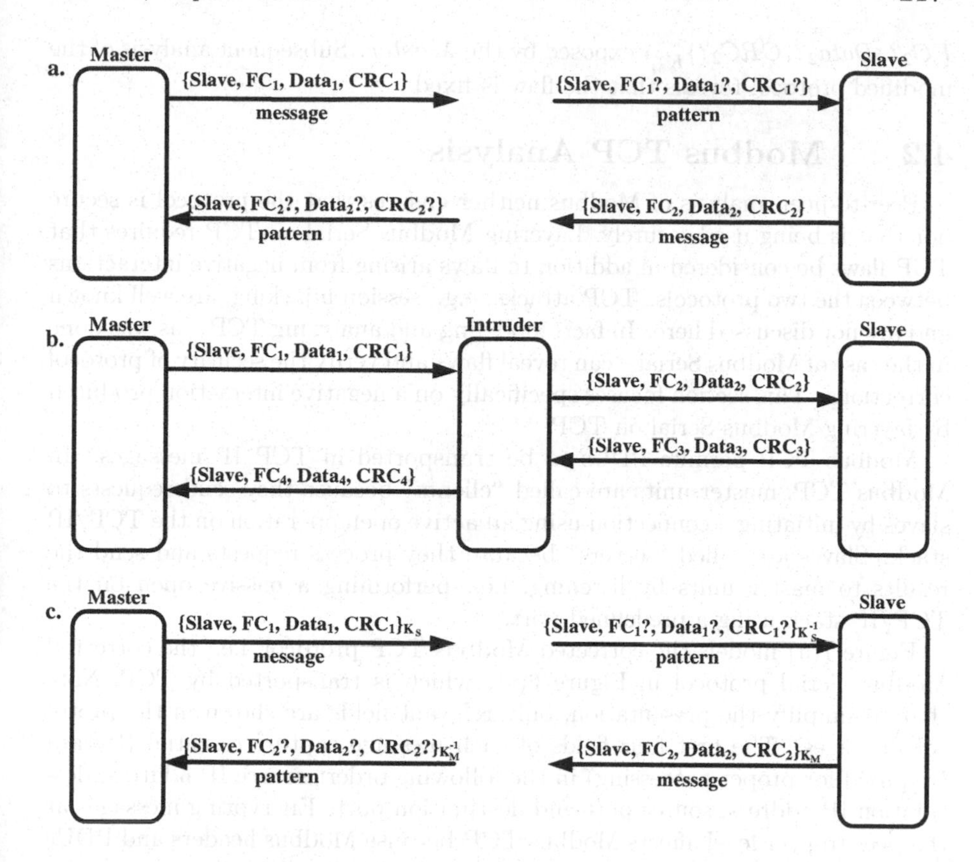

Figure 6. Modbus Serial attack and correction.

performs FC_2 with $Data_2$ instead of FC_1 with $Data_1$. Next, *Slave* responds with $\{Slave, FC_3, Data_3, CRC_3\}$ where $FC_3 = FC_2$ or $FC_3 = FC_2 + 128$ for positive/negative replies.

At this point, as shown in Figure 6(b), *Intruder* intercepts *Slave*'s message and sends the fabricated message $\{Slave, FC_4, Data_4, CRC_4\}$ where $FC_4 = FC_1$ or $FC_4 = FC_1 + 128$ to *Master*. Note that the fabricated message is constructed so that it matches the pattern exposed by *Master* to receive a response message from *Slave* regarding function FC_1.

One way to defeat this attack is to use asymmetric encryption for Modbus messages. The new specification of a Modbus transaction is shown in Figure 6(c). The private keys of the *Master* and *Slave* are K_M^{-1} and K_S^{-1}, respectively; the corresponding public keys are K_M and K_S. The *Master* uses the *Slave*'s public key K_S to encrypt the request message $\{Slave, FC_1, Data_1, CRC_1\}_{K_S}$, and the *Slave* exposes the pattern $\{Slave, FC_1?, Data_1?, CRC_1?\}_{K_S^{-1}}$. Matching is verified according to Definitions 2 and 5 (note that $K_S \overset{K}{\sim} K_S^{-1}$). The *Slave* responds by using the *Master*'s public key K_M to encrypt the message: $\{Slave, FC_2, Data_2, CRC_2\}_{K_M}$, which is matched by the pattern $\{Slave,$

$FC_2?, Data_2?, CRC_2?\}_{K_M^{-1}}$ exposed by the *Master*. Subsequent analysis of the modified protocol reveals that the flaw is fixed.

4.2 Modbus TCP Analysis

Peer-to-peer analysis of Modbus neither ensures that the protocol is secure nor that is being used securely. Layering Modbus Serial on TCP requires that TCP flaws be considered in addition to flaws arising from negative interactions between the two protocols. TCP attacks, e.g., session hijacking, are well known and are not discussed here. In fact, modeling and analyzing TCP – as was done in the case of Modbus Serial – can reveal flaws and verify the security of protocol corrections. This section focuses specifically on a negative interaction produced by layering Modbus Serial on TCP.

Modbus TCP permits PDUs to be transported in TCP/IP messages. In Modbus TCP, master units are called "clients" because they send requests to slaves by initiating a connection using an active open operation on the TCP/IP stack. Slaves are called "servers" because they process requests and send the results to master units by listening, i.e., performing a passive open on the TCP/IP stack using a predefined port.

Figure 7(a) models the corrected Modbus TCP protocol, i.e., the corrected Modbus Serial protocol in Figure 6(c), which is transported by TCP. Note that to simplify the presentation, only relevant fields are shown in the protocol messages. The first four fields of each message capture essential IP data (required for proper processing) in the following order: source IP address, destination IP address, source port and destination port. Encrypting messages at the peer-to-peer level affects Modbus TCP because Modbus headers and PDUs are encrypted (Figure 7(a)). Note also that the Modbus specifications require that messages contain additional MBAP fields (e.g., $transID$, PID, $length$ and $unitID$).

Figure 7(b) presents an attack that exploits a flaw arising from negative interactions between layers of the Modbus TCP protocol. In the attack, the *Intruder* intercepts the *Client*'s encrypted request message sent from *IP-C* (*Client*'s IP address) to *IP-S* (*Server*'s IP address). Since the *Intruder* cannot decrypt the Modbus message (it does not know K_S^{-1}), it changes the TCP/IP data associated with the source of the IP datagram and forwards the Modbus content as is. The *Server* responds to the *Intruder*'s IP address *IP-I* with $\{transID, PID, length_2, unitID, FC_2, Data_2\}$ encrypted with its private key K_S^{-1}. The *Intruder* decrypts the Modbus payload using K_S and creates a bogus (but valid) Modbus response by encrypting $\{transID, PID, length_3, unitID, FC_3, Data_3\}$ using the *Client*'s public key K_C.

Protocol analysis reveals that encryption – while it maintains message confidentiality – does not ensure message integrity. The attack in Figure 7(b) exploits the flaw, enabling the *Intruder* to intercept and modify messages and make the *Server* believe it is the *Client* (master unit). One might observe that this attack is defeated if the *Server* (a remote terminal unit) could be configured with the IP address of the *Client* (the Modbus payload itself does

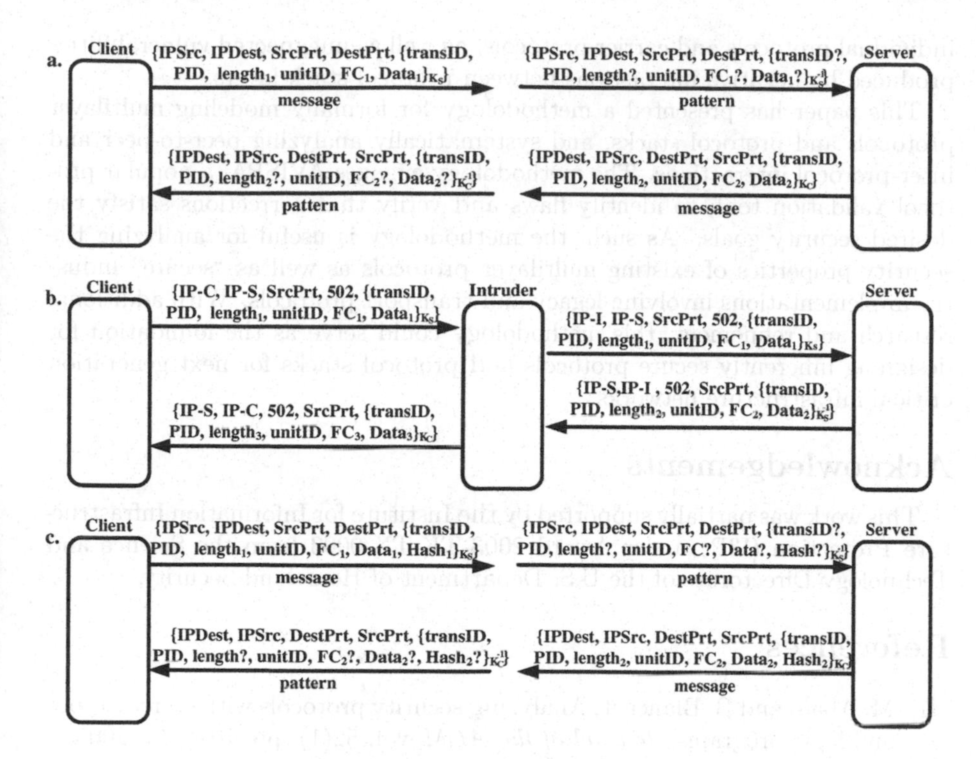

Figure 7. Modbus TCP attack and correction.

not contain any information identifying the *Client*). Clearly in this case, a message from *IP-I* would have been rejected and the attack would have failed. However, due to limited computational power, remote terminal units often deploy minimal TCP/IP stacks with few, if any, security settings.

The corrected protocol in Figure 7(c) appends a two-byte hash value of the IP source and destination addresses, the TCP source port and the Modbus transaction ID to the Modbus PDU. This has the effect of including an additional field (protected by encryption) that is used to establish integrity (by associating IP and Modbus-related data in a single field). Formal analysis of this corrected protocol reveals that it addresses the flaw by preserving Modbus agent authenticity and message integrity.

5. Conclusions

Using carrier protocols such as TCP/IP to transport control protocols in SCADA/distributed control systems, telecommunications and other critical infrastructure networks is efficient and cost effective. However, the layering of protocols raises serious security issues. The original control protocols were designed for use in isolated networks, not to be transported over WANs by carrier protocols. Protocol layering brings into play the vulnerabilities in the individual protocols and carrier protocols, as well as unexpected vulnerabilities produced by negative interactions between protocol stack layers.

This paper has presented a methodology for formally modeling multilayer protocols and protocol stacks, and systematically analyzing peer-to-peer and inter-protocol interactions. The methodology engages AVISPA, a popular protocol validation tool, to identify flaws and verify that corrections satisfy the desired security goals. As such, the methodology is useful for analyzing the security properties of existing multilayer protocols as well as "secure" industry implementations involving legacy and transport protocols. With additional research and refinement, this methodology could serve as the foundation for designing inherently secure protocols and protocol stacks for next generation critical infrastructure networks.

Acknowledgements

This work was partially supported by the Institute for Information Infrastructure Protection (I3P) under Award 2003-TK-TX-0003 from the Science and Technology Directorate of the U.S. Department of Homeland Security.

References

[1] M. Abadi and B. Blanchet, Analyzing security protocols with secrecy types and logic programs, *Journal of the ACM*, vol. 52(1), pp. 102–146, 2005.

[2] R. Anderson and R. Needham, Programming Satan's computer, in *Computer Science Today: Recent Trends and Developments (LNCS Vol. 1000)*, J. van Leeuwen (Ed.), Springer-Verlag, Berlin, Germany, pp. 426–440, 1995.

[3] A. Armando, D. Basin, Y. Boichut, Y. Chevalier, L. Compagna, J. Cuellar, P. Hankes Drielsma, P. Heam, O. Kouchnarenko, J. Mantovani, S. Modersheim, D. von Oheimb, M. Rusinowitch, J. Santiago, M. Turuani, L. Vigano and L. Vigneron, The AVISPA tool for the automated validation of Internet security protocols and applications, *Proceedings of the Seventeenth International Conference on Computer-Aided Verification*, pp. 281–285, 2005.

[4] D. Basin, S. Modersheim and L. Vigano, An on-the-fly model checker for security protocol analysis, *Proceedings of the Eighth European Symposium on Research in Computer Security*, pp. 253–270, 2003.

[5] D. Dolev and A. Yao, On the security of public key protocols, *IEEE Transactions on Information Theory*, vol. 29(2), pp. 198–208, 1983.

[6] L. Dryburgh and J. Hewitt, *Signaling System No. 7 (SS7/C7): Protocol, Architecture and Services*, Cisco Press, Indianapolis, Indiana, 2005.

[7] J. Edmonds, Security Analysis of Multilayer Protocols in SCADA Networks, Ph.D. Dissertation, Department of Computer Science, University of Tulsa, Tulsa, Oklahoma, 2006.

[8] S. Escobar, C. Meadows and J. Meseguer, A rewriting-based inference system for the NRL Protocol Analyzer and its meta-logical properties, *Theoretical Computer Science*, vol. 367(1-2), pp. 162–202, 2006.

[9] L. Lamport, The temporal logic of actions, *ACM Transactions on Programming Languages and Systems*, vol. 16(3), pp. 872–923, 1994.

[10] G. Lowe, A hierarchy of authentication specifications, *Proceedings of the Tenth Computer Security Foundations Workshop*, pp. 31–44, 1997.

[11] G. Lowe, Casper: A compiler for the analysis of security protocols, *Journal of Computer Security*, vol. 6, pp. 53–84, 1998.

[12] Modbus IDA, MODBUS Application Protocol Specification v1.1a, North Grafton, Massachusetts (www.modbus.org/specs.php), June 4, 2004.

[13] Modbus IDA, MODBUS Messaging on TCP/IP Implementation Guide v1.0a, North Grafton, Massachusetts (www.modbus.org/specs.php), June 4, 2004.

[14] Modbus.org, MODBUS over Serial Line Specification and Implementation Guide v1.0, North Grafton, Massachusetts (www. modbus.org/specs.php), February 12, 2002.

[15] L. Ong, I. Rytina, M. Garcia, H. Schwarzbauer, L. Coene, H. Lin, I. Juhasz, M. Holdrege and C. Sharp, Framework Architecture for Signaling Transport, RFC 2719, October 1999.

[16] M. Papa, O. Bremer, J. Hale and S. Shenoi, Formal analysis of E–commerce protocols, *IEICE Transactions on Information and Systems*, vol. E84-D(10), pp. 1313–1323, 2001.

[17] M. Papa, O. Bremer, J. Hale and S. Shenoi, Integrating logics and process calculi for cryptographic protocol analysis, in *Security and Privacy in the Age of Uncertainty*, D. Gritzalis, S. De Capitani di Vimercati, P. Samarati and S. Katsikas (Eds.), Kluwer, Boston, pp. 349–360, 2003.

[18] L. Vigano, Automated security protocol analysis with the AVISPA tool, *Proceedings of the Twenty-First Conference on the Mathematical Foundations of Programming Semantics*, pp. 61–86, 2006.

Chapter 16

REMOTE FORENSIC ANALYSIS OF PROCESS CONTROL SYSTEMS

Regis Friend Cassidy, Adrian Chavez, Jason Trent and Jorge Urrea

Abstract Forensic analysis can help maintain the security of process control systems: identifying the root cause of a system compromise or failure is useful for mitigating current and future threats. However, forensic analysis of control systems is complicated by three factors. First, live analysis must not impact the performance and functionality of a control system. Second, the analysis should be performed remotely as control systems are typically positioned in widely dispersed locations. Third, forensic techniques and tools must accommodate proprietary or specialized control system hardware, software, applications and protocols.

This paper explores the use of a popular digital forensic tool, EnCase Enterprise, for conducting remote forensic examinations of process control systems. Test results in a laboratory-scale environment demonstrate the feasibility of conducting remote forensic analyses on live control systems.

Keywords: Process control systems, digital forensics, live forensics, EnCase

1. Introduction

The personal computer that sits on a desk at work or at home is similar to the systems that are used to operate many critical infrastructure components. Power plants, oil and gas pipelines, and other large infrastructures that once mainly employed legacy systems with proprietary technologies have adopted commodity computer systems, software and networking technologies, including Internet connectivity.

While commodity computer systems and the Internet are efficient, cost effective solutions for operating critical infrastructure components, they introduce vulnerabilities in addition to those that are invariably present in specialized process control systems. Mechanisms should be in place for incident response in the event of an attack or system failure. Security specialists need to investigate the root cause of the problem, resolve the issue, and mitigate current and

Cassidy, R.F., Chavez, A., Trent, J. and Urrea, J., 2008, in IFIP International Federation for Information Processing, Volume 253, Critical Infrastructure Protection, eds. E. Goetz and S. Shenoi; (Boston: Springer), pp. 223–235.

future threats while minimizing or eliminating the downtime of control systems. This paper explores the application of a commercial software solution to perform secure, remote forensic analysis of process control systems while they are operating.

2. Process Control Systems

The United States critical infrastructure includes approximately 28,600 networked financial institutions, two million miles of pipeline, 2,800 power plants, 104 nuclear power plants, 80,000 dams, 60,000 chemical plants, 87,000 food processing plants, and 1,600 water treatment plants [3]. The National Strategy for Homeland Security states that these systems are so vital that their destruction "would have a debilitating impact on security, national economic security, national public health or safety, or any combination of [these] matters" [4].

Process control systems are responsible for the safe, reliable and efficient operation of many critical infrastructure components. One example is a supervisory control and data acquisition (SCADA) system, which performs tasks such as monitoring switches and valves, controlling temperature and pressure levels, and collecting and archiving field data. SCADA systems are required to maintain 24/7 availability and provide real-time (or near real-time) response. Estimated downtime costs in certain sectors range from $1 million to $4 million per hour [3].

The security of process control systems is a major concern. This is because current systems often use commodity hardware and commercial off-the-shelf software (operating systems, databases and applications) and because of increased network connectivity. Proprietary protocols have been replaced with Ethernet/IP-based protocols allowing for inexpensive, efficient solutions, but these expose process control systems to common network attacks. It is also increasingly common for process control systems to connect to enterprise networks (e.g., corporate IT networks), which are typically connected to the Internet. Figure 1 shows an industrial network that accesses real-time data from control systems for tasks such as statistical analysis, trending and budget analysis [3]. Even when control systems are isolated in their own internal networks, they are still vulnerable to attacks by malicious insiders or insiders who unwittingly introduce malicious code via removable media.

3. Digital Forensics

It is critical to implement security and auditing mechanisms for process control systems to combat vulnerabilities introduced by the underlying technology. Beyond network firewalls, monitoring tools and intrusion detection systems, there is a need for utilities that offer timely incident response and forensic analysis when protection systems fail. Identifying the problem and discovering the root cause of a system compromise or failure is important to mitigate its negative effects as well as to secure control systems from future breaches.

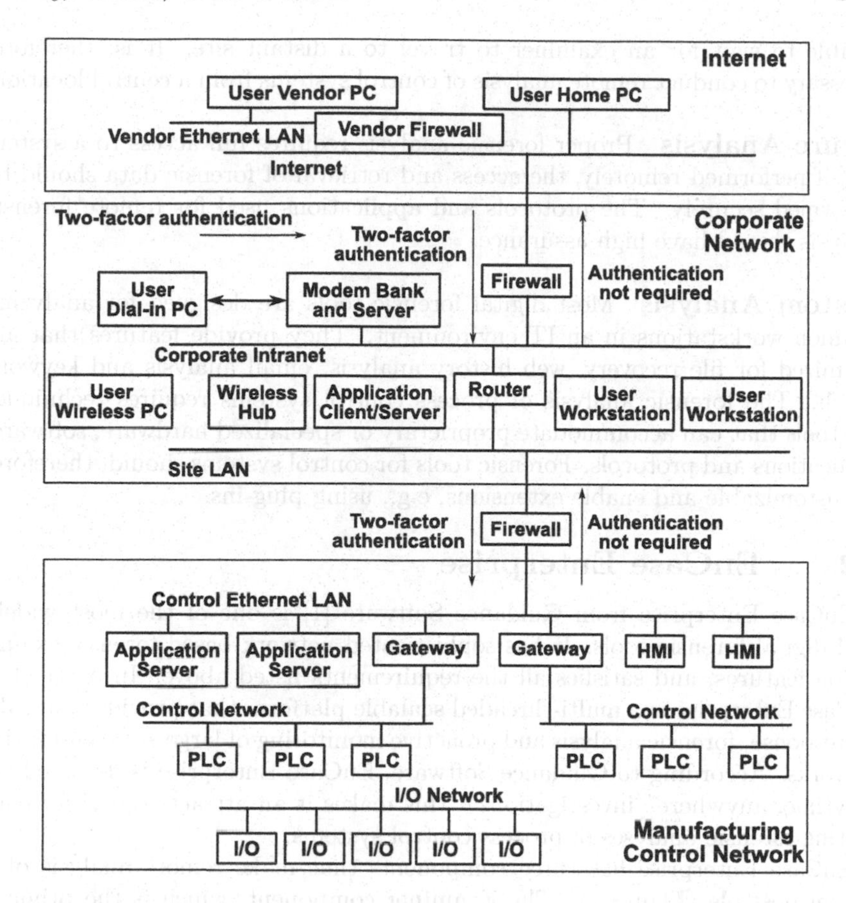

Figure 1. Process control network with Internet connectivity [3].

3.1 Forensic Analysis Requirements

This section lists the main requirements for performing forensic analysis on control systems.

Availability During a digital forensic investigation, a computer system is typically shut down and taken back to a laboratory where a specialist conducts a forensic examination. A process control system cannot be taken offline for forensic analysis, especially if it is monitoring or controlling plant operations. It is, therefore, necessary to conduct *in situ* analysis of a control system while it is operating.

Remote Analysis Control systems are widely distributed, often located hundreds of miles away from the control center and in hard-to-reach locations (e.g., offshore rigs). When responding to a security incident, it may not be feasible to wait for an examiner to travel to a distant site. It is, therefore, necessary to conduct remote analysis of control systems from a central location.

Secure Analysis Proper forensic analysis requires full access to a system and, if performed remotely, the access and retrieval of forensic data should be performed securely. The protocols and applications used for remote forensic analysis should have high assurance.

Custom Analysis Most digital forensic tools are designed for analyzing common workstations in an IT environment. They provide features that are optimized for file recovery, web history analysis, email analysis and keyword search. The forensic analysis of process control systems requires techniques and tools that can accommodate proprietary or specialized hardware, software, applications and protocols. Forensic tools for control systems should, therefore, be customizable and enable extensions, e.g., using plug-ins.

3.2 EnCase Enterprise

EnCase Enterprise from Guidance Software [1] is one of the most widely used digital forensic tools. It has sophisticated network-based forensic examination features, and satisfies all the requirements listed above. In particular, EnCase Enterprise is a multi-threaded scalable platform that provides immediate response, forensic analysis and proactive monitoring of large-scale enterprise networks. According to Guidance Software, EnCase Enterprise is designed for "anytime, anywhere" investigations – this makes it an attractive tool for conducting forensic analyses of process control systems.

EnCase Enterprise has three components that make remote analysis of a system possible (Figure 2). The Examiner component, which is the primary system used by a forensic examiner, houses the interface to EnCase forensic tools and applications. The Servlet component is a highly specialized service that runs on a target node and provides bit-level access to its hard drives. The SAFE (secure authentication for EnCase) component implements secure communications between the Examiner and Servlet components; it authenticates EnCase users and controls network access to remote servlets. SAFE is typically installed on a security-hardened server.

4. Customizing EnCase with EnScripts

EnCase's EnScript technology provides sophisticated customizable features for forensic examiners. It is a C++ based scripting language for interacting with live systems and analyzing volatile data and storage media.

Using the EnScript editor, scripts can be created to automate forensic processes and analyze large data sets that would be impractical to perform manually. Since EnCase Examiner provides bit-level access to a target system, EnScript's capabilities are limited only by the programming abilities and creativity of the script writer.

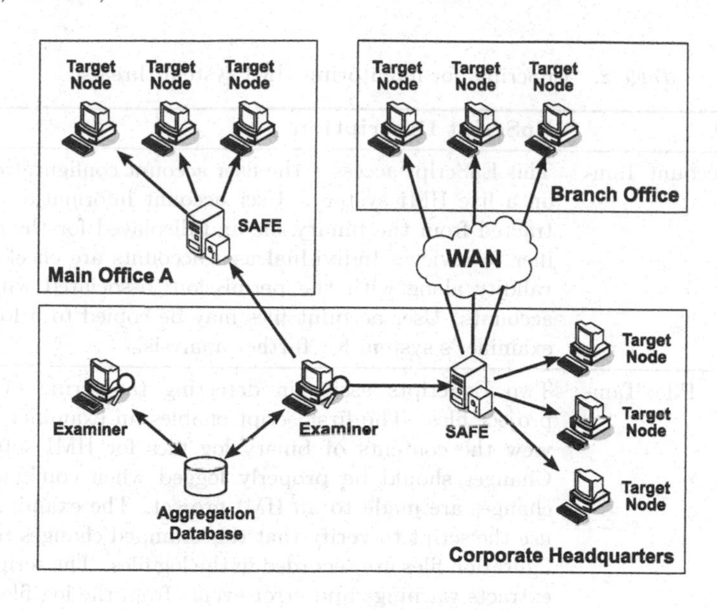

Figure 2. EnCase Enterprise architecture [2].

Table 1. HMI system threats.

Threat	Description
User Account Tampering	HMI software should implement a user authentication policy with role-based permissions. User permissions could be modified maliciously or unauthorized user accounts could be created.
Project File Tampering	Project files make up the graphical interface used by an operator to monitor and control devices in a process control network. Configurations specified in these files could be modified maliciously.
Trojaned HMI Processes and Services	HMI software typically has multiple running processes and services. Services have open network connections. A Trojan could cause unwanted processes to execute and also cause anomalous behavior by the HMI. A Trojan could also send malicious communications using network ports that should not be open.

Our research involved the analysis of human machine interface (HMI) software from two vendors. An HMI provides a graphical user interface for monitoring sensors and configuring programmable logic controllers (PLCs) in a process control network. Table 1 lists three main threats identified for HMI systems. EnScripts were written to identify the corresponding exploits.

Table 2. EnScripts for monitoring HMI system threats.

Threat	EnScript Description
User Account Tampering	This EnScript accesses the user account configuration file on a live HMI system. User account information is extracted from the binary file and displayed for the examiner to review. Individual user accounts are checked for validity along with the permissions associated with the accounts. User account files may be copied to a forensic examiner's system for further analysis.
Project File Tampering	Two EnScripts assist in detecting tampering of HMI project files. The first script enables an examiner to review the contents of binary log files for HMI software. Changes should be properly logged when configuration changes are made to an HMI project. The examiner can use the script to verify that timestamped changes to configuration files are recorded in the log files. The script also extracts warnings and error events from the log files. The second EnScript enables an examiner to create and compare hash values of selected files. For example, initial hash values can be computed for files in an HMI project that is known to be in a safe, operable and correct state. The hash values are periodically re-computed and compared with the known good set of hash values. Any discrepancy in hash values produces an alert that is recorded for further analysis.
Trojaned HMI Processes and Services	This EnScript provides detailed information about running processes and can be adjusted to focus on processes associated with HMI software. A timeline is given for the process execution order, and a visual process tree (or hierarchy) is constructed and displayed. A forensic examiner can study the instances, open files, dlls and open network ports associated with a process of interest.

The EnScripts described in Table 2 were written to identify exploits corresponding to the threats listed in Table 1. They are illustrative of the range of scripts that may be written to support forensic analyses of process control systems.

5. Benchmark Testing

Due to the critical nature of its operations, a process control system must run continuously without any downtime or delay in transmitting control signals and process data. Consequently, the load placed on the running control system during forensic analysis must be minimized. Furthermore, forensic analysis

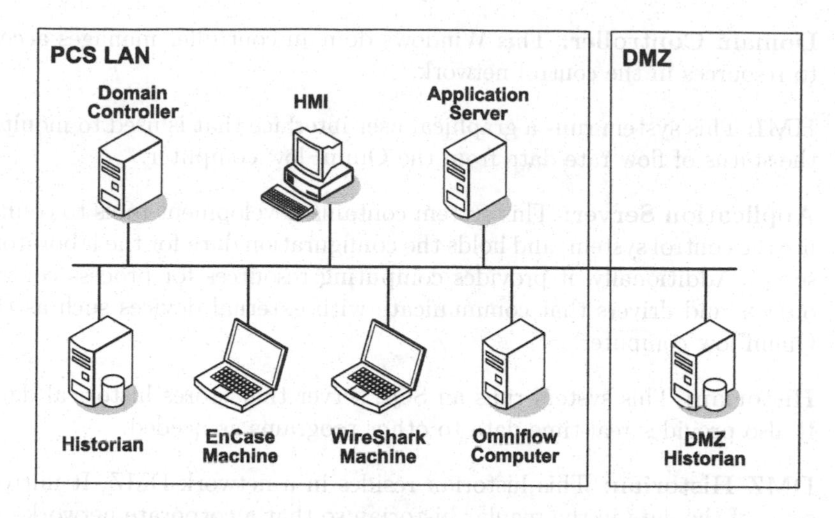

Figure 3. Benchmark test laboratory.

should be completely transparent to all control operations and should not incur additional overhead or maintenance on the part of an operator.

Benchmark testing was performed on the test systems to determine whether or not the forensic analysis would: (i) impact control system behavior, (ii) perform CPU and memory intensive procedures, and (iii) be detectable by monitoring CPU utilization, memory utilization, disk quotas, etc. As discussed above, forensic analysis should have little, if any, impact on the behavior of the control system. It is also important that forensic techniques that are CPU- and memory-intensive (e.g., imaging a hard drive) be performed without disturbing the normal mode of operation. Furthermore, it is desirable that forensic analysis be undetectable to the extent possible. If an adversary (or malicious operator) gained access to a control system and noticed high CPU or memory utilization, he/she might use the task manager to identify suspicious processes and stop the live forensic analysis.

EnCase Enterprise was used to perform forensic analysis in the benchmark tests. The tests used custom EnScripts that were written to analyze control systems running Wonderware software. Complete forensic images were acquired from the hard drives of the control system platforms. Several performance measures were computed while the forensic analysis was being performed. The laboratory setup, system specifications, procedures used, and results of the benchmark tests are described in the following sections.

5.1 Laboratory Setup

The laboratory setup for the benchmark tests is shown in Figure 3. It incorporates several control system components.

- **Domain Controller:** This Windows domain controller manages access to resources in the control network.

- **HMI:** This system runs a graphical user interface that is used to monitor the status of flow rate data from the OmniFlow computer.

- **Application Server:** This system contains development tools to configure the control system, and holds the configuration data for the laboratory setup. Additionally, it provides computing resources for process control objects and drivers that communicate with external devices such as the OmniFlow computer.

- **Historian:** This system runs an SQL server that stores historical data. It also provides real-time data to other programs as needed.

- **DMZ Historian:** This historian resides in a network DMZ. It mirrors some of the data in the regular historian so that a corporate network can access the data without connecting to the control system network.

Auxiliary systems included an EnCase machine and a Wireshark network protocol analyzer. An OmniFlow computer was used to generate the values monitored by the laboratory control system.

5.2 System Specifications

Five systems were benchmarked to ascertain the impact of the two EnScripts and hard drive imaging executed on control system hardware and software. The specifications of the systems used in the benchmark tests are summarized in Table 3.

Two auxiliary machines were used in the benchmark tests, the EnCase machine and a machine that ran Wireshark network protocol analyzer to evaluate the impact of hard drive imaging on alarm propagation. The specifications of the auxiliary systems are summarized in Table 4.

5.3 Test Procedure

Microsoft's Performance Monitor Wizard (Version 1.1.3) was used to log performance data during the execution of EnCase EnScripts. The following six tests were conducted for each control system component:

- Benchmark (no servlet and scripts).

- Servlet only.

- Servlet and hash script.

- Servlet and process tree script.

- Servlet and both scripts (executed sequentially).

Table 3. System specifications.

Function	Processor and Speed	Memory	Operating System	Control Software
Domain Controller	Pentium 4 (3 GHz)	1 GB	Microsoft Windows Server 2003 (Standard Edition) – Service Pack 1	NA
HMI	Pentium 4 (3 GHz)	1 GB	Microsoft Windows XP (Professional) – Service Pack 2	Wonderware
Application Server	Pentium 4 (3 GHz)	1 GB	Microsoft Windows Server 2003 (Standard Edition) – Service Pack 1	Wonderware
Historian	Pentium 4 (3 GHz)	1 GB	Microsoft Windows Server 2003 (Standard Edition) – Service Pack 1	MySQL
DMZ Historian	Pentium 4 (3 GHz)	1 GB	Microsoft Windows 2000 (5.00.2193) – Service Pack 4	NA

Table 4. Auxiliary system specifications.

Function	Processor and Speed	Memory	Operating System	Software
EnCase Machine	Intel T2600 (2.16 GHz)	2 GB	Microsoft Windows XP (Professional) – Service Pack 2	EnCase
Wireshark Machine	Pentium 4 (1.7 GHz)	512 MB	Linux Kernel 2.6.15	Wireshark

- Servlet and complete imaging of hard drive.

The following performance data was recorded for each test:

- Percentage of committed memory bytes in use.
- Pages swapped per second.
- Bytes received at the network interface per second.

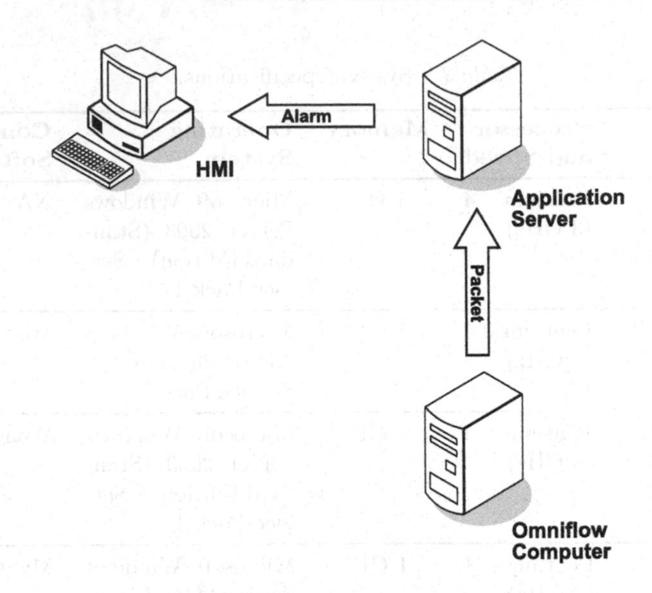

Figure 4. Alarm propagation path.

- Bytes sent from the network interface per second.

- Percentage of CPU time used.

Test data was collected for each performance measure for each control system component. For example, data collected from the application server can be used to compare the pages swapped per second for the baseline system, servlet only, servlet and hash script, servlet and process tree script, servlet and both scripts, and servlet and hard drive imaging. This data helps evaluate the impact of forensic analysis (in terms of a performance metric) on the control system component being investigated.

Tests were conducted to investigate if imaging a hard drive increased the time taken for an alarm to propagate from the OmniFlow computer to the HMI. The tests considered the alarm propagation path (Figure 4). Note that a packet containing an alarm triggering value is generated by the OmniFlow computer and sent to the application server. Next, the server recognizes the alarm value and sends an alarm to the HMI. Upon receiving the alarm, the HMI displays it on the operator's computer screen.

The first step was to arrange for an alarm to fire in the application server when the flow rate exceeded 1,500 bbl/hr. Next, the test machines and the Wireshark machine were linked to a Network Time Protocol (NTP) server (domain controller) to synchronize their clocks. Once this was done, the Wireshark machine was configured to capture packets going from the OmniFlow computer to the application server. The flow setting was then changed to a value below 1,500 bbl/hr.

When the HMI displayed a flow rate less than 1,500 bbl/hr, the flow setting was changed to a value above 1,500 bbl/hr. It was then possible to measure the time interval between the OmniFlow computer sending the first response packet with a value above 1,500 bbl/hr and the alarm being fired by the HMI. Knowing which packet contained a value above 1500 bbl/hr was simple because the application server only polled the OmniFlow computer every ten seconds; therefore, when the OmniFlow monitor value exceeded 1,500 bbl/hr, the next packet sent by the OmniFlow computer would be the alarm triggering packet. Unfortunately, the alarm settings on the application server had a resolution in seconds, so the measurement accuracy was limited to one second.

This test was performed three times each for three different cases. The first case was a control measurement with the system operating in its native state without any running EnCase processes. The second was the system running while a hard drive image of the application server was being taken by EnCase. The third was the system running while a hard drive image of the HMI was being taken.

6. Test Results

Using EnCase for remote forensic analysis of a live process control system was successful. It was also possible to create a bit-for-bit copy of a process control system's hard disk while it was in continuous operation. Custom forensic analysis of an HMI running different process control software was possible using EnCase's EnScript feature. Benchmarking was performed on a process control system to determine processor, memory and network resources required during remote analysis and imaging.

6.1 Custom EnScript Results

The two EnScripts (hash and process tree scripts) were executed on the domain controller without any major performance penalties. They produced a slight increase in memory use and a few spikes in network traffic and CPU utilization.

Similar results were obtained for the HMI, application server, historian and DMZ historian. The scripts were only applied to subsets of files and directories specific to process control software on the HMI, application server and historian; they took about one minute to execute. In the case of the domain controller and DMZ historian, the scripts were executed on a few chosen files and directories because these two machines did not run any process control software. In general, the custom scripts worked well in all instances and had little impact on the machines in the laboratory setup. The servlet also had no noticeable impact on system operation in all the tests.

The memory utilization benchmarks exhibited several anomalies. The most significant was that the baseline and servlet alone used more memory than some of the script executions. However, since the memory utilization in the benchmark tests differed by less than 0.5% (less than 5 MB of memory on the test systems), it is within the margin of experimental error. The memory utilization in the case of the DMZ historian had a similar anomaly with the benchmark tests being within approximately 2% of each other. However, the benchmark tests do show that forensic analysis does not have a detrimental effect on the available system memory.

The hash script had a significant impact on system operation, but should still be tolerable for most systems. The script produced one or two CPU utilization spikes to about 40% utilization, each lasting no more than five seconds. However, many of the hash script executions also resulted in CPU loads of 20% over a 40 second period. This 20% utilization did not impact the test systems, but should be scaled to the CPU resources available in control systems. The hash script also triggered bursts of page swapping when hash values were calculated. Increased network activity due to the hash script must also be considered, but this did not negatively impact system operation.

The process analysis script generally resulted in one or two CPU utilization spikes to about 50% utilization, each lasting less than five seconds. However, it is possible to scale the utilization according to processor speed. Increased network activity due to the process analysis script produced several small spikes, but these were close to those observed during normal system operations.

6.2 Imaging Results

In the case of the domain controller, the most noticeable performance decreases were seen in the numbers of bytes received and sent, and CPU utilization. While the hard drive was being imaged, peak values of 220,000 bytes/s received, 650,000 bytes/s sent and 45% CPU utilization were observed, each lasting about 30 seconds, 1 minute and 3 minutes, respectively. Similar results were obtained for the HMI, application server, historian and DMZ historian.

A future version of EnCase could permit users to set thresholds on the numbers of bytes sent and received per second, and on CPU utilization while forensic analysis is being performed. With this functionality, forensic analysis could be conducted without "evident" decreases in performance.

6.3 Alarm Propagation Results

The test results reveal that, even under the stress of imaging the entire hard drive of a control system component, there is no significant delay in alarm propagation. The time taken for a packet containing an alarm triggering value to manifest itself as an alarm in the HMI was not affected by the imaging process. In particular, the alarm delay was no more than one second, which was the resolution of HMI alarm timestamps.

7. Conclusions

Standard monitoring and forensic practices can enhance security in large-scale process control systems. The targeted areas include user authentication and permissions, configuration and log files, active processes, and open network connections. Process control software has begun to implement user-based and role-based authentication, and it is necessary to determine if these features have been circumvented. Analysis of log files, timestamps and hash values helps identify tampering of configuration files and other key files. It is also important to determine if process control software is behaving as intended by tracing process activity and monitoring open network connections.

Our test results demonstrate that EnCase Enterprise is an effective tool for conducting remote forensic examinations of live process control systems. Forensic processes, in particular, hashing, process analysis and hard drive imaging, did not strain CPU, memory and network resources to levels that impacted control system behavior or functionality. Furthermore, Encase Enterprise's scripting features make it possible to customize forensic techniques for proprietary hardware, software, applications and protocols used in process control networks.

References

[1] Guidance Software, EnCase Enterprise (www.guidancesoftware.com/products/ee_index.asp), 2006.

[2] Guidance Software, How it works – EnCase Enterprise (www.guidancesoftware.com/products/ee_HowItWorks.asp), 2006.

[3] A. Miller, Trends in process control systems security, *IEEE Security and Privacy*, vol. 3(5), pp. 57–60, 2005.

[4] Office of Homeland Security, The National Strategy for Homeland Security, The White House, Washington, DC (www.whitehouse.gov/homeland/book/nat_strat_hls.pdf), 2002.

Chapter 17

CREATING A EUROPEAN SCADA SECURITY TESTBED

Henrik Christiansson and Eric Luiijf

Abstract Supervisory control and data acquisition (SCADA) systems are commonly used to monitor and control critical infrastructure assets. However, over the past two decades, they have evolved from closed, proprietary systems to open networks comprising commodity platforms running common operating systems and TCP/IP stacks. The open architecture and increased connectivity provide more functionality and reduce costs, but they significantly increase the vulnerabilities and the exposure to threats. Since SCADA systems and the critical infrastructure assets they control must have 24/7 availability, it is imperative to understand and manage the risk. This paper makes the case for a European SCADA security testbed that can be used to analyze vulnerabilities, threats and the impact of attacks, ultimately helping design new architectures and robust security solutions. The paper also discusses testbed requirements, deployment strategies and potential hurdles.

Keywords: SCADA systems, risk assessment, security testbed

1. Introduction

Process control systems – often referred to as supervisory control and data acquisition (SCADA) systems – are commonly used to monitor and control industrial processes. SCADA systems have three main functions: (i) obtaining data from sensors, switches and other devices, (ii) managing industrial processes that are supervised and operated by humans, and (iii) adjusting process parameters by changing the states of relays, switches and actuators (e.g., opening a valve to increase gas flow, which raises the process temperature).

SCADA systems are used in practically every critical infrastructure asset. The term "critical infrastructure" is defined as "those physical and information technology facilities, networks, services and assets which, if disrupted or destroyed, have a serious impact on the health, safety, security or economic well-being of citizens or the effective functioning of governments" [11]. SCADA

Christiansson, H. and Luiijf, E., 2008, in IFIP International Federation for Information Processing, Volume 253, Critical Infrastructure Protection, eds. E. Goetz and S. Shenoi; (Boston: Springer), pp. 237–247.

systems come in myriad types, sizes and applications. They may monitor only a few devices as in a manufacturing plant or tens of thousands of sensors as in an oil or gas pipeline. They may coordinate a multitude of actuators, each controlling a different physical process as in a petrochemical refinery. The controlled processes may require monitoring cycles varying from milliseconds (e.g., in the power sector) to an hour or longer (e.g., at a sewage treatment facility). SCADA systems differ from "normal" information and communication technology (ICT) systems in that they must operate reliably and provide 24/7 availability. Moreover, their depreciation is much higher and their lifecycles are longer, with eight to fifteen years being quite common [4].

SCADA security is a growing concern; organizational, architectural, technical and implementation vulnerabilities abound [1, 2, 20]. Parks and Duggan [18] observe that the first principle in waging a cyber war is to have a "kinetic effect" such as shutting down an electrical substation or opening the spill gates in a dam. Such attacks can be perpetrated quite effectively by manipulating SCADA systems – the severity of an attack depends on the criticality of the infrastructure asset and the damage characteristics (nature, extent, duration, etc.). Indeed, the effect of an attack can range from a nuisance event to a major national disaster.

It is imperative to analyze the risk to SCADA systems in terms of vulnerabilities, threats and potential impact. This paper argues for the creation of a European testbed for understanding and analyzing the risk to SCADA systems used in critical infrastructure assets. The paper also discusses testbed requirements, deployment strategies and potential hurdles.

2. Problem Description

This section discusses security issues related to SCADA systems and the risk in terms of threats, vulnerabilities and potential impact.

2.1 SCADA Security

Since the early 1990s, proprietary, hard-wired automation systems used in critical infrastructure components have increasingly been replaced by modern SCADA systems [7]. Many of these modern systems incorporate commercial-off-the-shelf ICT solutions, including commodity computing and network equipment, standard operating systems, Internet protocols and open software.

This trend raises serious security issues concerning SCADA systems and the critical infrastructure assets they control. Asset owners and operators are generally unprepared to deal with information security in SCADA environments either due to a lack of expertise or an absence of security functionality and tools. Meanwhile, vulnerabilities in ICT components are becoming part of the SCADA environment. Advanced operator functionality and web-based control interfaces make it easy to change vital SCADA settings deliberately or by accident. Indeed, critical processes can no longer be controlled manually.

Table 1. Risk handling in ICT and SCADA environments.

	ICT Environment	SCADA Environment
Reliability	Occasional failures are tolerated Beta test in the field is acceptable	Outages are not tolerated Thorough *quality* assurance testing is expected
Risk Impact	Loss or unauthorized alteration of data Loss of data privacy and confidentiality	Loss of production, equipment and/or lives; potential for environmental damage; disruptions to the critical infrastructure
Information Handling Performance	High throughput is demanded Delays and jitter are accepted	Modest throughput is acceptable Delays are a serious concern
Risk Management	Recovery by rebooting Safety is not an issue	Fault tolerance is essential Explicit hazard analysis *related to the physical process* is expected

Therefore, if a SCADA system fails, the industrial process it controls is rendered non-operational or worse.

Limited emphasis has been placed on SCADA security because it is generally assumed that SCADA systems are based on proprietary hardware and software, and obscure protocols. Other common assumptions are that SCADA systems are isolated from ICT assets and that they operate in benign (if not trusted) environments. However, all these assumptions have been shown to be unwarranted [7, 14].

It is also incorrect to assume that techniques and tools designed to mitigate risk in ICT environments can be directly transferred to SCADA environments. Table 1 (based on [6] with our comments provided in italics) identifies the major differences in handling risk in ICT environments as opposed to SCADA environments. The concept of thorough quality assurance testing for SCADA systems typically focuses on safety and functionality instead of information security [4]. Also, hazard analysis in SCADA environments is generally related to the physical processes being controlled. These issues are not relevant to ICT environments.

2.2 Understanding the Risk

Establishing a suitable SCADA security framework requires an understanding of the risk in terms of threats, vulnerabilities and potential impact. Most SCADA personnel have backgrounds in automation and safety with little, if any, formal training in information security. ICT security staff often view SCADA systems simply as equipment with valves, switches and sensors.

The primary reason for the general lack of awareness about SCADA security is the scarcity of well-documented incidents. One exception is the British Columbia Institute of Technology's industrial security incident database, which contains data about 94 SCADA incidents from the period 1982 through 2004 [5]; however, details about the incidents are confidential and are released only to authorized entities. Another problem is the lack of a structured repository about specific SCADA vulnerabilities (some information about general vulnerabilities is available; see, e.g., [22]). Moreover, very little is known about attackers and their techniques and tools.

The following are some of the most widely publicized SCADA incidents [14, 15, 21, 24]:

- In January 1998, hackers seized control of GazProm's gas pipeline system. The attack was most likely launched in an attempt to extort money.

- Between January and April 2000, Vitek Boden, a disgruntled former contractor manipulated the SCADA system of Hunter Watertech in Maroochy Shire, Australia a total of 46 times. He released one million liters of untreated sewage to the environment.

- In November 2001, a SCADA software error in The Netherlands caused natural gas to be produced with the incorrect composition; 26,000 Dutch households were unable to heat their homes and cook food for three days.

- In January 2003, the SQL/Slammer worm shut down communications at an electric power substation in the United States. The same worm affected the telemetric system of a SCADA/energy management facility and attacked a security display station at the Davis-Besse nuclear power plant. These systems were unusable for more than five hours.

- The U.S. Department of Energy reported to the U.S. House of Representatives that it had identified several scenarios for unauthorized entry into SCADA systems in the power sector. It reported eight successful penetrations of SCADA systems in eight attempts.

- In January 2005, approximately 15,000 households in Weert, The Netherlands lost electrical power due to a failure in a SCADA system.

- In July 2005, a lack of situational awareness in a SCADA/emergency management system caused an explosion when a ground-wired switch at a new substation was connected to a 150 kV circuit.

We have learned that numerous SCADA security incidents in critical infrastructure facilities have gone unreported by asset owners and operators. These include processing plants being shut down by worms, a penetration testing team inadvertently causing a blackout, and hackers penetrating systems controlling refineries and electrical power transmission substations [14].

On the threat side of the risk spectrum, more than twenty nation states currently possess advanced cyber attack capabilities [16]. Seven types of actors are deemed to constitute a threat to SCADA systems [16, 20]:

- Nation states seeking to add electronic attacks on critical infrastructure assets to their set of capabilities
- Radical activists and terrorists intending to impact society by attacking critical infrastructure assets
- Activists seeking to publicize their cause by disrupting critical infrastructure services
- Criminal organizations intending to extort money from critical infrastructure asset owners and operators
- Virus/worm writers interested in demonstrating their ability to shut down critical infrastructure assets
- Insiders seeking revenge on their employers by attacking critical infrastructure assets
- Script kiddies experimenting with tools that could affect critical infrastructure assets

However, it is difficult to assess the expertise of potential attackers. The main reason is the absence of well-documented incidents (at least in the open literature). At a minimum, qualified attackers should have substantial expertise about: (i) physical systems and processes managed by SCADA systems, (ii) technical and operational aspects of SCADA systems, and (iii) techniques for circumventing security measures.

It would appear that attacking SCADA systems is a difficult task because of the complex knowledge, advanced skills and access needed for successful penetration. But the reality is that asset owners and operators have a distinct disadvantage. It is well-known that they operate SCADA systems to control important societal resources. Detailed information about SCADA architectures, protocols and configurations is freely available on the Internet or is obtainable from other sources; and system vulnerabilities and code for exploiting weaknesses are public knowledge. The geographic scale, remoteness and limited physical security of many critical infrastructure assets allow them to be penetrated quite easily. Finally, even when SCADA systems are designed to be isolated, the need to share information for business purposes or to perform remote maintenance results in interconnections with public networks, including the Internet.

3. Establishing a SCADA Security Testbed

A SCADA security testbed can be used to analyze vulnerabilities, threats and the impact of attacks. This section discusses the requirements of a testbed and makes a case for deploying a European SCADA testbed.

Table 2. Penetration testing in ICT and SCADA environments.

Activity	ICT Environment	SCADA Environment
Enumeration and identification of hosts, nodes and networks	Perform a ping sweep (e.g., nmap)	Examine channel access method (CAM) protocol tables on switches Examine router configuration files and router tables Verify physical configuration Perform passive scanning or intrusion detection (e.g., snort)
Identification of vulnerabilities in services	Perform a port scan (e.g., nmap)	Verify local ports (e.g., netstat) *Perform port scan of duplicate, development or test system*
Identification of services on hosts, nodes and networks	Perform a vulnerability scan (e.g., Nessus, ISS)	Capture local banners using version lookup in a CVE database *Perform scan of duplicate, development or test system*

3.1 Assessing SCADA Security

Several challenges are encountered when attempting to perform security-related analyses of SCADA systems. The following sections describe the primary challenges, all of which can be addressed using a well-designed SCADA security testbed.

Penetration Testing of Live Systems Penetration testing of live systems is an effective technique for discovering vulnerabilities and assessing attack impact. Unlike their ICT counterparts, SCADA systems control physical processes and have real-world consequences associated with their actions. Consequently, it is very dangerous to perform penetration tests on live SCADA systems; a SCADA testbed is most appropriate for this purpose.

According to [10], a penetration test of ICT systems involves three steps: (i) identification of hosts, nodes and networks; (ii) identification of services available on hosts, nodes and networks; and (iii) identification of possible vulnerabilities in services. However, performing penetration testing of SCADA systems requires a different approach, which is highlighted in Table 2 (our comments are italicized for emphasis).

Penetration testing techniques for SCADA environments are more complex because they must incorporate damage control and mitigation activities. Some researchers (e.g., [23]) have used active penetration methods on live systems, but this is not well advised [10, 14]. At best, passive penetration tests are recommended for operational SCADA systems. Active tests should be performed only on development systems or testbeds.

Validating Security Solutions It is important to ensure that classical ICT security solutions (e.g., firewalls, VPNs and anti-virus software) do not adversely impact operations, especially when SCADA environments use specialized protocols such as Modbus or DNP3. This requires the design and deployment of test plans, architectures and configurations, and extensive analysis of test results [12, 19]. Thorough testing is also required to evaluate potential negative side-effects of software updates and patches. These activities can only be performed using a SCADA testbed.

Establishing Risk Analysis Methods Relatively few risk assessment methods are available for SCADA systems. One of the more prominent is the relative risk assessment method developed for water utilities in the United States [26]. The method, which is based on joint assessments by sector experts and SCADA security experts, assumes that the potential consequences of a SCADA system failure are unique to an infrastructure asset. Therefore, risk assessment cannot be performed using generic information related to SCADA system security. As a consequence, developing an effective risk analysis method requires a realistic SCADA security testbed.

Establishing SCADA Security Standards Many ICT security standards such as ISO/IEC 17799:2005 conflict with requirements for SCADA environments [14]. Few security standards have been established for SCADA systems to date; however, recently, there has been a flurry of activity [1]. The risk to SCADA systems is so high that even incompatible and conflicting security standards and best practices are being considered. In the energy sector, for example, emphasis is being placed on addressing the technology gaps before specifying security policies and best practices [8]. The most effective way to address these challenges is to establish a SCADA security testbed.

3.2 Rationale for a European Testbed

The U.S. National SCADA Test Bed (NSTB) has had a major influence in developing security solutions. Testimony at a 2005 congressional hearing highlighted the effectiveness of the NSTB [1], a joint venture involving the national laboratories, and the SCADA and ICT vendor communities. The NSTB has helped identify several SCADA vulnerabilities, which were subsequently fixed by SCADA vendors and integrators. Validation of the fixes was also performed using the NSTB's extensive SCADA testing environment.

Other SCADA testbeds are located at NIST in Gaithersburg, Maryland and at the British Columbia Institute of Technology (BCIT) in Burnaby, Canada. In Europe, testbeds are operational in Grenoble, France; at CERN in Geneva, Switzerland; and at the European Joint Research Centre in Ispra, Italy [13].

Clearly, a large (possibly distributed) SCADA security testbed needs to be established in Europe. Many of the reasons for creating a testbed have already been discussed. Perhaps the most important reason, however, is the fact that the architectures of many European critical infrastructure components are quite unique. For example, the European power grid has a highly distributed structure with diverse power generation facilities; in contrast, the North American system has deregulated control [3]. A European testbed will help develop, assess and deploy security solutions and best practices that fit the European realm. Moreover, the testbed will help evaluate and frame standards and legislation related to SCADA security and critical infrastructure protection.

4. Towards a European Testbed

This section discusses the deployment strategy and the potential barriers to creating a European SCADA security testbed.

4.1 Strategy

Establishing a European SCADA security testbed requires a coherent strategy that addresses the issues of what to test, how to test, and (eventually) how to disseminate the results. The issue of what to test requires an assessment of what a European testbed can provide to its stakeholders. This requires an examination of the architectural characteristics of European infrastructures.

The NSTB identifies technology security, protocol security and infrastructure security as three major testing areas [17]; these can be used as the basis for a European approach. The NSTB checklist for the strategic impact of assumed attacks or failures [17] is also a good starting point as it prioritizes systems for testing based on aspects such as the extent of use and manufacturer's market share. A consistent and coordinated strategy is required for all SCADA components – from field devices to complex SCADA systems [9]. It is important to note the lack of coherent work conducted in Europe in the area of SCADA security will likely complicate the task of identifying the relevant competencies. Equally important is to identify deficiency areas that should be addressed.

No international standards exist for testing SCADA components and systems. To our knowledge, the only list of security characteristics to be tested is the one employed by the NSTB [25]. The list, which is determined based on risk, ease of attack and attack severity, includes clear text communications, authentication, system integration, web services and perimeter protection.

A large-scale European testbed should address the needs of SCADA manufacturers, critical infrastructure stakeholders and academic researchers, and should facilitate the testing of new SCADA security architectures and strategies, along with the analysis and evaluation of complex vulnerabilities in real-world environments. The testbed must support iterative, synergistic evaluation efforts and the integration of different competency areas such as infrastructure system engineering, ICT security and physical security.

4.2 Potential Problems

Europe has an excellent track record at running world-class joint research centers ranging from CERN to JET (nuclear fusion). However, a European

SCADA security facility would have a very different political and economical environment from that at CERN or JET (which focus on fundamental research) or at a U.S. SCADA testbed facility (which is managed by one national government). A major complexity arises because a European SCADA security testbed would have to balance the national security interests of multiple nations. Also, the needs of asset owners and operators and SCADA vendors from different countries would have to be balanced. Since a European facility is multinational in nature, the political, financial and strategic issues would have to be addressed to the satisfaction of all the participating entities.

4.3 Requirements

The requirements of a SCADA security testbed are complex, and cover the organizational and technical areas. The organization that operates the testbed should be an independent entity and should be able to handle and safeguard extremely sensitive information related to vulnerabilities, threats and attacks, in addition to proprietary information from owners, operators and vendors. Dissemination of Computer Emergency Response Team (CERT) data about SCADA security must be performed both rapidly and carefully as a release can affect thousands of operational systems around the world. At the same time, unauthorized leaks or the release of incorrect information could create havoc throughout the critical infrastructure, potentially resulting in economic losses, environmental damage and casualties.

A European SCADA testbed must leverage the resources provided by existing testbed facilities; simultaneously, it should identify and initiate efforts in specialty areas. International cooperation will be critical, especially in the areas of testing, research and development, and standards promulgation. Finally, the testbed should be highly reconfigurable and connect to other SCADA facilities using secure, long-haul communication links to create a state-of-the-art distributed testing environment.

5. Conclusions

The architectures of many European infrastructure components are unique. A state-of-the-art European testbed is, therefore, needed to analyze vulnerabilities, threats and the impact of attacks on SCADA systems that control vital infrastructure assets. Since a European facility would be multinational in nature, the political, financial and strategic exigencies will have to be addressed to the satisfaction of all the participating entities. However, given Europe's track record at running world-class research centers such as CERN, a European SCADA security testbed promises to be extremely successful. The testbed would engage industry stakeholders, academic researchers and government scientists, helping design new SCADA security architectures and strategies that would significantly enhance global critical infrastructure protection efforts.

References

[1] K. Ananth, Testimony of Dr. K. P. Ananth, Associate Laboratory Director, National and Homeland Security, Idaho National Laboratory, Idaho Falls, Idaho, Idaho Hearing on SCADA and the Terrorist Threat: Protecting the Nation's Critical Control Systems, House Committee on Homeland Security, Subcommittee on Economic Security, Infrastructure Protection and Cyber Security, October 18, 2005.

[2] M. Assante, R. Wells and W. Pelgrin, The SCADA and process control security procurement project update, SANS Special Webcast, SANS Institute, Bethesda, Maryland, May 18, 2006.

[3] D. Bakken, What good are CIP test beds? And what CIP test beds are good? Some observations from the field, presented at the *Joint U.S.-E.U. Workshop on ICT-Enabled Critical Infrastructures and Interdependencies: Control, Safety, Security and Dependability*, 2006.

[4] K. Barnes, B. Johnson and R. Nickelson, Review of Supervisory Control and Data Acquisition (SCADA) Systems, Technical Report INEEL/EXT-04-01517, Idaho National Engineering and Environmental Laboratory, Idaho Falls, Idaho, 2004.

[5] E. Byres, The British Columbia Institute of Technology's confidential industrial security incident database, presented at the *NISCC SCADA Security Conference*, 2005.

[6] E. Byres, J. Carter, A. Elramly and D. Hoffman, Test your system five ways, *ISA InTech Magazine*, vol. 50(3), pp. 24–27, 2003.

[7] E. Byres and J. Lowe, The myths and facts behind cyber security risks for industrial control systems, presented at the *VDE Congress*, 2004.

[8] R. Carlson, J. Dagle, S. Shamsuddin and R. Evans, A summary of control system security standards activities in the energy sector, National SCADA Test Bed, U.S. Department of Energy, Washington, DC (www.oe.energy.gov/DocumentsandMedia/Summary_of_CS_Standards_Activities_in_Energy_Sector.pdf), 2005.

[9] J. Davidson, M. Permann, B. Rolston and S. Schaeffer, ABB SCADA/EMS System INEEL Baseline Summary Test Report, Technical Report INEEL/EXT-04-02423, Idaho National Engineering and Environmental Laboratory, Idaho Falls, Idaho, 2004.

[10] D. Duggan, M. Berg, J. Dillinger and J. Stamp, Penetration Testing of Industrial Control Systems, Technical Report SAND2005-2846P, Sandia National Laboratories, Albuquerque, New Mexico, 2005.

[11] European Commission, Critical Infrastructure Protection in the Fight Against Terrorism, Communication COM(2004) 702 Final, Communication from the Commission to the Council and the European Parliament, Brussels, Belgium, 2004.

[12] J. Falco, Use of antivirus on industrial control and SCADA systems, presented at the *Process Control Security Requirements Forum Spring Meeting*, 2005.

[13] S. Lueders, Control systems under attack? presented at the *International Conference on Accelerator and Large Experimental Physics Control Systems*, 2005.

[14] H. Luiijf and R. Lassche, SCADA (on)veiligheid: Een rol voor de overhead? TNO-KEMA Report, TNO Defence, Security and Safety, The Hague, The Netherlands, 2006.

[15] M. Naedele and D. Dzung, Industrial information system security – IT security in industrial plants – An introduction, *ABB Review*, issue 2, pp. 66–70, 2005.

[16] National Infrastructure Security Co-ordination Centre (NISCC), The Electronic Attack Threat to Supervisory Control and Data Acquisition Control and Automation Systems, NISCC Briefing 02/04, London, United Kingdom, 2004.

[17] R. Parks, National control system security testing plan, presented at the *SANS Process Control and SCADA Security Summit*, 2006.

[18] R. Parks and D. Duggan, Principles of cyber-warfare, *Proceedings of the IEEE Workshop on Information Assurance and Security*, pp. 122–125, 2001.

[19] R. Parks, J. Hills, S. Smith, T. Davis, A. Baros and P. Cordeiro, Network Security Infrastructure Testing, Version 1.2, Center for SCADA Security, Sandia National Laboratories, Albuquerque, New Mexico (sandia.gov/scada/documents/NSTB_NSIT_V1_2.pdf), 2005.

[20] A. Priore, Hacking for dollars, *Newsweek International*, December 22, 2005.

[21] T. Smith, Hacker jailed for revenge sewage attacks, *The Register*, October 31, 2001.

[22] J. Stamp, J. Dillinger and W. Young, Common Vulnerabilities in Critical Infrastructure Control Systems, Technical Report SAND2002-0435C, Sandia National Laboratories, Albuquerque, New Mexico, 2002.

[23] V. Virta, The red team tool box: A method for penetration tests, *Proceedings of the European Institute for Computer Antivirus Research Conference*, 2005.

[24] J. Visser, M. Berkom, J. Spiekhout, Y. Suurenbroek, J. Wessels, B. Smolders and C. Pietersen, Storing Gasmengstation (Faults in Gas Mixing Stations), Technical Report CB-2-02.060, Raad voor de Transportveiligheid, The Hague, Netherlands, 2002.

[25] R. Wells, Measurements, presented at the *SANS Process Control and SCADA Security Summit*, 2006.

[26] W. Young and J. DePoy, Relative Risk Assessment for Water Utility SCADA Systems, Technical Report SAND2003-1772C, Sandia National Laboratories, Albuquerque, New Mexico, 2003.

IV

NETWORK INFRASTRUCTURE SECURITY

Chapter 18

PROTECTING INTERNET SERVICES FROM LOW-RATE DOS ATTACKS

Yajuan Tang, Xiapu Luo and Rocky Chang

Abstract Feedback control is an important element in the engineering of stable Internet services. However, feedback channels are vulnerable to various Internet attacks. This paper shows analytically that the recently proposed low-rate denial-of-service (DoS) attacks can degrade Internet services by generating intermittent false feedback signals. The effectiveness of the attacks is evaluated using a control-theoretic approach for a general feedback control system and detailed analysis for a specific system. A nonparametric algorithm based on changes in traffic distribution is proposed for detecting attacks.

Keywords: Feedback control, low-rate DoS attacks, detection, countermeasures

1. Introduction

Feedback control is a fundamental building block for many dependable computing systems, network protocols and Internet services that are required to handle dynamic service demands. A classic example is modeling TCP congestion control dynamics with an active queue management (AQM) scheme at a router as a feedback control system. Web servers increasingly rely on feedback controllers to provide stable and scalable performance (see, e.g., [11, 17, 19]). Moreover, feedback control is a central element in emerging autonomic computing and communications systems (see, e.g., [4, 10]).

However, relatively little attention has been paid to the lack of security of feedback control mechanisms. This paper focuses on denial-of-service (DoS) attacks; in particular, low-rate DoS (LRDoS) attacks that send out intermittent pulses of malicious requests to victims. Examples of these attacks include reduction of quality (RoQ) attacks [6, 7] and pulsing denial-of-service (PDoS) attacks [14, 16]. These low-rate attacks are much more flexible than shrew attacks [9], which require a fixed time period between attack pulses. In the rest

Tang, Y., Luo, X. and Chang, R., 2008, in IFIP International Federation for Information Processing, Volume 253, Critical Infrastructure Protection, eds. E. Goetz and S. Shenoi; (Boston: Springer), pp. 251–265.

of this paper, we do not distinguish between RoQ and PDoS attacks; instead, we refer them to as low-rate DoS (LRDoS) attacks.

LRDoS attacks are particularly effective on feedback control systems. When a system encounters an attack pulse, it is temporarily overloaded. There are two consequences to this overloading: (i) new requests are refused during the attack, because resources are depleted by the malicious requests, and (ii) it takes some time for the system to recover to its normal state using a feedback controller. Many new requests are also turned down during this recovery period. Therefore, a sequence of properly-spaced attack pulses induces intermittent false feedback signals, which could force the server to persistently operate in a low-throughput region.

This paper has two parts. The first part examines the potential effects of LRDoS attacks on feedback-based Internet services. A control-theoretic approach is used to model these services and analyze the performance degradation of a web server under different attack scenarios. The second part of the paper presents a new nonparametric algorithm to detect LRDoS attacks based on changes in traffic distribution. Simulation results are used to analyze the attacks and evaluate the detection algorithm.

2. Related Work

Several researchers have studied LRDoS attacks. Guirguis, *et al.* [6, 7] originally proposed the RoQ attack, which exploits the transients of adaptation. They specifically considered the effects on a web server equipped with a feedback-based admission controller. Chan, *et al.* [1] proposed a related attack, which exploits the relative update scheme in computer systems to prevent normal users from joining the service. The procedure for generating the arrival time of the next update is essentially a feedback loop. Luo, *et al.* [14, 15] analyzed the effects of PDoS attacks on TCP throughput with different AQM schemes and proposed a two-stage detection algorithm.

Sun, *et al.* [18] presented an LRDoS attack detection scheme based on dynamic time warping (DTWP), but the scheme incurs high computation complexity. Chen and Hwang [2] devised a spectral template matching approach to identify shrew attacks. However, the template is generated from simulation and the test is based on parametric distributions, which may not be representative of real-world environments. Furthermore, the DTWP- and spectrum-based methods may not be able to handle aperiodic LRDoS attacks. Luo and Chang [14] developed a two-stage detection scheme. They also proposed the Vanguard scheme [13] to cover situations where the attack rate is less than or equal to a bandwidth bottleneck that cannot be handled [14]. However, both these schemes require bi-directional data to be effective.

3. Vulnerabilities to LRDoS Attacks

We model feedback-based Internet services as a typical feedback control loop shown in Figure 1. The two major components are the "process" and

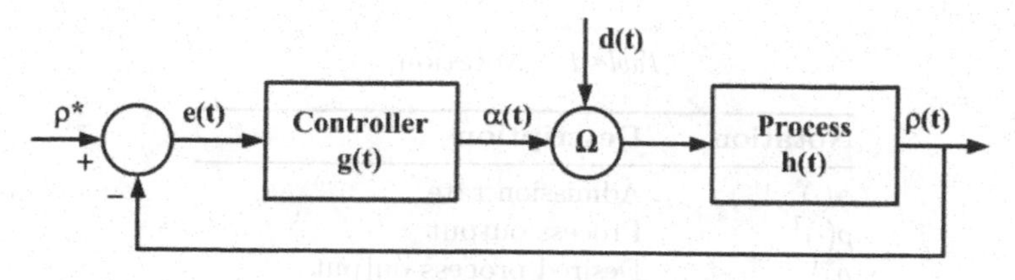

Figure 1. Feedback control loop.

the "controller." The process could represent any Internet service (e.g., email, web services, routing or streaming media) [8]. The output of the process $\rho(t)$ is any measurable "process output" (e.g., system utilization or queue length) that is fed back to the controller. $\alpha(t)$ is the "control signal" generated by the controller to move the process output to the desired value ρ^*. The controller is driven by a "control error" $e(t) = \rho^* - \rho(t)$.

On the other hand, the combination of normal requests for services and malicious requests from an LRDoS attack are modeled as a "disturbance input" $d(t)$. Moreover, we use $\lambda_n(t)$ to denote the arrival rate of normal requests. And we model an LRDoS attack as a sequence of Dirac signals: $\sum_{k=1}^{N} \lambda_a \delta(t - k\tau)$, where λ_a is the attack intensity of each pulse, τ is the time elapsed between two adjacent attack pulses, and N is the total number of pulses in the attack. Thus, the attack pulses are periodic with period τ. The input to the process is driven by both $\alpha(t)$ and $d(t)$ through an operator Ω. We consider additive [12] and multiplicative [7] operators Ω in this paper.

In this section, we first use a control-theoretic approach to analyze how an LRDoS attack can degrade the performance of Internet services. Note that the results obtained here apply to any controller and process. In the next section, we will analyze the effect on a web server consisting of a proportional controller, a constant service rate model and a multiplicative operator Ω.

Table 1 summarizes the symbols used in this paper. The upper rows list the parameters associated with the process, some of which are used for the web server in Section 4. The middle rows list the parameters associated with the controller, and K is used for the proportional controller in Section 4. The bottom rows list the parameters for the disturbance inputs.

Due to the lack of space, we will derive the results only for the additive operator Ω; the results for the multiplicative Ω can be derived in a similar manner. Let $d(t) = \lambda_n(t) + \sum_{k=1}^{N} \lambda_a \delta(t - k\tau) = d_n(t) + d_a(t)$; its Laplace transform is given by $D(s) = \mathcal{L}(\lambda_n(t)) + \lambda_a \sum_{k=1}^{N} e^{-k\tau s} = D_n(s) + D_a(s)$. Moreover, let $G(s)$ and $H(s)$ be the Laplace transforms of the transfer functions of the controller and the process, respectively. Therefore, the system output for the additive Ω in the s-plane is:

$$Y(s) = \frac{R(s)G(s) + D_n(s)}{1 + G(s)H(s)} H(s) + \frac{D_a(s)}{1 + G(s)H(s)} H(s), \tag{1}$$

where $Y(s)$ and $R(s)$ are the Laplace transforms of $\rho(t)$ and ρ^*, respectively.

Table 1. Notation.

Notation	Description
$\alpha(\cdot)$	Admission rate
$\rho(\cdot)^1$	Process output
ρ^{*1}	Desired process output
$n(\cdot)$	Number of backlogged requests
μ	Servicing rate
A, B, C, D, ℓ	Constants for determining $\rho(\cdot)$
$e(\cdot)$	Control error
$\alpha(\cdot)^2$	Control signal
$d(\cdot)$	Disturbance input
K	Controller parameter
$\lambda_n(\cdot)$	Arrival rate of normal requests
$\lambda(\cdot)$	Total arrival rate
λ_a	Attack intensity
τ	Attack period
N	Total number of attack pulses

[1]We use $\rho(\cdot)$ and ρ^* to refer to system utilization in Section 4.

[2]We use $\alpha(\cdot)$ to refer to admission rate in Section 4.

In an attack-free environment, the feedback control loop enables the process output $\rho(t)$ to converge to ρ^*. Consequently, the entire system could attain the best performance according to its design. However, Theorem 1 shows that an LRDoS attack impedes this convergence by introducing oscillations to the output $\rho(t)$. This is an undesirable phenomenon for Internet services, because the oscillations result in performance degradation and unstable services. Moreover, Corollary 2 shows that $e(t)$, which affects the control signal $\alpha(t)$, will also fluctuate periodically, and its amplitude is modulated by the attack intensity. Therefore, $e(t)$ cannot converge to zero as long as attack pulses are present. In other words, the attacker could inflict different scales of damage by tuning the attack intensity.

THEOREM 1 *Under an LRDoS attack, the system output comprises a response caused by the normal requests and an additional oscillating component due to the attack:* $\rho(t) \sim \rho_n(t) + \lambda_a \sum_{k=1}^{N} f(t - k\tau)$.

PROOF 1 *We prove the theorem for an additive* Ω. *By taking an inverse Laplace transform of Equation 1,* $\rho(t)$ *comprises an attack-free component and an attack-induced component:* $\rho(t) = \rho_n(t) + \rho_a(t)$. *Moreover,*

$$\rho_a(t) = \mathcal{L}^{-1}\left(\frac{\lambda_a \sum_{k=1}^{N} e^{-k\tau s}}{1 + G(s)H(s)} H(s)\right) = \lambda_a \sum_{k=1}^{N} f(t - k\tau). \tag{2}$$

It is not difficult to see that $f(t) = \mathcal{L}^{-1}(\frac{H(s)}{1+G(s)H(s)})$ *is the system output excited by* $\delta(t)$ *when* $\rho^* = 0$*, because* $\mathcal{L}(\delta(t)) = 1$*. Moreover, being a stable system,* $\rho_n(t)$ *converges to a steady state. Therefore, the trajectory of* $\rho(t)$ *is a stable, periodic function.*

COROLLARY 2 *Under an LRDoS attack,* $e(t)$ *oscillates in the time domain and its magnitude is proportional to the intensity of the pulse* $e(t) \sim e_n(t) - \lambda_a \sum_{k=1}^{N} f(t - k\tau)$*, where* $e_n(t)$ *is the error caused by the normal requests and* $f(\cdot)$ *is a function introduced by the attack.*

PROOF 2 *We prove the corollary for an additive* Ω*. Since* $E(s) = R(s) - Y(s)$*, we have* $E(s) = E_n(s) - E_a(s)$*. From Equation 2,* $e_a(t) = \lambda_a \sum_{k=1}^{N} f(t - k\tau)$*. Moreover, being a stable system,* $e_n(t) = \mathcal{L}^{-1}(E_n(s))$ *vanishes as* $t \to \infty$*. Therefore, the attack introduces an oscillation to the error signal with an amplitude proportional to the attack intensity.*

4. LRDoS Attack on a Web Server

Having established the general results in the previous section, we examine a specific feedback-based Internet service – a web server. First, we describe the service model and analyze the service degradation caused by a single attack pulse. Next, we consider a sequence of attack pulses and analyze the service degradation for various attack periods.

The service model under consideration follows Figure 1 with the following components. First, the utilization ($\rho(t)$) is employed as the system output; the utilization is a piecewise linear function of $n(t)$ (see Equation 5). The controller is a PI controller with parameter K, which takes in $\rho^* - \rho(t)$ and generates an admission rate ($\alpha(t)$) as the control signal. Therefore, the rate of the admitted requests is given by $\lambda(t)\alpha(t)$; the unadmitted requests are dropped. As a result, the state vector of the service model comprises $\alpha(t)$, $\rho(t)$ and $n(t)$; their evolution and relationships are summarized below:

$$\dot{\alpha}(t) = K(\rho^* - \rho(t)),\ \alpha(t) \in [0,1] \tag{3}$$

$$\dot{n}(t) = \lambda(t)\alpha(t) - \mu,\ n(t) \in [0, +\infty) \tag{4}$$

$$\rho(t) = \begin{cases} An(t) + B & \text{if } n(t) < \ell \\ Cn(t) + D & \text{if } n(t) \geq \ell \end{cases},\ \rho(t) \in [0,1] \tag{5}$$

Note that this service model is the same as the one in [7], except that it uses a constant μ and a continuous-time model, both of which are essential for analytical tractability. In the rest of the paper, we assume a constant rate for normal requests, i.e., $\lambda_n(t) = \lambda_n$.

4.1 Analysis of a Single Attack Pulse

Suppose that an attack pulse arrives at $t = 0$ when the system is in the steady state and its state vector is $[\alpha_0, \rho_0, n_0]$. The system will evolve through three

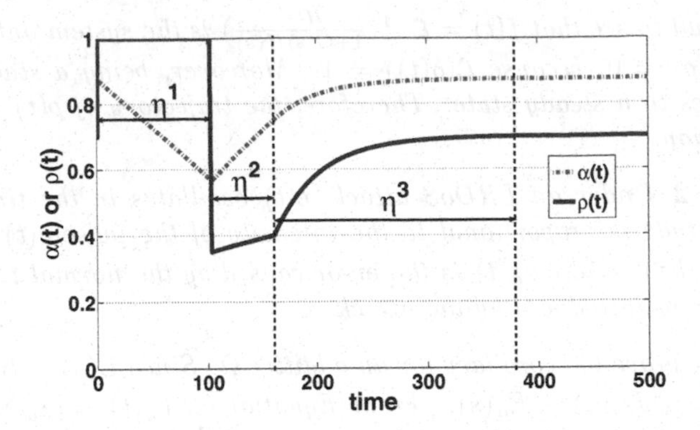

Figure 2. Effect of one attack pulse at $t = 0$ on $\alpha(t)$ and $\rho(t)$ ($A = 0.00267$, $B = 0.2$, $C = 0.024$, $D = -1.4$, $\ell = 75$, $K = 0.01$, $\mu = 90$, $\rho^* = 0.7$ (from [7])).

different stages before reaching the same state after the attack: saturation, recovery I and recovery II. The durations of these three stages are denoted by η_1, η_2 and η_3, respectively. The two recovery stages are due to the two piecewise linear relationships between $\rho(t)$ and $n(t)$.

Saturation Stage: As soon as the first attack pulse arrives, the system enters into a saturation stage in which we assume that the aggregated arrival rate results in a 100% utilization (i.e., $\rho(t) = 1$). The utilization stays at 100% throughout this period because $n(t) > \mu$. Since $\rho(t) = 1$, according to Equation 3, the admission rate decreases linearly as shown in Figure 2. Therefore, the state evolution during this stage is characterized by $\rho(t) = 1$, $\dot{\alpha}(t) = K(\rho^* - 1)$ and $\dot{n}(t) = \lambda_n \alpha(t) - \mu$.

This stage ends when all the pending requests have been processed, i.e., the total number of processed requests is equal to the total number of admitted requests. Therefore, we can obtain η_1 by solving $\lambda_a \alpha_0 + \int_0^{\eta_1} \lambda_n \alpha(t) dt = \eta_1 \mu$ with the initial conditions $[\alpha_0, \rho_0, n_0]$, where $\alpha_0 = \alpha(0^-) = \alpha(0^+)$, $n_0^+ = (\lambda_n + \lambda_a)\alpha_0 + n_0^-$ (this is due to the arrival of the attack pulse at $t = 0$), and $\rho_0 = \rho(0^+) = 1$:

$$\eta_1 = \frac{(\lambda_n \alpha_0 - \mu) + \sqrt{(\lambda_n \alpha_0 - \mu)^2 - 2\lambda_n K(\rho^* - 1)((\lambda_n + \lambda_a)\alpha_0 + n_0)}}{\lambda_n K(1 - \rho^*)}. \quad (6)$$

Recovery Stage I: At the beginning of this recovery stage, we have $n(\eta_1^-) = n(\eta_1^+) = \lambda_n \alpha(\eta_1^+)$, $\alpha(\eta_1^-) = \alpha(\eta_1^+) = \alpha_0 + K(\rho^* - 1)\eta_1$ and $\rho(\eta_1^+) = A\lambda_n \alpha(\eta_1^+) + B$. Since the utilization is now below the desired level, both the admission rate and utilization increase in this stage. Their evolutions are given by $\rho(t) = A\lambda_n \alpha(t) + B$, $\dot{\alpha}(t) = K(\rho^* - \rho(t))$ and $\dot{n}(t) = \lambda_n \alpha(t) - \mu$. Since this stage ends when $n(t) = \ell$, we can obtain η_2 by solving $\rho(\eta_2) = A\ell + B$ with the initial conditions $(\alpha(\eta_1^+), \rho(\eta_1^+), \lambda_n \alpha(\eta_1))$:

$$\eta_2 = \frac{1}{A\lambda_n K} \ln \frac{A\lambda_n \alpha(\eta_1) + B - \rho^*}{A\ell + B - \rho^*}. \quad (7)$$

Recovery Stage II: The two recovery stages differ only in their parameters and initial conditions. The initial conditions for the second recovery stage are: $\alpha(\eta_2^-) = \alpha(\eta_2^+) = \frac{\ell}{\lambda}$, $\rho(\eta_2^-) = \rho(\eta_2^+) = A\ell + B$, and $n(\eta_2^-) = \dot{n}(\eta_2^+) = \lambda_n\alpha(\eta_2^+) - \mu$. This stage ends when the utilization reaches the desired value. Therefore, we can obtain η_3 by solving $\rho(\eta_3) = \rho^*$ with the initial conditions $(\alpha(\eta_2^+), \rho(\eta_2^+), \lambda_n\alpha(\eta_2))$:

$$\eta_3 = \frac{1}{C\lambda_n K} \ln \frac{C\lambda_n\alpha(\eta_2) + D - \rho^*}{b\rho^* - \rho^*}, \text{ where } b \approx 1 \text{ and } \alpha(\eta_2) = \frac{\ell}{\lambda}. \tag{8}$$

4.2 Analysis of Multiple Attack Pulses

When there are multiple attack pulses, different degrees of damage are produced for different attack periods. This section considers four different choices of τ (only one choice was examined in [7]). Figure 3 illustrates how an attack launched at $t = 0$ degrades the admission rates for the four cases. In all four cases there is a relatively long saturation period at the beginning of the attack (this period is more noticeable for smaller values of τ). After that, the admission rates converge to oscillating patterns, similar to what we have discussed in Section 3. Moreover, the oscillating periods and the peaks of the admission rates increase with τ.

Case 1 ($0 < \tau \leq \eta_1$): As in the single pulse case, the admission rate drops linearly (i.e., $\dot{\alpha} = K(\rho^* - 1)$). During this declining period more attack pulses arrive at the victim. However, they do not cause further damage, because the admission rate is already very low. Again, as in the single pulse case, the system eventually serves all the pending requests and the recovery stage starts. However, another attack pulse arrives before the system can restore the admission rate to the normal pre-attack level. As a result, the admission rate drops linearly again. But this time, the system recovers much faster because the admission rate is already at a very low value when the attack pulse arrives. Consequently, the admission rate converges to an oscillation pattern with a small peak value.

Case 2 ($\eta_1 < \tau \leq \eta_1 + \eta_2$): As in Case 1, the admission rate drops linearly in the beginning and the additional attack pulses arriving during this period do not cause further damage. When the recovery stage first starts, the next attack pulse, say the kth pulse, arrives when the admission rate has not yet been restored (i.e., $\alpha((k-1)\tau) < \alpha_0$). This $\alpha((k-1)\tau)$ induces a shorter η_1 for the next attack period because η_1 is an increasing function with respect to the initial admission rate (i.e., $\frac{\partial \eta_1}{\partial \alpha_0} > 0$). Consequently, the time to recover before the next pulse arrival, which is given by $k\tau - \eta_1$, is longer. Unfortunately, the admission rate still cannot climb back to α_0. To see why, suppose that at $t = k\tau^-$ the admission rate is large enough that $\alpha(k\tau^-) = \alpha((k-1)\tau^-)$. Therefore, when the next attack pulse arrives, the same number of attack requests is accepted, which forces the system to oscillate again. As a result, the admission rate converges to an oscillating pattern with a peak value less than α_0.

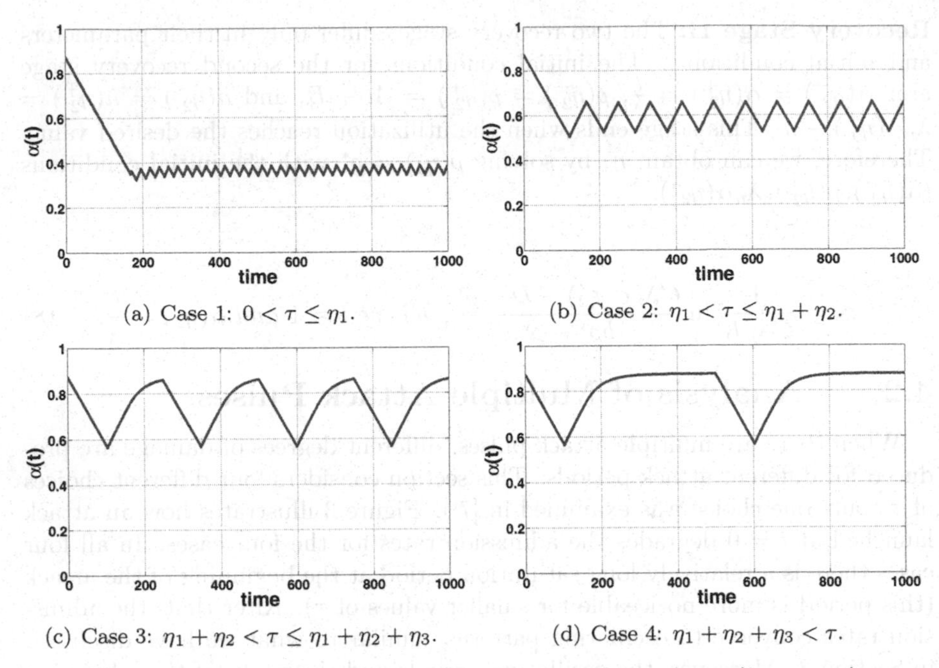

(a) Case 1: $0 < \tau \leq \eta_1$.

(b) Case 2: $\eta_1 < \tau \leq \eta_1 + \eta_2$.

(c) Case 3: $\eta_1 + \eta_2 < \tau \leq \eta_1 + \eta_2 + \eta_3$.

(d) Case 4: $\eta_1 + \eta_2 + \eta_3 < \tau$.

Figure 3. Effects of the attack period on the admission rate (four cases).

Case 3 ($\eta_1+\eta_2 < \tau \leq \eta_1+\eta_2+\eta_3$): The evolution of the system state is similar to that in Case 2, except that there is an additional recovery part governed by parameters C and D. The details are, therefore, omitted.

Case 4 ($\tau > \eta_1 + \eta_2 + \eta_3$): In this case, the system state always returns to the steady state before the next pulse arrives. Since this case has already been analyzed in [7], we do not discuss it again.

This proves that the system state converges in all four cases. We have derived the maximal and minimal values of $\alpha(t)$ after convergence, denoted by α_{max} and α_{min}, respectively. However, due to a lack of space, we present the expressions for α_{max} and α_{min} without proof:

$$\alpha_{max} = \frac{e^{-A\lambda_n K\tau}}{A\lambda_n}(Ay + A\lambda_n\alpha_{\max} + B - \rho^*)e^{\frac{A}{\rho^*-1}y} + \frac{\rho^* - B}{A\lambda_n}. \tag{9}$$

$$\alpha_{min} = K(\rho^* - 1)\eta_1 + \alpha_{max}, \tag{10}$$

where $y = -(\lambda_n\alpha_{max} - \mu) - \sqrt{(\lambda_n\alpha_{max} - \mu)^2 - 2\lambda_n K(\rho^* - 1)(\lambda_n + \lambda_a)\alpha_{max}}$. Note that $\alpha_{max} - \alpha_{min}$ measures the magnitude of the oscillations, and as shown in Figure 3, the magnitude increases with τ.

5. Detecting LRDoS Attacks

This section describes a new anomaly-based detection scheme for LRDoS attacks. The approach is based on the fact that high-intensity request bursts in an attack disturb the distribution of the arrival rates of normal requests. The detection scheme, therefore, has two components: (i) modeling the distribution using a histogram, and (ii) using a nonparametric outlier detection algorithm to determine whether there is a change in the histogram (assumed to be due to an LRDoS attack). A similar outlier detection approach has been proposed in [5]. However, it differs from our histogram approach in that it uses a clustering technique to group samples under various resolutions.

Suppose that x_i, $i \in \mathbb{Z}$, are request rate samples. For every window of W samples, say $\{x_{m-W+1}, \ldots, x_m\}$, our detection algorithm determines whether the latest sample x_m has disturbed the distribution. This is accomplished by using a histogram to model the distribution. A histogram consists of a set of equally-spaced intervals of sample values each of which is called a "bin;" the total number of bins is called the "bin resolution." Given a set of samples, the histogram plots the number of samples falling into each bin ("bin size"). An attack is detected when changes are seen in the histogram for $\{x_{m-W+1}, \ldots, x_m\}$ compared with the histogram for $\{x_{m-W+1}, \ldots, x_{m-1}\}$.

Determining the proper bin resolution is the main drawback of the histogram approach. The issue is resolved by applying the detection strategy to a range of bin resolutions. We first let $\beta_{x_m}(r)$ be the size of the bin that contains the sample x_m when the bin resolution is r. Figure 4 plots the values of $\beta_{x_m}(r)$ for $r \in [1, 60]$ obtained from simulation experiments for normal requests and malicious requests. Note that the $\beta_{x_m}(r)$ values for normal requests decrease more gradually from 60 (when $r = 1$) to 1 (when $r = 60$). On the other hand, the $\beta_{x_m}(r)$ values for malicious requests drop drastically from $r = 1$ to $r = 2$, because x_m, a sample from the attack pulse, is an outlier compared with the normal request samples. Therefore, the attack can be detected by measuring the changes in $\beta_{x_m}(r)$ values as r increases. For this purpose, we define a cumulative ratio for x_m:

$$R(x_m) = \sum_{r=1}^{W-1} \frac{\beta_{x_m}(r)}{\beta_{x_m}(r+1)}. \tag{11}$$

To see how the statistic in Equation 11 is used to detect an attack, let $R_n(x_m)$ (or $R_a(x_m)$) be the value of $R(x_m)$ when x_m is a sample from normal (or attack) traffic. If the attack intensity is high enough, the sample x_m from the attack traffic will most likely be the first sample that is separated from other samples when r is increased beyond one. In the most extreme case, $\beta_{x_m}(1) = W$ and $\beta_{x_m}(r) = 1$, $r > 1$; therefore, $R_a(x_m) = 2W - 2$. On the other hand, suppose that x_m is from normal traffic. Then, if the normal traffic intensity is uniformly distributed, $\beta_{x_m}(r) = \frac{1}{r}$. Therefore, $R_n(x_m) = \sum_{r=1}^{W-1} \frac{r+1}{r} < \sum_{r=1}^{W-1} \frac{r+r}{r} = 2(W-1) = R_a(x_m)$.

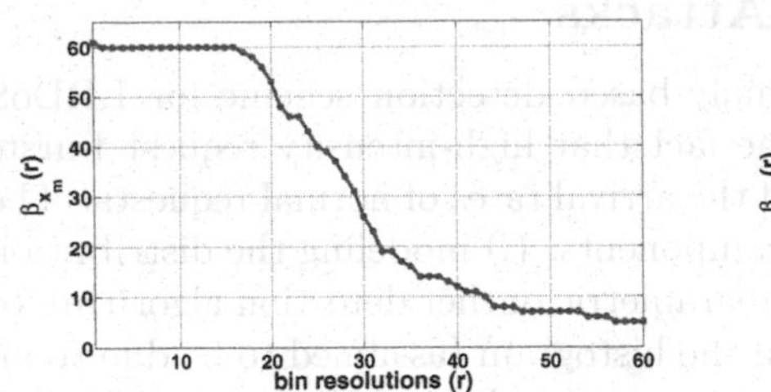

(a) x_m is a sample from normal requests.

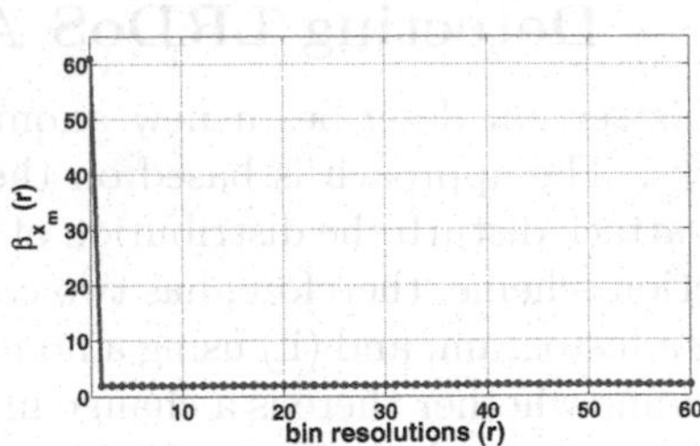

(b) x_m is a sample from malicious requests.

Figure 4. Change in x_m's bin size when the bin resolution is increased from 1 to 60.

However, to deal with the fact that the normal traffic distribution is usually heavy tailed, we introduce appropriate weights to the ratios in Equation 11 by assigning a higher weight to a $\beta_{x_m}(r)$ that has a higher traffic intensity:

$$R(x_m) = \sum_{r=1}^{W-1} \left(\frac{\beta_{x_m}(r)}{\beta_{x_m}(r+1)} \left| \frac{\bar{x}_n(r+1) - \bar{x}}{\bar{x}} \right| \right), \tag{12}$$

where $\bar{x}_n(r)$ is the mean of the samples in x_m's bin and $\bar{x}$ is the mean of all W samples. Moreover, if x_m is from normal traffic, $\bar{x}_n(r)$ should not be too far away from $\bar{x}$. If x_m is from attack traffic, $\bar{x}_n(r)$ is much closer to x_m because of the intensity of the attack traffic.

Therefore, the $R(x_m)$ values for a normal traffic sample and an attack traffic sample are revised as follows:

$$R_a(x_m) = (2W-2) \left| \tfrac{\bar{x}_n - \bar{x}}{\bar{x}} \right| \approx (2W-2) \left| \tfrac{\lambda_a - \bar{x}}{\bar{x}} \right|. \tag{13}$$

$$R_n(x_m) = \textstyle\sum_{r=1}^{W-1} \left(\tfrac{r+1}{r} \left| \tfrac{\bar{x}_n(r) - \bar{x}}{\bar{x}} \right| \right) < (2W-2) \left| \tfrac{\bar{x}_n - \bar{x}}{\bar{x}} \right| = R_a(x_m). \tag{14}$$

The final step is to choose a threshold θ such that the detection outcome is positive if $R(x_m) \geq \theta$. The threshold θ is determined as follows. Denote σ_x as the standard deviation of the first $W-1$ samples in the detection window: $\sigma_x = \sqrt{\frac{1}{W-1} \sum_{i=m-W+1}^{m-1} (x_i - \bar{x})^2}$. Note that if x_m is from attack traffic, then $\bar{x}_m - \bar{x} > \sigma_x$; if x_m is from normal traffic, $\bar{x}_m - \bar{x} \approx \sigma_x$. Also, we have $\sum_{r=2}^{W-1} \frac{1}{r} < W-1$. Taking these into consideration, we set $\theta = (2W-2)\sigma_x/\bar{x}$. To handle the burstiness in normal traffic, we introduce a weight w_d to the threshold value: $\theta = (2W-2)w_d\sigma_x/\bar{x}$.

6. Simulation Results

This section evaluates the performance of the detection algorithm for different values of w_d. MATLAB simulation results are used to assess attack capabilities as well as detection performance. The simulation experiments use

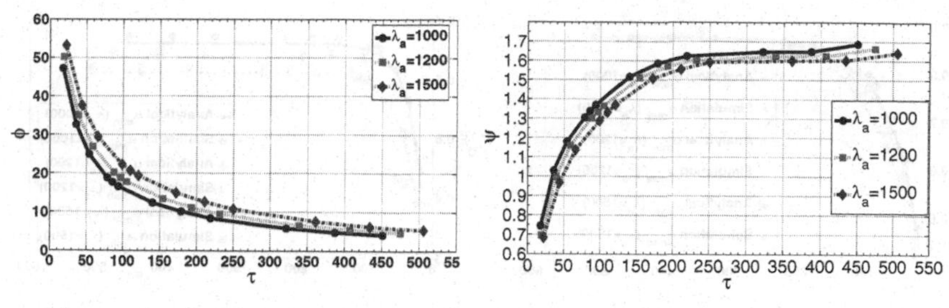

(a) Attack capability in terms of ϕ. (b) Attack capability in terms of ψ.

Figure 5. Capability of LRDoS attacks for different values of τ and λ_a.

the same parameters as before: $A = 0.00267$, $B = 0.2$, $C = 0.024$, $D = -1.4$, $\ell = 75$, $K = 0.01$, $\mu = 90$, and $\rho^* = 0.7$.

Attack Capability: In Section 4, we analyzed the effects of τ on the system output and admission rate of a victim system. Here we use simulations to further quantify the effects. We also study the effects for different values of λ_a. First, we define two metrics that characterize the capability of LRDoS attacks: (i) the percent of normal requests dropped due to an attack (denoted by ϕ), and (ii) the number of normal requests dropped due to an attack per λ_a (denoted by ψ). Therefore,

$$\phi = \frac{\int_0^T (\alpha^c - \alpha(t))\lambda_n dt}{\int_0^T \alpha^c \lambda_n dt} \times 100 \quad and \quad \psi = \frac{\int_0^T (\alpha^c - \alpha(t))\lambda_n dt}{N\lambda_a},$$

where T is the observation period (all N attack pulses arrive during T), and α^c is the admission rate when the system is in the steady state and not under attack. Therefore, ϕ measures the absolute service degradation. On the other hand, ψ measures the attack effectiveness in terms of the amount of service degradation caused by one attack request.

Figure 5 presents the ϕ and ψ values for attacks with $\lambda_a = 1000, 1200$ and 1500 requests per second, and $\tau \in [20, 500]$ seconds. For the three λ_a values, it is easy to verify that the range of τ covers the four cases discussed in Section 4. Figures 5(a) and 5(b) show that ϕ increases with λ_a while ψ decreases with λ_a. Furthermore, for a given value of λ_a, ϕ decreases with τ while ψ increases with τ. Moreover, as $\tau \to \infty$, $\phi \to 0$, because this is similar to the case of one attack pulse being encountered over a very long observation period. On the other hand, ψ converges to a value below 2, which is the maximal service degradation in terms of ψ.

Figure 6 presents the values of α_{max} and α_{min} obtained from simulations; it also includes the analytical results from Equations 9 and 10 for comparison. Note that the simulation results closely match the analytical results. Also, both α_{max} and α_{min} are increasing functions of τ, which can be validated by

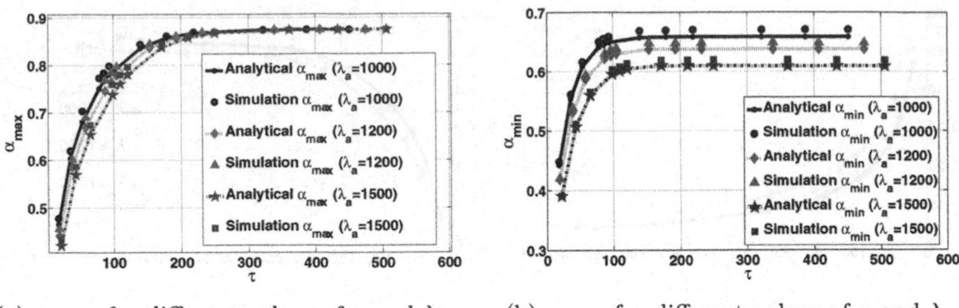

(a) α_{max} for different values of τ and λ_a.

(b) α_{min} for different values of τ and λ_a.

Figure 6. Analytical and simulation results for α_{max} and α_{min}.

computing the derivatives of Equations 9 and 10. Furthermore, α_{max} and α_{min} eventually reach plateaus, which indicates that the range of τ corresponds to Case 4 in Section 4.2. Finally, the α_{max} values for the three λ_a values converge to the same value, but the α_{min} values do not—a higher λ_a gives a lower α_{min}. In other words, a higher attack intensity increases the magnitude of the oscillations.

Detection Performance: To evaluate the performance of our detection algorithm, normal traffic was generated using log-normal, Pareto and Poisson distributions. For the log-normal and Pareto distributions, the location parameter was set to 4.6027 and 91.6667, respectively, and the scale parameter to 0.0707 and 12, respectively. For the Poisson distribution, the rate was set to 100. These parameter values yielded mean arrival rates of 100 requests per second for all three distributions. Also, samples for the request arrival rates were computed every second.

Figures 7(a) and 7(b) show the simulation results for the detection rates and false alarm rates, respectively. The detection rate increases with $\frac{\lambda_a}{\lambda_n}$ for all three distributions. Also, all the attacks can be detected (i.e., detection rate is 1) when $\frac{\lambda_a}{\lambda_n}$ is around 1.5. Moreover, the detection algorithm achieves the highest detection rate for the log-normal distribution before the detection rate reaches 1.0. Note that the variance of the log-normal distribution is approximately 50; this shows that the detection algorithm works well even under bursty normal traffic. The false alarm rate also improves (decreases) with $\frac{\lambda_a}{\lambda_n}$. The false alarm rates for the log-normal and Pareto distributions exhibit similar decreasing trends, whereas the rate for the Poisson distribution is at a low (albeit decreasing) level.

7. Conclusions

Low-rate DoS (LRDoS) attacks can significantly degrade feedback-based Internet services. By sending intermittent attack pulses, these attacks induce victim systems to generate false feedback signals, which cause them to decrease

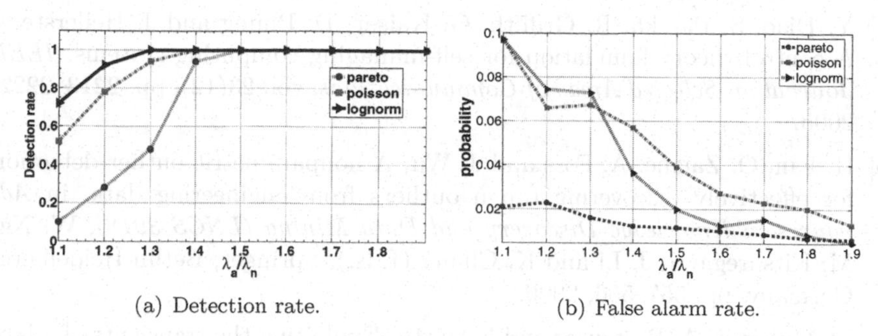

(a) Detection rate.

(b) False alarm rate.

Figure 7. Performance of the new detection algorithm for values of $\frac{\lambda_a}{\lambda_n}$.

their request acceptance rates. The nonparametric algorithm presented in this paper analyzes changes in traffic distribution to detect attacks. Extensive simulation results demonstrate that the algorithm is very effective at detecting LRDoS attacks.

Our current research is investigating strategies for optimizing LRDoS attacks and improving detection capabilities. We are also experimenting with several TCP variants, especially those targeting Linux systems (e.g., Veno, Hybla, Westwood+).

Acknowledgements

This work was partially supported under Project No. PolyU 5080/02E from the Research Grant Council of the Hong Kong Special Administrative Region, China, and by a grant from the Cisco University Research Program Fund.

References

[1] M. Chan, E. Chang, L. Lu and S. Ngiam, Effect of malicious synchronization, in *Applied Cryptography and Network Security (LNCS 3989)*, J. Zhou, M. Yung and F. Bao (Eds.), Springer, Berlin-Heidelberg, Germany, pp. 114–129, 2006.

[2] Y. Chen and K. Hwang, Collaborative detection and filtering of shrew DDoS attacks using spectral analysis, *Journal of Parallel and Distributed Computing*, vol. 66(9), pp. 1137–1151, 2006.

[3] Y. Diao, J. Hellerstein, S. Parekh, R. Griffith, G. Kaiser and D. Phung, Self-managing systems: A control theory foundation, *Proceedings of the Twelfth IEEE International Conference and Workshops on the Engineering of Computer-Based Systems*, pp. 441-448, 2005.

[4] Y. Diao, S. Parekh, R. Griffith, G. Kaiser, D. Phung and J. Hellerstein, A control theory foundation for self-managing computing systems, *IEEE Journal on Selected Areas of Communications*, vol. 23(12), pp. 2213–2222, 2005.

[5] H. Fan, O. Zaïane, A. Foss and J. Wu, A nonparametric outlier detection for effectively discovering top n outliers from engineering data, in *Advances in Knowledge Discovery and Data Mining (LNCS 3918)*, W. Ng, M. Kitsuregawa, J. Li and K. Chang (Eds.), Springer, Berlin-Heidelberg, Germany, pp. 557–566, 2006.

[6] M. Guirguis, A. Bestavros and I. Matta, Exploiting the transients of adaptation for RoQ attacks on Internet resources, *Proceedings of the Twelfth IEEE International Conference on Network Protocols*, pp. 184–195, 2004.

[7] M. Guirguis, A. Bestavros, I. Matta and Y. Zhang, Reduction of quality (RoQ) attacks on Internet end-systems, *Proceedings of the Twenty-Fourth Annual Joint Conference of the IEEE Computer and Communications Societies*, vol. 2, pp. 1362–1372, 2005.

[8] J. Hellerstein, Y. Diao, S. Parekh and D. Tilbury, *Feedback Control of Computing Systems*, John Wiley, New York, 2004.

[9] A. Kuzmanovic and E. Knightly, Low-rate TCP-targeted denial-of-service attacks: The shrew vs. the mice and elephants, *Proceedings of the Conference on Applications, Technologies, Architectures and Protocols for Computer Communications*, pp. 75–86, 2003.

[10] R. Lotlika, R. Vatsavai, M. Mohania and S. Chakravarthy, Policy schedule advisor for performance management, *Proceedings of the Second International Conference on Autonomic Computing*, pp. 183–192, 2005.

[11] Y. Lu, T. Abdelzaher, C. Lu, L. Sha and X. Liu, Feedback control with queueing-theoretic prediction for relative delay guarantees in web servers, *Proceedings of the Ninth IEEE Real-Time and Embedded Technology and Applications Symposium*, pp. 208–217, 2003.

[12] C. Lu, J. Stankovic, G. Tao and S. Son, Feedback control real-time scheduling: Framework, modeling and algorithms, *Journal of Real-Time Systems*, vol. 23(1-2), pp. 85–126, 2002.

[13] X. Luo, E. Chan and R. Chang, Vanguard: A new detection scheme for a class of TCP-targeted denial-of-service attacks, *Proceedings of the Tenth IEEE/IFIP Network Operations and Management Symposium*, pp. 507–518, 2006.

[14] X. Luo and R. Chang, On a new class of pulsing denial-of-service attacks and the defense, *Proceedings of the Twelfth Annual Network and Distributed System Security Symposium*, 2005.

[15] X. Luo and R. Chang, Optimizing the pulsing denial-of-service attacks, *Proceedings of the International Conference on Dependable Systems and Networks*, pp. 582–591, 2005.

[16] X. Luo, R. Chang and E. Chan, Performance analysis of TCP/AQM under denial-of-service attacks, *Proceedings of the Thirteenth IEEE International Symposium on Modeling, Analysis and Simulation of Computer and Telecommunication Systems*, pp. 97–104, 2005.

[17] A. Robertsson, B. Wittenmark, M. Kihl and M. Andersson, Design and evaluation of load control in web-server systems, *Proceedings of the American Control Conference*, vol. 3(30), pp. 1980–1985, 2004.

[18] H. Sun, J. Lui and D. Yau, Defending against low-rate TCP attacks: Dynamic detection and protection, *Proceedings of the Twelfth IEEE International Conference on Network Protocols*, pp. 196–205, 2004.

[19] M. Welsh and D. Culler, Adaptive overload control for busy Internet servers, *Proceedings of the Fourth USENIX Symposium on Internet Technologies and Systems*, p. 4, 2003.

[20] R. Zhang, C. Lu, T. Abdelzaher and J. Stankovic, Controlware: A middleware architecture for feedback control of software performance, *Proceedings of the Twenty-Second International Conference on Distributed Computing Systems*, p. 301, 2002.

Chapter 19

DETECTING WORMHOLE ATTACKS IN WIRELESS SENSOR NETWORKS

Yurong Xu, Guanling Chen, James Ford and Fillia Makedon

Abstract Wormhole attacks can destabilize or disable wireless sensor networks. In a typical wormhole attack, the attacker receives packets at one point in the network, forwards them through a wired or wireless link with less latency than the network links, and relays them to another point in the network. This paper describes a distributed wormhole detection algorithm for wireless sensor networks, which detects wormholes based on the distortions they create in a network. Since wormhole attacks are passive in nature, the algorithm uses a hop counting technique as a probe procedure, reconstructs local maps for each node, and then uses a "diameter" feature to detect abnormalities caused by wormholes. The main advantage of the algorithm is that it provides the locations of wormholes, which is useful for implementing countermeasures. Simulation results show that the algorithm has low false detection and false toleration rates.

Keywords: Wireless sensor networks, wormhole detection, distributed algorithm

1. Introduction

Wireless sensor networks (WSNs) [1, 15] are constructed using numerous small, low-power devices that integrate limited computation, sensing and radio communication capabilities. They provide flexible infrastructures for numerous applications, including healthcare, industry automation, surveillance and defense.

Currently, most WSN applications are designed to operate in trusted environments. However, security issues are a major concern when WSNs are deployed in untrusted environments. An adversary may disable a WSN by interfering with intra-network packet transmission via wormhole attacks, sybil attacks [11], jamming or packet injection attacks [17].

This paper focuses on wormhole attacks [2, 6, 12]. In a typical wormhole attack, the attacker receives packets at one point in the network, forwards them

Xu, Y., Chen, G., Ford, J. and Makedon, F., 2008, in IFIP International Federation for Information Processing, Volume 253, Critical Infrastructure Protection, eds. E. Goetz and S. Shenoi; (Boston: Springer), pp. 267–279.

through a wired or wireless link with less latency than the network links, and relays the packets to another point in the network. Such an attack does not require any cryptographic knowledge; consequently, it puts the attacker in a powerful position compared with other attacks (e.g., sybil attacks and packet injection attacks), which exploit vulnerabilities in the network infrastructure. Indeed, a wormhole attack is feasible even when the network infrastructure provides confidentiality and authenticity and the attacker does not have the cryptographic keys.

Several methods have been proposed for detecting wormhole attacks. However, these methods usually require that some nodes in the network be equipped with special hardware. Solutions such as SECTOR [2] and Packet Leashes [6] need time synchronization or highly accurate clocks to detect wormholes. The method of Hu and Evans [4] requires a directional antenna to be deployed at each node. LAD [3], SerLoc [8] and the approach of Hu, Perrig and Johnson [5] involve anchor nodes (nodes that know their exact locations), which requires the manual setup of a network.

This paper presents the wormhole geographic distributed detection (WGDD) algorithm, which requires neither anchor nodes nor any additional hardware. Since a wormhole attack is passive, the algorithm employs a hop counting technique as a probe procedure, reconstructs local maps using multidimensional scaling at each node, and uses a novel "diameter" feature to detect distortions produced by wormholes. The principal advantage of the algorithm is that it provides the approximate location of a wormhole, which can assist in implementing defense mechanisms. Simulation results show that the wormhole detection algorithm has low false detection and false toleration rates.

2. Related Work

Early approaches proposed for detecting wormhole attacks in wireless ad hoc networks include Packet Leashes [6] and SECTOR [2], which employ the notions of geographical and temporal leashes. The assumption is that each network node knows its exact location, and embeds the location and a timestamp in each packet it sends. If the network is synchronized, then any node that receives these packets can detect a wormhole based on differences in the observed locations and/or calculated times. Such a solution requires a synchronized clock and each node to know its location. The algorithm proposed in this paper does not have these requirements.

Kong, *et al.* [7] have studied denial-of-service (DoS) attacks (including wormhole attacks) on underwater sensor networks. Because these networks typically use acoustic methods to propagate messages, the detection techniques cannot be applied directly to wireless sensor networks.

Hu and Evans [4] have attempted to detect wormholes by equipping network nodes with directional antennas so they can all have the same orientation. Lazos and Poovendran [8] have applied a similar idea in their secure localization scheme called SeRLoc. SeRLoc employs about 400 anchor nodes (called "beacon nodes") in a 5,000-node network. Each anchor node has a directional antenna and knows its physical location. Other nodes in the network use anchor nodes to locate themselves. Since a wormhole produces shortcuts in a network, the directional antennas deployed at anchor nodes help detect the attack; nodes can then defend against the attack by discarding incorrect localization messages. However, SeRLoc is unable to detect wormhole attacks when anchor nodes are compromised, especially nodes located near one of the ends of a wormhole.

More recently, Liu, *et al.* [3, 9] have proposed an anchor-based scheme for detecting several attacks, including wormhole attacks. The scheme uses a hop counting technique to estimate the distance between a node and an anchor node (called a "location reference"). Since a wormhole changes the distance from a node to an anchor node, a simple threshold method can be used to determine if the change in distance is caused by a wormhole or by a localization error. Our approach also uses a hop counting technique, but it does not involve anchor nodes and, consequently, does not require the manual setup of a sensor network.

A graph-theoretic framework has also been proposed for detecting wormhole attacks [13]. However, the framework relies on "guard nodes," which are functionally similar to anchor nodes.

MDS-VOW [16] provides visualization facilities to detect the distortions produced by a wormhole in a computed network map. The principal limitation of MDS-VOW is that it is a centralized approach; also, as noted in [13], MDS-VOW cannot be applied to networks with irregular shapes. Our approach also detects wormholes based on the distortions they produce in a network map, but it employs a distributed algorithm and can detect wormholes in irregularly-shaped networks.

3. Wormhole Attacks

In a typical wormhole attack, the attacker receives packets at one point in the network, forwards them through a wireless or wired link with much less latency than the default links used by the network, and then relays them to another location in the network. In this paper, we assume that a wormhole is bi-directional with two endpoints, although multi-end wormholes are possible in theory.

A wormhole receives a message at its "origin end" and transmits it at its "destination end." Note that the designation of wormhole ends as origin and destination is dependent on the context. We also assume a wormhole is passive (i.e., it does not send a message without receiving an inbound message) and static (i.e., it does not change its location).

4. Wormhole Detection Algorithm

Our wormhole geographic distributed detection (WGDD) algorithm uses a hop counting technique as a probe procedure. After running the probe procedure, each network node collects the set of hop counts of its neighbor nodes that are within one/k hops from it. (The hop count is the minimum number of node-to-node transmissions to reach the node from a bootstrap node.) Next, the node runs Dijkstra's (or an equivalent) algorithm to obtain the shortest path for each pair of nodes, and reconstructs a local map using multidimensional scaling (MDS). Finally, a "diameter" feature is used to detect wormholes by identifying distortions in local maps.

The main steps involved in the wormhole detection algorithm are described in the following sections.

4.1 Probe Procedure

Since a wormhole attack is passive, it can only occur when a message is being transmitted in the region near a wormhole. To detect a wormhole attack, we use a probe procedure that floods the network with messages from a bootstrap node to enable all network nodes to count the hop distance from themselves to the bootstrap node. The probe procedure is based on the hop coordinates technique [18].

- **Bootstrap Node:** The bootstrap node x creates a probe message with $(i = id_x)$ to flood the network. Next, the bootstrap node drops all probe messages that originated from itself. The bootstrap node has the hop coordinate $hop_x = 0$ and $offset_x = 0$.

- **Other Nodes:** The probe procedure is presented in Algorithm 1. The algorithm computes the hop distance for node a. Node b is a neighbor of node a; hop_a is the minimum number of hops to reach node a from the bootstrap node (x) and its initial value is MAXINT. The combination of hop_a and $offset_a$ is the hop coordinate for node a. N_a is the set of nodes that can be reached from node a in one hop, and $|N_a|$ is the number of nodes in N_a.

4.2 Local Map Computation Procedure

In this step, each node computes a local map for its neighbors based on the hop coordinates computed in the previous step. After the hop coordinates are generated by the probe procedure, each node requests its neighbor nodes that are within one/k hops to send it their hop coordinates.

After a node receives the hop coordinates from its neighbors, it computes the shortest paths between all pairs of nodes one/k hops away using Dijkstra's algorithm (or a similar algorithm).

Next, multidimensional scaling (MDS) is applied to the $(|N_a|+1 \times |N_a|+1)$ shortest path matrix to retain the first two (or three) largest eigenvalues and eigenvectors for constructing a 2-D (or 3-D) local map. Note that $|N_a|$ is the number of nodes that can be reached from node a in one/k hops.

This step has a computational cost of $O(|N_a|^3\, n)$ and a memory cost of $O(|N_a|^2)$ per node. No communication cost is associated with this step.

Algorithm 1 : Probe Procedure (for Node a).

```
1: INPUT: message (hop_b) from node b ∈ N_a
2: for message (hop_b) from any B ∈ N_a and not TIMEOUT do
3:    if hop_b < hop_a then
4:       hop_a = hop_b + 1
5:       forward (message (hop_a)) to MAC
6:    else
7:       drop (message (hop_b))
8:    end if
9: end for
10: if |N_a| == 0 then
11:    offset_a = 0
12: else
13:    offset_a = (Σ_{b∈N_a} (hop_b − (hop_a − 1)) + 1) / (2(|N_a| + 1))
14: end if
15: return hop_a and offset_a
```

4.3 Detection Procedure

The detection procedure uses a local map created in the previous step. To help clarify the methodology, we examine the effect of a wormhole on a computed map.

Wormhole in a Reconstructed Map In order to observe a wormhole, we implemented the probe procedure and the local map computation procedure as routing agents, and the bootstrap node for the probe procedure as a protocol agent in ns-2 version 2.29 [10]. The RF range was 15 m.

The first experiment used 2,500 nodes in a uniform placement. Specifically, 2,500 nodes were placed on a grid with $\pm 0.5r$ randomized placement error, where $r = 2$ m is the width of a grid square. A wormhole was implemented as a wired connection.

Figure 1 shows two views of the sensor network. Each "x" mark represents a node; the circles indicate wormhole ends. The wormhole in Figure 1(a) is located in the center of the network. The two ends of the wormhole in Figure 1(b) are at the edges of the network.

Feature for Detecting Wormhole Attacks Since each node has limited resources and cannot store global information, a node can only use local information to detect wormhole attacks.

Figure 2 shows the portions of the network in the vicinity of the two ends of the wormhole in Figure 1(a). Nodes are represented by "x" marks and triangles; dotted circles are used to represent the neighborhoods corresponding to the circled node's transmission range R. After the circled node has completed its computations for the nodes in its local range, it generates the local map shown

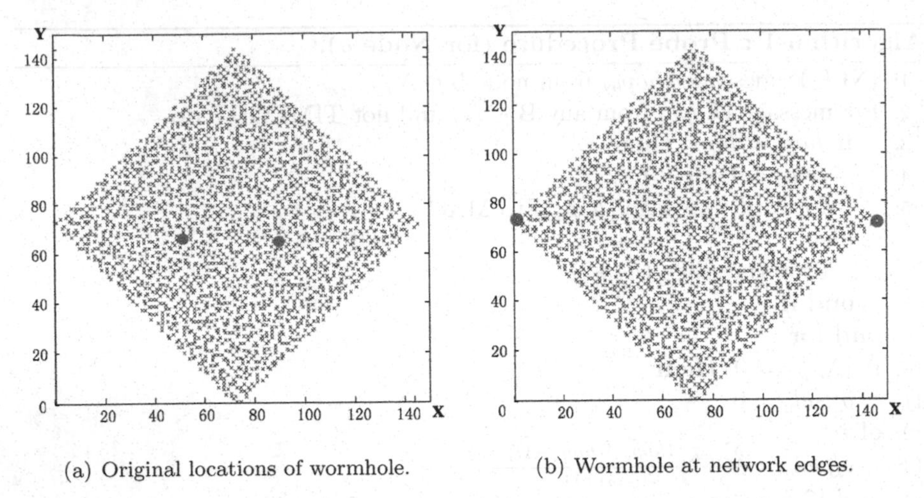

(a) Original locations of wormhole. (b) Wormhole at network edges.

Figure 1. A 2,500-node network ($r = 2$ m) with one wormhole.

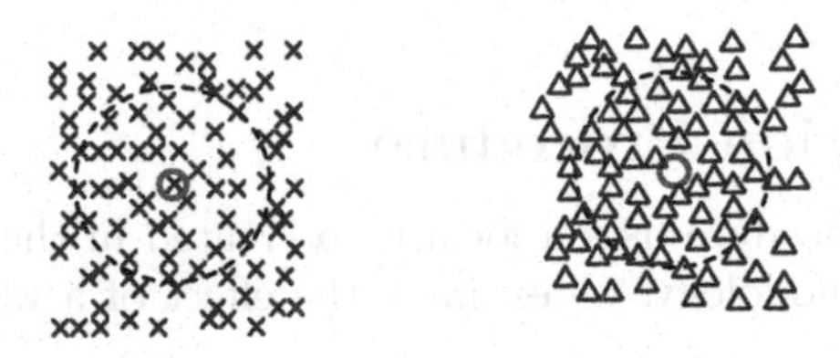

Figure 2. Portions of the network near the wormhole ends ($r = 4$ m; $R = 15$ m).

in Figure 3. The figure shows that, because the wormhole shortcuts the two portions of the network, the circled node can reach farther than before (the longest distance in the local map is 49 m), although the computed local map is distorted by the wormhole.

Based on the above observation, we employ the diameter of the computed local map as a feature to detect wormholes. We define the diameter d for a node a as:

$$d = max(distance(b, c))/2 \tag{1}$$

where $b, c \in N_a$. Note that N_a is the set of neighbor nodes of node a, and $distance(a, b)$ in the 2-D case is computed as $\sqrt{((x - x')^2 + (y - y')^2)}$, where (x, y) and (x', y') are the coordinates of nodes a and b, respectively, in the local map computed in the previous step.

In theory, the diameter of the neighborhood of a node is no more than R because a node can only hear from its neighbors within the transmission range R. However, the "shortcuts" created by a wormhole distort the computed map in the neighborhood of a node. Therefore, the diameter of the computed local

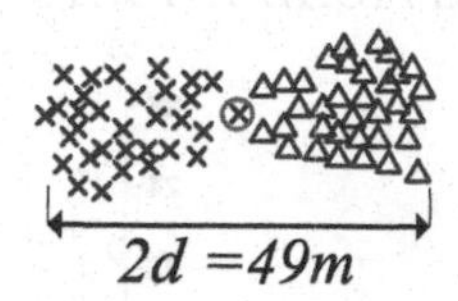

Figure 3. Local map of the circled node in Figure 2.

map is larger than the physical map. This is seen in the local map in Figure 3 where $2d = 49$ m.

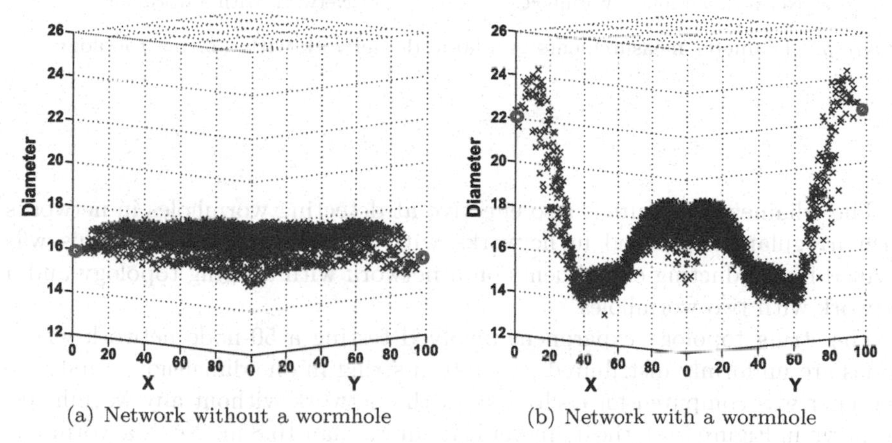

(a) Network without a wormhole (b) Network with a wormhole

Figure 4. Diameter measurements in a 2,500-node network.

To verify the effectiveness of the diameter feature in detecting wormholes, we computed the diameter for each node in the original 2,500-node network (Figure 2(a)) without and with a wormhole. The results are shown in Figures 4(a) and 4(b), respectively.

The diameters of the local maps of nodes close to a wormhole (i.e., near the circles in Figure 4(b)) are noticeably increased because of their proximity to the wormhole in comparison with the diameters for the same nodes in the network without a wormhole (Figure 4(a)). In Figure 4(b), the diameters of the local maps are roughly equal to R (14 to 18 m for $R = 15$ m) unless there is a wormhole attack, in which case the diameters of the local map become larger when the corresponding nodes are closer to the wormhole. On the other hand, the diameters of the local maps of nodes farther away from the wormhole or located in a distant part of the network (e.g., middle area in Figure 4(b)) are almost the same as those for nodes located in the same regions in Figure 4(a), which does not have a wormhole.

The diameter of a local map has the highest value (25 m) for nodes located about 7 m from the ends of the wormhole. The diameter values decrease for nodes closer to the network edges, but the values remain above 22 m.

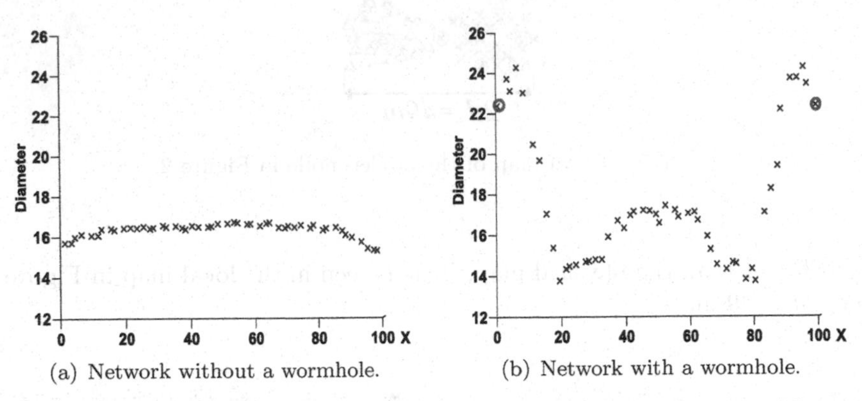

(a) Network without a wormhole. (b) Network with a wormhole.

Figure 5. Diameter measurements in a 50-node network with a string topology.

The "diameter" feature is also effective at detecting wormholes in networks with irregular shapes and in networks with multiple wormholes. This was verified by conducting experiments on a network with a string topology and a network with two wormholes.

The string topology experiment involved testing a 50-node network whose nodes are uniformly distributed in a 100 m string in one dimension. First, the diameter was computed for each node in the network without any wormholes; as shown in Figure 5(a), the diameter is no more than 16.8 m. Next, a wormhole was added to the network; the ends of the wormhole were located at the two ends of the string. As shown in Figure 5(b), the diameters for nodes close to the wormhole ends are larger than 22 m.

To test the effectiveness of the "diameter" feature in detecting multiple wormholes in a network, we deployed two wormholes in the network of Figure 2(a). The diameter measurements for all the nodes are shown in Figure 6 (the shading bar indicates the diameter value). The locations of the ends of the two wormholes are represented as circles; the dashed lines are the wormhole tunnels.

Figure 6 shows that even when two wormholes are very close to each other, the peak diameter values still occur for nodes that are close to a wormhole end. The four peak values are 24.8 m, 25.2 m, 22.2 m and 22.6 m. Therefore, by computing the diameter d for a local map, the detection algorithm can run independently for each node and in conjunction with the computation of its local map. Since all the nodes in this area are within one/k hops of the calculating node, the detection algorithm can compute the diameters for the local maps after determining the location of each neighbor node.

Wormhole Detection Procedure The wormhole detection procedure is shown in Algorithm 2. The "diameter" feature is used to determine whether or not there is a wormhole attack. The experimental results in Figures 4(a)

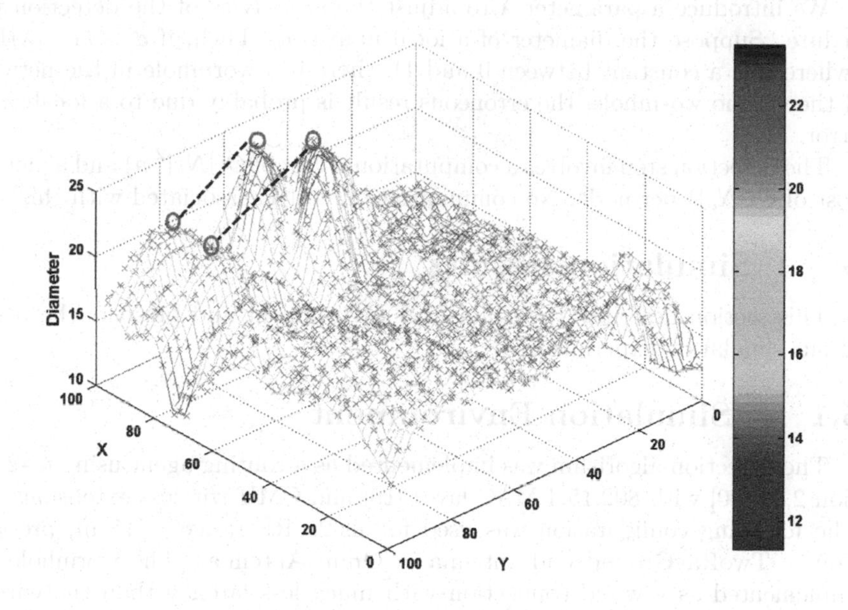

Figure 6. Diameter measurements in a 2,500-node network with two wormholes.

Algorithm 2 : Wormhole Detection Procedure (for Node a).

1: INPUT: local map G in node a for $N_a \cup \{a\}$
2: diameter $d = 0$
3: **for** each $b \in N_a \cup \{a\}$ **do**
4:    **for** each node $c \in N_a \cup \{a\} - \{b\}$ **do**
5:       **if** $2d <$ distance(b, c) in local map G **then**
6:          $2d =$ distance(a, b) in local map G
7:       **end if**
8:    **end for**
9: **end for**
10: **if** $d > (1 + \lambda) \times 1.4R$ **then**
11:    **return** "FOUND WORMHOLE" to sink node.
12: **end if**

---

and 4(b) show that the diameters for the local maps are around R when there is no wormhole. However, when there is a wormhole, the diameters for the local maps computed for nodes close to a wormhole end are higher (more than $1.5R$ in the example). Therefore, we can define a diameter threshold for detecting wormholes. Based on our experimental results, we define the threshold as $1.4R$ ($= 21$ m since $R = 15$ m). In general, the lower the value of the threshold, the higher the likelihood of false positives.

We introduce a parameter λ to adjust the sensitivity of the detection procedure. Suppose the diameter of a local map is d. Then, if $d > (1 + \lambda)1.4R$ (where λ is a constant between 0 and 1), there is a wormhole in the network. If there is no wormhole, the erroneous result is probably due to a localization error.

The detection step involves a computational cost of $O(|N_a|^2 n)$ and a memory cost of $O(|N_a|)$ per node. No communication cost is associated with this step.

5. Simulation Results

This section describes the simulation environment and presents the results of our simulation experiments.

5.1 Simulation Environment

The detection algorithm was implemented as a routing agent using ns-2 version 2.29 [10] with 802.15.4 MAC layer [19] and CMU wireless extensions [14]. The following configuration was used for ns-2: RF range = 15 m, propagation = TwoRayGround and antenna = Omni Antenna. The wormhole was implemented as a wired connection with much less latency than the wireless connections.

Uniform placement of nodes was used in the simulation experiments: n nodes were placed on a grid with $\pm 0.5r$ randomized placement error (r is the width of a grid square). We constructed a total of 24 placements for values of $n =$ 400, 900, 1,600 and 2,500, and $r = 2, 4, 6, 8, 10$ and 12 m. The reason for using uniform placement with $\pm 0.54r$ error is that it usually produces node holes and islands in just one placement. The location of the wormhole was completely randomized within the network.

5.2 Detection Results

As the value of λ is decreased, the accuracy of detecting wormhole attacks is increased, but the likelihood of false alarms is increased. To evaluate the accuracy of attack detection under different λ values, we introduce the following measures:

- **False Detection Rate (FDR):** This is the frequency with which a detection system falsely recognizes identical characteristics as being different, thus failing to tolerate, for example, a normal localization error. FDR is computed as the number of normal localization errors flagged as detected wormholes divided by the total number of trials.

  To compute an FDR value, we count the number of nodes that sent "FOUND WORMHOLE" messages but that are "far away" from the ends of a wormhole multiplied by the number of normal localization errors flagged as detected wormholes. We assume that if a node is $R = 15$ m away from the ends of a wormhole, then the node is essentially unaffected by the wormhole and is, therefore, considered to be "far away" from the

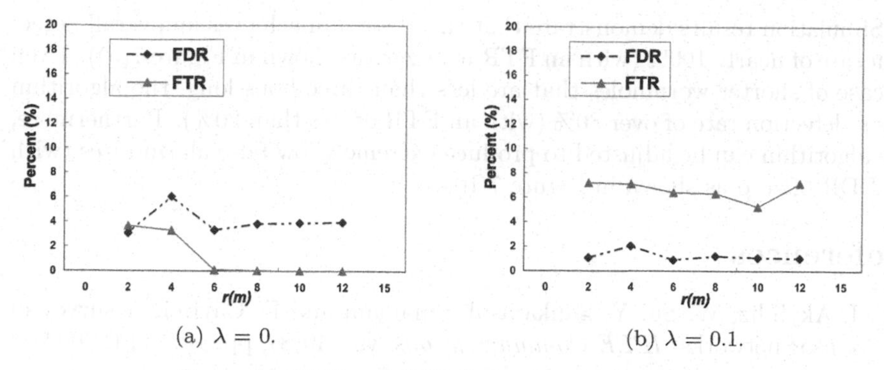

(a) $\lambda = 0$. (b) $\lambda = 0.1$.

Figure 7. FDR and FTR for various node spacings.

wormhole. An FDR value of zero means that there are no false alarms when detecting wormholes.

- **False Toleration Rate (FTR):** This is the frequency with which a detection system falsely recognizes different characteristics as identical, thus failing to detect a wormhole attack. FTR is computed as the number of wormhole attacks that are not detected divided by the total number of trials.

  If a wormhole is present in an experiment, but there is no node to send "FOUND WORMHOLE" messages, we count it as an undetected wormhole. Therefore, an FTR value of zero means that the detection algorithm is successful at detecting wormholes in all experiments.

We used the experimental setup described above with one wormhole in each placement. The FDR and FTR values for the experiments are presented in Figure 7. The detection algorithm has a low FTR value with FDR = 0 when $\lambda = 0$ as shown in Figure 7(a). When $\lambda = 0.1$, as shown in Figure 7(b), the detection algorithm achieves a low FDR value with FTR = 0.

6. Conclusions

The wormhole geographic distributed detection (WGDD) algorithm presented in this paper employs a hop counting technique as a probe procedure for wormholes, reconstructs local maps using multidimensional scaling at each node, and uses a novel "diameter" feature to detect distortions produced by wormholes. Unlike other wormhole detection algorithms, it does not require anchor nodes, additional hardware (e.g., directional antennas and accurate clocks) or the manual setup of networks. Even so, it can rapidly provide the locations of wormholes, which is useful for implementing countermeasures. Because the algorithm is distributed, each node can potentially detect the distortions produced by a wormhole, which increases the likelihood of wormhole detection.

Simulation results demonstrate that the algorithm achieves an overall detection rate of nearly 100% (with an FTR near zero as shown in Figure 7(a)). Even in case of shorter wormholes that are less than three hops long, the algorithm has a detection rate of over 80% (with an FTR of less than 20%). Furthermore, the algorithm can be adjusted to produce extremely low false alarm rates (with an FDR of zero as shown in Figure 7(b)).

References

[1] I. Akyildiz, W. Su, Y. Sankarasubramaniam and E. Cayirci, A survey of sensor networks, *IEEE Communications*, vol. 40(8), pp. 102–114, 2002.

[2] S. Čapkun, L. Buttyán and J. Hubaux, SECTOR: Secure tracking of node encounters in multi-hop wireless networks, *Proceedings of the First ACM Workshop on Security of Ad Hoc and Sensor Networks*, pp. 21–32, 2003.

[3] W. Du, L. Fang and P. Ning, LAD: Localization anomaly detection for wireless sensor networks, *Journal of Parallel and Distributed Computing*, vol. 66(7), pp. 874–886, 2006.

[4] L. Hu and D. Evans, Using directional antennas to prevent wormhole attacks, *Proceedings of the Eleventh Network and Distributed System Security Symposium*, pp. 131–141, 2004.

[5] Y. Hu, A. Perrig and D. Johnson, Wormhole Detection in Wireless Ad Hoc Networks, Technical Report TR01-384, Department of Computer Science, Rice University, Houston, Texas, 2002.

[6] Y. Hu, A. Perrig and D. Johnson, Packet leashes: A defense against wormhole attacks in wireless networks, *Proceedings of the Twenty-Second Annual Joint Conference of the IEEE Computer and Communications Societies*, vol. 3, pp. 1976–1986, 2003.

[7] J. Kong, Z. Ji, W. Wang, M. Gerla, R. Bagrodia and B. Bhargava, Low-cost attacks against packet delivery, localization and time synchronization services in underwater sensor networks, *Proceedings of the Fourth ACM Workshop on Wireless Security*, pp. 87–96, 2005.

[8] L. Lazos and R. Poovendran, SeRLoc: Robust localization for wireless sensor networks, *ACM Transactions on Sensor Networks*, vol. 1(1), pp. 73–100, 2005.

[9] D. Liu, P. Ning and W. Du, Attack-resistant location estimation in sensor networks, *Proceedings of the Fourth International Symposium on Information Processing in Sensor Networks*, pp. 99–106, 2005.

[10] S. McCanne and S. Floyd, The network simulator – ns-2 (nsnam.isi.edu/nsnam/index.php/User_Information), 2007.

[11] J. Newsome, E. Shi, D. Song and A. Perrig, The sybil attack in sensor networks: Analysis and defenses, *Proceedings of the Third International Symposium on Information Processing in Sensor Networks*, pp. 259–268, 2004.

[12] P. Papadimitratos and Z. Haas, Secure routing for mobile ad hoc networks, *Proceedings of the SCS Communication Networks and Distributed Systems Modeling and Simulation Conference*, 2002.

[13] R. Poovendran and L. Lazos, A graph theoretic framework for preventing the wormhole attack in wireless ad hoc networks, *Wireless Networks*, vol. 13(1), pp. 27–59, 2007.

[14] The Rice Monarch Project, Wireless and mobility extensions to ns-2 (www.monarch.cs.cmu.edu/cmu-ns.html), 2007.

[15] M. Vieira, C. Coelho Jr., D. da Silva Jr. and J. da Mata, Survey of wireless sensor network devices, *Proceedings of the IEEE Conference on Emerging Technologies and Factory Automation*, vol. 1, pp. 537–544, 2003.

[16] W. Wang and B. Bhargava, Visualization of wormholes in sensor networks, *Proceedings of the ACM Workshop on Wireless Security*, pp. 51–60, 2004.

[17] A. Wood and J. Stankovic, Denial of service in sensor networks, *IEEE Computer*, vol. 35(10), pp. 54–62, 2002.

[18] Y. Xu, J. Ford and F. Makedon, A variation on hop counting for geographic routing, *Proceedings of the Third IEEE Workshop on Embedded Networked Sensors*, 2006.

[19] J. Zheng, Low rate wireless personal area networks: ns-2 simulator for 802.15.4 (release v1.1) (ees2cy.engr.ccny.cuny.edu/zheng/pub), 2007.

Chapter 20

DETECTING NON-DISCOVERABLE BLUETOOTH DEVICES

Daniel Cross, Justin Hoeckle, Michael Lavine, Jason Rubin
and Kevin Snow

Abstract Mobile communication technologies such as Bluetooth are becoming ubiquitous, but they must provide satisfactory levels of security and privacy. Concerns about Bluetooth device security have led the specification of the "non-discoverable" mode, which prevents devices from being listed during a Bluetooth device search process. However, a non-discoverable Bluetooth device is visible to devices that know its address or can discover its address. This paper discusses the detection of non-discoverable Bluetooth devices using an enhanced brute force search attack. Our results indicate that the average time to attack a non-discoverable Bluetooth device using multiple search devices and condensed packet timing can be reduced to well under 24 hours.

Keywords: Bluetooth security, device discovery, non-discoverable mode

1. Introduction

Bluetooth devices are growing in popularity, despite security concerns. A Bluetooth device in the "discoverable" mode is easily scanned using a computer; moreover, private information can be downloaded from the device. This technique has been used in high profile attacks against celebrities whose devices were operating in the discoverable mode.

To address some of these concerns, the Bluetooth Special Interest Group (SIG) recommends that devices be placed in the non-discoverable mode, which prevents them from being listed during a Bluetooth device search process. However, a non-discoverable Bluetooth device can still be attacked if its address is already known or is determined by brute force. Most brute force methods take about a week, which alleviates the security concerns to some extent. However, a brute force search for non-discoverable Bluetooth devices can be sped up significantly using certain details about device operation.

Cross, D., Hoeckle, J., Lavine, M., Rubin, J. and Snow, K., 2008, in IFIP International Federation for Information Processing, Volume 253, Critical Infrastructure Protection, eds. E. Goetz and S. Shenoi; (Boston: Springer), pp. 281–293.

This paper presents a novel technique for detecting non-discoverable Bluetooth devices. It leverages the constraints imposed on the connection process and uses multiple search devices to enhance the brute force search for device addresses. Results indicate that the average time to successfully attack a non-discoverable Bluetooth device using 79 search devices and condensed packet timing is well under 24 hours.

2. Background

The Bluetooth specification [1] establishes certain constraints and parameters to ensure the interoperability of Bluetooth devices. Our method for accelerating the search for non-discoverable devices leverages the constraints on the Bluetooth connection process.

2.1 Bluetooth State Transitions

The Bluetooth specification defines a state transition sequence for Bluetooth devices. A device in the Standby state can enter the Inquiry, Inquiry Scan, Page or Page Scan states. A Bluetooth device enters the Inquiry state when it sends inquiry packets. A device enters the Inquiry Scan state to listen for and respond to inquiry messages broadcast by other devices. The Inquiry and Inquiry Scan states are used for device discovery. The Page and Page Scan states are reached when a connection is being established between two devices. A Bluetooth device enters the Page state when it transmits page packets; it enters the Page Scan state to listen for and respond to page packets with its address. The Master Response and Slave Response states are entered when packets are exchanged as a connection is being established. Upon successfully completing a connection, a Bluetooth device enters the Connection state.

2.2 MAC Address Components

Every Bluetooth device is assigned a unique 48-bit MAC address. The 48-bit address has three segments. The sixteen most significant bits are dedicated to the non-significant address part (NAP). The upper address part (UAP) constitutes the next eight bits of the address. The NAP and UAP are assigned to companies that manufacture Bluetooth devices. The last 24 bits of the address make up the lower address part (LAP), which is designated by the manufacturer. The addressing of page packets is based on the 24-bit LAP.

2.3 Discoverable and Non-Discoverable Modes

Bluetooth devices discover and connect to each other using inquiry and paging procedures, respectively. An inquiry procedure is initiated by an inquiring device. Discoverable Bluetooth devices send responses to inquiry packets, making the inquiring device aware of its presence. Bluetooth devices in the non-discoverable mode do not reply to inquiry packets and, thus, remain invisible to the inquiring device.

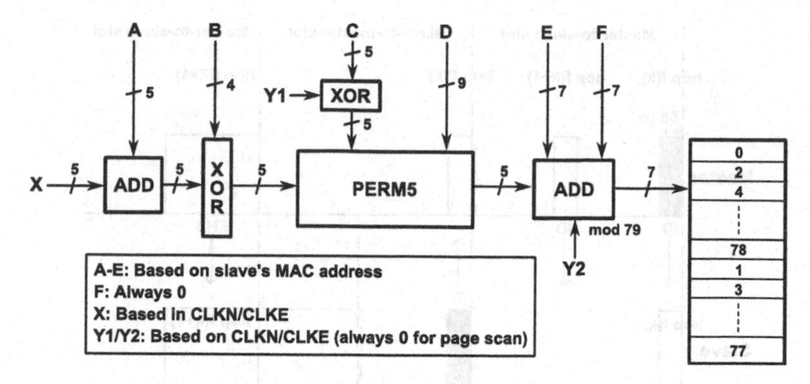

Figure 1. Hop selection kernel for page, page scan and response.

2.4 Connection Process

The paging procedure uses the address of a nearby Bluetooth device. Two devices are involved in a paging procedure: the device that seeks a connection by issuing a paging packet and the device that listens for a paging packet using a page scan. Only the device with the correct address responds to a paging packet. The channel used by the paging procedure is dependent on the characteristics of the connectable device.

The paging device attempts to approximate the clock of the connectable device by estimating its offset and adding the offset to its own clock. This approximation determines the timing of the page scan channel of the connectable device. The hopping sequence is determined by the address of the connectable device. The page hopping sequence and page response hopping sequence both utilize only 32 of the 79 available frequencies. The frequencies used by the two sequences are in one-to-one correspondence with each other.

2.5 Hop Channel Calculation

A Bluetooth device calculates a hop channel on-the-fly as it is dependent on the time and the address of the device with which it is communicating. The set of channels and the order in which they are used are determined by the hop selection kernel (Figure 1). According to the Bluetooth specification, the order and phase are determined by portions of the lower 28 bits of the slave's MAC address and the paging device's clock. The lower seven odd bits of the MAC address are used to determine the channels in the set. The inputs X, Y1 and Y2 vary depending on the current mode (page scan, inquiry scan, page, inquiry, responses, etc.). Inputs A–F remain constant for the majority of modes.

2.6 Page Packets

A page packet is 68 bits in length. Unlike other packets, it has no header, payload or trailer, only a device access code (DAC). The DAC consists of a 4-bit

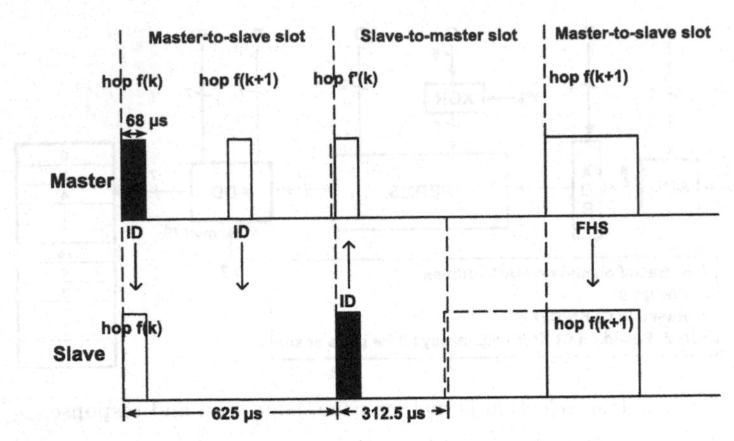

Figure 2. Paging process (first packet).

preamble and a 64-bit sync word. The preamble is an alternating sequence of 0s and 1s based on the least significant bit of the sync word. The sync word is created by appending six bits to the end of the LAP. If the most significant bit of the LAP is 0, then 001101 is appended to the LAC; otherwise, 110010 is appended. The thirty bits are then XORed with a pseudo-random noise (PN) sequence. The result is then XORed with a previously generated codeword to create the 64-bit sync word.

2.7 Paging Process

The paging process hops channels 3,200 times per second. Two page packets are sent in every transmission (TX) slot, each on a different channel. A single TX slot covers 625 μs. Since there are two packets, 312.5 μs are used for each frequency. Out of the 312.5 μs, 68 μs are spent sending a packet.

Following every TX slot is a reception (RX) slot, which also lasts 625 μs. The RX slot is used by a paging device to receive the first page slave response packet from a connectable device. The paging response procedure used by the connectable device hops the same channels as the paging procedure and at the same rate. Upon receiving the page packet in the RX slot, the connectable device waits until it receives the corresponding packet in the next TX slot. If the connectable device receives the page packet in the second 312.5 μs half of its RX slot, then the first page slave response packet is sent in the second 312.5 μs half of the next TX slot. Thus, there is a consistent 625 μs between when the page packet is sent and when the first page slave response is received by the paging device.

Figures 2 and 3 illustrate the initial packet exchange in the paging process. The diagrams show that a reply to a page packet is sent 625 μs after the page packet. As shown in Figure 2, a page packet transmitted by a paging device as the first page packet in the TX slot results in a page reply 625 μs later in the

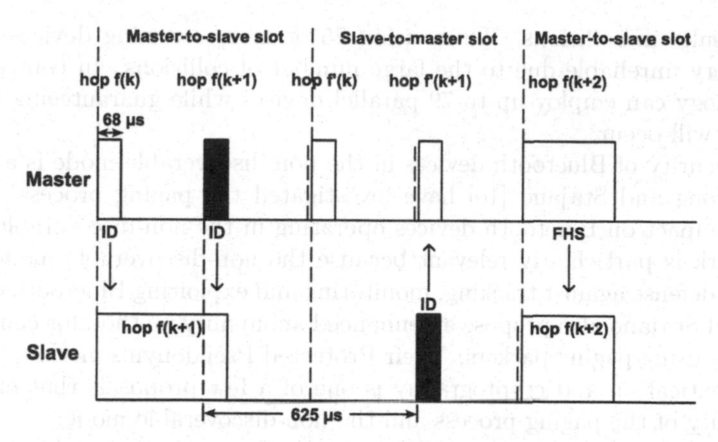

Figure 3. Paging process (second packet).

paging device's RX slot (also the first TX slot of the paged device). Similarly, a page packet transmitted as the second page packet in the TX slot results in a page reply 625 μs later in the paging device's RX slot (Figure 3). The paging process involves additional packet exchanges, but they are not relevant because our goal is to discover devices, not to establish connections with them.

3. Related Work

While a variety of *ad hoc* tools have been developed for brute force searches of non-discoverable Bluetooth devices, little research exists on enhancing brute force techniques. One exception is the work of Haataja [4]. Haataja reasons that the address space to be searched can be reduced by assuming that the manufacturer is known; this assumption yields a reduced search space of 2^{24} addresses. Haataja used a Bluetooth-compatible radio unit and a protocol analyzer to attempt ACL link connections to remote devices for each address. In one experiment, 2,000 addresses were scanned in 174 minutes. Based on these results, it is estimated that, on the average, 1.4 years of scanning would be required to discover a single device. Using 25 scanning devices would reduce the average time to 20.3 days.

However, some of Haataja's assumptions are problematic. First, it is not reasonable to assume that the device manufacturer is known. It should be possible to detect devices from any manufacturer. Therefore, the approach requires at least 20.3 days for each manufacturer. Our methodology, on the other hand, is faster and makes no assumptions about the device manufacturer.

The second problem is that the 20.3 day estimate relies on 25 devices scanning in parallel. Bluetooth operates on 79 unique frequencies and a reliable brute force search of one address requires connection attempts over 32 unique frequencies within a short time period. Parallel scanning offers no guarantees that the devices will not concurrently send requests on identical frequencies, which results in collisions. Thus, using 25 or more scanning devices in parallel is very unreliable due to the large number of collisions. In contrast, our methodology can employ up to 79 parallel devices while guaranteeing that no collisions will occur.

The security of Bluetooth devices in the non-discoverable mode is a serious issue. Wong and Stajano [10] have investigated the paging process and the security impact on Bluetooth devices operating in the non-discoverable mode. Their work is particularly relevant because the non-discoverable mode is the principal defense against tracking, monitoring and exploiting Bluetooth devices. Wong and Stajano also propose an enhanced anonymity method for connecting to devices using paging packets. Their Protected Pseudonyms method employing authentication and cryptography is one of a few proposals that enhances the security of the paging process and the non-discoverable mode.

A white paper by Gehrmann [3] focuses on the encryption and authentication architectures built in the baseband layer of Bluetooth devices. The paper discusses the need to keep a Bluetooth device in a secure environment when pairing. But it does not discuss the use of the non-discoverable mode as a security function, nor does it provide recommendations for using the mode to secure devices.

A more recent document released by the Bluetooth SIG [2] addresses several security exploits and concerns. The document explicitly cites the non-discoverable mode as the chief security mechanism and advocates its use to protect against a number of exploits and attacks against Bluetooth-enabled devices. It even states that the non-discoverable mode can protect devices from viruses and worms. Unfortunately, this premise is based on the assumption that a non-discoverable Bluetooth device cannot be detected and will not respond to an attacking device. Our methodology, which is capable of detecting Bluetooth devices in the non-discoverable mode, shatters this assumption.

4. Detection Methodology

A straightforward brute force search of the address space based on the Bluetooth specification is trivial, but incredibly time consuming. The best brute force approach [4] is estimated to take an average of 1.4 years using one search device, and just under a week with 79 devices (the maximum number of devices used in our methodology). Our methodology is faster because it: (i) reduces the number of addresses to be searched, and (ii) decreases the time taken to search addresses. Searching one address entails sending the correct page packet on each page scan frequency with the appropriate timing. Therefore, a brute force technique involves not only searching for all possible addresses, but also each of their corresponding paging channels.

The following sections describe our address space and search time reduction techniques. The results obtained using the reduction techniques are presented along with some practical considerations.

4.1 Address Space Reduction

The number of addresses to be searched is determined by the DAC sent in a page packet and the address inputs into the channel hop selection kernel. As mentioned above, one component of the DAC is the 24-bit LAP, which is the only portion of the address included in a page packet. Since there are 2^{24} unique LAPs, only 2^{24} addresses instead of all 2^{48} addresses need to be searched. Unfortunately, this also means that the number of addresses to be searched is at least 2^{24} without detailed address space profiling. However, paging a single address involves transmitting the page packet at the correct time on the appropriate channel.

As mentioned in Section 2, 28 bits of the address are used for hop channel selection. Using a brute force technique to identify the address corresponding to a channel set increases the search space from 2^{24} to 2^{28}. However, this increase is avoided because only certain bits of an address are used to select the channels in the page scan channel set. Specifically, the lower seven odd address bits 13, 11, 9, 7, 5, 3 and 1 are used to determine the channel set. Some of the remaining address bits determine the order of the channels selected, but this is not relevant to our methodology.

Since the address bits mentioned above are contained in the LAP, the size of the search space is still 2^{24}. Assuming a uniform distribution of address assignments, an average of 2^{23} addresses need to be searched before a response is received.

4.2 Search Time Reduction

Search time reduction is achieved through two approaches: condensed packet timing, which increases the rate at which page packets are sent; and parallelized paging, which enables simultaneous page requests over each page channel in one TX slot.

Condensed Packet Timing To decrease the amount of time taken to search an address, the number of packets sent per page scan window (N_{pw}) can be increased from the value in the Bluetooth specification. N_{pw} is computed using the following equation:

$$N_{pw} = \left\lfloor \frac{T_{w\,page\,scan}}{T_{page} + T_{delay}} \right\rfloor .$$

Figure 4 presents the timing diagram represented by the equation. Since the page scan window ($T_{w\,page\,scan}$) and the paging packet transmit time (T_{page}) are variables outside the scope of a paging device's control, the delay between page packets (T_{delay}) is the only controllable factor for determining the number of packets that can be sent in a single page scan window. In a standard page sequence, packets are sent at a rate corresponding to a T_{delay} of 244.5 μs. This allows the sending device enough time to change channels if needed. However,

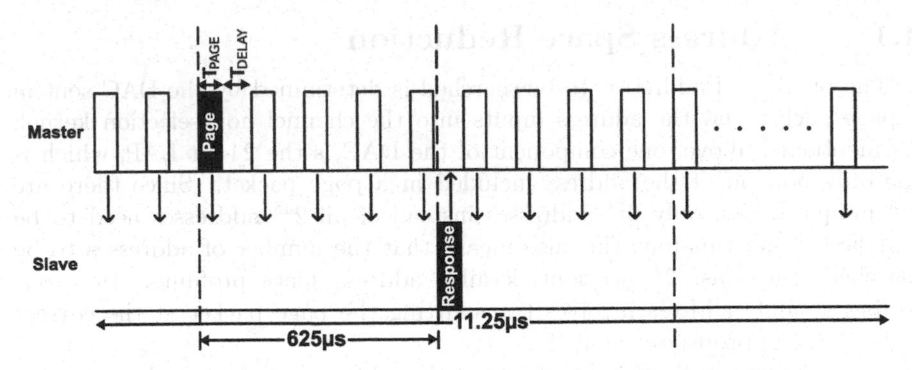

Figure 4. Page packet timing diagram.

our modified approach does not require a paging device to change channels; this permits the use of a lower T_{delay}.

Certain restrictions are imposed on T_{delay}. One is that T_{delay} must be large enough to allow a response packet to be received without colliding with other page packets. Since a page packet takes 68 μs to transmit, the lower bound on T_{delay} is 68 μs.

Another restriction is that the period during which a page response is returned (and no transmission is allowed) must be 625 μs after the respective page packet is sent to ensure that the packet is received. Therefore, a targeted device must not transmit during periods when a response page packet might be sent.

The minimum T_{delay} is 68 μs because a page packet must fit in the reception window. This yields 82 packets per page scan window. Unfortunately, transmitting and receiving packets during these intervals causes packet collisions. Since the number of packets must be reduced in increments of one, the number of packets per page scan window is reduced from 82 to 81, yielding a T_{delay} of 70.88 μs, which does not cause packet collisions.

Thus, a T_{delay} value of 70.88 μs is selected. It satisfies all the constraints and is significantly smaller than the value in the Bluetooth specification (244.5 μs). The result is that condensed timing allows more page packets to be sent in a single page scan window. Since we use the default page scan window value of 11.25 ms, N_{pw} is computed as:

$$N_{pw} = \left\lfloor \frac{11.25\ ms}{68\ \mu s + 70.88\ \mu s} \right\rfloor = 81\ pages/window.$$

Note that there is no way to control when a target device starts its page scan. This can occur while a packet is being transmitted, which would cause the device to miss a packet addressed to it. If the first and last packets sent in a single window are the same, then all unique packets (N_{upw}) could be received by the target device, but this comes at the expense of an additional packet per page scan window:

$$\begin{aligned} N_{upw} &= N_{pw} - 1 \\ &= 81 \; pages/window - 1 \; redundant \; page/window \\ &= 80 \; pages/window. \end{aligned}$$

Parallelized Paging In addition to increasing the number of packets that are transmitted per page scan window via condensed timing, multiple page packets may be sent in parallel during a single TX slot. A device may be listening on any of the 79 possible page scan channels depending on its address, each of which can be transmitted simultaneously using multiple devices. Previous approaches have failed to address the fact that collisions increase as more devices are added to increase the scanning speed. Collisions decrease the reliability of address space scanning, which ultimately increases the search time.

These problems can be overcome using a simple matrix representation that models more complex timing and channel selection issues. Based on the assumption that 79 devices are being used and that each is transmitting in blocks of N_{upw}, matrices of size $N_{upw} \times 79$ can be created with <address, channel> pairs as their elements. Each column of a matrix is deemed to be a "transmission slot." The task is to fill the matrices as densely as possible. The next two sections describe how matrix elements are generated and how the elements are placed in matrices.

Paging Channel Set Generation A formula for generating the 32 paging channels for each address is a prerequisite for packet scheduling. We have previously described the main aspects of hop channel selection. Recall that it requires the set of channels, not the specific order of the set. Inputs E and F in Figure 1 are the only inputs that determine the unordered set of channels. Since input F is used in the Connection state, not in any of the paging sequence states, this leaves input E and the 5-bit output of a permutation to determine the channel set. A simple iteration from 0 to 31 (representing the 32 possible permutation values) added to E gives the 32 indices into a channel mapping register. Therefore, the formula for calculating the paging channel set given $i \in 0..31$ is:

$$Channel_i = (((E + i) \; mod \; 79) \times \; 2) \; mod \; 79.$$

$(E + i) \; mod \; 79$ generates the output of the final addition of the selection box. The modulo 79 computation maps the output of the addition (channel index) to the mapping register, producing the actual channel number.

A set of <address, channel> pairs is generated for each address. Since each 7-bit E value corresponds to a set of 32 channels, 128 groups with 32 channels each are created. Some of these sets are identical because of the modulo 79 computation. Each LAP address therefore belongs to one of the 128 groups.

Thus, $2^{24}/128$ or 2^{17} addresses belong to each group, which must then be scheduled into matrices.

Packet Scheduling The goal is to fill all the matrices as densely as possible, where each matrix element corresponds to an <address, channel> pair. Two restrictions apply: (i) channels must be unique within a transmission slot (matrix column), and (ii) <address, channel> pairs for an address must fit in one matrix or be divided among matrices in multiples of 32.

The first restriction guarantees that no collisions occur between targeted devices. The second ensures that the listening device can successfully receive a page packet for each address. Since a device could be listening on any of its 32 paging channels during each page scan window (matrix window), each channel must be tried. However, the listening device increments the channel it listens on for each new matrix window. If half the channels for an address are tried in a matrix, the second half cannot be tried in a second matrix because nothing is known about the channel set order or phase. The only assumption that can be made is that 32 matrices later, the listening device will be on the same channel. This is because a listening device repeatedly scans the same 32 channel sequence.

A matrix can be created by scheduling the 32 channels of each of the 128 groups mentioned above into one matrix. Each element of the matrix contains the group number (0–127). This fills most of the first 64 of 80 slots, leaving the remaining 16 slots unused. The result is convenient because 16 is one quarter of 64: one of the 64-slot matrices can be split up into quarters, which can fill the remaining 16 slots of 4 sequential matrices. Thus, five 64-slot matrices fit into four 80-slot (full) matrices. The four full matrices may be used as a template by replacing the group number in each element with an <address, channel> pair from the respective group.

Unfortunately, this does satisfy the restriction that an address split across matrices must be 32 matrices apart. Therefore, instead of splitting one 64-slot matrix among four sequential full matrices, 32 64-slot matrices are split among 128 full matrices. The first quarters of the 32 64-slot matrices are split among the first 32 sequential full matrices, the 32 second quarters are split among the second 32 sequential full matrices, and so on (see Figure 5). This forces the matrices to be generated in blocks of 128, which cover 20,480 addresses. The generation of 128 matrix blocks is performed until all the addresses are scheduled. In total, 104,863 matrices are generated.

4.3 Results

Given that the page channels are known, but not their order or phase, page packets must be sent in a redundant manner to guarantee reception within the page scan interval. Therefore, if the phase of a targeted device is not known, the timing of a page scan window occurrence is completely unknown to the sending device. Thus, it is necessary to transmit the same sequence of N_{upw} packets for a duration equal to $T_{page\ scan}$ to guarantee that regardless of when

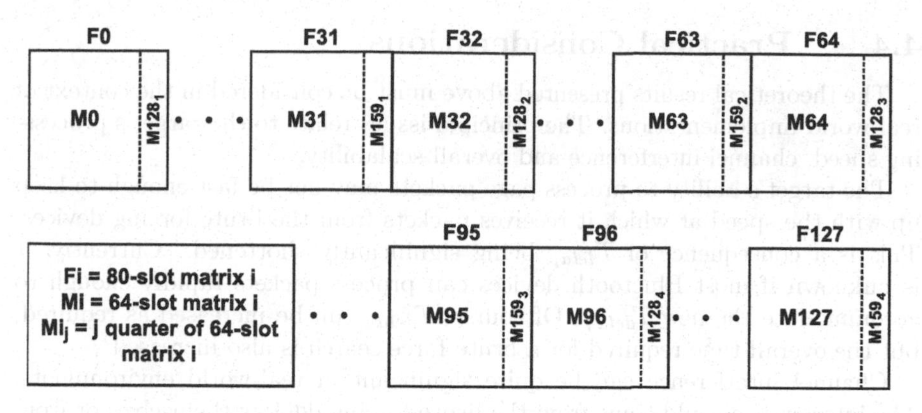

Figure 5. 128 matrix block.

the listening device wakes up it will receive all N_{upw} packets required for a successful brute force search.

The average time taken for a brute force search of an address (T_{bf}) can be calculated as:

$$T_{bf} = \frac{T_{page\,scan} \times f(N_a,\, N_d,\, N_{upw})}{2}.$$

N_a represents the number of addresses to be guessed and N_d is the number of devices used in the brute force search. The function f is determined by the packet schedule and represents the number of matrices needed to search for all the addresses. The denser the matrices, the lower the f value and the lower the T_{bf} value.

Table 1. Average time required for brute force search.

Mode	$T_{page\,scan}$	T_{bf}
R0	11.25 ms	19.66 min
R1	1.28 s	18.64 hrs
R2	2.56 s	37.28 hrs

The Bluetooth specification defines three page scan modes, R0, R1 and R2, which differ only in their page scan intervals. Table 1 lists the average times to find addresses for the three modes of operation. In the best case (mode R0), an address is found in under 10 minutes. However, the majority of Bluetooth devices operate in mode R1. A sample calculation for mode R1 is given by:

$$\begin{aligned} T_{bf} &= \frac{1.28\,s \times f(2^{24},\; 79,\; 80)}{2} \\ &= \frac{1.28\,s \times 104,863\; matrices}{2} \\ &= 18.64\; hours. \end{aligned}$$

4.4 Practical Considerations

The theoretical results presented above must be considered in the context of real-world implementations. The principal issues relate to the target's processing speed, channel interference and overall scalability.

The target's ability to process page packets may not be fast enough to keep up with the speed at which it receives packets from the brute forcing devices. This is a consequence of T_{delay} being significantly shortened. Currently, it is unknown if most Bluetooth devices can process packets rapidly enough to accommodate the new T_{delay}. Of course, T_{delay} can be increased as required, but the overall time required for a brute force search is also increased.

Channel interference can be quite significant in real-world environments. The interference could come from the brute forcing devices themselves or from environmental noise (including other Bluetooth devices). Packet scheduling ensures that the brute forcing devices do not interfere with each other because each device transmits on its own channel. Environmental noise is more difficult to mitigate; future research should attempt to properly model the noise and identify possible mitigation strategies. Since packet scheduling is never able to completely fill all the packet matrices, the potential exists to utilize unused matrix slots for redundant address searches. A trade-off procedure could be developed that balances the number of unique guesses (and total search time) with the number of redundant guesses that could be adjusted based on the noise model.

Finally, with respect to scalability, it may be feasible to use 79 devices, but this may not be practical. It is essential that the model be capable of scaling down to fewer than 79 devices. The time required for a brute force search scales linearly with the number of devices used. When one device is available, everything is done the same way as with 79 devices, except that only one channel is transmitted per address space search. Page packets would then be sent for all addresses on channel 1, then channel 2, etc. Similarly, in the case of two devices, two channels could be utilized simultaneously (and so on).

5. Conclusions

Mobile phones, PDAs, input devices, smart card readers, computers and automobiles have all become Bluetooth-enabled devices. More than 1 billion Bluetooth devices are in use worldwide, and another 13 million devices are shipped each week [9]. The ability to glean information from the devices is a serious concern; due to the ubiquity of Bluetooth devices, this represents a threat to the critical infrastructure.

The non-discoverable mode is intended to serve as a protection mechanism for Bluetooth devices. However, the ability to detect non-discoverable devices threatens security and privacy. Detecting a device is a precursor to tracking its location; once the device is located, other exploits can be launched.

The methodology presented in this paper drastically reduces the time needed for a brute force attack on Bluetooth devices. The combination of collision avoidance, multiple scanning devices and condensed packet timing enables the average device discovery time to be reduced to a mere 20 minutes.

This work opens several avenues for future research. One extension is to verify the theoretical results via a software simulation using a coded extension to IBM's BlueHoc 2.0 [8]. Other extensions include designing a hardware solution for adjusting detection parameters based on environmental variables, refining the packet scheduling technique, and reducing the address search space via a statistical analysis of assigned MAC addresses. Of course, the most pressing research issue is to devise mitigation strategies that will render Bluetooth devices immune to brute force attacks.

Acknowledgements

The authors gratefully acknowledge the support of Professor Gerald Masson and the suggestions provided by Jeff Cua.

References

[1] Bluetooth Special Interest Group, Bluetooth core specification v2.0 + EDR (bluetooth.com/Bluetooth/Learn/Technology/Specifications), 2004.

[2] Bluetooth Special Interest Group, Wireless security (www.bluetooth.com/Bluetooth/Learn/Security), 2007.

[3] C. Gehrmann, Bluetooth security white paper, Bluetooth SIG Security Expert Group (grouper.ieee.org/groups/1451/5/Comparison%20of%20PHY/Bluetooth_24Security_Paper.pdf), 2002.

[4] K. Haataja, Two practical attacks against Bluetooth security using new enhanced implementations of security analysis tools, *Proceedings of the IASTED International Conference on Communication, Network and Information Security*, pp. 13–18, 2005.

[5] J. Hallberg, M. Nilsson and K. Synnes, Bluetooth positioning, *Proceedings of the Third Annual Symposium on Computer Science and Electrical Engineering*, 2002.

[6] M. Herfurt, and C. Mulliner, Remote device identification based on Bluetooth fingerprinting techniques, White Paper (version 0.3) (trifinite.org/Downloads/Blueprinting.pdf), 2004.

[7] IEEE Registration Authority, Public OUI listing (standards.ieee.org/reg auth/oui/index.shtml), 2006.

[8] A. Kumar, BlueHoc: Bluetooth performance evaluation tool (bluehoc.sou rceforge.net).

[9] M. Lev-Ram, Bluetooth's amazing makeover, *Business 2.0*, June 14, 2007.

[10] F. Wong and F. Stajano, Location privacy in Bluetooth, *Proceedings of the Second European Workshop on Security and Privacy in Ad Hoc and Sensor Networks (LNCS 3813)*, R. Molva, G. Tsudik and D. Westhoff (Eds.), Springer-Verlag, Berlin-Heidelberg, pp. 176–188, 2005.

V

INFRASTRUCTURE INTERDEPENDENCIES

Chapter 21

RISK ANALYSIS IN INTERDEPENDENT INFRASTRUCTURES

Yacov Haimes, Joost Santos, Kenneth Crowther, Matthew Henry, Chenyang Lian and Zhenyu Yan

Abstract Human activities are defined and influenced by interdependent engineered and socioeconomic systems. In particular, the global economy is increasingly dependent on an interconnected web of infrastructures that permit hitherto unfathomable rates of information exchange, commodity flow and personal mobility. The interconnectedness and interdependencies exhibited by these infrastructures enable them to provide the quality of life to which we have become accustomed and, at the same time, expose seemingly robust and secure systems to risk to which they would otherwise not be subjected. This paper examines several analytical methodologies for risk assessment and management of interdependent macroeconomic and infrastructure systems. They include models for estimating the economic impact of disruptive events, describing complex systems from multiple perspectives, combining sparse data to enhance estimation, and assessing the risk of cyber attack on process control systems.

Keywords: Risk analysis, systems engineering, interdependent systems

1. Introduction

Critical infrastructure and industry sectors in the United States and abroad are becoming more interdependent, due largely to the increasing integration and application of information technology in business operations such as manufacturing, marketing and throughout the supply chain. New sources of risk to critical infrastructures and national security emerge from the dynamics of large-scale, complex systems that are highly interconnected and interdependent.

Over several years, researchers at the Center for Risk Management of Engineering Systems at the University of Virginia have addressed these emergent risks and their association with interdependent infrastructures by developing

Haimes, Y., Santos, J., Crowther, K., Henry, M., Lian, C. and Yan, Z., 2008, in IFIP International Federation for Information Processing, Volume 253, Critical Infrastructure Protection, eds. E. Goetz and S. Shenoi; (Boston: Springer), pp. 297–310.

new analytical and methodological frameworks for gaining insight into complex systems, their interdependencies, and the means by which risk can be effectively managed by public policy makers and corporate decision makers. The portfolio of analytical and methodological tools spans several operational domains at the macroeconomic, industry and facility levels. The work is founded in the broad conception that interdependent infrastructures are themselves characterized by interdependent facilities that produce, transport and consume commodities that are distributed over physical and cyber networks. Furthermore, at a more abstract level, the commodity production and consumption patterns of industries can be modeled at the macroeconomic level to gain insight into the dynamics of commodity disruptions at the regional or national levels.

This paper highlights several methodologies for modeling, assessing and managing risk in complex, interdependent systems. Also, it discusses the contexts in which the methodologies are useful from a systems perspective. For reasons of space, we focus on analytical methods developed at our center at the University of Virginia. Our purpose is not to discount the contributions of other research groups. Instead, we advocate the use of our models in combination with other approaches to arrive at more robust analyses of system interdependencies.

2. Risk Assessment

Risk assessment is a process for understanding the result of destructive forces acting on systems of interest in terms of the potential adverse consequences and their associated likelihoods. By understanding how fundamental characteristics of a system contribute to its vulnerability to different sources of risk, a risk assessment methodology provides insight into how to manage risk by changing the state of the system to reduce vulnerability, improve resilience and mitigate potential consequences. Kaplan and Garrick [13] posed the risk assessment triplet of questions:

- What can go wrong?
- What is the likelihood?
- What are the consequences?

Ideally, the process of risk assessment fully develops answers to these questions and, thus, holistically captures all the sources of risk and assesses their associated likelihoods and consequences. Current assessment methodologies decompose systems into isolated subsystems for analysis and recombination to create system-level measures [14]. This approach, however, is inadequate for analyzing complex, interdependent systems of systems. Rinaldi and coworkers [18] underscore the need to enhance interdependency analysis. In their words, "it is clearly impossible to adequately analyze or understand the behavior of a given infrastructure in isolation from the environment or other infrastructures; rather, we must consider multiple interconnected infrastructures and their interdependencies in a holistic manner." Current work seeks to address this gap and improve methods for interdependency assessment.

3. Modes of Coupling

Risk assessment and management in large-scale systems requires an understanding of how and to what degree composing subsystems are interdependent. For any given analysis, a subset of particularly relevant interdependencies will tend to dominate the modeling activity, depending on the modeling objectives and the decision maker who will ultimately use the analytical results for developing risk management policies. The role of the modeler is to isolate the relevant interdependencies and build analytical tools to answer the questions posed by decision makers. This section reviews several fundamental modes of coupling, each of which is characterized by different functional and structural relationships. In addition, each mode of coupling is subject to risk in different ways. This is due to the variety of vulnerabilities that can be exploited by potential adversaries; the differing degrees of robustness, resilience and redundancy that provide risk-mitigating mechanisms; and the diverse types and levels of associated consequences.

Physical Coupling Physical coupling between components exists when energy, information or matter is physically transferred from one component to another. In the case of interdependent infrastructures, physical couplings are manifested in the transmission of (i) electricity from distribution networks to electromechanical loads via transformers and transmission lines, (ii) water and gas from distribution infrastructures to points of consumption via plumbing, (iii) materials from one process to another or from one facility to another via plumbing, pipeline or other transport, and (iv) information from one network component to another via the transmission and reception of electromagnetic signals. As such, physical couplings have the capacity to render multiple systems inoperable if critical nodes are disrupted. For example, refineries cannot ship their products to consumers by way of a pipeline if the valves that enable flow from holding tanks to the pipeline are immovably shut. Due to their high degree of criticality, physical couplings tend to be highly robust and are often redundant. However, they are typically neither adaptable nor resilient due to structural and mechanical constraints. Therefore, the risks associated with physical couplings tend to be characterized by significant consequences, yet with relatively low degrees of likelihood. Moreover, risk analysis of physical couplings is typically performed by comparing a set of disruptive scenarios against design or operational specifications.

Logical and Information Coupling Logical couplings provide mechanisms by which coupled systems will conditionally behave based on shared measurements and functional relationships. Information couplings involve mechanisms by which information is physically transferred from one device to another by way of signal transmission. Many infrastructure sectors have become extremely dependent on networked information systems for efficient operations and timely delivery of products and services. The ubiquity of networked information systems in the various infrastructure sectors introduces risks associated with the three main security goals: confidentiality, integrity and availability [1].

As a case in point, the June 1999 rupture of the Olympic Pipeline in Washington State resulted in the leakage of 277,000 gallons of gasoline and the shutdown of the pipeline for more than a year. Tanker trucks and barges were used for gasoline transport during this time, which led to higher retail prices. The National Transportation Safety Board [17] report indicated that the incident was caused by the "slow response" or "non response" of a supervisory control and data acquisition (SCADA) system. From a homeland security perspective, the fact that such an event could have been triggered by a malicious agent is a grave concern, especially since a well-placed attack could cause widespread disruption due to infrastructure interdependencies. Therefore, in order to ensure the security of critical infrastructure sectors, it is imperative not only to understand their inherent physical and economic linkages, but also the information and logical interdependencies associated with networked information systems.

In distributed control systems, logical couplings are implemented in the payloads of data packets; information coupling, on the other hand, is implemented in the routing headers of data packets. In other words, logical coupling is embedded in the messages being communicated, and information coupling is associated with the sequence of relay points in carrying messages from their origins to their destinations. Locally, logical coupling is characterized by the rules embedded in automation software that govern the functionality of controlled processes in response to other processes with which they are interdependent.

Logically coupled systems are by nature prone to risk associated with the propagation of erroneous data or control signals. Using knowledge about the logical coupling in a system, an attacker could potentially disrupt its operation by manipulating measurements or other data used to make control decisions. A well-executed attack of this type would be difficult to detect if the manipulated data is within the normal ranges. For this reason, risk analysis of logically interdependent systems must also take into account the propagation of apparently innocuous manipulations of data and erroneous data.

Inter-Regional Economic Couplings These couplings exist when the production, distribution and consumption of commodities are dictated in part by regional interdependencies defined by physical infrastructures, import and export flows, and relative geographic distances. These couplings are often evident in the aftermath of massively disruptive events such as natural disasters, major plant closures and adversarial geopolitical activity. Typically, inter-regional couplings act to dampen the propagation of disruptions by way of locational redundancies and consumption patterns provided by competitive markets, excess capacities and consumer adaptation in the form of substitution and income effects. In the case of oil and gas infrastructures, geographic couplings were evident in the wake of hurricanes Katrina and Rita, where, immediately following the storms, the supply of crude oil to refineries increased with distance from the epicenter of the storm damage (this observation is based on an analysis of numerous EIA Hurricane Rita situation reports). In other words, supplies of crude from other regions were more available to refineries that were less geographically dependent on Gulf sources.

Risk associated with inter-regional interdependencies is often manifested in economic effects; however, other relationships can create and propagate risk. For example, the water distribution infrastructure poses risk by way of geographic coupling due to the fixed nature of water assets. Hazardous chemical releases in one region threaten consumers in neighboring regions by way of natural hydrology and engineered water distribution infrastructures. Similarly, through geographic coupling, ecological risks associated with oil and gas infrastructures are propagated to regions not directly associated with the infrastructures. Therefore, any analysis of the degree to which communities in the vicinity of accident-prone systems are at risk must take into account geographic interdependencies.

Inter-Sector Economic Couplings These couplings yield insight into how disruptions in one sector will affect dependent sectors. Interdependencies are characterized by the production functions used by the manufacturers of a commodity and the commodities upon which they are dependent for production. Furthermore, as production is driven by demand, disruptions in the marketplace, where commodities are consumed by households, will propagate back to the producers that supply the end products as well as constituent ingredients and other support commodities. A thorough understanding of these interdependencies enables regional and national preparedness planners to better pre-position materials for rapid rehabilitation of critical sectors in the aftermath of a major disaster.

4. Modeling Interdependent Systems

In order to provide answers to the triplet of risk assessment questions, it is necessary to construct models of the systems being considered, potential sources of risk and the couplings to other systems that might provide insights into the dynamics of risk propagation. The models provide descriptions of the state of the system and how changing the system state can reduce the likelihood of adverse consequences, thereby providing a means for evaluating the efficacy of different risk management options. This section describes several methodologies for analyzing interdependent systems: (i) the Input-output Inoperability Model (IIM) [9, 19] and its derivatives, the Multi-Regional IIM (MR-IIM) developed by Crowther [2], and the Dynamic IIM (DIIM) developed by Lian and Haimes [16]; (ii) the Hierarchical Holographic Model (HHM) developed by Haimes [4] and its derivatives, the Adaptive Multi-Player HHM (AMP-HHM) developed by Haimes and Horowitz [7], and the Risk Filtering and Ranking Method (RFRM) developed by Haimes, Kaplan and Lambert [10]; (iii) the Hierarchical Coordinated Bayesian Model (HCBM) being developed by Yan, Haimes and Waller [20]; and (iv) the Network Security Risk Model (NSRM) being developed by Henry and Haimes [11, 12].

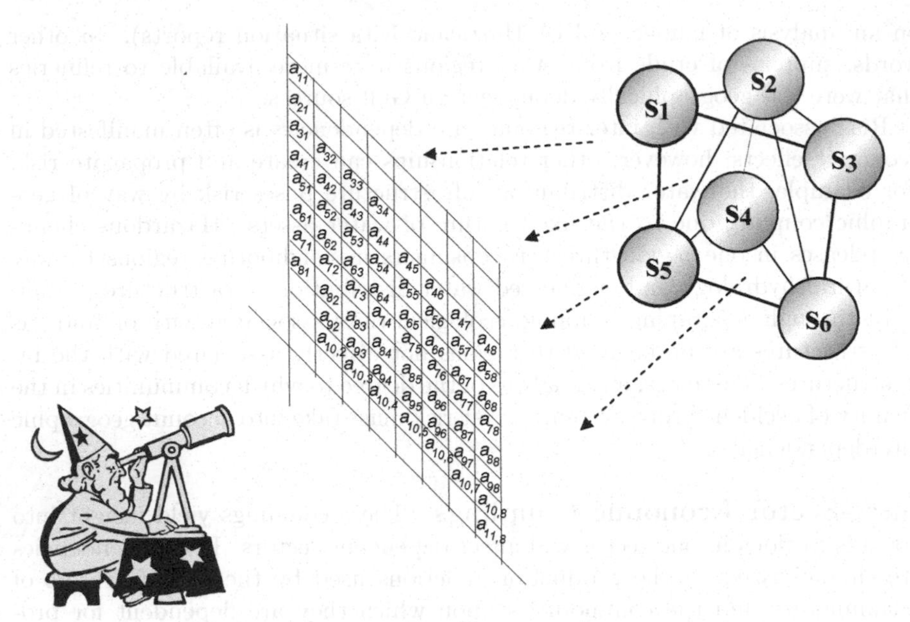

Figure 1. IIM modeling principle as a snapshot of interdependencies.

4.1 Inoperability Input-Output Model

Several models have been proposed to study economic couplings. Input-output analysis, based on the Nobel Prize winning work by Wassily Leontief, is a useful tool for determining the economic ripple effects associated with a disruption in a particular sector of an economy. The Inoperability Input-output Model (IIM) [6, 8, 9, 19] extends the input-output analysis methodology to model the interconnectedness and interactions of different sectors of an economy. Given a perturbation from one or more sectors, IIM estimates the ripple effects measured in terms of industry inoperability and economic loss. For example, a disruption in the oil and gas sector will impact dependent sectors: petroleum and coal products, manufacturing, pipeline transportation, utilities, air transportation, chemical manufacturing and mining. Figure 1 presents IIM as a mapping of sector interdependencies, where s_i, $i = 1, 2, \ldots, 6$ notionally represents a sector with financial, physical and commercial linkages to other sectors (depicted by dotted lines). These linkages are mapped to a series of linear equations whose parameters a_{ij} that populate the matrix quantify the linkages between sectors i and j based on inter-sector transaction data collected and processed by the U.S. Bureau of Economic Analysis.

IIM is an inexpensive, holistic method for estimating economic impacts and sector interdependencies. It can model a nation or regions of contiguous states or counties as an interdependent set of linear causal relationships with perfect communication between all economic sectors. Thus, the resulting effects of a perturbation are estimated uniformly across the entire region without temporal recovery details. The lack of spatial and temporal explicitness in IIM risk analysis produces average estimates across geography and time. These estimates may overlook geographically-concentrated risks and significant cross-regional interdependencies and dynamic effects associated with post-event recovery.

Several extensions to IIM have been developed to address these problems. The Dynamic IIM (DIIM) [16] describes the temporal recovery of sectors after an attack or natural disaster. The concept of resilience is incorporated so that sector improvements can be quantified and managed over time. Like IIM, DIIM shows economic loss and the number of sectors affected when considering different policy options, which directly or indirectly change the recovery dynamics of different sectors as quantified by resilience coefficients in the dynamic model. The Multi-Regional IIM (MR-IIM) [2] estimates higher-order impact propagations across multiple regions and industry sectors by integrating regional models with cross-regional flows gleaned from geospatial databases.

4.2 Hierarchical Holographic Model

The Hierarchical Holographic Model (HHM) [4, 6] provides a construct for capturing the multifarious nature of a complex system to drive subsequent detailed analysis. For example, the HHM in Figure 2 presents a simplified taxonomy of interdependency analysis. The major topics, displayed in the second row of double-lined blocks, describe considerations for interdependency models. The corresponding subtopics cover ranges that may be included in the modeling effort. The value in approaching complex modeling in this way is that questions and analytical activities can be more narrowly and appropriately defined by way of careful system decomposition. Moreover, the reconstruction of the model and analysis follow the reverse process and yield a more comprehensive and useful product for policy analysis and formulation.

The Adaptive Multi-Player HHM (AMP-HHM) [7] and the Risk Filtering and Ranking Method (RFRM) [10], which are derived from HHM, provide more extensive frameworks for collaborative and resource allocation analyses, respectively. In particular, AMP-HHM is a framework for making more structured use of experts with different points of view when analyzing risk in specific assets or classes of systems. In conducting an AMP-HHM exercise, each of several teams of experts is charged with constructing an HHM from its point of view, after which the HHMs are combined to build a richer model of the system of interest. For example, two teams, one representing asset owners and the other representing potential adversaries, might build separate HHMs to capture, from their perspective, the possible paths of attack, methods of defense, etc. The combined HHM serves as a seed for future HHM adaptation on the part of each team. RFRM makes use of HHM development to construct risk scenarios, which are then filtered and prioritized according to their likelihood and consequence assessments to make reasoned judgments for risk management.

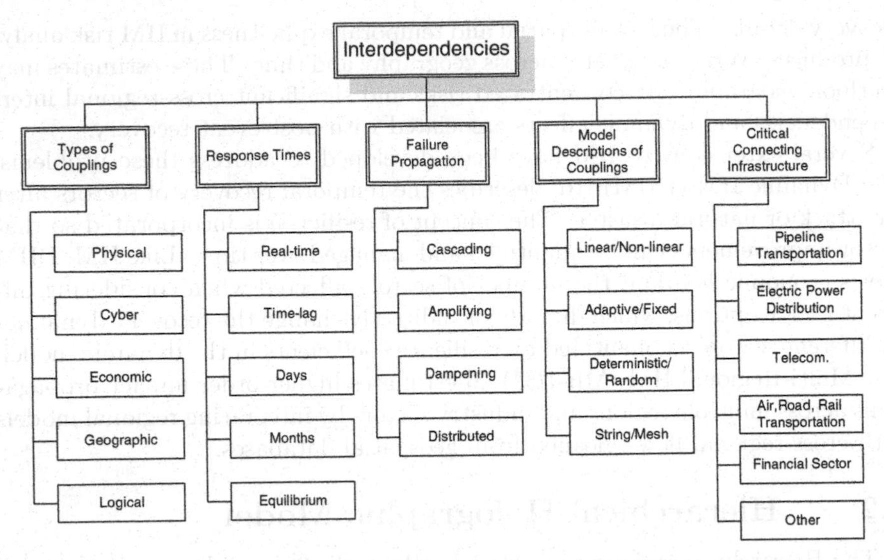

Figure 2. Introductory taxonomy for interdependency analysis.

4.3 Hierarchical Coordinated Bayesian Model

It is well known that when estimating the distributions of parameters with traditional statistical methods (e.g., maximum likelihood estimation), larger data sets give more accurate estimates with smaller confidence intervals and standard errors. However, when statistical methods are applied to small data sets, they produce confidence intervals and errors so large that they are described as unstable. Because problems in risk analysis often involve extreme events, which rarely occur or have never occurred, direct empirical data for these problems are almost always lacking. Therefore, a methodology for analyzing sparse data would be a great asset in risk analysis.

The Hierarchical Coordinated Bayesian Model (HCBM) [20] is a statistical data analysis tool for analyzing sparse data related to extreme events. By decomposing data into multiple perspectives, HCBM can integrate direct data and indirect data from multiple sources and make inferences about extreme event likelihoods and consequences using hierarchical coordination. HCBM reduces the estimation variance and enhances estimation accuracy compared with direct estimation methods.

4.4 Network Security Risk Model

At the facility level, interdependencies exist between system components within the facility, between system components and facility objectives, and between system components and adversary objectives. The Network Security Risk Model (NSRM) [11, 12] was developed to assess the risk of cyber attacks on process control networks in facilities that produce or distribute commodities over large infrastructures. The models are scenario-based to reflect the different attack progressions and consequences arising from different entry points and different attacker objectives. Furthermore, the models are formulated so that risk management policies map directly to the model parameter space, permitting an evaluation of the efficacy of risk management policies as each policy implementation induces a new measure of risk. Dynamic risk assessment results from the sequential implementation of policies. The efficacy of long-term strategies can be evaluated by measuring the average risk due to the state trajectory induced by each risk management strategy.

Several modeling paradigms have been employed, including scenario development, stochastic shortest path models and dynamic risk management. Stochastic shortest path modeling provides a state machine analysis that yields insight into how an attack on an asset might proceed because of the interdependencies between adversary objectives and facility system response. These interactions also provide insight into how attacks might disrupt or disable facility operability as a result of the interdependencies between facility objectives and system components, some or all of which may be disabled by an attack on the facility.

5. Managing Risks in Interdependent Systems

Risk management is a process for developing a set of decisions that place decision makers in a position where they understand and recognize the range of possible consequences and trade-offs for actions in an uncertain environment. The intertwined processes of risk assessment and risk management provide an analysis and decision structure for policy formulation in interdependent systems that accounts for uncertainty and extreme events. The development of risk management policies is guided by the risk management triplet of questions posed by Haimes [5, 6]:

- What can be done and what options are available?
- What are the trade-offs in terms of costs, benefits and risks?
- What are the impacts of current decisions on future options?

The previous section reviewed several methodologies that provide answers to the first two questions. Specifically, the identification of candidate risk management policies can be accomplished through HHM and AMP-HHM, where measures are elicited to mitigate either the likelihood or consequences of disruptive events. Furthermore, RFRM can assist in setting priorities for addressing specific risk scenarios.

Evaluating tradeoffs requires the quantitative assessment of risk for comparison with the costs of risk management. For large-scale economic systems, IIM and its extensions DIIM and MR-IIM provide quantitative estimates of the economic impact stemming from disruptions in commodity production and distribution. NSRM and HCBM provide tools for assessing the risk of cyber attacks on process control networks at a facility level. These risk models provide a means for evaluating the efficacy of candidate risk management policies

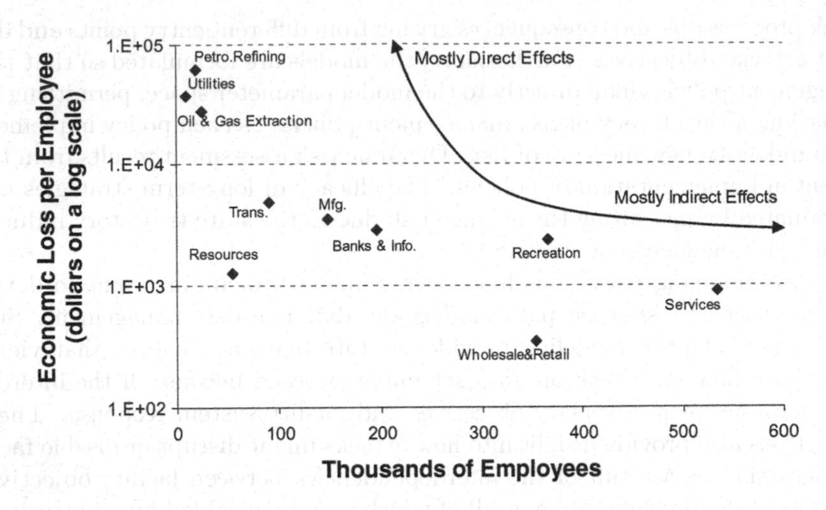

Figure 3. Distribution of direct and indirect impacts across Louisiana economic sectors during the month after Hurricane Katrina.

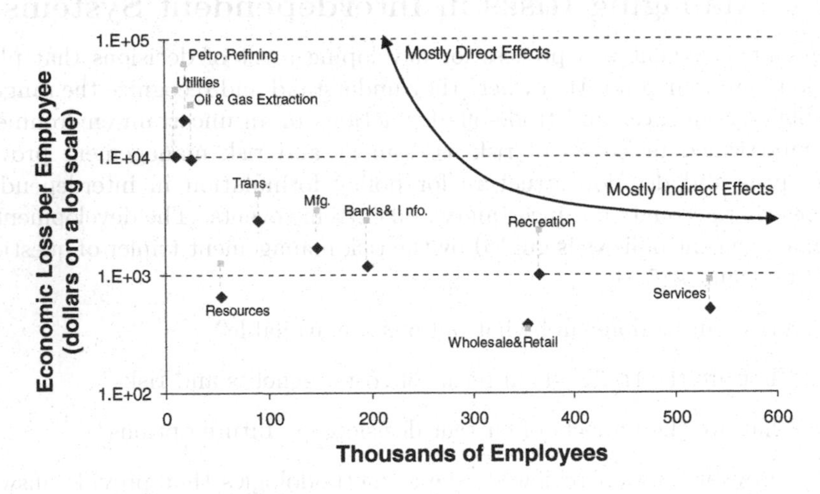

Figure 4. Hypothetical redistribution of impacts from specific preparedness activity.

by producing a measure of risk with and without the policy in place. These assessments, when compared against the estimated cost of risk management policies, permit an evaluation of cost-benefit-risk tradeoffs.

For example, Figures 3 and 4 illustrate the results of an MR-IIM assessment of the benefits of proactive risk management to Gulf Coast residents prior to Hurricane Katrina in 2005 [3]. The analysis also clarifies how cost and benefit could be distributed amongst different interest groups.

Addressing the third question requires a new approach for employing risk models in a dynamic decision framework that evaluates the cost-benefit-risk tradeoffs in the context of constrained future options due to past and present

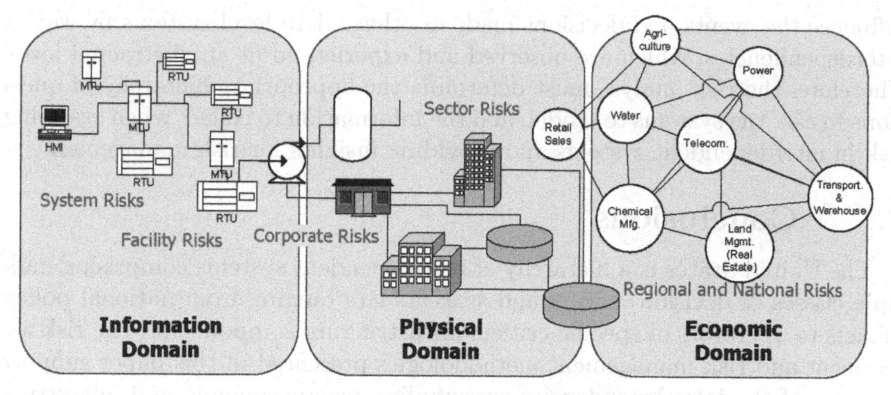

Figure 5. Types and layers of interdependencies.

decisions. A minimax methodology [11, 12], based on the envelope approach to multiobjective optimization [15], has been developed to evaluate the efficacy of risk management policies under scenario uncertainty. For facility-level analysis, NSRM is used as a risk assessment engine to provide measures of risk for evaluation of candidate policies over the course of several decision periods that correspond to corporate resource allocation cycles. Analyses based on minimax envelopes are robust in the face of the uncertainty associated with cyber attack scenarios. At a macroeconomic level, MR-IIM is embedded in the minimax envelope framework to evaluate preparedness and emergency response policies at a regional level.

6. Layers of Interdependencies

Interdependencies may be characterized by different modes of coupling to facilitate modeling and analysis. Similarly, systems can be modeled from different perspectives and abstraction levels to provide analytical support to decision makers at various levels within an organization or system of organizations.

Consider the interdependent systems illustrated in Figure 5. At the lowest level, a process control system manages petrochemical plant operations. This information level connects organizations, protocols, operators and machines based on defined operations, and it allows the vulnerabilities present in any aspect of the system to affect other parts of the system. The middle layer of the diagram illustrates the larger physical and business interconnections. Plants and buildings are physically connected, and products flow between plants and are shared by the plants. At the highest level, plant units interoperate with other businesses, economic sectors and infrastructure sectors.

Risk is experienced and analyzed at each level of this hierarchy according to the objectives and requirements of the respective decision makers. Correspondingly, analyses require hierarchies of models and simulations to understand how micro-level activities affect the behavior of macro-level systems. These interactions are bi-directional in the sense that events in one micro-level system will influence the events and decisions made in other micro-level systems by way of interdependencies, which are observed and experienced at an abstracted level. Therefore, the risk analyst must determine the appropriate hierarchy of questions to ask, the systems to model, and the information to collect when assessing risk in interdependent systems and providing insights for risk management.

7. Conclusions

The United States is a hierarchy of interdependent systems comprising multiple classes of decision makers and stakeholders ranging from national policy makers to operators of specific critical infrastructure components. The risk assessment and risk management methodologies presented in this paper support analyses of the interdependencies surrounding macroeconomic and infrastructure systems. The analyses may be conducted at multiple levels of system resolution and can be integrated to develop hierarchies of insights and recommendations. IIM and its dynamic and multi-regional extensions support analyses of the ripple effects of disruptive events across interdependent macroeconomic sectors and regions. In contrast, NSRM models cyber and logical interconnections among components of a process control network and its infrastructure for the purpose of assessing the risk of cyber attacks on specific facilities.

The many dimensions of interdependencies coupled with the data-sparse nature of extreme risk scenarios make model parameterization a challenge. HHM identifies critical sources of risk; its collaborative extension enables the pooling of parameter estimates from multiple experts along with the associated uncertainties. To complement the parameter estimation and risk quantification processes, HCBM is being developed to integrate multiple databases to improve confidence in statistical inference when data scarcity is a significant factor.

Acknowledgements

This work was partially supported by the Institute for Information Infrastructure Protection (I3P) under Award 2003-TK-TX-0003 from the Science and Technology Directorate of the U.S. Department of Homeland Security. Additionally, we wish to acknowledge the contributions of Bayard Gennert, Grace Zisk and Joanne Foster, who edited versions of this manuscript, and Professors Barry Horowitz and James Lambert, who provided their expertise and insight through discussions and critical reviews.

References

[1] R. Bace, *Intrusion Detection*, MacMillan Technical Publishing, Indianapolis, Indiana, 2000.

[2] K. Crowther, Development and Deployment of the Multiregional Inoperability Input-Output Model for Strategic Preparedness of Interdependent Regions, Ph.D. Dissertation, Department of Systems and Information Engineering, University of Virginia, Charlottesville, Virginia, 2006.

[3] K. Crowther, Y. Haimes and G. Taub, Systemic valuation of strategic preparedness through application of the inoperability input-output model with lessons learned from Hurricane Katrina, to appear in *Journal of Risk Analysis*, 2007.

[4] Y. Haimes, Hierarchical holographic modeling, *IEEE Transactions on Systems, Man and Cybernetics*, vol. 11(9), pp. 606–617, 1981.

[5] Y. Haimes, Total risk management, *Risk Analysis*, vol. 11(2), pp. 169–171, 1991.

[6] Y. Haimes, *Risk Modeling, Assessment and Management*, Wiley, New York, 2004.

[7] Y. Haimes and B. Horowitz, Adaptive two-player hierarchical holographic modeling game for counterterrorism intelligence analysis, *Journal of Homeland Security and Emergency Management*, vol. 1(3) (www.bepress.com/jhsem/vol1/iss3/302), 2004.

[8] Y. Haimes, B. Horowitz, J. Lambert, J. Santos, C. Lian and K. Crowther, Inoperability input-output model for interdependent infrastructure sectors, *ASCE Journal of Infrastructure Systems*, vol. 11(2), pp. 67–92, 2005.

[9] Y. Haimes and P. Jiang, Leontief-based model of risk in complex interconnected infrastructures, *Journal of Infrastructure Systems*, vol. 7(1), pp. 1–12, 2001.

[10] Y. Haimes, S. Kaplan and J. Lambert, Risk filtering, ranking and management framework using hierarchical holographic modeling, *Risk Analysis*, vol. 22(2), pp. 383–398, 2002.

[11] M. Henry, Mimimax Envelopes for Total Cyber Risk Management in Process Control Networks, Ph.D. Dissertation, Department of Systems and Information Engineering, University of Virginia, Charlottesville, Virginia, 2007.

[12] M. Henry and Y. Haimes, A new dynamic risk assessment and management model for supervisory control and data acquisition networks, presented at the *Society of Risk Analysis Annual Meeting*, 2006.

[13] S. Kaplan and B. Garrick, On the quantitative definition of risk, *Risk Analysis*, vol. 1(1), pp. 11–27, 1981.

[14] S. Kaplan, Y. Haimes and B. Garrick, Fitting hierarchical holographic modeling into the theory of scenario structuring and a resulting refinement to the quantitative definition of risk, *Risk Analysis*, vol. 21(5), pp. 807–819, 2001.

[15] D. Li and Y. Haimes, The envelope approach for multiobjective optimization problems, *IEEE Transactions on Systems, Man and Cybernetics*, vol. 17(6), pp. 1026–1038, 1987.

[16] C. Lian and Y. Haimes, Managing the risk of terrorism to interdependent systems through the dynamic inoperability input-output model, *Systems Engineering*, vol. 9(3), pp. 241–258, 2006.

[17] National Transportation Safety Board, Pipeline Accident Report: Pipeline Rupture and Subsequent Fire in Bellingham, Washington, June 10, 1999, Washington, DC, 2002.

[18] S. Rinaldi, J. Peerenboom and T. Kelly, Identifying, understanding and analyzing critical infrastructure interdependencies, *IEEE Control Systems*, vol. 21(6), pp. 11–25, 2001.

[19] J. Santos and Y. Haimes, Modeling the demand reduction input-output inoperability due to terrorism of interconnected infrastructures, *Risk Analysis*, vol. 24(6), pp. 1437–1451, 2004.

[20] Z. Yan, Y. Haimes and M. Waller, Hierarchical coordinated Bayesian model for risk analysis with sparse data, presented at the *Society of Risk Analysis Annual Meeting*, 2006.

Chapter 22

ANALYSIS OF INTERDEPENDENCIES BETWEEN ITALY'S ECONOMIC SECTORS

Roberto Setola

Abstract The infrastructure sectors of developed countries have direct and indirect interdependencies. These interdependencies make national infrastructures extremely prone to the cascading effects of perturbations or failures. A negative event that reduces the operability of one infrastructure sector rapidly spreads to other sectors and back to the original sector in a feedback loop, amplifying the negative consequences throughout the national economy. This paper uses the Input-output Inoperability Model (IIM) to analyze interdependencies in Italy's economic sectors. Economic data from 1995 to 2003 provided by the Italian National Institute of Statistics (ISTAT) is used to investigate the interdependencies in 57 sectors. The results demonstrate that interdependencies between economic sectors have an overall increasing trend, which can dramatically enhance the negative consequences of any sector perturbation or failure.

Keywords: Italy, economic sectors, interdependencies, input-output inoperability model

1. Introduction

During the last two decades, for a variety of economic, social, political and technological reasons, significant changes have been seen in the organizational, technical and operational frameworks of practically every infrastructure sector in developed countries. Indeed, to reduce costs, improve quality and efficiency, and provide innovative services, infrastructure sectors have become highly interoperable. This enables infrastructure owners and operators to share common services and resources, and to better focus their efforts on their core businesses.

But this interoperability has increased the interdependencies between infrastructure components and sectors. Sector interdependence makes the entire

Setola, R., 2008, in IFIP International Federation for Information Processing, Volume 253, Critical Infrastructure Protection, eds. E. Goetz and S. Shenoi; (Boston: Springer), pp. 311–321.

national infrastructure prone to the cascading effects of perturbations or failures. A negative event that reduces the operability of one infrastructure sector can rapidly spread to other sectors and back to the original sector in a feedback loop, amplifying the negative consequences throughout the national economy.

Haimes and colleagues [3] proposed the Input-output Inoperability Model (IIM) to quantify the global impact of negative events in interdependent sectors. Their approach is based on the well-known theory of market equilibrium developed by Nobel laureate Wassily Leontief [5]. IIM uses Leontief's theoretical framework, but instead of considering how the provision of goods or services by one firm influences the levels of production of other firms, it focuses on the degradation of operability throughout a networked system. To this end, IIM introduces the notion of "inoperability," which is defined as the inability of a system to perform its intended functions.

IIM helps analyze how a given amount of inoperability of one component influences other components in a network. It is been used to evaluate the impact of a high-altitude electromagnetic pulse (HEMP) on the U.S. economy [2], to investigate economic losses due to a reduction in air transportation services [9], to study the recovery process in the aftermath of Hurricane Katrina [6], and to analyze the extent of cascading failures in a highly networked modern hospital compared with one that uses less information and communications technology [10]. IIM has also been extended to account for the spread of faults and the presence of uncertain data (using fuzzy numbers) [7].

This paper uses IIM to analyze interdependencies in Italy's economic sectors based on data from the period 1995 to 2003 provided by the Italian National Institute of Statistics (ISTAT). The results demonstrate that interdependencies between economic sectors have an overall increasing trend. Thus, any reduction in the operability of one sector – due to malicious acts, accidents or natural disasters – can cascade through all sectors, dramatically increasing the negative consequences to the country's entire economy.

2. Input-Output Inoperability Model

The Input-output Inoperability Model (IIM) is a theoretical framework for analyzing how interdependencies existing between different sectors of a complex society can propagate the spread of degradation [1, 3]. The framework requires each sector to be modeled as an atomic entity, whose level of operability depends on external causes as well as on the availability of "resources" supplied by other entities. An event (e.g., a failure) that reduces the operational capability of the i-th sector may induce degradations in other sectors that require goods or services produced by the i-th sector. The degradations may propagate to other sectors in a cascade effect, and can even exacerbate the situation in the i-th sector due to the presence of feedback loops.

IIM models this phenomenon using a level of inoperability associated with each sector. The inoperability of the i-th sector is expressed using the variable $x_i \in [0, 1]$. Note that $x_i = 0$ means that the i-th sector is fully operable, while $x_i = 1$ means that the sector is completely inoperable.

IIM evaluates the impact of external events that produce a given amount of inoperability using the dynamic equation:

$$\mathbf{x}(k+1) = \mathbf{x}(k) + \mathbf{K}\left[(\mathbf{\Lambda} - \mathbf{I})\,\mathbf{x}(k) + \mathbf{c}(k)\right] \quad (1)$$

where $\mathbf{x} \in [0,\ldots,1]^n$ and $\mathbf{c} \in [0,\ldots,1]^n$ are vectors specifying the levels of inoperability and external failure, respectively, that are associated with each of the n sectors considered in the scenario. $\mathbf{A} \in \mathcal{R}^{n\times n}$ is the matrix of Leontief coefficients and $\mathbf{K} \in \mathcal{R}^{n\times n}$ is the resilience matrix, which represents the capability of each sector to absorb the negative effects of a perturbation and its ability to restore the nominal conditions after a failure.

Matrix $\mathbf{\Lambda}$ can be decomposed into its main-diagonal and off-diagonal elements:

$$\mathbf{\Lambda} = diag\,(\mathbf{\Lambda}) + \mathbf{A} \quad (2)$$

where the first term models the restoring dynamics while matrix $\mathbf{A}$ models the functional dependencies existing between different sectors. Specifically, each entry a_{ij} of matrix $\mathbf{A}$ represents the influence of the inoperability of the j-th sector on the inoperability of the i-th sector. Obviously, when $a_{ij} < 1$, the i-th sector suffers a level of inoperability smaller than that exhibited by the j-th sector. On the other hand, when $a_{ij} > 1$, there is an amplification in the inoperability level.

Limiting the study to impact analysis, we can omit the first term in Equation 2. Then, assuming $\mathbf{K} = \mathbf{I}$, as proposed in [1], Equation 1 reduces to:

$$\mathbf{x}(k+1) = \mathbf{A}\mathbf{x}(k) + \mathbf{c} \quad (3)$$

where $a_{ii} = 0 \;\forall\; i = 1,\ldots,n$.

To evaluate the dependency of each sector with respect to the others, we introduce a "dependency index," which is defined as the sum of the Leontief coefficients along a single row:

$$\delta_i = \sum_{j\neq i} a_{ij} \qquad \text{(row summation)} \quad (4)$$

The dependency index δ_i measures the resilience of the i-th sector. When the index is less than 1, the i-th sector preserves some working capabilities (e.g., because of stocks, buffers, etc.) despite supplier inoperability. On the other hand, when $\delta_i > 1$, the operability of the i-th sector may be completely nullified even when some of its supplier sectors have residual operational capabilities.

The influence that a sector exercises on the entire system is expressed by its "influence gain," i.e., the column sum of the Leontief coefficients:

$$\rho_j = \sum_{i\neq j} a_{ij} \qquad \text{(column summation)} \quad (5)$$

A large value of ρ_j means that the inoperability of j-th sector induces significant degradation to the system. When $\rho_j > 1$, the negative effects (in terms of inoperability) induced by cascading phenomena on the other sectors are amplified. The opposite occurs when $\rho_j < 1$.

Note that parameters defined in Equations 4 and 5 represent one-step-ahead estimations, and the overall consequences have to be evaluated based on a steady-state solution to Equation 3. When the constraints on x_i are satisfied, the closed form solution is given by:

$$\overline{\mathbf{x}} = \mathbf{G}^{-1}\mathbf{c} \qquad \text{where } \mathbf{G} = (\mathbf{I} - \mathbf{A}). \tag{6}$$

The entries g_{ij} of $\mathbf{G} \in \mathcal{R}^{n \times n}$ represent the consequences (in terms of induced inoperability) that an external event affecting the j-th sector has on the i-th sector. The term g_{ii} represents the amplification of inoperability registered by the i-th sector due to feedback with respect to the amount of inoperability directly induced by the external cause c_i.

3. Economic Formulation of IIM

The most difficult task when applying IIM is to estimate the Leontief coefficients. In [1] the coefficients were evaluated using U.S. economic statistics provided by the Bureau of Economic Analysis. This paper follows a similar approach using data on the Italian economy supplied by ISTAT [4].

ISTAT recently released the input-output tables for the Italian economy during the period 1995 to 2003. The data was grouped into 59 sectors in accordance with the European Sec95 Standard [4]. We use the ISTAT data, but restrict our analysis to 57 sectors because two sectors (Extraction of Uranium and Thorium Minerals, and Domestic Services) have no dependencies and influences on the other sectors. The ISTAT data included the **U** (*Use*) and **S** (*Supply*) matrices for each year from 1995 to 2003. These commodity-per-industry matrices represent the amount of goods used (**U**) and services provided (**S**) by each economic sector expressed in millions of Euros.

Due to the symmetry of the ISTAT data, the main-diagonal elements of the *Use* and *Supply* matrices correspond to the commodities directly used and provided by each sector, respectively. The off-diagonal elements capture the functional dependencies existing between sectors.

Over the 1995–2003 period, the *Supply* matrix has uniform increments for the main-diagonal entries and the total volumes. The *Use* matrix, which is illustrated in Figure 1, shows considerable increments for the off-diagonal elements, which confirms the increased relevance of cross-sector relationships.

Starting with the ISTAT data and using the technique described in [1], we calculated the Leontief coefficients for the $\mathbf{\Lambda}$ matrix. The normalized matrices $\mathbf{U}^*$ and $\mathbf{S}^*$ were first computed using the equations:

$$u_{ij}^* = \frac{u_{ij}}{\sum_{i=1}^{n} u_{ij}} \qquad s_{ij}^* = \frac{s_{ij}}{\sum_{i=1}^{n} s_{ij}}. \tag{7}$$

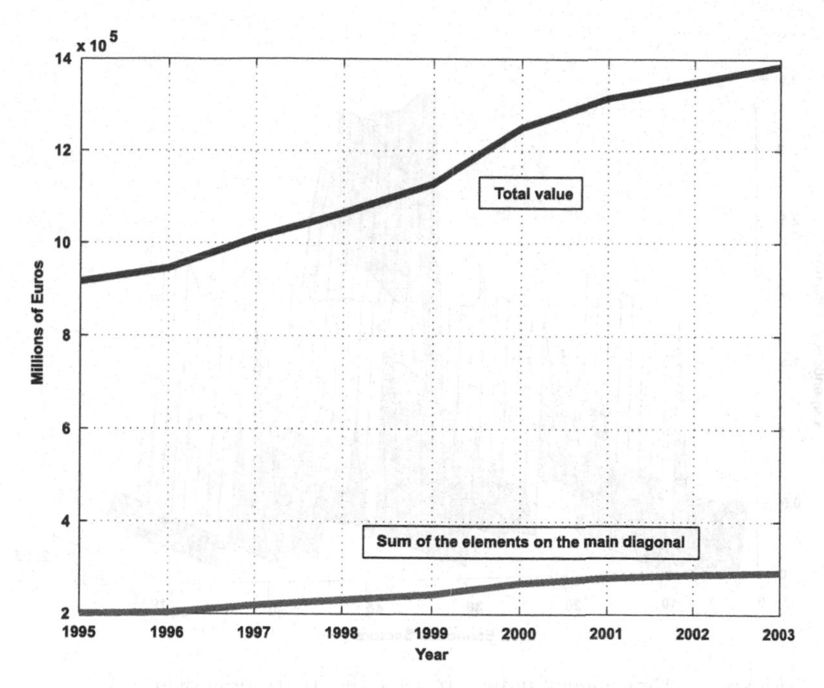

Figure 1. *Use* matrix values (1995 to 2003).

The Leontief coefficients were then calculated using the normalized matrices:

$$\mathbf{\Lambda} = \left(\mathbf{S}^{*T}\right)\mathbf{U}^{*}. \tag{8}$$

Having computed the Leontief coefficient matrix in Equation 8, the matrix $\mathbf{A}$ was obtained by nullifying the elements on the main diagonal.

Figure 2 shows the dependency indices for the 57 sectors in the Italian economy. The sectors that are more dependent on other sectors have larger dependency index values. The most dependent sectors are Building (Id = 33), Wholesale Trade (Id = 35), Retail Trade (Id = 36) and Public Administration (Id = 51). Although there are no dramatic variations in the indices for different sectors over the time period, the values are slightly reduced for the Building (Id = 33) and Wholesale Trade (Id = 35) sectors, while the values for the other sectors show increments. Note that 18 sectors (19 sectors in 2003) have dependency index values close to 1 or greater. This means that the operability levels of these sectors largely depend on external resources; therefore, they can have dramatic degradations due to domino effects.

On the other hand, the influence gain values (Figure 3) are very stable from 1995 to 2003. The largest values are assumed by the Wholesale Trade (Id = 35), Retail Trade (Id = 36) and Terrain Transportation (Id = 38) sectors, with peak values ranging from 1.2 to 1.6. Moreover, 19 sectors (20 sectors in 2003) have influence gain values greater than 1. This implies that the consequences,

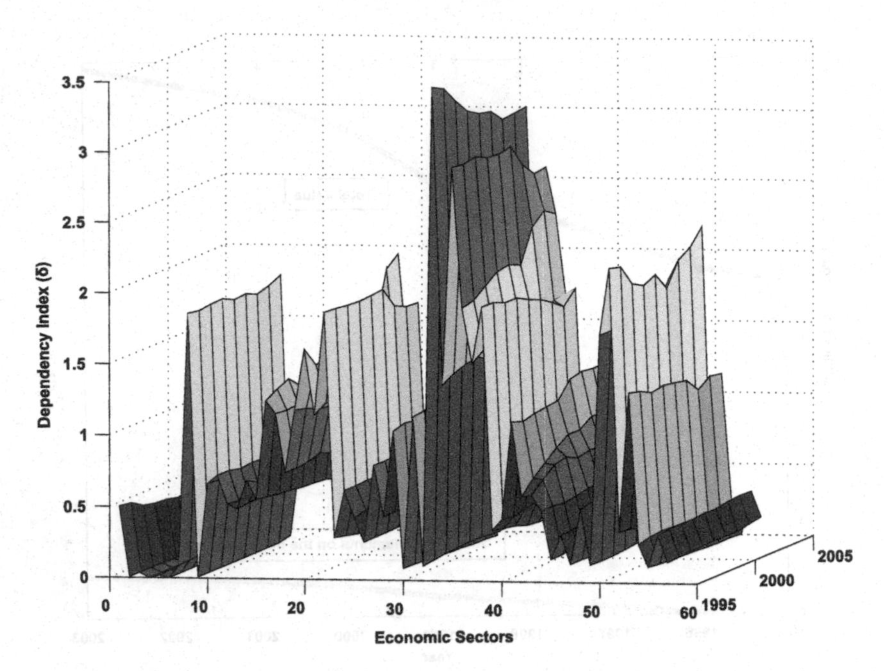

Figure 2. Dependency indices (δ_i) for the 57 sectors (1995 to 2003).

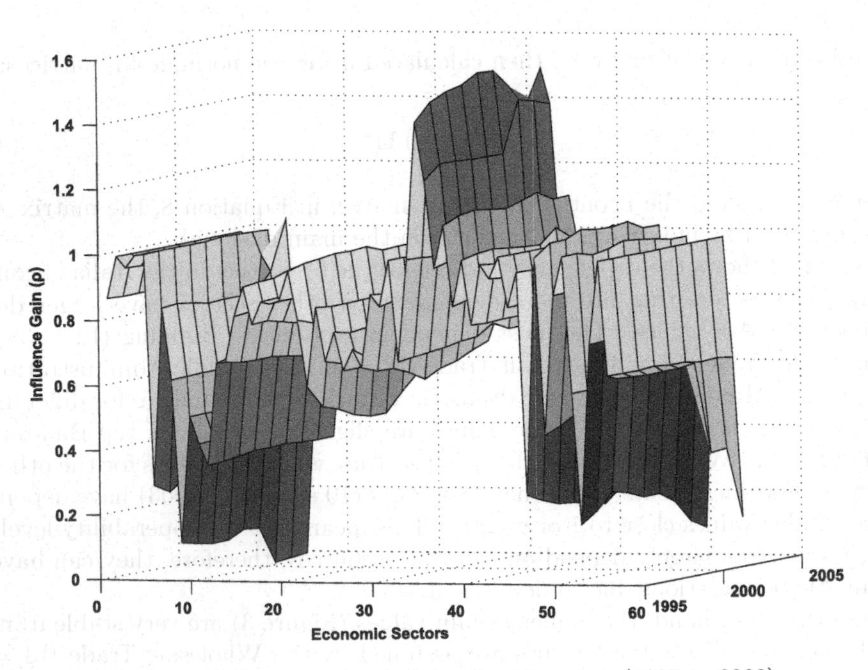

Figure 3. Influence gains (ρ_i) for the 57 sectors (1995 to 2003).

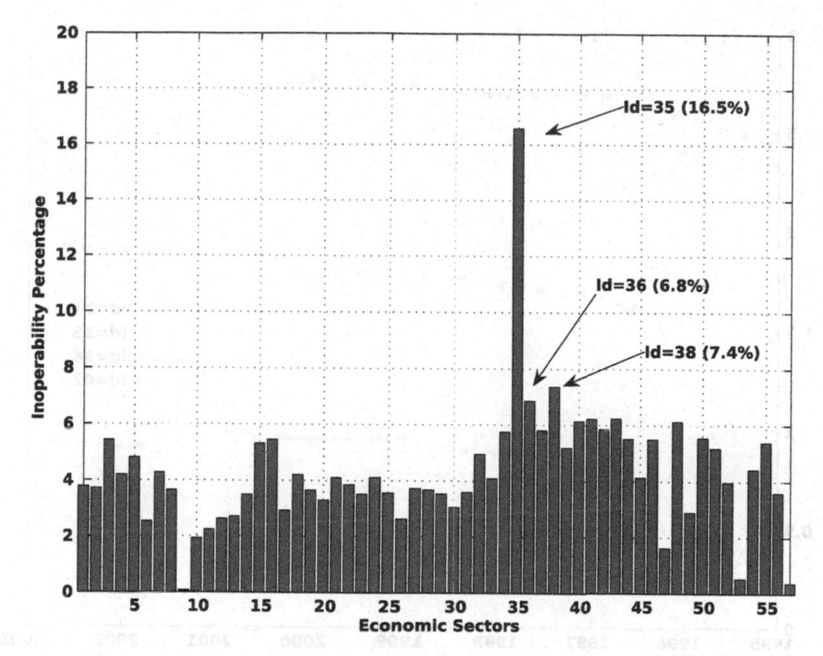

Figure 4. Sector inoperability at steady state given an initial perturbation (2003).

in terms of inoperability, induced on the entire system are more than double those that are produced directly by external causes.

It is important to note that the indices discussed above provide only one-step-ahead information. Therefore, to estimate the overall consequences induced by external failures, it is necessary to solve Equation 3.

4. Application of Dynamic IIM

Equation 3 above must be solved to estimate the overall system impact of an external event that reduces the operability of a single sector. If we assume that all the variables are constrained in their domains of definition, then Equation 6 provides the corresponding steady-state solution in closed form.

Figure 4 shows the levels of inoperability attained by the various sectors when the Wholesale Trade sector (Id = 35) is externally perturbed to reduce its operability by 10%. As noted above, due to cascade effects, this perturbation affects almost every sector quite substantially: 19 sectors have levels of inoperability greater than 5% and only four sectors have levels of operability greater than 98%. Moreover, due to feedback effects, the level of inoperability of the Wholesale Trade sector grows to 16.5%. The most degraded sectors, as predicted by their large dependency index values, are Terrain Transportation (Id = 38) and Retail Trade (Id = 36), which reach inoperability levels of 7.4% and 6.8%, respectively. This analysis clearly demonstrates that sector interdependencies can significantly affect the overall consequences of a negative event.

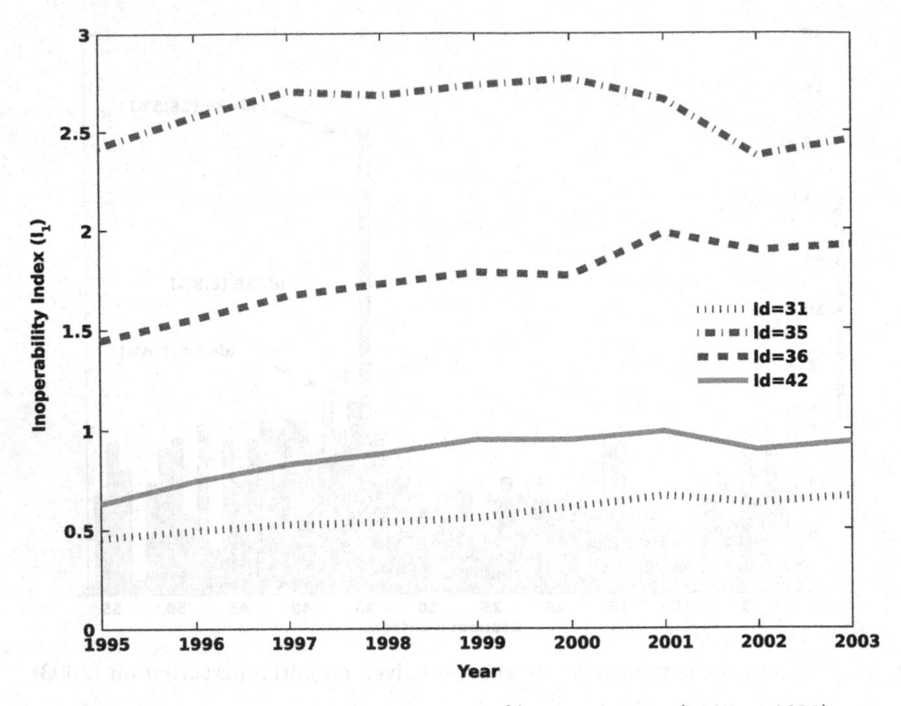

Figure 5. Overall inoperability index for a 10% perturbation (1995 to 2003).

A global index is required to codify the impact of a perturbation on the entire system. The simplest index, which we call the "overall inoperability index," is defined as:

$$I_1^{year}(I_d = \alpha) = \sum_{i=1}^{57} \overline{x}_i. \tag{9}$$

The index is the sum of the inoperability levels (at steady state) over all sectors for a given year given a perturbation of I_d with amplitude α.

Figure 5 shows that the same perturbation produces a different effect for each year in the period from 1995 to 2003. The same initial perturbation of 10% is applied to each sector (Energy (Id = 31), Wholesale Trade (Id = 35), Retail Trade (Id = 36), and Post and Communications (Id = 42)). Note that the index increases uniformly during the period. In the years when interdependencies between sectors increase, the entire system becomes much more fragile. An abrupt change in the trend is seen in 2002, most likely due to the impact of the 9/11 attacks on the world economy.

The overall inoperability index provides a global measure, but it gives the same weight to every economic sector, discounting the relative importance of each sector in the national economy. To address this issue, we define an index,

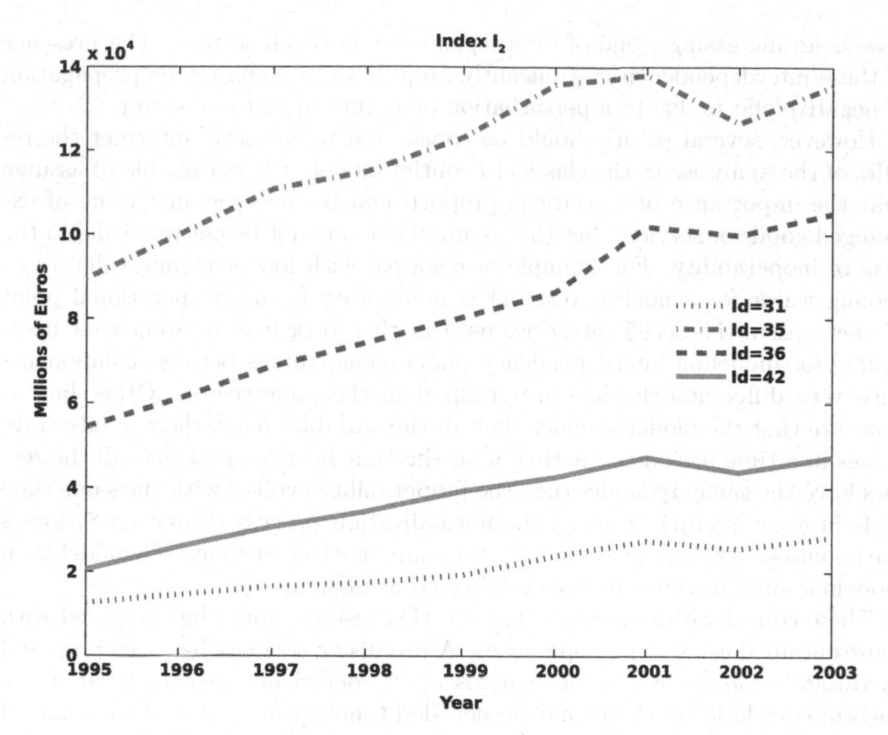

Figure 6. Weighted inoperability index for a 10% perturbation (1995 to 2003).

which is normalized with respect to the economic value of each sector. This "weighted inoperability index" is defined as:

$$I_2 = \sum_{i=1}^{57} \left[\left(\sum_j s_{ij} \right) \overline{x}_i \right]. \tag{10}$$

The index weights the inoperability of each sector based on the sum of corresponding row in the *Supply* matrix.

Figure 6 shows the weighted inoperability index for each year in the period from 1995 to 2003. Once again, the data is generated by applying the same initial perturbation of 10% to each sector (Energy (Id = 31), Wholesale Trade (Id = 35), Retail Trade (Id = 36), and Post and Communications (Id = 42)). The trend in the overall level of inoperability is the same as in Figure 5. Note also that the same results are obtained when the inoperability of a sector is weighted according to the sum of its corresponding row in the *Use* matrix.

5. Conclusions

The Input-output Inoperability Model (IIM) is a powerful approach for investigating the interdependencies existing between various sectors of a national economy. Our study, which analyzes data from Italy's 57 economic sectors, reveals an increasing trend of interdependence between sectors. The presence of these interdependencies significantly amplifies the system-wide propagation of negative effects due to a perturbation or failure in just one sector.

However, several points should be considered to correctly interpret the results of the analysis. In the classical Leontief model, it is reasonable to assume that the importance of a sector is proportional to the economic value of exchanged goods or services, but this assumption may not be entirely valid in the case of inoperability. For example, a resource with low economic value (e.g., cooling water for a nuclear reactor) is mandatory from an operational point of view. Also, the Sec95 categories used in this work may be somewhat inadequate for modeling interdependency phenomena; this is because components with very different behaviors are grouped in the same sector. Other limitations are that the model assumes that all the variables reach their steady-state values in a time period compatible with the time horizon, and that all the sectors have the same dynamics (i.e., the inoperability evolves with the same time scale in every sector). Finally, the normalization process (Equation 8) forces the Leontief coefficients to be no greater than one; this prevents the model from modeling amplifications in inoperability transmission.

These considerations suggest that the IIM results should be compared with those obtained using other approaches. A promising strategy has been proposed by Rosato, *et al.* [8], where the "macroscopic" coefficients are calculated on the basis of correlations existing among detailed topological models of each pair of sectors. Another approach is to obtain values for the coefficients by conducting interviews with experts from each sector. The comparison of the results of these and other approaches is the subject of our future research.

Acknowledgements

The author would like to thank Angela Forte for her assistance in interpreting the ISTAT economic data, and Stefano De Porcellinis for his advice and support of this research effort.

References

[1] Y. Haimes, B. Horowitz, J. Lambert, J. Santos, C. Lian and K. Crowther, Inoperability input-output model for interdependent infrastructure sectors I: Theory and methodology, *ASCE Journal of Infrastructure Systems*, vol. 11(2), pp. 67–79, 2005.

[2] Y. Haimes, B. Horowitz, J. Lambert, J. Santos, C. Lian and K. Crowther, Inoperability input-output model for interdependent infrastructure sectors II: Case studies, *ASCE Journal of Infrastructure Systems*, vol. 11(2), pp. 80–92, 2005.

[3] Y. Haimes and P. Jiang, Leontief-based model of risk in complex interconnected infrastructures, *Journal of Infrastructure Systems*, vol. 7(1), pp. 1–12, 2001.

[4] Istituto Nazionale di Statistica, Tavole di dati delle risorse e degli impieghi (o tavole supply e use), Rome, Italy, 2006.

[5] W. Leontief, *The Structure of the American Economy 1919–1939*, Oxford University Press, Oxford, United Kingdom, 1953.

[6] D. Newman, B. Nkei, B. Carreras, I. Dobson, V. Lynch and P. Gradney, Modeling of infrastructure interdependencies, *Proceedings of the Third International Conference on Critical Infrastructures*, 2006.

[7] S. Panzieri and R. Setola, Failures in critical interdependent infrastructures, to appear in *International Journal of Modeling, Identification and Control*, 2007.

[8] V. Rosato, F. Tiriticco, L. Issacharoff, S. Meloni, S. De Porcellinis and R. Setola, Modeling interdependent infrastructures using interacting dynamical networks, to appear in *International Journal of Critical Infrastructures*, 2007.

[9] J. Santos, Inoperability input-output modeling of disruptions to interdependent economic systems, *Journal of Systems Engineering*, vol. 9(1), pp. 20–34, 2006.

[10] R. Setola, Availability of healthcare services in a network-based scenario, *International Journal of Networking and Virtual Organizations*, vol. 4(2), pp. 130–144, 2007.

Chapter 23

THE ISE METAMODEL FOR CRITICAL INFRASTRUCTURES

Felix Flentge and Uwe Beyer

Abstract The implementation-service-effect (ISE) metamodel is a general framework for modeling critical infrastructures that can integrate several different perspectives. The metamodel has a technical basis and also provides the abstractions needed for risk assessment and management of critical infrastructures in complex environments. ISE supports an iterative modeling approach that continuously refines models based on new information. By focusing on the services provided by critical infrastructures, the approach bridges the gap between the business and engineering views of critical infrastructures. The technical realization of services is described in the implementation layer of ISE; the effects of the successful (or unsuccessful) delivery of services are described in the effect layer. A sound mathematical foundation provides the basis for analyses ranging from topological evaluations of dependency structures to statistical analyses of simulation results obtained using agent-based models.

Keywords: Infrastructure modeling, interdependencies, ISE metamodel

1. Introduction

Modern societies rely to a large extent on the undisturbed availability of services provided by critical infrastructures. The massive use of information and communications technology, and deregulation and globalization trends have led to the emergence of new dependencies between infrastructures while aggravating existing dependencies. The increased complexity of critical infrastructures as a whole raises security issues that cannot be addressed appropriately using a narrow view of a single infrastructure. Some of the problems include cascading, escalating and common cause infrastructure failures [11], which require new approaches for risk assessment and management. Models must be constructed to describe complex dependencies and support detailed analysis. Furthermore,

Flentge, F. and Beyer, U., 2008, in IFIP International Federation for Information Processing, Volume 253, Critical Infrastructure Protection, eds. E. Goetz and S. Shenoi; (Boston: Springer), pp. 323–336.

simulation methods must be developed to understand the dynamic behavior of critical infrastructures and evaluate risk management solutions.

Several approaches have been proposed for modeling and simulating dependencies between infrastructures [1, 2, 4, 13–15]. Most approaches focus on dependencies in only a small portion of the overall infrastructure, e.g., Aspen-EE [3], which examines the economic aspects of the electric power infrastructure. Wolthusen [16] uses geographic information systems (GISs) to identify and analyze geographical dependencies. Hopkinson, *et al.* [8] employ simulations to investigate interdependencies between the telecommunications and electric power infrastructures. However, the modeling and simulation of complex dependencies between infrastructures is still in its infancy. While several commercial simulators are available for analyzing single infrastructures, there is a lack of systems that can handle multiple infrastructures or address the technical and human aspects.

The implementation-service-effect (ISE) metamodel described in this paper is a general modeling framework that combines viewpoints from different sectors and professions. It provides a strong technical basis as well as abstractions needed for modeling and analyzing risk in critical infrastructures.

2. Critical Infrastructure Modeling

Interdependencies between critical infrastructures are due to many non-linear factors that can vary dramatically from case to case. Furthermore, there are several levels of possible interactions among the components of large, complex infrastructure networks. Reliable models for analysis and simulation can only be developed by taking real data into consideration. This leads to a "chicken and egg problem." Data availability is a limiting factor [9]. Infrastructure providers are generally unwilling to release technical data before risks have been identified (if at all); but risk analysis cannot proceed without appropriate data. The ISE model of critical infrastructures offers a solution by providing an iterative modeling approach that starts with an abstract model and publicly-available data. General problems can be discovered using this data, which helps refine the initial model. The iterative approach progressively refines the new model at each step based on new data.

Another problem encountered when modeling complex interrelationships is the "particular answers dilemma." This problem arises because system behavior is often dependent on low-level technical details. A small change in a technical detail can have a significant impact on overall system behavior. However, it is difficult – if not impossible – to model a system down to its lowest level. In fact, some of the data needed for system modeling may not even be observable. One way to deal with this problem is to develop taxonomies of dependencies and develop general strategies for dealing with classes of dependencies. A modeling approach with a sound mathematical background can facilitate the identification and description of dependency classes. This problem is closely related to that of choosing the right abstraction level. If the level of abstraction is too high, trivial results are obtained. If the level is too low, too much data is involved and it may not be possible to identify the underlying structures.

The analysis that follows the modeling process is also somewhat problematic. Few, if any, general methods exist for analyzing complex infrastructures and their dependencies (most methods only deal with abstract networks). The lack of common modeling and analysis methodologies also makes it difficult to evaluate models and compare results. The ISE metamodel provides a sound mathematical foundation to build a variety of models with the same underlying structure. Systems of dependent critical infrastructures can be described in a well-defined manner and analysis can proceed using well-established methods.

Critical infrastructure protection is a problem that straddles several disciplines. According to Dunn [6], critical infrastructure protection involves at least four different perspectives: a system-level technical perspective, a business perspective, a law-enforcement perspective and a national security perspective. Since it is difficult to reconcile different views, most models only focus on a single perspective. The ISE model, on the other hand, integrates the technical and business perspectives while accommodating the national security perspective.

3. Implementation-Service-Effect Metamodel

Infrastructure dependencies must be modeled at the right level of abstraction to facilitate analysis. The ISE metamodel supports an iterative approach that starts with limited data and an abstract model, which is refined in a step-by-step manner to permit more accurate analysis. The approach also facilitates the modeling of a critical infrastructure from different viewpoints and the integration of the different viewpoints to produce a single coherent model. A critical infrastructure may be modeled from a business perspective, which focuses on business continuity, risk analysis and risk mitigation. Alternatively, one may construct a detailed physical model, which provides insight into the critical infrastructure at the engineering level and helps determine weak points in the design.

The gap between a business model and a technological model is bridged by introducing a service layer. This layer models the services produced by infrastructures along with their mutual dependencies. Since all services are directly or indirectly based on some technical implementation, a natural mapping exists from the implementation layer to the service layer. On the other hand, because services are either products sold by private companies or are at least guaranteed by public sector (or quasi public sector) providers, the delivery of services and the quality of delivery have an effect on the service provider's business and overall approval. Thus, a natural mapping exists from services to effects. The focus on services guarantees that relevant functions and effects of real systems are taken into account, leading to a practical model.

An ISE model comprises several ISE submodels that describe different infrastructures or different components. The submodels contain three types of elements: implementation elements, services and effect factors. A complete ISE model is created by combining several submodels, describing their dependencies

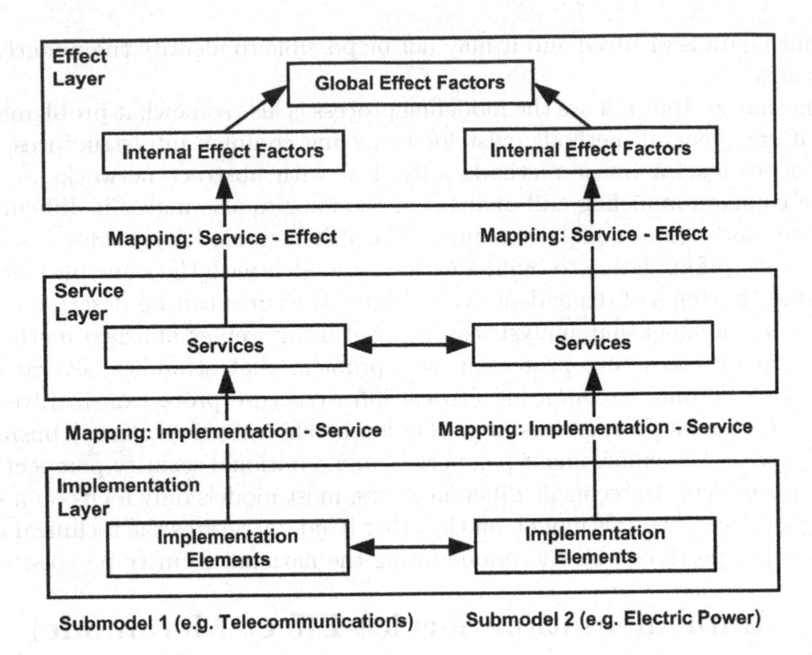

Figure 1. Structure of an ISE model with two submodels.

(within and across submodels) and adding global effect factors. The resulting model has three layers: implementation layer, service layer and effect layer. The relationships between these layers are described by two mappings, the implementation-service mapping and the service-effect mapping. The general structure of an ISE model with two submodels is shown in Figure 1. Note that dependencies between elements of different submodels can only appear within the same layer. Dependencies in one submodel always appear within the same layer or in a top-down manner; therefore, they can be modeled as directed graphs.

The following sections describe each layer in detail. A formalism that facilitates the analysis of ISE models is also introduced.

3.1 Service Layer

The purpose of critical infrastructures, regardless of their ownership, is to provide services in a reliable manner. These services are delivered to the end-customer, to another critical infrastructure (public services) or to some other part of the same infrastructure (internal services). Services can be viewed at various levels of abstraction. One approach is to describe services in the form of trees. For example, in the electric power infrastructure, the abstract service "delivery of electricity to the end-consumer" could be subdivided into "generation of electricity," "transmission of electricity from the generation level

Table 1. Infrastructure services.

Telecommunications	Electric Power
Fixed Line Telephony	Generation
GSM	Transmission
SMS	Distribution
DSL	Maintenance
GPRS	Control

to the distribution level," and "delivery of electricity from the distribution level to the end-consumer."

The reliability of service delivery depends on various aspects of a critical infrastructure (physical equipment, organization, human resources, etc.) and to some extent on the reliability of other services. For example, the delivery of communications services depends on the availability of electricity. An entire network of services is exchanged between different infrastructures and end-consumers. Therefore, it is extremely important to ensure the reliable delivery of services. Of course, protecting physical equipment and securing information technology assets are important, but critical infrastructure protection encompasses much more than just these tasks:

> "More often than not, the actual objects of protection interests are not static infrastructures, but rather the services, the physical and electronic (information) flows, their role and function for society, and especially the core values that are delivered by the infrastructures. This is a far more abstract level of understanding of essential assets, with a substantial impact on how we should aim to protect them [6]."

The service layer is the central layer of an ISE model. In the case of private companies, services are products that are usually accompanied by service level agreements (SLAs). In the case of (quasi) governmental infrastructure providers, there may be SLAs as well as other kinds of regulations. Therefore, services should be easily identifiable as they provide a good starting point for modeling. Internal services usually can be identified by examining the internal structure and organization of enterprises. Table 1 lists examples of services in the telecommunications and electric power infrastructures.

Of course, services may be considered at different levels of abstraction. For example, in one case, the delivery of electricity might be modeled as a service; in another, the delivery of electricity to a specific customer. In general, what should be considered as a single service depends on the purpose of the model. If the focus is on dependencies between infrastructures, one would most certainly distinguish between services delivered to other infrastructures and services delivered to the general public.

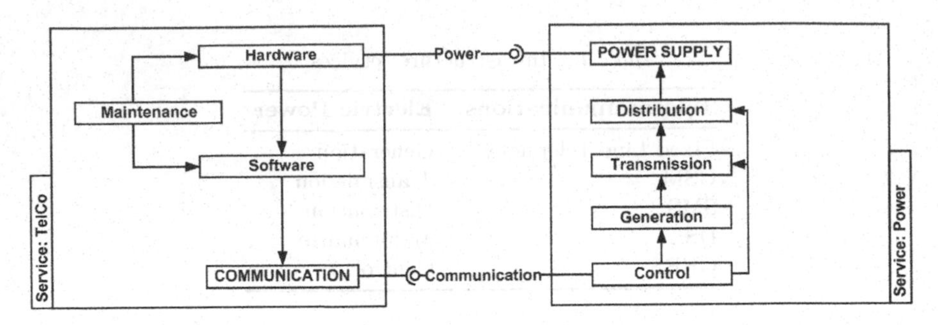

Figure 2. Service layers.

Formally, the service layer S of an ISE model consists of internal services IS^i and public services PS^i of all submodels i:

$$\begin{aligned} S &= \bigcup_{i=1,\ldots,n} (IS^i \cup PS^i) \\ IS^i &= IS^i_1, \ldots, IS^i_k \\ PS^i &= PS^i_1, \ldots, PS^i_l \end{aligned}$$

The dependencies between services in an ISE model are described by a service dependency graph $SDG = (S, DS)$ with $DS \subseteq S \times S$. The vertices of a service dependency graph are services and the edges are dependencies between services. Edges are directed according to the direction of influence: an edge (a, b) exists when b is dependent on a.

The ISE model requires certain constraints to be satisfied by dependencies. Using graph theoretic notation, we define the set of predecessors of a vertex a in a graph $G = (V, E)$ as:

$$N_G^-(a) = \{a_i | \, (a_i, a) \in E\}$$

The constraints on a service dependency graph are formally defined as:

$$N_{SDG}^-(a) \subseteq IS^k \cup \bigcup_{i=1,\ldots,n} PS^i \quad \text{for all } a \in IS^k \cup PS^k$$

Note that a service of a submodel k cannot be dependent on the internal services of other submodels.

Figure 2 shows an example of a simple service topology with dependencies between the telecommunications and electric power infrastructures. The vertices of the service dependency graph represent public services (all capitals) and internal services (upper and lower case). The edges describe how services are dependent on other services (i.e., "subservices" that guarantee the proper operation of dependent services). Interdependencies exist between infrastructures when there are mutual exchanges of services between the infrastructures.

3.2 Implementation Layer

Services are realized by technical or organizational measures in the implementation layer. This is done by offering "implementation elements" to the service layer. The implementation layer is very heterogeneous because it encapsulates individual details of infrastructures. It includes physical equipment as well as all that is needed to provide services (e.g., human operators, organizational measures and procedures). Often, three elements are distinguished as in the U.S. National Infrastructure Protection Plan of 2006 [5]: physical (physical components that produce and deliver infrastructure services), cyber (hardware, software and information used to monitor and control physical components), and human (people who monitor and control the infrastructure and service delivery).

Table 2. Implementation elements.

Telecommunications	**Electric Power**
Base Stations	Generators
Base Station Controllers	Transmission Lines
Network Operation Control Centers	Distribution Lines
Operators	Consumers
Communication Links	Control Centers

Table 2 provides examples of items included in the implementation layer. There is almost no limit to the level of detail. However, if one starts with the service layer, it is usually sufficient to model the implementation elements at the subsystem level and not at the component level.

The implementation layer comprises the implementation elements IE^i of all submodels i:

$$I = \bigcup_{i=1,\ldots,n} IE^i$$

$$IE^i = IE^i_1, \ldots, IE^i_j$$

Once again, dependencies are modeled as a directed graph, the implementation dependency graph $IDG = (I, DI)$ with $DI \subseteq I \times I$. There are no special constraints on this graph; each implementation element may depend on any other implementation element. However, dependencies between submodels in this layer usually have counterparts in the service layer.

Figure 3 shows the implementation layer of an electric power infrastructure and a supporting telecommunications infrastructure along with the dependencies between them. The implementation layer of the electric power infrastructure includes a control center, substation, generators, transmission lines and distribution lines. The telecommunications infrastructure is modeled more abstractly with human resources, four communication units and a communication

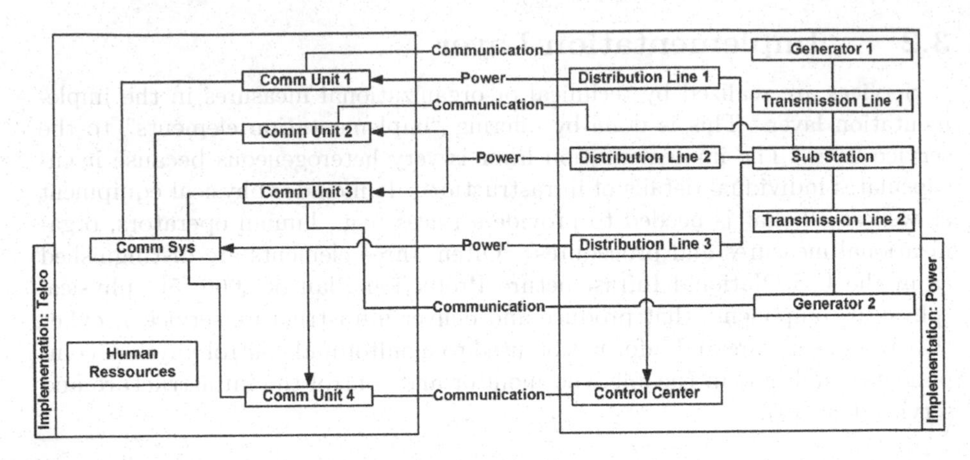

Figure 3. Implementation layer.

system that connects the communication units. The telecommunications equipment is powered by distribution lines. In turn, the communication system and the communication units enable communications between the control center and other system components (generators, substation). The communications are necessary to monitor and control the generation and transmission of electricity.

3.3 Effect Layer

The effect layer, which lies on top of the service layer, describes the effects of the successful or unsuccessful delivery of services. Effects may be expressed in terms of revenues or profits/losses, risk, affected people, public opinion, etc. Internal effect factors describe effects specific to a submodel. Global effect factors combine the internal effect factors of submodels to describe the effects of multiple infrastructures. Formally, the effect layer E of an ISE model consists of the global effect factors EF^* and the effect factors EF^i of all submodels i:

$$E = EF^* \cup \bigcup_{i=1,\ldots,n} EF^i$$

$$EF^* = EF_1^*, \ldots, EF_l^*$$

$$EF^i = EF_1^i, \ldots, EF_k^i$$

The dependencies between effect factors are given by the effect dependency graph $EDG = (E, DE)$ with $DE \subseteq E \times E$. The only constraint on the effect dependency graph is:

$$N_{EDG}^-(a) \subseteq EF^k \quad \text{for all } a \in EF^k$$

i.e., internal effect factors cannot depend on internal effect factors of other infrastructures or on global effect factors.

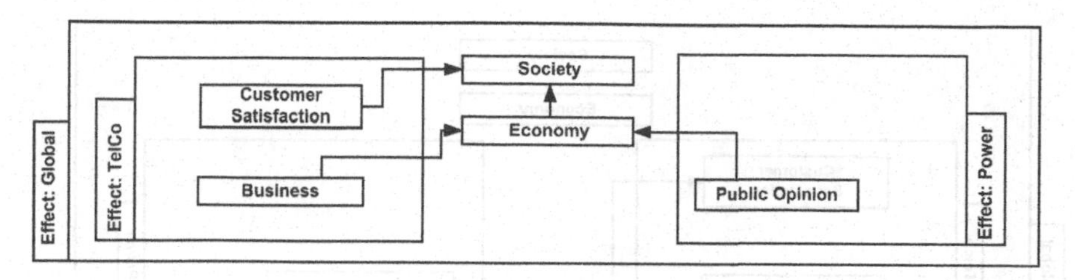

Figure 4. Effect layer based on services.

The effect layer is important from the business point of view, especially for performing business impact analyses and risk assessments. Furthermore, existing approaches for modeling risk in the context of critical infrastructures (e.g., [12]) may be integrated. Figure 4 shows a simple example of an effect layer.

3.4 Implementation-Service Dependencies

Services are based on the implementation layer: several implementation elements have to interoperate correctly to provide a service. These dependencies are described by the implementation service dependency graph $ISDG = (I \cup S, DIS)$ with $DIS \subseteq I \times S$. Edges in $ISDG$ always originate from an implementation element to a service, i.e., only dependencies between the two layers, not within each layer, are considered in the graph. An additional constraint is that the dependencies have to be in the same submodel k:

$$N^{-}_{ISDG}(a) \subseteq IE^k \quad \text{for all } a \in IS^k \cup PS^k$$

Figure 5 shows examples of vertical dependencies in a telecommunications infrastructure and an electric power infrastructure. The service Hardware in the telecommunications service layer is dependent on technical equipment in the implementation layer. Also, Maintenance is dependent on Human Resources. The electric power infrastructure has more dependencies. The service Control is dependent on the implementation element Control Center that may include technical equipment along with human operators. The services Generation, Transmission and Distribution are dependent on their specific elements in the implementation layer.

3.5 Service-Effect Dependencies

Internal effects are based on the states of the services of the respective infrastructures. These dependencies are described by the service effect dependency graph $SEDG = (S \cup E', DSE)$ with $DSE \subseteq S \times E'$ and $E' = E \setminus E^*$, i.e., only internal effect factors are considered. Once again, dependencies exist between the two involved layers, not within the layers. The following condition ensures

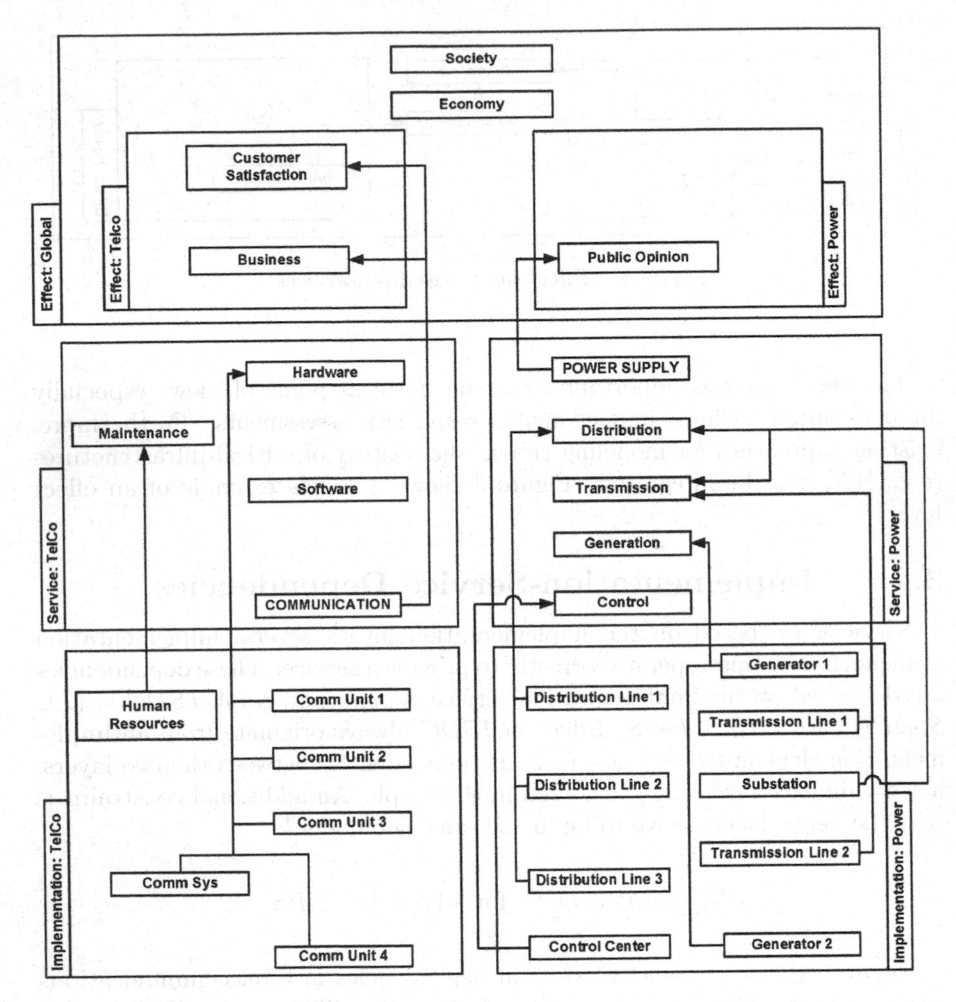

Figure 5. Vertical dependencies between submodels.

that dependencies appear only within the same submodel k:

$$N^{-}_{SEDG}(a) \subseteq PS^k \cup IS^k \quad \text{for all } a \in EF^k$$

Figure 5 shows effects that are dependent on services in the telecommunications and electric power infrastructures. Note that different effects can be based on the same service, e.g., communication service influences company revenue as well as consumer satisfaction.

4. Iterative Modeling and Analysis

The ISE metamodel supports an iterative modeling approach: the process starts with an abstract topological model of the service layer, which is iteratively refined by including additional layers and/or submodels. The elements in each layer and the associated dependencies are described in more detail in each refinement step. We distinguish between four principal types of models based on their elements and dependencies: topological models, Boolean models, numerical models and simulation models. Different models may be combined; moreover, based on the nature of the elements and dependencies in a specific model, it is possible to perform different types of analyses.

4.1 Topological Models

A topological model only uses information contained in the five ISE model graphs. For example, the service dependency graph and the implementation dependency graph may be analyzed for cycles, which could indicate possible problems in infrastructure recovery after a disruption. Also, the implementation service dependency graph and the service effect dependency graph can be used to express the relationships between paths in one layer and paths in another layer. For example, a path in the service layer should have a counterpart in the implementation layer and vice versa:

$$\text{Let } (i_1, s_1), (i_2, s_2) \in ISDG:$$

$$\text{Path } (i_1, \ldots, i_2) \text{ exists in } IDG \quad \Leftrightarrow \quad \text{Path } (s_1, \ldots, s_2) \text{ exists in } SDG$$

Statements of this kind can be used to check the consistency of a model and to relate dependencies in one layer to elements and dependencies in another layer. Moreover, taxonomies of dependencies can be constructed, general structures can be detected and strategies for dealing with problematic dependencies can be devised.

4.2 Boolean Models

Topological models indicate where possible problems may arise; however, topological analyses can only make very limited statements about the nature of these problems. For example, in the implementation layer in Figure 3, the failure of Generator 1 may not have severe consequences if Generator 2 is working and produces enough electricity to supply all the loads connected to the distribution lines. Such a situation is modeled more easily using a Boolean model. Each element has a Boolean value, which indicates whether the element is working or not. A Boolean expression is used to calculate the Boolean value of an element based on the values of other elements. Since cycles may exist in the dependency structure, a notion of time must be introduced. In particular, the value of an element at time t is calculated based on values at time $t-1$. For example, the Boolean value of a substation at time t, $b_t(\text{substation})$, depends on the Boolean values of two transmission lines at time $t-1$:

$$b_t(\text{substation}) = b_{t-1}(\text{transmission line 1}) \text{ OR } b_{t-1}(\text{transmission line 2})$$

Boolean models support "what-if" analyses. Different initial settings can be assumed and the effects of failures can be investigated. Boolean expressions for various elements can be adjusted to account for different conditions. For example, if one generator cannot produce enough electricity for the distribution system, the OR operator in the expression above could be changed to an AND. However, Boolean models cannot handle time-based effects such as the slow degradation or recovery of a service. More complex, numerical models are required for these and other situations.

4.3 Numerical Models

A wide range of numerical models have been proposed. The simplest models extend the Boolean model by replacing Boolean values with real numbers and Boolean expressions with mathematical functions. For example, numerical values could be assigned to service inoperability levels as in Leontief-based models [7, 10]. More complex numerical models use vectors to specify properties of elements (e.g., quality of service (QoS) parameters). Some models employ differential equations to model temporal aspects. Others use random variables or fuzzy variables to account for objective or subjective uncertainty, respectively.

4.4 Simulation Models

When conducting a simulation, each infrastructure element can be modeled as an autonomous agent with specific attributes and behavior. The behavior of an agent depends on its own state as well as on the states of other agents that influence it; agents influence other agents in the direction of the dependencies. Generally, the complexity of a simulation model decreases from the implementation layer to the effect layer. Implementation elements may be modeled and simulated using existing tools. Usually, services are described by real number values (for availability, quality of service, etc.); effects (e.g., profits/losses, revenues, risk, etc.) are also described by real number values. Time-based simulations may be conducted with different initial values and for different scenarios (e.g., changes in service consumption or failures of certain elements). The systematic manipulation of factors in the implementation layer allows the sampling of sets of service qualities at the service layer. Based on these values, the corresponding effect factors may be evaluated. Producing sample sets of possible effects as a function of infrastructure elements facilitates the application of a range of statistical analysis methods.

5. Conclusions

The ISE metamodel is a novel approach for modeling critical infrastructures along with their dependencies and interdependencies. ISE supports an iterative modeling approach that starts with an abstract model and publicly-available data, and continuously refines the model at each iteration based on new information; this addresses problems posed by the unavailability of data and the particular answers dilemma. The metamodel also provides a framework that combines viewpoints from different sectors and professions. By focusing on the services provided by critical infrastructures, ISE bridges the gap between the business and engineering views of critical infrastructures and accommodates the national security perspective. Furthermore, the sound mathematical foundation provided by the ISE metamodel supports analyses ranging from topological evaluations of dependency structures to statistical analyses of simulation results obtained using agent-based models.

Drawing from our experience with the telecommunications and electric power infrastructure modeling effort, we are currently creating detailed models of multiple critical infrastructures using the ISE metamodel. An integrated simulation environment called SimCIP based on the ideas presented in this paper is also under development.

Acknowledgements

This research was undertaken in the context of the IRRIIS Project, which is partially funded by the European Community's Sixth Framework Programme.

References

[1] M. Amin, Restructuring the electric enterprise: Simulating the evolution of the electric power industry with intelligent adaptive agents, in *Electric Pricing in Transition*, A. Faruqui and K. Eakin (Eds.), Kluwer, Norwell, Massachusetts, pp. 51–64, 2002.

[2] M. Baran, R. Sreenath and N. Mahajan, Extending EMTDC/PSCAD for simulating agent-based distributed applications, *IEEE Power Engineering Review*, vol. 22(12), pp. 52–54, 2002.

[3] D. Barton and K. Stamber, An Agent-Based Microsimulation of Critical Infrastructure Systems, Technical Report SAND2000-0808C, Sandia National Laboratories, Albuquerque, New Mexico, 2000.

[4] E. Casalicchio, R. Setola and S. Tucci, An overview of modeling and simulation techniques for critical infrastructures, *Proceedings of the Twelfth IEEE International Symposium on Modeling, Analysis and Simulation of Computer and Telecommunications Systems*, pp. 630–633, 2004.

[5] Department of Homeland Security, National Infrastructure Protection Plan, Washington, DC (www.dhs.gov/xlibrary/assets/NIPP_Overview.pdf), 2006.

[6] M. Dunn, Understanding critical information infrastructures: An elusive quest, in *International CIIP Handbook 2006 – Volume II*, M. Dunn and V. Mauer (Eds.), Center for Security Studies, ETH Zürich, Zürich, Switzerland, pp. 27–53, 2006.

[7] Y. Haimes and P. Jiang, Leontief-based model of risk in complex interconnected infrastructures, *Journal of Infrastructure Systems*, vol. 7(1), pp. 1–12, 2001.

[8] K. Hopkinson, X. Wang, R. Giovanini, J. Thorp, K. Birman and D. Coury, EPOCHS: A platform for agent-based electric power and communication simulation built from commercial off-the-shelf components, *IEEE Transactions on Power Systems*, vol. 21(2), pp. 548–558, 2006.

[9] S. Panzieri, R. Setola and G. Ulivi, An agent-based simulator for critical interdependent infrastructures, *Proceedings of the Second International Conference on Critical Infrastructures*, 2004.

[10] D. Reed, S. Chang and T. McDaniels, Modeling of infrastructure interdependencies, *Proceedings of the Third International Conference on Critical Infrastructures*, 2006.

[11] S. Rinaldi, J. Peerenboom and T. Kelly, Identifying, understanding and analyzing critical infrastructure interdependencies, *IEEE Control Systems*, vol. 21(6), pp. 11–25, 2001.

[12] J. Saunders, A dynamic risk model for information technology security in a critical infrastructure environment, in *Risk-Based Decision Making in Water Resources X*, Y. Haimes, D. Mosher and E. Stakhiv (Eds.), American Society of Civil Engineers, Reston, Virginia, pp. 23–39, 2003.

[13] D. Schoenwald, D. Barton and M. Ehlen, An agent-based simulation laboratory for economics and infrastructure interdependency, *Proceedings of the American Control Conference*, vol. 2, pp. 1295–1300, 2004.

[14] W. Tolone, D. Wilson, A. Raja, W. Xiang, H. Hao, S. Phelps and E. Johnson, Critical infrastructure integration modeling and simulation, in *Intelligence and Security Informatics (LNCS 3073)*, H. Chen, R. Moore, D. Zeng and J. Leavitt (Eds.), Springer, Berlin-Heidelberg, Germany, pp. 214–225, 2004.

[15] W. Tolone, D. Wilson, A. Raja, W. Xiang and E. Johnson, Applying Cougaar to integrated critical infrastructure modeling and simulation, *Proceedings of the First Open Cougaar Conference*, 2004.

[16] S. Wolthusen, GIS-based command and control infrastructure for critical infrastructure protection, *Proceedings of the First IEEE International Workshop on Critical Infrastructure Protection*, pp. 40–47, 2005.

Chapter 24

MULTIGRAPH DEPENDENCY MODELS FOR HETEROGENEOUS INFRASTRUCTURES

Nils Svendsen and Stephen Wolthusen

Abstract The identification and mitigation of interdependencies among critical infrastructure elements such as telecommunications, energy and transportation are important steps in any protection strategy and are applicable in preventive and operative settings. This paper presents a graph-theoretical model and framework for analyzing dependencies based on a multigraph approach and discusses algorithms for automatically identifying critical dependencies. These algorithms are applied to dependency structures that simulate the scale-free structures found in many infrastructure networks as well as to networks augmented by random graphs.

Keywords: Infrastructure interdependencies, multigraph models, simulation

1. Introduction

One of the defining characteristics of critical infrastructures is the level of interdependence among individual infrastructure components such as energy, telecommunications and financial services. While the interdependencies act on different timescales and may exhibit buffering characteristics (e.g., in the case of emergency power supplies) or delays in the effects (e.g., an inability to schedule transportation services after a communication system failure), direct and transitive (often also circular interdependencies) can be identified in a large number of cases.

An area of particular interest in critical infrastructure protection research is the avoidance and analysis of widespread effects on large parts of the population and economies, which may, for example, result from cascading and circular effects among infrastructure components – as exemplified by the August 2003 power outages in the northeastern U.S. and Canada and the November 2006 power outages throughout much of continental Europe. While elaborate

Svendsen, N. and Wolthusen, S., 2008, in IFIP International Federation for Information Processing, Volume 253, Critical Infrastructure Protection, eds. E. Goetz and S. Shenoi; (Boston: Springer), pp. 337–350.

models, also incorporating physical characteristics and effects and with predictive capabilities exist for many of the individual critical infrastructure services (e.g., for electrical power grids at the national and transnational levels), it is desirable to also investigate larger-scale interactions among multiple infrastructure sectors. Specific questions include cascading effects that would occur if one infrastructure component becomes unavailable for an extended period, along with possible circular effects that might inhibit or at least severely impede the resumption of regular infrastructure services. This, however, requires the development of models that exhibit acceptable computational complexity and at the same time provide adequate modeling capabilities. The level of detail that can be incorporated in such models is of necessity a limited one compared to sector-specific models. However, in many cases the basic identification of the existence of interdependencies and critical dependency paths among infrastructure components already provides valuable information, which may be investigated further using more refined modeling processes.

This paper presents a model framework based on a simple graph-theoretic model that forms the basis of several models of increasing capabilities (and computational complexity) in which additional constraints are introduced and infrastructure characteristics such as the ability to buffer resources are added. Connectivity-based interdependency models, however, can provide important insights into the vulnerabilities introduced by interlinking infrastructure components, particularly if the interdependency characteristics differ significantly as in the case of power and telecommunication networks discussed in this paper.

The remainder of this paper is structured as follows: Section 2 summarizes the basic multigraph model, which forms the foundation for a family of models with increasing expressiveness and computational complexity. Section 3 provides several simplified case studies, which are intended to be illustrative and hence represent abstractions, not actual network structures. These model instances are further illustrated through simulation results described in Section 4. Section 5 briefly reviews related research. Section 6 provides conclusions and an outlook on current and future research.

2. Multigraph Model

Interactions among infrastructure components and infrastructure users are modeled in the form of directed multigraphs, which can be further augmented by response functions defining interactions between components. In the model, the vertices $\mathcal{V} = \{v_1, \ldots, v_k\}$ are interpreted as producers and consumers of m different types of services. A single vertex can act as a producer and consumer at the same time. If a node is not able to generate a needed type, the node is dependent on some other node delivering this service. Such a dependability has the dependability type d_j, which is chosen from the set $\mathcal{D} = \{d_1, \ldots, d_m\}$.

Pairwise dependencies between nodes are represented with directed edges, where the head node is dependent on the tail node. The edges of a given infrastructure are defined by a subset $\mathcal{E}$ of $\boldsymbol{\mathcal{E}} = \{e_1^1, e_2^1, \ldots, e_{n_1}^1, e_1^2, \ldots, e_{n_m}^m\}$, where $n_1, \ldots, n_m$ are the numbers of dependencies of type $d_1, \ldots, d_m$, respectively, and e_i^j is the edge number i of dependency type j in the network. A dependency between nodes v_a and v_b is uniquely determined by $e_i^j(v_a, v_b)$. In addition to the type, two predicates $C_{\text{Max}}(e_i^j(v_a, v_b)) \in \mathbb{N}_0$ and $C_{\text{Min}}(e_i^j(v_a, v_b)) \in \mathbb{N}_0$ are defined for each edge. These values represent the maximum capacity of the edge $e_i^j(v_a, v_b)$ and the lower threshold for flow through the edge, respectively.

The first studies of large complex networks evaluated the robustness of infrastructure attacks based on static failures [6, 9]. This is accomplished by removing a certain percentage of nodes in the network and estimating how the performance or connectivity of the network is affected by the induced failure. In dependency networks, such as the power distribution network and the telephony transport network, the breakdown of a node may cause cascading failures and have other time-dependent effects on the networks that are only detectable via a dynamic approach. We assume a discrete time model with the system in an initial state at time $t = 0$. Let $r_a^j(t) \in \mathbb{Z}$ be the amount of resource j produced in node v_a at time t. We define $D(t)$ to be a $k \times m$ matrix over $\mathbb{Z}$ describing the amount of resources of dependency type j available at the node v_a at time t. It follows that the initial state of D is given by

$$D_{aj}(0) = r_a^j(0). \tag{1}$$

For every edge in $\mathcal{E}$ a response function

$$\begin{aligned} R_i^j(v_a, v_b, t) &= f(D_{a1}(t-1), \ldots, D_{am}(t-1), \\ &\qquad C_{\text{Max}}(e_i^j(v_a, v_b)), C_{\text{Min}}(e_i^j)(v_a, v_b)) \end{aligned} \tag{2}$$

is defined, which determines the i-th flow of type j between the nodes v_a and v_b. The function f w.l.o.g. is defined as a linear function mapping $\mathbb{Z} \times \cdots \times \mathbb{Z} \times \mathbb{N}_0 \times \mathbb{N}_0$ to $\mathbb{N}_0$ (see below for a rationale for limiting f to linear functions), and may contain some prioritizing scheme over i and v_b. As seen from Equation 2, a single-step model with one state memory has been chosen, as we are currently not concerned with long-term feedback, although the model naturally extends to longer-term state retention.

Given the responses at time t, the available resources in a node v_a at time t in any node are given by

$$D_{aj}(t) = \sum_{i,s | e_i^j(v_s, v_a) \in \mathcal{E}} R_i^j(v_s, v_a, t). \tag{3}$$

A node v_a is said to be functional at time t if it receives or generates the resources needed to satisfy its internal needs, i.e., $D_{aj}(t) > 0$ for all dependency types j which are such that $e_i^j(v_b, v_a) \in \mathcal{E}$, where $b \in \{1, \ldots, a-1, a+1, \ldots k\}$. If this is the case for only some of the dependency types the node is said to be partially functional; if no requirements are satisfied the node is said to be dysfunctional.

The implemented model investigates how high-level network effects (functionality of nodes) and interrelations (connectivity of nodes) in interconnected infrastructures react to different attack scenarios. The presented model can be used to represent any topology given a set of infrastructures and their interconnections. The model cannot achieve the level of accuracy found in devoted network simulators (described in Section 5), but it has the advantage of being able to estimate the consequences of cascading failures in interconnected infrastructures.

By constraining the response function to a linear function and discrete values for both time steps and resources, linear programming approaches can be employed for optimization of the relevant parameters. Interior point methods such as [18] can achieve computational complexity on the order of $O(n^{3.5})$, making the analysis of large graphs feasible.

3. Dependency Analysis

This section explores how two interconnected networks influence each other. Two clearly interdependent networks are the electrical power distribution network and the telephony transport layer network. The analysis is based on several abstractions and represents an approximation to actual network topologies. The motivation for choosing these two infrastructure elements as the first subject of investigation is primarily due to their key enabling role in modern society. The BAS study [16], carried out by the Norwegian Defense Research Establishment in 1997, established the criticality of power supply and telecommunications to Norwegian society. In addition, the networks are interesting candidates for model verification as there is a fundamental difference in how service deliveries flow through the networks. In the power distribution network all the power originates from a small number of power plants or generators. A transportation network, which may well interconnect several power plants, delivers power to a large number of transformers that serve the low voltage distribution network. As a consequence, the resulting graph is a directed network where multiple edges of different orientation between two nodes rarely occur.

Traditionally, the telephony transport layer has been a hierarchical network (see, e.g., [14]). Although there has been a decided trend away from this due to progress in transmission and switching technology since the early 1990s, we have chosen to use this model because it is representative of much of the currently-deployed telecommunications infrastructure. The telephony transport layer may be idealized as an onion structure with a very low diameter. The signal always starts from the outer layer; depending on the range of the connection, it goes through the core of the network before retuning to a local switch in the outer layer of the network. All edges are bidirectional, thus all connected nodes are connected by an edge in each direction.

3.1 Electrical Power Distribution Network

One of the early studies of power distribution networks was the analysis of the Western (U.S.) States Power Grid carried out by Watts and Strogatz [27] in 1998. The degree distribution of the network was found to be exponential-like, but the clustering coefficients were too large for the network to be a classical random graph. The observed network consisted of approximately 3,500 nodes, a number which might be too small for being conclusive regarding the categorization of the network [12]. For the purposes of the present study, however, an exact representation of the power distribution grid is not necessary as we are primarily interested in topological characteristics. To this end, a network topology generator was implemented based on the assumptions that the number of source nodes is small compared to the number of transport and sink nodes, power generating nodes are not directly interconnected, the network is constructed to cover a topological area as efficiently as possible, and some links are forced on the network to interconnect distribution networks and create redundancy. Based on these assumptions, a tree-like model for the power distribution network is a reasonable approximation, although binary and k-trees are much too regular to represent the topology. The basic Barabási-Albert (BA) model [1] with some modifications provides a tree-like structure together with the level of irregularity found in real networks. The original BA model is initiated with a connected graph. In the power distribution network case, the source nodes are not interconnected. This is solved by simply providing the originating nodes with an initial degree $k_{\mathrm{Init}} \geq 1$ that does not represent any real edges, just the centrality of the node in the network.

Given that one node is added at each time step in the BA model, as many disconnected trees as there are initial nodes in the network are generated. A sparse random graph is placed on top of the scale-free networks to connect lower-level nodes with each other. Since the network is very sparse, its statistical properties are not affected, but there is a major influence on network connectivity and the possible generation of feedback loops. The procedure used to generate the power distribution network topology involves network properties such as growth (a new node, defining the head of a new edge, is added to the network at every time step), preferential attachment (the tail of the edge is selected among the existing nodes with probability proportional to the degree of the node), and redundant connections (after the final time step a sparse random graph is placed on top of the network). As the network grows large, the influence of the sparse random graph becomes small and the probability of a node having k edges follows a power law with exponent $\gamma = 3$ [12].

Finally, a response function is defined for each edge. In the case of quantitative analysis of service delivery this function should be an implementation of Kirchhoff's first law, ensuring that the flow into a node along with the flow generated by the node equals the output and the consumption of the node. Such a detailed approach is not necessary to explore the model, as the model focuses on the functionality of the node. The principal issue is that electricity is consumed as it propagates through the networks and cannot be stored e.g., using subgraph cycles. Thus, the implemented response function only illustrates a resource which is being consumed as it flows through the network. Introducing a threshold function $T(x, c) = \delta(x - c)x$, where

$$\delta(x) = \begin{cases} 0, & x < 0 \\ 1, & x \geq 0. \end{cases} \tag{4}$$

The implemented response function is of the form

$$R_i(v_a, v_b, t)) = T(\frac{1}{2}D_a(t), C_{\text{Min}}(e_i(v_a, v_b))), \tag{5}$$

where D_a is the current available in node a at time t. Equation 5 indicates that two units of input current to the node are required to produce one unit of output current along an outgoing edge. The dependency type is not specified because there is only one dependency in the network. We assume that only one power dependency exists between two nodes and no prioritization scheme is defined for the outgoing edges.

A node in the power distribution network is defined to be functional if it has incoming current or generates current. The given response function can provide information on whether a node is functional or not, but it does not provide any physical representation of the level of functionality of a node in the network, which provides a sufficient level of detail for the purpose of this study.

3.2 Telephony Transport Layer Network

Compared with the electric grid, Internet and autonomous system networks [21], the telephony transport layer network has received relatively little attention by the critical infrastructure modeling community. In this work, we assume the telephony transport layer has a traditional hierarchical network structure. The network is optimized locally for complete connectivity and globally to minimize the number of switches in an average connection circuit. In order to be functional, a switch must be connected to other switches and to a power supply, which is the focus of our analysis.

The network, which is modeled as a number of disconnected trees, is connected to a fully-connected transportation network through their root nodes. The response function of the telephony network depends on whether or not the node has power as input. If no power is available, circuit switching cannot take place and no communication is possible. The response function for edges in the telephony transport layer is thus a threshold function given by

$$R_i(v_a, v_b, t) = \delta(D_a(t) - C_{\text{Min}}(e_i(v_a, v_b))), \tag{6}$$

where D_a is the current available in node a at time t and δ is as defined in Equation 4. It follows from Equation 2 that a directed edge between nodes v_a and v_b is defined if power is available to node v_a. Again, no redundant links are defined between two nodes and no prioritization scheme is defined for the edges. As mentioned earlier, each connection in the telephony transport layer is bidirectional (one-way communications are of no interest). The functionality of a node thus depends on whether the node and the node it is connected to have power supply (i.e., the switch can deliver the two-way service it is meant to deliver).

3.3 Network Interconnections

The dependency between the electrical power distribution network and the telephony transport layer is assumed to be one-way. The power distribution network is fully functional when switches in the telephony transport layer are not functional. Conversely, the flow along an edge in the telecommunications network will halt if either the head node or the tail node lose power. The connection of the telephony transport layer to the power grid is randomized in the present model (i.e., it does not take into account geospatial proximity and other factors that result in functional clustering). However, this is deemed to be adequate for the purpose of our analysis. Readers are referred to [25] for an extension of the theoretical model with two-way dependencies between the electrical power distribution network and the telephony transport layer.

Telephony transportation layer nodes have two inputs (current and information) and produce one output (information). At every time step, the response functions for power distribution and telephony transportation edges can be computed given the network state in the previous time step. The functionality of the telephony transport layer follows directly from this. Since a one-way dependency is defined, failure can only propagate from the power distribution network into the telephony transportation layer.

3.4 Attack Scenarios

Studies of complex networks frequently conclude that many man-made and natural networks are scale-free in nature, and thus possess the well-known Achilles heel of robustness against random breakdown and vulnerability to targeted attacks [2]. The first item investigated in Section 4 is whether the introduction of a very sparse random graph on top of a scale-free infrastructure will reduce some of the vulnerability to targeted attacks.

Several possible scenarios may cause the failure of a node in an infrastructure. The cause may be an intentional or unintentional act by a human, or a change in the network environment (e.g., flooding), or a technical error. We consider three attack scenarios in our analysis: single node removal (consequence of a targeted terrorist attack or a single technical failure), removal of a small connected component (non-localized failure such as flooding or some other natural disaster), and removal of disconnected components (result of a coordinated terrorist attack).

4. Simulation Study

Small topologies were generated artificially to illustrate the properties of the model. A power distribution topology based on two power sources and 28 power distribution nodes was connected to a telephony transport network with 21 total switches, including three core switches. The switches were connected to randomly selected lower-level power distribution nodes (i.e., no power generating nodes were connected directly to the telephony transport layer). None of the nodes of the telephony transport layer were assumed to have an independent power supply.

The attacks involve the removal of one or two nodes with the following steps: (i) remove a node from the network, (ii) run the response function until the number of functional nodes in the network stabilizes, (iii) count the number of functional nodes in the network, and (iv) reinsert the node. This procedure is repeated for all nodes in the network. The pairwise removal of nodes follows a similar procedure, except that two nodes are removed at a time.

The results are presented as the fraction of functional nodes that remain after removing one or two nodes from the network. The results are presented as histograms in Figures 1, 2 and 3. The x-axis represents the fraction of functional nodes in a run, and the y-axis represents number of runs of the algorithm. The results are deduced from one topology generated as described in Section 3. A single topology is not sufficient to draw general conclusions about the properties of the proposed topologies, but it illustrates the ability and flexibility of the model.

4.1 Coordinated Failures in a Single Domain

This scenario considers the single, non-buffered power distribution network. While atypical of the interdependencies existing between real-world critical infrastructures, the network permits the exposition of core elements of the model and the simulation environment.

4.1.1 Scale-Free Power Distribution Network. This scenario illustrates the well-known vulnerability of scale-free networks to targeted attacks. The electrical power distribution network is represented as a scale-free network and two scenarios are considered: (i) removal of one node, and (ii) removal of two random-selected power nodes.

Figure 1a shows that removing one node has limited influence on the network. Specifically, in almost 50% of the cases, more than 95% of the nodes are functional, which is very high as the simulated power distribution network has 28 nodes. We also note the high influence of removing one particular node – the generator in the largest sub-distribution network. As the distribution networks of the two generators are not interconnected due to the BA construction, removing the generator takes out the entire subgraph. The gap observed between 0.85% and 0.90% of functional nodes is most likely due to the small size of the network.

The results of the attacks are shown in Figure 1, which nicely illustrates the properties of a scale-free network.

Figure 1b shows that removing two nodes from the network also has a limited effect on the network – more than 70% of the nodes are functional in the

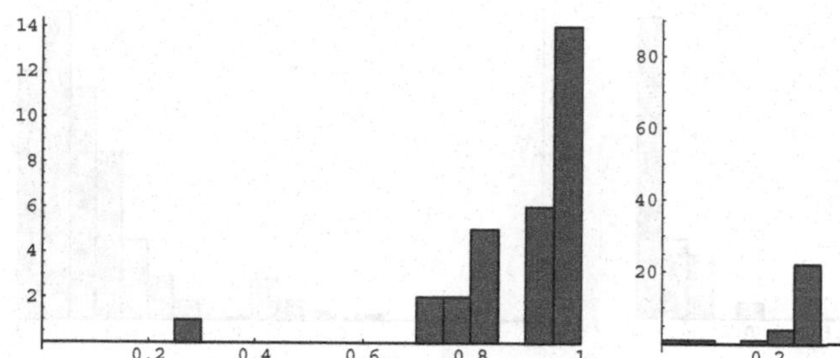

(a) Fraction of functional nodes after random removal of one node (28 runs).

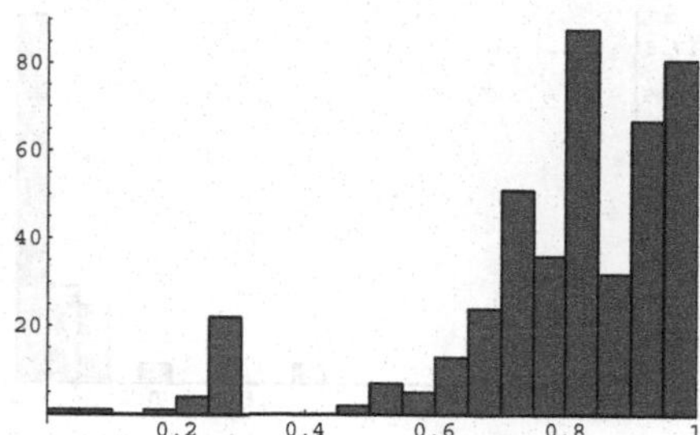

(b) Fraction of functional nodes after random removal of two nodes (378 runs).

Figure 1. Consequences of node removal on a scale-free topology.

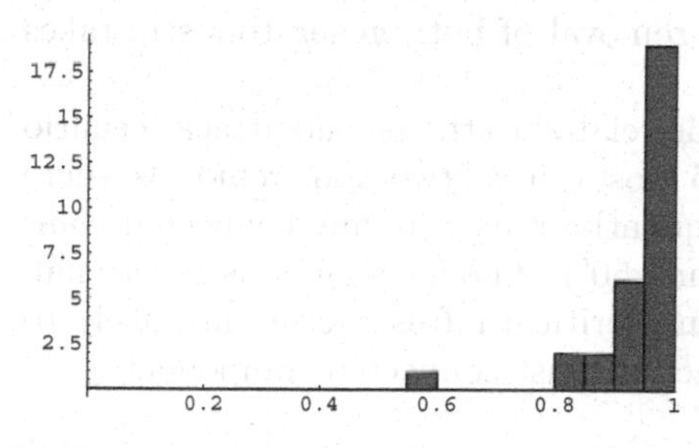

(a) Fraction of functional nodes after random removal of one node (51 runs).

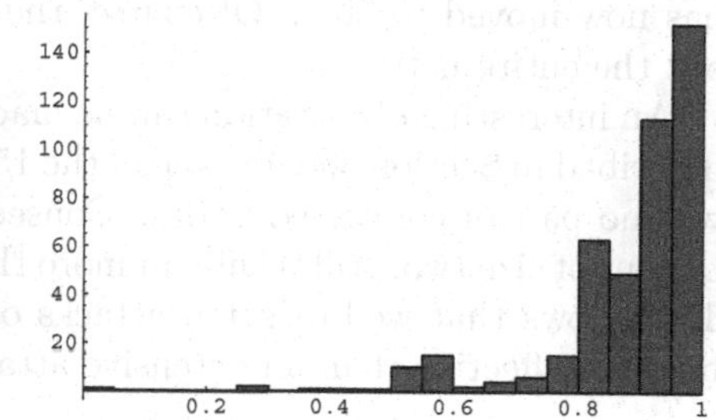

(b) Fraction of functional nodes after random removal of two nodes (1,275 runs).

Figure 2. Consequences of node removal on a scale-free network with redundancy.

majority of the cases. Obviously, taking out both generators paralyzes the network. The peak observed around 30% is due to the removal of the largest generator plus a central node in the second power distribution network.

4.1.2 Scale-Free Network with Added Redundancy. In this scenario, a sparse random graph is placed on top of the scale-free graph to provide redundancy. The results of the simulation are presented in Figure 2. Figure 2a shows that the introduced redundancy improves the robustness of the network considerably. When one node is removed, the functionality of the network rarely drops below 90%, and never below 50%. Thus, the cost of adding redundant edges may pay off in terms of robustness. The same holds for the scenario involving the removal of two nodes (Figure 2b). The functionality rarely drops below 80% and the peak that was formerly located around 30%

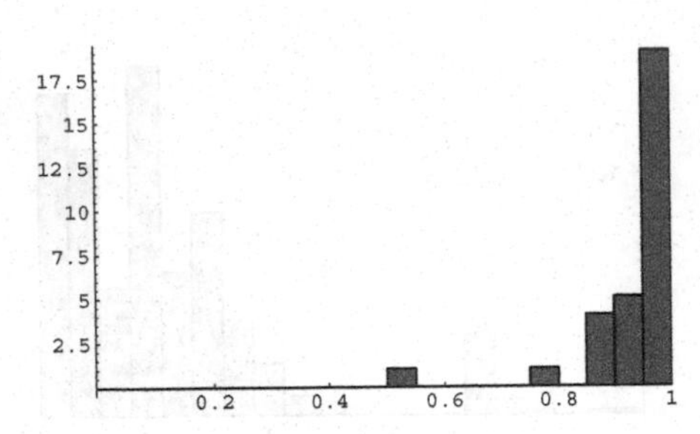

(a) Fraction of functional telecommunication nodes after random removal of one power node (51 runs).

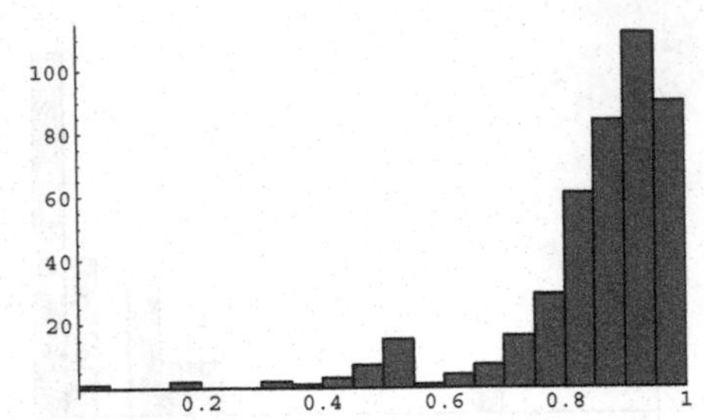

(b) Fraction of functional telecommunication nodes after random removal of two power nodes (1,275 runs).

Figure 3. Consequences of node removal from two networks.

has now moved to 60%. Of course, the removal of both generators still takes out the entire network.

An interesting observation can be made related to the second attack scenario described in Section 3.4. In each of the 15 most critical two-node removals, there was no pair of connected nodes. Consequently, removing any connected component of size two, still results in more than 50% of nodes remaining functional. This shows that well-targeted attacks on a critical infrastructure are likely to be more effective than an extensive attack against connected components.

4.2 Multi-Domain Dependencies

The final simulation illustrates how failures in the electrical power distribution network propagate into the telephony transport layer. Each node of the telephony transport layer is connected to a node in the power distribution network, and its functionality depends on the power supplied to itself and its neighbors. Figure 3 shows the fraction of functional telecommunication nodes as one or two nodes are removed from the power distribution network.

The results clearly illustrate the dependency between the two networks and validates the basics of the model. In our future work, we will explore more exiting features such as circular dependencies, multiple network interdependencies and metrics for identifying critical network components.

4.3 Discussion

In our opinion, pure scale-free topologies are not suitable for representing for real-world infrastructures. Unlike most man-made infrastructures, the pure BA topology contains very few redundant links. Imposing random connections on top of the BA structure makes the model more realistic; at the same time, the vulnerability of the network is reduced. As illustrated in our simulation study, when redundancy is introduced, the network is less sensitive to removing single nodes.

Future analyses should consider the removal of random nodes and random pairs of nodes from the network, and observe failure propagation throughout the network. This will identify the nodes that are central to network functionality and help determine where resources should be invested to increase operational reliability and infrastructure security.

5. Related Work

Research activities related to the monitoring and simulation of critical infrastructures are being conducted worldwide, although generally at a qualitative level. One of the earliest and most widespread methodologies involves the application of a control systems approach [24], including hybrid mechanisms [17]. Other approaches for modeling infrastructures include agent-based systems [4, 20, 26]. Such qualitative efforts also include the Critical Infrastructure Modeling and Assessment Program (CIMAP) and the European Project ACIP [23]. Additional approaches (e.g., [3, 22]) vary considerably in the level of detail considered, ranging from simple dependency analysis to elaborate models containing continuous physical submodels (e.g., for pipelines and electrical power grids) as well as behavioral models.

For the more constrained case of individual infrastructures such as pipelines and power grids, however, rich modeling and simulation environments already exist including the PSIcontrol system and proprietary mechanisms employed by operators. However, interconnections and interdependencies can only be modeled to a limited extent in such environments. Several properties are immediately derivable from interconnection characteristics alone as shown for power grid and Internet connectivity [5, 8, 13, 28]. Frequently, the underlying structure of the networks can be identified as being wholly or partially scale-free [7, 11, 15, 19]. This has significant implications for the vulnerability of interconnected and interdependent networks of critical infrastructure components to random failure [6, 9] as well as to targeted attacks [10].

6. Conclusions

This paper has presented the foundational elements of a family of models for investigating interdependencies among heterogeneous critical infrastructures in abstract topologies. To this end, we have provided an extensible graph-theoretical model, which incorporates a flexible response function for modeling vertex behavior, including activities internal to vertices and the provision of buffered and unbuffered infrastructure services.

With the help of simplified abstract models, we have demonstrated how the addition of random components to an otherwise scale-free network can influence the overall robustness of the network to vertex removal. The observations are verified by a simulation study involving a simple interconnection model for two unbuffered networks, an electrical power distribution grid and a fixed-line telephony network.

Our future research will focus on validating the model using simulations of large-scale power and telephony network topologies. We will also work on extensions to the model, including the ability to store dependency types within nodes, incorporating cyclic interdependencies between infrastructures, prioritizing resources within nodes, and introducing component failure as known from reliability theory. Furthermore, we will attempt to refine our analytic approach by using graph-theoretical and combinatorial optimization techniques to identify critical interdependencies and effective mechanisms for enhancing the robustness of critical infrastructures.

References

[1] R. Albert and A. Barabási, Statistical mechanics of complex networks, *Reviews of Modern Physics*, vol. 74(1), pp. 47–97, 2002.

[2] R. Albert, H. Jeong and A. Barabási, Error and attack tolerance of complex networks, *Nature*, vol. 406, pp. 378–382, 2000.

[3] M. Amin, Toward self-healing infrastructure systems, *IEEE Computer*, vol. 33(8), pp. 44–53, 2000.

[4] D. Barton and K. Stamber, An Agent-Based Microsimulation of Critical Infrastructure Systems, Technical Report SAN02000-0808C, Sandia National Laboratories, Albuquerque, New Mexico, 2000.

[5] A. Broder, R. Kumar, F. Maghoul, P. Raghavan, S. Rajagopalan, R. Stata, A. Tomkins and J. Wiener, Graph structure in the web, *Computer Networks*, vol. 33(1-6), pp. 309–320, 2000.

[6] D. Callaway, M. Newman, S. Strogatz and D. Watts, Network robustness and fragility: Percolation on random graphs, *Physical Review Letters*, vol. 85(25), pp. 5468–5471, 2000.

[7] B. Casselman, Networks, *Notices of the American Mathematical Society*, vol. 51(4), pp. 392–393, 2004.

[8] Q. Chen, H. Chang, R. Govindan, S. Jamin, S. Shenker and W. Willinger, The origin of power laws in Internet topologies revisited, *Proceedings of the Twenty-First Annual Joint Conference of the IEEE Computer and Communications Societies*, vol. 2, pp. 608–617, 2002.

[9] R. Cohen, K. Erez, D. ben-Avraham and S. Havlin, Resilience of the Internet to random breakdowns, *Physical Review Letters*, vol. 85(21), pp. 4626–4628, 2000.

[10] R. Cohen, K. Erez, D. ben-Avraham and S. Havlin, Breakdown of the Internet under intentional attack, *Physical Review Letters*, vol. 86(16), pp. 3682–3685, 2001.

[11] S. Dorogovtsev and J. Mendes, Effect of the accelerating growth of communications networks on their structure, *Physical Review E*, vol. 63, pp. 025101-1–025101-4, 2001.

[12] S. Dorogovtsev and J. Mendes, *Evolution of Networks, From Biological Nets to the Internet and WWW*, Oxford University Press, Oxford, United Kingdom, 2003.

[13] M. Faloutsos, P. Faloutsos and C. Faloutsos, On power law relationships of the Internet topology, *Proceedings of the Conference on Applications, Technologies, Architectures and Protocols for Computer Communication*, pp. 251–262, 1999.

[14] R. Freeman, *Fundamentals of Telecommunications*, John Wiley, New York, 1999.

[15] K. Goh, B. Kahng and D. Kim, Spectra and eigenvectors of scale-free networks, *Physical Review E*, vol. 64, pp. 0519031-1–0519031-5, 2001.

[16] O. Hæsken, T. Olsen and H. Fridheim, Beskyttelse av Samfunnet (Bas) – Sluttrapport, Technical Report FFI/RAPPORT-97/01459, Norwegian Defence Research Establishment, Kjeller, Norway, 1997.

[17] J. James and F. Mabry, Building trustworthy systems: Guided state estimation as a feasible approach for interpretation, decision and action based on sensor data, *Proceedings of the Thirty-Seventh Annual Hawaii International Conference on System Sciences*, p. 20056, 2004.

[18] N. Karmarkar, A new polynomial time algorithm for linear programming, *Combinatorica*, vol. 4(4), pp. 373–395, 1984.

[19] M. Newman, The structure and function of complex networks, *SIAM Review*, vol. 45(2), pp. 167–256, 2003.

[20] M. North, Agent-based modeling of complex infrastructures, *Proceedings of the Simulation of Social Agents: Architectures and Institutions Workshop*, pp. 239–250, 2000.

[21] R. Pastor-Satorras and A. Vespignani, *Evolution and Structure of the Internet: a Statistical Physics Approach*, Cambridge University Press, Cambridge, United Kingdom, 2004.

[22] S. Rinaldi, Modeling and simulating critical infrastructures and their interdependencies, *Proceedings of the Thirty-Seventh Annual Hawaii International Conference on System Sciences*, p. 20054.1, 2004.

[23] W. Schmitz, Analysis and Assessment for Critical Infrastructure Protection (ACIP), Final Report, IST-2001-37257 Deliverable D7.5, ACIP Consortium, Ottobrunn, Germany, 2003.

[24] K. Sullivan, J. Knight, X. Du and S. Geist, Information survivability control systems, *Proceedings of the Twenty-First International Conference on Software Engineering*, pp. 184–192, 1999.

[25] N. Svendsen and S. Wolthusen, Connectivity models of interdependency in mixed-type critical infrastructure networks, *Information Security Technical Report*, vol. 12(1), pp. 44–55, 2007.

[26] W. Thomas, M. North, C. Macal and J. Peerenboom, From Physics to Finances: Complex Adaptive Systems Representation of Infrastructure Interdependencies, Technical Report, Naval Surface Warfare Center, Dahlgren, Virginia, 2003.

[27] D. Watts and S. Strogatz, Collective dynamics of small-world networks, *Nature*, vol. 393, pp. 440–442, 1998.

[28] S. Yook, H. Jeong and A. Barabási, Modeling the Internet's large-scale topology, *Proceedings of the National Academy of Sciences*, vol. 99(21), pp. 13382–13386, 2002.

Chapter 25

VISUALIZING CASCADING FAILURES IN CRITICAL CYBER INFRASTRUCTURES

Jason Kopylec, Anita D'Amico and John Goodall

Abstract This paper explores the relationship between physical and cyber infrastructures, focusing on how threats and disruptions in physical infrastructures can cascade into failures in the cyber infrastructure. It also examines the challenges involved in organizing and managing massive amounts of critical infrastructure data that are geographically and logically disparate. To address these challenges, we have designed Cascade, a system for visualizing the cascading effects of physical infrastructure failures into the cyber infrastructure. Cascade provides situational awareness and shows how threats to physical infrastructures such as power, transportation and communications can affect the networked enterprises comprising the cyber infrastructure. Our approach applies the concept of punctualization from Actor-Network Theory as an organizing principle for disparate infrastructure data. In particular, the approach exposes the critical relationships between physical and cyber infrastructures, and enables infrastructure data to be depicted visually to maximize comprehension during disaster planning and crisis response activities.

Keywords: Cyber infrastructure, infrastructure dependencies, cascading failures, actor-network theory, situational awareness

1. Introduction

Research efforts by the critical infrastructure protection (CIP) community that focus on the cyber infrastructure are primarily directed at vulnerabilities that expose cyber assets to software-based attacks by hackers, viruses, worms and denial-of-service attacks, and the effects of the digital threats on physical infrastructures. Less attention has been directed at the impact of physical infrastructures on the cyber infrastructure [17]. This paper explores how disruptions to physical infrastructures can cascade to the cyber infrastructure. Also, it examines how the cyber infrastructure can be better incorporated into

Kopylec, J., D'Amico, A. and Goodall, J., 2008, in IFIP International Federation for Information Processing, Volume 253, Critical Infrastructure Protection, eds. E. Goetz and S. Shenoi; (Boston: Springer), pp. 351–364.

the larger context of CIP, and presents the design of a software system that integrates information from physical and cyber infrastructures.

The intricate web of dependencies between cyber assets and physical infrastructures enables the cyber assets to function and communicate. From the power grid that provides electricity to roads that deliver workers to the data center, a complex orchestration of services exists to keep an enterprise network up and running [16]. In addition, categories of vulnerabilities that are tied to geographic locations (e.g., earthquake faults and flood plains) must be considered when assessing risk and planning for recovery. The individuals who maintain critical information technology (IT) systems must understand both the internal (cyber) and external (physical) infrastructures on which their assets rely.

We began our efforts by studying how IT disaster planners and crisis responders analyze the effects of other infrastructures on the cyber infrastructure. In addition to reviewing existing technologies and literature, we interviewed CIP experts and IT professionals, evaluating their work practices and the challenges they face. The interviewees were drawn from federal, state and local government agencies as well as from academia and commercial entities. They stressed the need to make time-sensitive decisions based on critical infrastructure data and diverse sensor data, both for proactive disaster planning as well as reactive crisis response. Although they came from a variety of backgrounds and had different responsibilities, these diverse individuals were linked by their shared concern for the planning, protection and recovery of critical cyber infrastructures. Collectively, we refer to this group as "IT crisis managers."

IT crisis managers are required to protect large-scale enterprise networks from cyber threats (viruses, worms and targeted attacks) as well as from physical threats (hurricanes, floods and acts of terror). Nevertheless, we found that the IT crisis managers focused their efforts almost exclusively on cyber threats, largely ignoring the effects that disruptions to physical infrastructures could have on their systems. They had a poor understanding of the dependencies between infrastructures, which are complex and difficult to comprehend, especially in crisis situations. They did not adequately comprehend the cascading effects that disruptions in other critical infrastructures have on the cyber infrastructure. Moreover, they are deluged with massive volumes of disparate data that must be considered for effective crisis planning and response.

These challenges guided the requirements and use cases involved in our design of Cascade, a software system that visually presents the physical vulnerabilities of an enterprise network and how the vulnerabilities can propagate due to the network's dependence on other critical infrastructures (e.g., electrical power). The design incorporates the locations of critical computing assets and man-made or natural threats specific to the geographic regions that could affect the enterprise network. The system presents information to IT crisis managers to support rapid vulnerability analysis and course-of-action evaluation when planning responses to potential threats, as well as command and control activities for individuals engaged in crisis management.

2. Related Work

Several researchers have examined how digital attacks can disrupt the cyber infrastructure and how these disruptions cause failures in other critical infrastructures [4, 20]. Others have attempted to provide quantitative metrics for measuring risk associated with digital threats (see, e.g., [5, 10]). In our work, we examine the relationships between cyber and physical infrastructures from the opposite perspective. Instead of investigating how cyber threats affect other critical infrastructures, we focus on how disruptions to physical infrastructures cascade into and interact with the cyber infrastructure.

Infrastructure interdependence is fundamental to the propagation of threats between infrastructures. Therefore, understanding and documenting infrastructure dependencies is an essential step in coordinating disaster planning and emergency response activities [19]. There are two main approaches to understanding these dependencies and their role in infrastructure failure: surveying historical disasters, and modeling and simulating disasters.

Much of what is known about infrastructure failure comes from actual disasters. Identifying the causes and effects of previous failures and the infrastructures involved helps to better plan for the future. Zimmerman [18] has conducted extensive research in this area, surveying a large number of disasters in various infrastructures; her results strongly support the use of infrastructure dependency information in decision-making. Rinaldi and co-workers [15] have developed a foundation for learning from disasters and mapping the results into a framework of interdependent infrastructures.

The development of computer models and simulations for critical infrastructure dependencies is a new and rapidly evolving area of research that has yielded a number of techniques and tools with varying maturity levels. Robinson, *et al.* [16] describe the benefits of simulation-based infrastructure models. Pederson and colleagues [13] have completed an extensive survey of work in the area. Dudenhoeffer, *et al.* [1] have designed a simulation framework (CIMS) for multiple interacting infrastructures. CIMS introduces disaster scenarios on the modeled infrastructures and simulates the effects of infrastructure failures.

Unfortunately, the results of disaster studies and simulations rarely reach IT crisis managers and emergency responders who can benefit from them. Indeed, the individuals we interviewed were unaware of the work and had never used any infrastructure simulation technologies. This is unfortunate because much of this work is directly applicable to the cyber infrastructure, and the results of infrastructure simulations could help disaster planners better understand infrastructure dependencies and vulnerabilities. The Cascade system described in this paper helps translate simulation results into actionable information for IT crisis managers.

3. Linking Infrastructure Data

There are key challenges to linking cyber and physical infrastructures, mainly due to the deluge of data and the unique aspects of cyber data. To overcome these challenges, we propose the process of "induced depunctualization" as an organizing principle for linking cyber and physical infrastructures. We demonstrate how this principle can be used to organize and filter infrastructure data.

3.1 Physical Infrastructure Data Challenges

There is a concerted effort by federal, state and county government agencies to collect data about critical physical infrastructures. Geographic Information Systems (GISs) are often used to provide the robust storage, visualization and analysis solutions that are required. A GIS allows for the use of geographic location as a baseline for bringing data from different infrastructures together. Within these geodatabases, infrastructure information takes the form of map layers, where each layer depicts some aspect of an infrastructure. For example, when storing information about the telecommunications infrastructure, multiple map layers separately show the locations of telephone switching stations, fiber optic lines, telephone poles and cell phone towers. Surprisingly, very few layers are dedicated directly to capturing data about the cyber infrastructure (e.g., locations of government data centers). Without such location information, it is difficult to determine whether a flood, explosion or power outage will damage or impede access to important cyber assets.

The collection of physical infrastructure data can be thought of as a large stack of map layers, growing taller as new layers are added. When historical data is included, the number of layers grows even faster, making it difficult to discern the unfolding of a crisis. It is difficult, if not impossible, to view all of these layers at once; nor can one easily select those most likely to affect the cyber infrastructure. As the information density grows, users are overloaded with data and potentially important data is occluded. This makes it difficult to find the information most relevant to any single infrastructure. For example, an IT crisis manager may have to decide where to place a back-up facility, or determine which data centers are at risk during a hurricane. When presented with hundreds of infrastructure map layers, it is an arduous task to home in on the layers that provide relevant information.

Another problem is that there is no straightforward method for connecting map layers and, therefore, no way to relate different infrastructures. States like New York [12] and Montana [2] have created massive databases of infrastructure map layers and have begun efforts to provide search capabilities for map layers of interest. Still, these systems lack support for associating map layers from different infrastructures.

3.2 Cyber Infrastructure Data Challenges

The cyber infrastructure has certain characteristics that affect its total representation within a GIS: it is geographically dispersed, it incorporates components beyond the IT crisis manager's control, and it is often dynamically reconfigured. Large enterprise networks have mission-critical servers in geographically dispersed locations. These servers may support one organizational mission, yet they are housed in separate locations and may be vulnerable to quite different physical threats (e.g., hurricanes on the Gulf Coast and earthquakes on the Pacific Coast). Displaying such widely dispersed assets within a single GIS display would require a scale that affords little space for details. The other side of this issue is that a single facility may incorporate systems with very different missions. Separate database servers containing medical records and transportation records may be co-located and, therefore, share a common physical vulnerability even though they have no logical relationship. Furthermore, large enterprise networks rely on other entities (e.g., Internet service providers and backbone providers) that are outside the enterprise owners' control; moreover, the locations and status of the assets may be unknown. Finally, large enterprise networks are dynamic. Networks are reconfigured with new hardware, software is updated or replaced, and file content is changed at a frequency that far exceeds any configuration document or disaster plan. Thus, the current state of the system is often partially unknown. Consequently, it is important to allow for frequent display refreshes and to provide the IT crisis manager with information about the age and reliability of network-related data.

Whereas physical infrastructure data is collected and managed as GIS map layers, cyber data is gathered by sensors such as network monitors and intrusion detection systems. This data is collected at different rates from the various sensors and is often stored in multiple formats. Some of these systems can generate huge amounts of data. All this data must be linked to the physical infrastructure to fully understand threats to the cyber infrastructure. But this is very difficult because cyber data is typically not stored in the GIS format of physical data.

3.3 Infrastructure as an Actor-Network

This section describes a methodology for organizing the massive, complex data discussed in the previous section in a way that highlights only the relevant interaction effects between infrastructures. This principle forms the basis for our design and allows IT crisis managers to rapidly home in on the data they require while filtering out irrelevant details. Malone and Crowston's coordination theory [11] supports these requirements, helping address the important and pervasive need to study the dependence between interacting systems. We apply concepts from Actor-Network Theory (ANT) [6, 7] to address these challenges. ANT provides a perspective on how to view and analyze complex systems and interactions with disparate, yet coordinated, parts. In particular, ANT combines processes seamlessly with the objects and interactions that constitute them. Law has used ANT to study disasters [9] and system failures [8].

A key concept in ANT is punctualization [7], where different, interacting parts of a complex system are abstracted and named by their collective emergent behavior [3]. In a punctualized system, the individual parts are hidden. The concept of punctualization can be applied very effectively to the problem of infrastructure protection. For example, an IT crisis manager may view the electrical infrastructure as a single entity whose mission is to provide reliable power. In actuality, it comprises thousands of power lines, generators and transformers, all working together to supply electricity. As long as these components work seamlessly to provide the needed power, they remain concealed.

This process of hiding component parts and only acknowledging the larger whole contributes to the challenge of studying infrastructure interactions and dependencies. Due to punctualization, interactions within and between infrastructures are hidden, so identifying vulnerabilities and threats to these invisible systems is extremely difficult. Perrow [14] defines the complexities of such physical systems, outlining the visible and hidden interactions among them, motivating the question of how to make the hidden interactions visible. Our work also attempts to understand why we cannot see some interactions and what we can do to make them visible.

Returning to our example, when there is a power outage at a critical data center, the IT crisis manager no longer sees the electrical infrastructure as a single entity. Downed power lines, back-up generators, utility companies and repairmen that go unseen during normal operation all become visible, exposing the infrastructure's parts, couplings and dependencies. The hidden elements are rediscovered when an actor-network suffers from disruption or failure.

Although not explicitly described in ANT, but essential to the study of infrastructure dependencies, is that not all the parts are revealed when a failure is introduced into a punctualized system. For example, if a critical data center loses power, only those systems that rely on that power become important. The status of back-up generators and possible failure of critical computer systems become the focus of attention. Data center operations may also rely on other elements (e.g., staff and telecommunications), but they remain hidden during the power infrastructure failure. In fact, a failure causes a partial depunctualization of the system, where the parts that become visible are those that are directly relevant to and affected by the failure; the rest of the punctualized system remains hidden.

Applied to CIP, this partial depunctualization is useful because even though the infrastructure interactions may be too complex to fully understand, the most relevant interactions are exposed. So although all the interactions between complex infrastructures may be difficult to define, it is possible to discern the interactions that are of most interest by studying and simulating failures in these systems. By purposefully inducing or simulating failure into punctualized systems, the relevant facets and connections between infrastructures can be uncovered while keeping the non-relevant portions hidden.

We refer to the process that purposefully deconstructs an entity into its separate, dependent parts as "induced depunctualization." This process can be accomplished through either of the two methods discussed previously: surveying historical disasters or computer simulation. To illustrate the use of induced depunctualization to reveal the cascading effects of other infrastructures on the cyber infrastructure, consider the example of a hurricane hitting a critical data

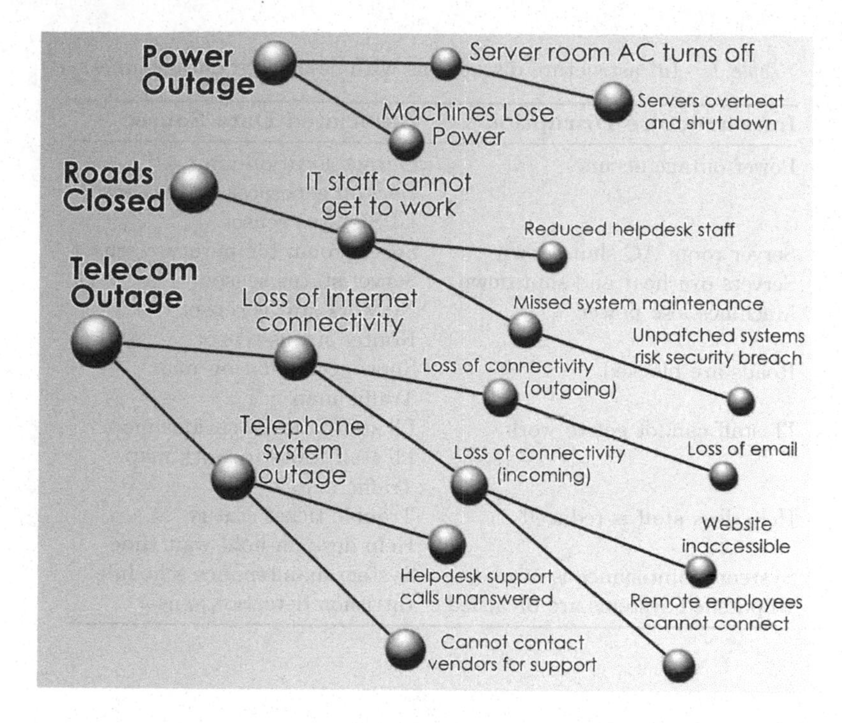

Figure 1. Cascading effects on a data center resulting from a hurricane.

center. Figure 1 shows the cascading failures that can result from disruptions to the electrical power, transportation and telecommunications infrastructures.

The disaster scenario shows how three separate physical infrastructure failures, namely electrical power, transportation and telecommunications, can affect an enterprise computer network. Failures propagate across infrastructures, exposing otherwise hidden portions of the infrastructures. For example, data centers often connect critical servers to back-up power supplies, but do not provide back-up power to the air conditioning units that cool the servers. When a power failure occurs, the air conditioning goes down, causing the servers to overheat and shut down, which reduces the effectiveness of the back-up power. Depunctualization reveals this hidden dependency. Induced depunctualization provides a method for determining the relevant component dependencies and cascading disruptions of a physical infrastructure failure.

3.4 Organizing Infrastructure Data

As discussed earlier, there are massive collections of infrastructure data. As more sensors are added to critical computing networks and other infrastructures, the deluge of incoming data will increase. Missing from these collections is a filtering mechanism or organizing principle that can guide an IT crisis manager to the right information in a timely manner. Induced depunctualization

Table 1. Infrastructure disruptions with associated data sources.

Infrastructure Disruption	Associated Data Source
Power outage occurs	Outage location map Backup generator status sensor UPS status sensor
Server room AC shuts down	Server room temperature sensor
Servers overheat and shut down	Server status sensor
Machines lose power	Network status sensor Router status sensor
Roads are blocked	Snow accumulation map Traffic map
IT staff cannot get to work	IT staff house locations map IT staff route to work map Traffic map
Help desk staff is reduced	Trouble ticket status Help desk on-hold wait time
System maintenance is missed	System maintenance schedule
Unpatched systems are breached	Intrusion detection sensor

analysis is useful because it shows the potential disruptions that could cascade from an infrastructure failure.

Using the cascading effects from an induced depunctualization of the hurricane scenario in Figure 1, each step in the scenario can be paired with infrastructure GIS map layers or network sensor data. Table 1 shows the failures from the hurricane scenario with the associated data sources (map layers or cyber sensors). For example, an electrical outage map from the utility company would show if a data center is in danger of losing power; this can be coupled with the status of back-up power supply and generator sensors to provide better situational awareness. On their own, the individual physical and cyber components do not describe the power outage threat, but in combination they can help define the threat to IT systems.

Table 1 shows that at each possible disruption point, there are map layers or cyber sensors that provide insight about how a network could be, or is being, affected. In addition, the large number of data sources can be organized by pairing them only with the relevant failure entries. Combining the physical and cyber infrastructure data enables IT crisis managers to fully understand the threats to their cyber assets. However, the data can be difficult to comprehend without visual aids. The next section demonstrates how the data can be displayed using the organizing principle of induced punctualization in a manner that assists IT crisis managers in planning for and responding to threats to their cyber assets.

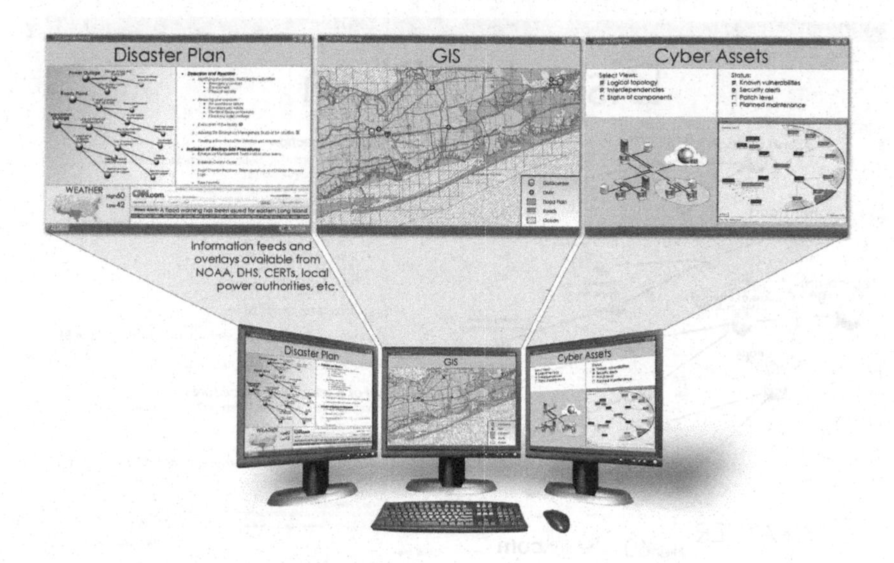

Figure 2. Coordinated views of cascading effects.

4. Visualizing Interdependent Infrastructures

Presenting information about cyber and physical infrastructures to IT crisis managers in an intuitive manner is of paramount importance. This section describes our design for providing this capability. Figure 2 shows the organization of the Cascade user interface. The design provides multiple coordinated views, which present potential infrastructure disruptions and their cascading effects, and support GIS infrastructure map layers and network topology.

Combining physical and cyber infrastructure data within these views enables IT crisis managers to easily determine if a threat or disruption is occurring or may occur. Specifically, the design incorporates: (i) cascading infrastructure failures that show cause-effect relationships of what can go wrong; (ii) disaster plan documents that suggest what to do when failures occur; (iii) infrastructure GIS data that describes the status of physical threats to the network; and (iv) network topology that connects infrastructure data to affected network function.

4.1 Cascading Effects and Disaster Plans

The first view, shown in Figure 3, provides information about what can fail and what to do about it. Presenting the cascading effects of vulnerabilities on network operations illuminates the possible failures. Specific scenarios – such as hurricane, fire or pandemic – can be chosen and displayed. These scenarios can either be hand-crafted or generated from underlying infrastructure dependency simulations.

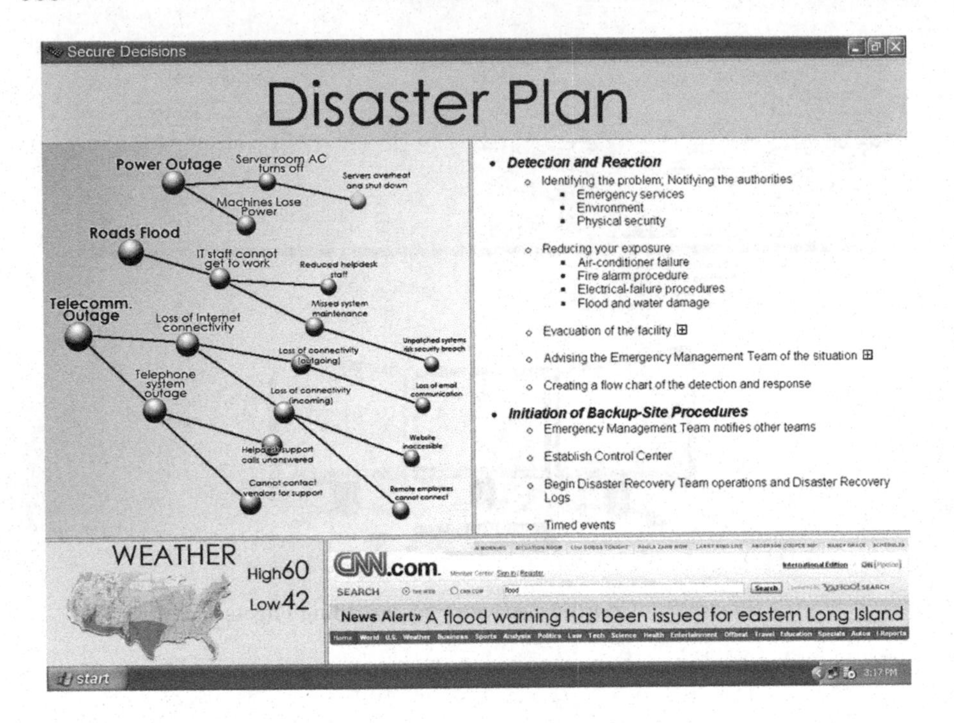

Figure 3. Cascade view of failures and disaster plans.

Including disaster planning documents directly into the interface puts them at the fingertips of IT crisis managers and affords coordination with the other views. For example, a user can link to staff contact lists, news feeds or weather reports. A user who clicks on the node for the failure "Help desk staff is reduced" is directed to the portion of the disaster plan that outlines how to deal with the problem.

4.2 Viewing GIS Infrastructure Data

As discussed earlier, much of the critical infrastructure data is stored in the form of GIS map layers. The second view, shown in Figure 4, incorporates map layers in the presentation. The advantage of map displays lies in the ability to overlay very different kinds of information in the same space, using physical location as the underlying connection. GIS displays and analysis tools have a central role in collecting and using critical infrastructure information.

Cascade leverages GIS technology to present a familiar view of infrastructure data. By coordinating the disaster plan view with the GIS view, failure-to-data associations can be used to organize the map layers that should be viewed. This provides the fundamental mechanism for organizing large catalogs of map layers and implicitly shows the dependencies between infrastructures.

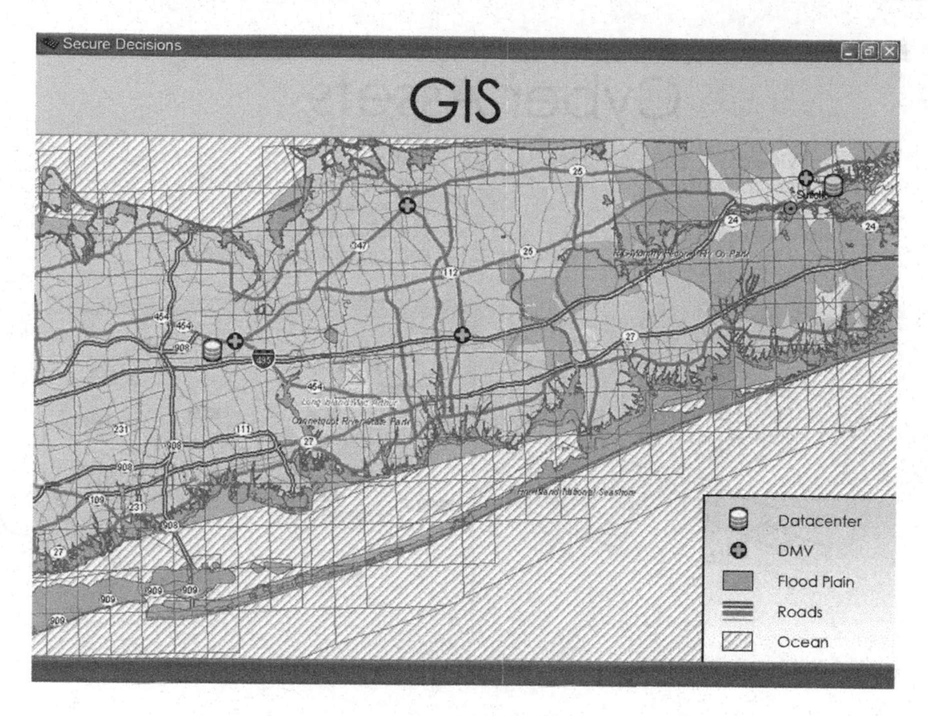

Figure 4. Associated infrastructure map layers.

4.3 Coordinating Physical and Cyber Views

The final view, presented in Figure 5, closes the loop between the physical locations of critical cyber assets and where they function in the network topology by showing the logical layout of the network. This view depicts how workstations, servers and network hardware are organized and connected into logical subnets, showing how connections can be made between machines and to Internet gateways. Additional information may be visually layered on this logical network base view, such as the status of software patches, power availability, temperature and connectivity.

Cascade combines the network topology view into a coordinated application with a disaster planning and infrastructure GIS, allowing interactive exploration of how infrastructure effects cascade to physical and cyber assets, and the network impact of failures. For example, an IT crisis manager in the midst of a hurricane might click on the failure "Server room AC shuts down." This brings up a GIS status map of all the data center's air conditioning systems. Spotting one that has failed in a particular building, he or she clicks on it. The corresponding critical servers in the network topology window light up, showing which servers are at risk of overheating. This intuitive and seamless integration of asset status, infrastructure data and network information provides the IT crisis manager with a comprehensive picture of the impact of failures on the network.

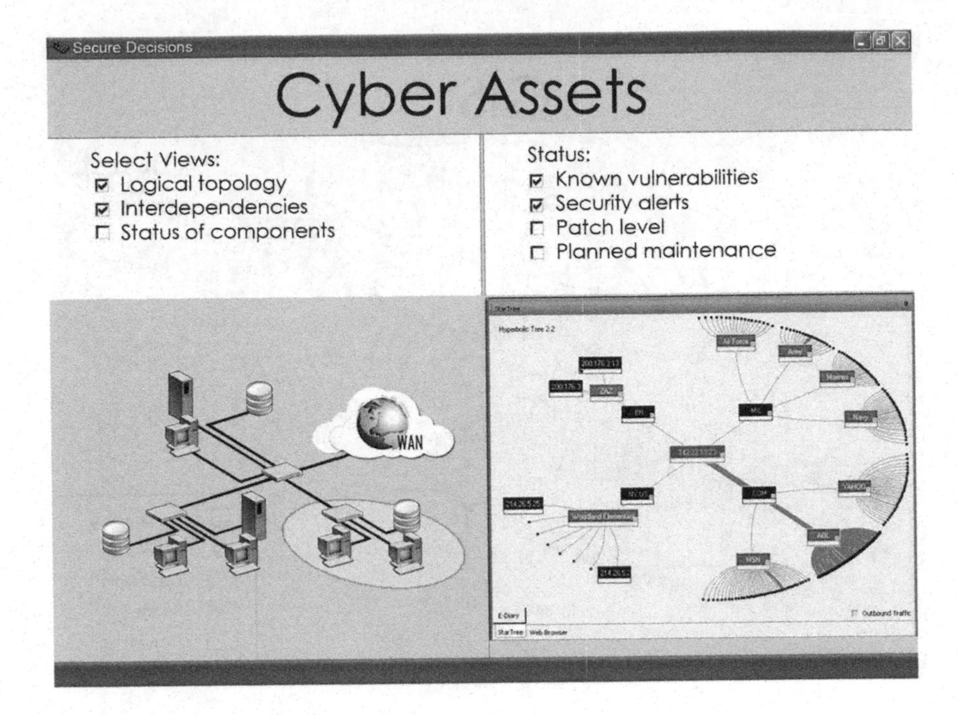

Figure 5. Network topology and critical cyber assets.

5. Conclusions

IT crisis managers, who must keep mission-critical enterprise networks operating during all types of disasters, need accurate, timely information about how vulnerabilities and failures in other critical infrastructures can cascade to their networks. To address this issue, we have engaged Actor-Network Theory, which provides powerful constructs for organizing diverse critical infrastructure data and deconstructing how the cyber infrastructure can be affected by failures in other critical infrastructures. The resulting Cascade system accommodates massive amounts of infrastructure sensor and GIS data, and provides sophisticated visualization facilities for understanding how failures in physical infrastructures can cascade to cyber assets. Cascade's coordinated geographic and network topological views provide situational awareness about the physical and logical aspects of large-scale enterprise networks. Furthermore, the intuitive, interactive visualization of disaster plans illuminates the cascading effects of infrastructure failures, which is essential to maintaining the stability and survivability of critical cyber assets. The implementation and operational use of tools like Cascade coupled with maturing infrastructure simulation systems and risk management tools will contribute to enhancing the reliability and trust of all critical infrastructures.

Acknowledgements

This research was funded by the Office of Naval Research under Contract N00014-06-M-0146.

References

[1] D. Dudenhoeffer, M. Permann and M. Manic, CIMS: A framework for infrastructure interdependency modeling and analysis, *Proceedings of the Winter Simulation Conference*, pp. 478–485, 2006.

[2] E. Eidswick, Montana spatial data infrastructure: Enhancing an all-hazards approach to emergency preparedness, *Proceedings of the ESRI Homeland Security GIS Summit*, 2006.

[3] J. Goldstein, Emergence as a construct: History and issues, *Emergence*, vol. 1(1), pp. 49–72, 1999.

[4] V. Kumar, J. Srivastava and A. Lazarevic (Eds.), *Managing Cyber Threats: Issues, Approaches and Challenges*, Springer, New York, 2005.

[5] G. Lamm and Y. Haimes, Assessing and managing risks to information assurance: A methodological approach, *Systems Engineering*, vol. 5(4), pp. 286–314, 2002.

[6] B. Latour, *Reassembling the Social: An Introduction to Actor-Network Theory*, Oxford University Press, Oxford, United Kingdom, 2005.

[7] J. Law, Notes on the theory of actor-network: Ordering, strategy and heterogeneity, *Systems Practice and Action Research*, vol. 5(4), pp. 379–393, 1992.

[8] J. Law, Ladbroke Grove, or how to think about failing systems, Technical Report, Lancaster University, Lancaster, United Kingdom, 2000.

[9] J. Law, Disasters, a/symmetries and interferences, Technical Report, Lancaster University, Lancaster, United Kingdom, 2003.

[10] T. Longstaff, C. Chittister, R. Pethia and Y. Haimes, Are we forgetting the risks of information technology? *IEEE Computer*, vol. 33(12), pp. 43–51, 2000.

[11] T. Malone and K. Crowston, The interdisciplinary study of coordination, *ACM Computing Surveys*, vol. 26(1), pp. 87–119, 1991.

[12] New York State, Geographic Information Systems Clearinghouse (www.nysgis.state.ny.us).

[13] P. Pederson, D. Dudenhoeffer, S. Hartley and M. Perman, Critical Infrastructure Interdependency Modeling: A Survey of U.S. and International Research, Technical Report INL/EXT-06-11464, Idaho National Laboratory, Idaho Falls, Idaho, 2006.

[14] C. Perrow, *Normal Accidents: Living with High-Risk Technologies*, Princeton University Press, Princeton, New Jersey, 1999.

[15] S. Rinaldi, J. Peerenboom and T. Kelly, Identifying, understanding and analyzing critical infrastructure interdependencies, *IEEE Control Systems*, vol. 21(6), pp. 11–25, 2001.

[16] C. Robinson, J. Woodward and S. Varnado, Critical infrastructure: Interlinked and vulnerable, *Issues in Science and Technology*, vol. 15(1), pp. 61–67, 1998.

[17] U.S. Department of Homeland Security, National Infrastructure Protection Plan, Washington, DC (www.dhs.gov/nipp), 2006.

[18] R. Zimmerman, Decision-making and the vulnerability of interdependent critical infrastructure, *Proceedings of the IEEE International Conference on Systems, Man and Cybernetics*, vol. 5, pp. 4059–4063, 2004.

[19] R. Zimmerman, Critical infrastructure and interdependency, in *The McGraw-Hill Homeland Security Handbook*, D. Kamien (Ed.), McGraw-Hill, New York, pp. 523–545, 2006.

[20] R. Zimmerman and C. Restrepo, The next step: Quantifying infrastructure interdependencies to improve security, *International Journal of Critical Infrastructures*, vol. 2(2-3), pp. 215–230, 2006.

VI

RISK ASSESSMENT

Chapter 26

A SERVICE-ORIENTED APPROACH FOR ASSESSING INFRASTRUCTURE SECURITY

Marcelo Masera and Igor Nai Fovino

Abstract The pervasive use of information and communication technologies (ICT) in critical infrastructures requires security assessment approaches that consider the highly interconnected nature of ICT systems. Several approaches incorporate the relationships between structural and functional descriptions and security goals, and associate vulnerabilities with known attacks. However, these methodologies are typically based on the analysis of local problems. This paper proposes a methodology that systematically correlates and analyzes structural, functional and security information. The security assessment of critical infrastructure systems is enhanced using a service-oriented perspective, which focuses the analysis on the concept of service, linking the interactions among services – modeled as service chains – with vulnerabilities, threats and attacks.

Keywords: Security assessment, vulnerabilities, threats, attacks, services, system-of-systems

1. Introduction

Security threats are a serious problem in this computer-based era. Any system that makes use of information and communication technologies (ICT) is prone to failures and vulnerabilities that can be exploited by malicious software and agents. Critical infrastructure components, especially industrial installations, have key features that differentiate them from more conventional ICT systems. In particular, industrial facilities combine traditional information systems (e.g., databases) with real-time elements that implement process control functions. Recently, these hybrid infrastructures have begun to be connected to internal and external communication networks, which raises serious security concerns.

Masera, M. and Fovino, I.N., 2008, in IFIP International Federation for Information Processing, Volume 253, Critical Infrastructure Protection, eds. E. Goetz and S. Shenoi; (Boston: Springer), pp. 367–379.

Risk assessment and management in critical infrastructures is a relatively new discipline. Most efforts concentrate on corporate information systems. But industrial systems have certain unique features – the co-existence of heterogeneous environments (e.g., real-time and desktop applications) and constraints deriving from physical phenomena (e.g., power stability) and business objectives (e.g., productivity and performance). These factors determine how IT systems in industrial environments can be handled. For example, it may not be possible to stop industrial operations in order to install security patches.

An effective security assessment and management methodology must take into account information about system characteristics (vulnerabilities, assets, security policies), threats (intentions, resources, capabilities), and potential attack mechanisms and countermeasures. In addition, it is necessary to consider the interactions of malicious actions with accidental failures and human error.

The evolution of systems into infrastructures adds a further level of complexity. Infrastructures are systems-of-systems, greatly interconnected (mainly due to the pervasive use of ICT) and characterized by interdependencies that induce system-wide propagations of negative effects. Several approaches have been proposed for analyzing critical infrastructure systems. These approaches generally focus on linking structural and functional descriptions to security goals, and associating vulnerabilities with known attacks.

This paper describes a novel approach, which builds on the embryonic security assessment methodology of Masera and Nai [14]. The approach, which involves the systematic correlation and analysis of security-relevant information, reveals dependencies within infrastructure systems and relationships between different "information sets" that describe a system-of-systems from the security standpoint. The security assessment of critical infrastructure systems is enhanced using a service-oriented perspective, which links the interactions among services with vulnerabilities, threats and attacks.

2. The State of The Art

The scientific literature has very limited work tailored to the comprehensive assessment of industrial ICT security. However, there is relevant work in the field of ICT security, system modeling and system safety. This section provides an overview of the principal approaches related to ICT security.

Safety and risk have traditionally been the focus of assessments of industrial systems. Only recently have security issues begun to be considered. Keeney, *et al.* [12] have conducted a study on computer system sabotage in critical infrastructures. Stoneburner, Goguen and Feringa [24] have developed a nine-step procedure for risk assessment of information systems. Swiderski and Snyder [25] introduced the concept of threat modeling, and a structured approach for identifying, evaluating and mitigating risks to system security. A similar approach has been proposed for web application environments [4]. Several general purpose tools have been developed, including Microsoft's Security Assessment Tool [20] and Citicus [6]. The first tool supports a traditional "check list" assessment process, which goes through a series of question-and-answer sessions, guiding the analysis through an iterative process and producing a set of recommendations and best practices. The process is quick and easy, but can only provide rough results. The second tool, Citicus, is based on the concept of perceived information risk, categorizing risk according to customized criteria.

The OCTAVE approach [1] introduced in late 1990s is an exhaustive methodology for information systems, but it has not been used for industrial applications. The CORAS methodology [7] was developed in the early 2000s to perform model-based risk analyses of security-critical systems – but the methodology has been applied to e-government and e-commerce systems, not to industrial control systems or, more generally, complex heterogeneous systems.

In our opinion, a security assessment is inadequate if it does not rely on a comprehensive description of the system of interest. The description should cover all relevant perspectives: policies and operations, structure and function, physical links and information flows, among others.

Infrastructure modeling has used mainly for design and operational purposes, but the analysis of security requires additional considerations. Alberts and Dorofee [1] have proposed a risk assessment methodology based on a system description. However, the description is relatively informal; more importantly, it cannot deal with complex systems. den Braber, *et al.* [7] have also presented a risk assessment approach that is partially based on a system description. The approach attempts to capture the concept of an adverse environment by introducing the concept of a "threat scenario." This, of course, represents an advance in system representation that could be adapted to modeling interacting systems (although this was not the intention of the authors).

Masera and Nai Fovino [15–17] have presented an approach based on the concept of a "system-of-systems," which preserves the operational and managerial independence of the individual components while capturing the relationship between components, services and subsystems. The present work adopts this approach as a starting point.

A security assessment has limited effectiveness unless it considers attack scenarios. An early approach to incorporating attack information was the creation of vulnerability databases (e.g., Bugtraq [22]). However, these databases merely describe vulnerabilities, not how they can be exploited in a successful attack. Graph-based attack models [23], which include Petri net models and attack trees models, are popular approaches for modeling attacks. The attack net model introduced by McDermott [19] is an exemplar; in this model, the places of a Petri net represent the attack steps and the transitions capture the actions performed by an attacker. Attack trees proposed by Schneier [21] use expansion trees to show the different attack lines that could affect a system, describing their steps and their interrelationships. The attack tree approach has been extended by Masera and Nai [18] who introduced the concept of an attack projection. This paper adopts this method of representing attacks as a reference.

3. Preliminary Definitions

A risk assessment of industrial ICT infrastructures requires two types of characterizations: security definitions and system definitions. These characterizations and related concepts are described below.

3.1 Security Description

A security description involves security-related concepts such as "threat," "vulnerability," "attack" and "risk." A "threat" is defined in [11] and in the Internet RFC glossary of terms as a potential for violation of security, which exists when there is a circumstance, capability, action or event that could breach security and cause harm. A "vulnerability" a weakness in the architectural design or implementation of an application or a service [2, 5]. As a direct consequence, an "attack" is the entire process implemented by a threat agent to exploit a system by taking advantage of one or more vulnerabilities. Finally, "risk," according to the ISO/IEC 17799:2000 [10], is the probability that a damaging incident is happening (i.e., when a threat is actualized by exploiting a vulnerability) times the potential damage.

3.2 System Description

A system description involves concepts required for system modeling such as "system," "subsystem," "component," "service," "dependency," "information flow" and "asset." A "system" is a collection of entities that collaborate to realize a set of objectives [9]. The same definition holds for a "subsystem" using an inheritance principle. Masera and Nai [16, 17] define a "component" as an atomic object able to fulfill actively- or passively-defined tasks. "Services" are tasks performed by components or subsystems (such services can be "on request").

The same authors define the concept of a "dependency" – a system object A depends on a system object B if B is required by A to accomplish its mission. "Information flow" is a set of point-to-point relationships describing the entire lifecycle of an information item [16]. Finally, an "asset" is any element with value to the relevant stakeholders of the system of interest [14].

As the loss (or impairment) of an asset will negatively affect its value, the objective of security management is to protect assets. Assets are security-relevant entities of a system because (i) their destruction, inability to perform the intended functions, or disclosure to unauthorized agents might cause a detrimental effect, (ii) malicious threats agents might have an interest in targeting them, and (iii) they can be exposed to malicious actions by component vulnerabilities and faults, or by errors on the part of system operators.

In general, an asset could take two main forms: (i) an internal set of components whose loss will cause detriment to the owner/operator of the system, or (ii) an external service supplied to users of the system. Examples of internal assets are a costly component or a set of sensitive data. A control function is an example of external asset. IT-based systems are distinguished from physical systems because of the presence of "information assets" [16].

4. Service-Oriented Paradigm

Beyond the basic descriptions of components, vulnerabilities, attacks, etc., there is a need for a paradigm to capture the interconnections of the different elements that need to be analyzed. It is necessary to identify and examine, for example, the potential effect that a component vulnerability might have on the entire system (e.g., on the business objectives of an industrial facility). As the elements to be considered in a "system-of-systems" situation are manifold, a key challenge is to avoid an excess of data that would hamper the analysis by obfuscating the significant aspects.

To deal with this issue, we make use of the concept of a "service" [16, 17]. Viewed in this light, objects in a system are producers/consumers of services. This concept permits the creation of detailed descriptions of the relationships and dependence mechanisms, which are at the core of the security issues for infrastructure systems.

DEFINITION 1 *A service s is a tuple* $< name, description, ID, sdr >$ *where name identifies the service, description is a brief functional description of the service, ID is the identifier of the producer of the service, and sdr represents information about the dependencies of the service (i.e., in order to fulfill its duty a service x needs the direct support of the services k, z, m).*

The converse of service is "disservice," the lack of provision of the service. The concept of disservice is used in the field of dependability, but its importance has not yet been recognized in the field of ICT security assessment. Upon applying a service-oriented description, the system assumes a "network" aspect. In particular, components and subsystems are directly or indirectly interconnected by what we call "service chains," where all the components/subsystems are in some way necessary for the proper provision of the intended services.

As far as assets are concerned, it is possible to describe them as a mix of internal and external services – more than just a set of hardware and software elements. This is a more operative approach that permits linking the system and the security descriptions of a system. Information, components and subsystems provide/require services to/form other information, components and subsystems. Certain services coalesce through service chains in elements of specific value to the stakeholders of a system; these are called "system assets."

To clarify the concept, consider a system, which provides an "information service" (IS) to external customers (e.g., a power plant might supply data about the energy it produced). This is performed by a "web application service" (WAS) at the subsystem level. The data forwarded to the customers are stored in a database, which provides a "storage service" (SS). The data are the results of computations based on raw data retrieved by remote field sensors, which provide a "field monitoring service" (FMS). The high-level service IS is linked to WAS in a functional way. Moreover, information flow links exist between

WAS and SS, and between SS and FMS. In other words, there is an indirect service link between IS, WAS and FMS. This set of links, which constitutes a service chain, could show how a failure of FMS could affect IS.

DEFINITION 2 *A system* S_n *is defined by* $\{s_1, \ldots, s_n, desc\}$, *where* s_1, ..., s_n *are services provided by* S_n, *and desc is the general description of the system. The concepts of subsystem and component can be defined in the same way without as loss of generality.*

DEFINITION 3 *Let SoS be a system-of-systems defined by* $\{S_a, S_b, \ldots, S_n\}$ *(i.e., set of systems, subsystems and components in SoS), and let Serv be the set of services of SoS. A service dependency record sdr is a tuple* $< s, s_{id}, inset, outset, lf >$, *where s is a service,* S_{id} *is the identifier of the system, subsystem or component* S_a *in SoS (which "produces" the service); inset* $= \{< d, w > | d \in Serv, w \in \aleph\}$ *represents the collection of services directly contributing to the realization of the service with an associated relevance w; outset is the list of services to which the service s directly provides a contribution; lf is a second-order logic expression that describes (when combined with the weights w of inset) the manner and relevance to which the contributing services are logically linked. For example, the provision of a service A may require the combination of services B, C and D according to the logical expression* $[(w_b.B \wedge w_c.C) \vee w_d.D)]$.

Applying this definition to a system-of-systems, *SoS*, it is possible to reconstruct all the links between services. We call this the "service chain" of the object under analysis. This is an oriented graph describing the direct and indirect links between all the services provided by and within *SoS*. From a security perspective, service chains help identify all the dependencies that play a role in a security event (e.g., propagation of failures, cascading effects, etc.). As defined in Masera [13], a "security dependency" exists when there is a relationship between two systems A and B such that an internal fault in B can be propagated through a chain of faults, errors and failures to system A. Drawing from [3], we refer to such chains as "pathological chains."

Pathological chains can be caused by (i) accidental events due to internal faults or human errors, or (ii) malicious attacks. Since every component in a system description has an associated set of known vulnerabilities (each vulnerability affects a target component with a certain plausibility y), we can enrich the description of the pathological chain by adding information related to the vulnerabilities. In this way, the appraisal of service chains considering dependencies and vulnerabilities result in what we call "vulnerability chains" (see Figure 1). The notion of a vulnerability chain offers three main advantages:

- It allows the identification of low-level vulnerabilities (associated with low-level components) that can have an effect on high-level services (typically services provided by the system to the external world).
- It permits the capture of the potential non-negligible side effects of an identified vulnerability.

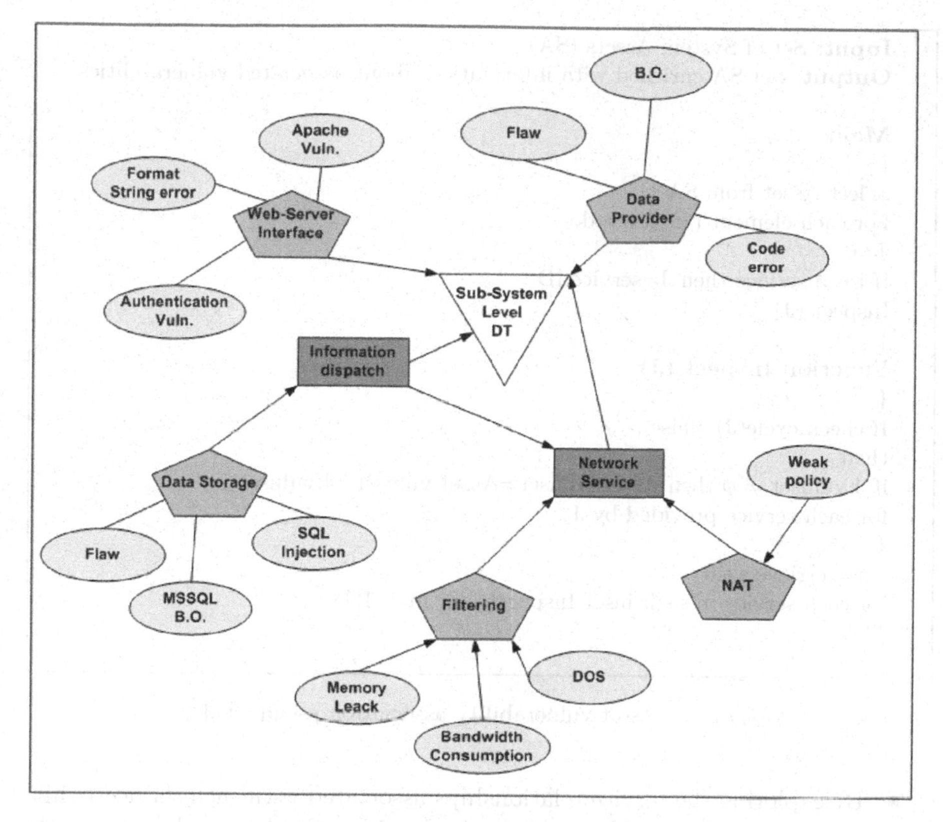

Figure 1. Vulnerability chains.

- It constitutes the glue that links system description knowledge (components, services, assets, etc.) with security knowledge (vulnerabilities, attacks and threats)

4.1 Service-Oriented Vulnerability Analysis

By adopting the description paradigm presented above, it is possible to identify which low-level vulnerabilities (i.e., those affecting low-level components) can have a negative security effect on the assets. The approach involves the following steps:

- The dependencies are computed for each asset.

- For each element in the asset, the services it provides are retrieved. Note that an asset may be composed of physical and logical subsystems, services and components.

```
Input: Set of System Assets (SA)
Output: Set SA enriched with information about associated vulnerabilities

Main
{
Select Asset from SA
For each element i in Asset do
J=i
If i is a service then J=service.ID
Inspect (J)
}
Function Inspect (J)
{
If check_cycle(J)=false
then
if J.vulnset ≠ φ then Asset.vulnset=Asset.vulnset+J.vulnset
for each service provided by J
{
sdr=retrieve s.sdr
for each service in s.sdr.inset Inspect(s.sdr.inset.ID)
}}
```

Figure 2. Asset-vulnerability association pseudo code.

- By exploring the service relationships associated with each service (while taking care of possible cyclic dependencies), the low-level components that contribute to the service in some way are identified.

- The vulnerabilities that potentially affect the low-level components are associated with the asset.

Applying this procedure, we can identify which vulnerability associated a component may have an impact on the asset and to what degree. This knowledge facilitates the analysis of the effects of threats and attacks, decisions about the effectiveness of current policies, the benchmarking of potential solutions and the running of security scenarios.

In our approach, vulnerabilities are classified according to their estimated relevance following an identification of potential threats. Figure 2 presents the pseudo code for this procedure.

4.2 Service-Oriented Threat Assessment

Determining the vulnerability of a system is not enough. It is also necessary to analyze the threats that might exploit the identified vulnerabilities. In this section, we expand the security analysis process described by Masera and Nai [14] into a "service-oriented threat assessment process," whose objective is to determine the vulnerable assets that are exposed to different types of threats taking into consideration the vulnerability chains.

When this kind of analysis is applied to relatively small systems, it is usually solved by assigning known threats to possible target assets on the basis of some (possibly not well-documented) hypotheses made by the analyst. But such an approach, in addition to not being systematic, says nothing about the proportion of security situations being considered from the total number of possible negative events.

Threat analysis can be improved by using information derived from vulnerability analysis. A threat is relevant only if there is the real possibility that it can be realized. In particular, ICT threats have to be correlated with the assets that – from the vulnerability viewpoint – can be affected by them. Service-oriented threat analysis proceeds in a similar manner to service-oriented vulnerability analysis that was presented in the previous section:

- A subset of assets affected by significant vulnerabilities (identified by service-oriented vulnerability analysis) is selected from the set of assets.
- The subsystem services involved for each element of the subset of vulnerable assets are identified.
- The hypothesized threats (derived from some parallel identification of plausible threats applicable to the type of system under analysis) are instantiated and correlated with the previously-identified subsystem services (an effective way to conduct this analysis is to assign threats only to subsystem services [14]).
- The threats whose effects can be propagated to the vulnerable assets are verified by exploring the service dependencies and relationships.

Using this procedure, it is possible to obtain a focused, motivated and documented set of "exposed" subsystem services. Also, it is possible to demonstrate how threats can affect services – and therefore assets – directly by targeting components, or indirectly by effects on correlated assets that propagate through service dependency chains.

4.3 Service-Oriented Attack Analysis

Attack analysis involves identifying the potential attacks that can be successfully developed by the previously identified threats. Validating the possibility that an attack can take place against a target system is not a simple task, especially in the case of large or complex systems.

Attack trees are a popular means for representing the steps and the conditions required to perpetrate offensive actions against vulnerable assets. However, attack trees are usually too abstract because they refer to the types of components. To validate attacks, attack trees have to be instantiated for the specific elements and characteristics of the system under analysis. This requires the consideration of all the interconnections and relative interdependencies, and potential alternative paths. An attack validation conducted without this knowledge will produce a large number of false positives (i.e., valid attacks that are not exploitable), or it will discard potential attacks derived from vulnerabilities that are coupled in non-obvious ways.

The information derived from service-oriented analysis is useful for mitigation efforts as it helps focus the examination of attacks on vulnerable disservice chains. In other words, by applying this knowledge to disservice chains, it is possible to identify whether there is some connection between vulnerable components that can be attacked by one of the verified threats. All the other chains may be considered safe with respect to potential attacks.

Attack validation using a service-oriented perspective proceeds as follows:

- The attacks that can be associated to the verified threats are identified and presented as hypotheses to be validated.

- The associated subsystems and all the respective relationships are identified for each verified threat.

- The attack trees associated with each verified threat are validated by applying existing information about disservice chains, dependency relationships and conditional assertions (i.e., assertions describing some additional conditions needed to realize the attack).

- The potential impact on the assets due to validated attacks are computed by considering all direct and indirect effects on the affected subsystems.

The procedure described above identifies the set of realizable attacks, while minimizing the number of false positives.

5. Preliminary Results

To test the performance, quality and benefits of the service-oriented approach, we developed a software tool named InSAW (Industrial Security Assessment Workbench). InSAW implements the analysis steps presented in this paper (system description, vulnerability assessment, threat assessment and attack assessment). In addition, it implements an additional phase for overall risk assessment. InSAW uses a MSSQL relational database with an intermediate object-oriented layer based on Hibernate and a set of modular analysis engines developed using Microsoft .Net technology.

The testing phase involved the following steps:

- Selection of a set of industrial case studies (remote control of primary substations, control of power plants), and performance of security assessments using the methodology with desktop tools.

- Application of InSAW to the automatic determination of service/disservice chains and related vulnerability, threat and attack analyses (it is, of course, necessary to input a description of the target system).

- Comparison of the results obtained by manual and automatic analyses.

Although the tests are preliminary in nature, the results (see, e.g., [8]) are promising. They enable us to make the following observations:

- A service-oriented approach provides an analyst with a better, more comprehensive understanding of the relations, connections and dependencies between system components.
- Service-oriented vulnerability and threat assessments benefit from the analysis of service dependencies as it is possible to identify side-effect connections between vulnerabilities and assets that are not readily observable by manual means.
- The service-oriented approach greatly augments the precision of attack validation. This is because each attack step can be related to all the aspects that might influence it.

6. Conclusions

The service-oriented methodology described in this paper is a novel approach for assessing the security of critical infrastructure systems. The methodology has as its core the concept of service and the description of service dependencies, which greatly facilitate vulnerability analysis, threat assessment and attack analysis and verification. Automating security assessment procedures is undoubtedly of value to analysts, mainly because of the dynamic nature of security events and the need to consider new information about vulnerabilities, threats, exploits and countermeasures. Our future work will concentrate on conducting extensive tests of the methodology and its implementation. In addition, we will attempt to link the approach with other security-relevant activities such as early warning, diagnostics and information sharing.

References

[1] C. Alberts and A. Dorofee, *Managing Information Security Risks: The OCTAVE (SM) Approach*, Addison-Wesley, Boston, Massachusetts, 2002.

[2] O. Alhazmi, Y. Malaiya and I. Ray, Security vulnerabilities in software systems: A quantitative perspective, in *Data and Applications Security XIX (LNCS 3654)*, S. Jajodia and D. Wijesekera (Eds.), Springer, Berlin-Heidelberg, Germany, pp. 281–294, 2005.

[3] A. Avizienis, J. Laprie, B. Randell and C. Landwehr, Basic concepts and taxonomy of dependable and secure computing, *IEEE Transactions on Dependable and Secure Computing*, vol. 1(1), pp 11–33, 2004.

[4] E. Bertino, D. Bruschi, S. Franzoni, I. Nai Fovino and S. Valtolina, Threat modeling for SQL servers, *Proceedings of the Eighth IFIP TC-6 TC-11 Conference on Communications and Multimedia Security*, pp. 189–201, 2004.

[5] M. Bishop, *Computer Security: Art and Science*, Addison-Wesley, Boston, Massachusetts, 2003.

[6] Citicus, Citicus ONE (www.citicus.com).

[7] F. den Braber, T. Dimitrakos, B. Gran, M. Lund, K. Stølen and J. Aagedal, The CORAS methodology: Model-based risk management using UML and UP, in *UML and the Unified Process*, L. Favre (Ed.), IGI Publishing, Hershey, Pennsylvania, pp. 332–357, 2003.

[8] G. Dondossola, J. Szanto, M. Masera and I. Nai Fovino, Evaluation of the effects of intentional threats to power substation control systems, *Proceedings of the International Workshop on Complex Network and Infrastructure Protection*, 2006.

[9] Institute of Electrical and Electronics Engineers, IEEE Standard Glossary of Software Engineering Terminology (IEEE Standard 610.12-1990), Piscataway, New Jersey, 1990.

[10] International Organization for Standardization, Code of Practice for Information Security Management (ISO/IEC 17799:2000), Geneva, Switzerland, 2000.

[11] A. Jones and D. Ashenden, *Risk Management for Computer Security: Protecting Your Network and Information Assets*, Elsevier Butterworth-Heinemann, Oxford, United Kingdom, 2005.

[12] M. Keeney, E. Kowalski, D. Cappelli, A. Moore, T. Shimeall and S. Rogers, Insider Threat Study: Computer System Sabotage in Critical Infrastructure Sectors, Technical Report, U.S. Secret Service and CERT Coordination Center, Software Engineering Institute, Carnegie Mellon University, Pittsburgh, Pennsylvania, 2005.

[13] M. Masera, Interdependencies and security assessment: A dependability view, *Proceedings of the IEEE International Conference on Systems, Man and Cybernetics*, Taipei, 2006.

[14] M. Masera and I. Nai Fovino, A framework for the security assessment of remote control applications of critical infrastructures, *Proceedings of the Twenty-Ninth ESReDA Seminar*, 2005.

[15] M. Masera and I. Nai Fovino, Emergent disservices in interdependent systems and systems-of-systems, *Proceedings of the IEEE International Conference on Systems, Man and Cybernetics*, 2006.

[16] M. Masera and I. Nai Fovino, Modeling information assets for security risk assessment in industrial settings, *Proceedings of the Fifteenth EICAR Annual Conference*, 2006.

[17] M. Masera and I. Nai Fovino, Models for security assessment and management, *Proceedings of the International Workshop on Complex Network and Infrastructure Protection*, 2006.

[18] M. Masera and I. Nai Fovino, Through the description of attacks: A multidimensional view, *Proceedings of the Twenty-Fifth International Conference on Computer Safety, Reliability and Security*, pp. 15–28, 2006.

[19] J. McDermott, Attack net penetration testing, *Proceedings of the New Security Paradigms Workshop*, pp. 15–22, 2002.

[20] Microsoft Corporation, Microsoft Security Assessment Tool (www.securityguidance.com).

[21] B. Schneier, Attack trees: Modeling security threats, *Dr. Dobb's Journal*, December 1999.

[22] SecurityFocus, Bugtraq vulnerability database (securityfocus.com).

[23] J. Steffan and M. Schumacher, Collaborative attack modeling, *Proceedings of the ACM Symposium on Applied Computing*, pp. 253–259, 2002.

[24] G. Stoneburner, A. Goguen and A. Feringa, Risk Management Guide for Information Technology Systems, Special Publication 800-30, National Institute of Standards and Technology, U.S. Department of Commerce, Gaithersburg, Maryland, 2002.

[25] F. Swiderski and W. Snyder, *Threat Modeling*, Microsoft Press, Redmond, Washington, 2004.

Chapter 27

ANALYSIS OF ELECTRICAL POWER AND OIL AND GAS PIPELINE FAILURES

Jeffrey Simonoff, Carlos Restrepo, Rae Zimmerman and Zvia Naphtali

Abstract This paper examines the spatial and temporal distribution of failures in three critical infrastructure systems in the United States: the electrical power grid, hazardous liquids (including oil) pipelines, and natural gas pipelines. The analyses are carried out at the state level, though the analytical frameworks are applicable to other geographic areas and infrastructure types. The paper also discusses how understanding the spatial distribution of these failures can be used as an input into risk management policies to improve the performance of these systems, as well as for security and natural hazards mitigation.

Keywords: Electrical power, oil and gas pipelines, risk, count regression models

1. Introduction

The energy infrastructure is required to operate practically every other infrastructure; failures in the energy sector can cascade to other sectors, often creating widespread disruptions. This paper provides an analysis of the vulnerabilities of the electrical power, oil and gas sectors, three major components of the energy infrastructure. For simplicity, we refer to hazardous liquids pipelines as oil pipelines, although they carry other hazardous liquids, e.g., anhydrous ammonia. It is vital to understand the nature of outage trends in the three sectors as a means for identifying areas of specific vulnerability and susceptibility to widespread damage in the event of human-initiated or natural catastrophes.

Evidence over roughly the past decade seems to point to the growing importance of weather-related events as at least partially responsible for U.S. outages. In the electricity sector, the proportion of outages attributed to weather-related events appears to be growing [10, 11]. In the oil and gas sectors, outages in transmission pipelines and production facilities are also often weather-related. For example, the Gulf Coast hurricanes of 2005 resulted in the Colonial pipeline, which serves much of the east coast of the U.S., not being fully operational for

Simonoff, J., Restrepo, C., Zimmerman, R. and Naphtali, Z., 2008, in IFIP International Federation for Information Processing, Volume 253, Critical Infrastructure Protection, eds. E. Goetz and S. Shenoi; (Boston: Springer), pp. 381–394.

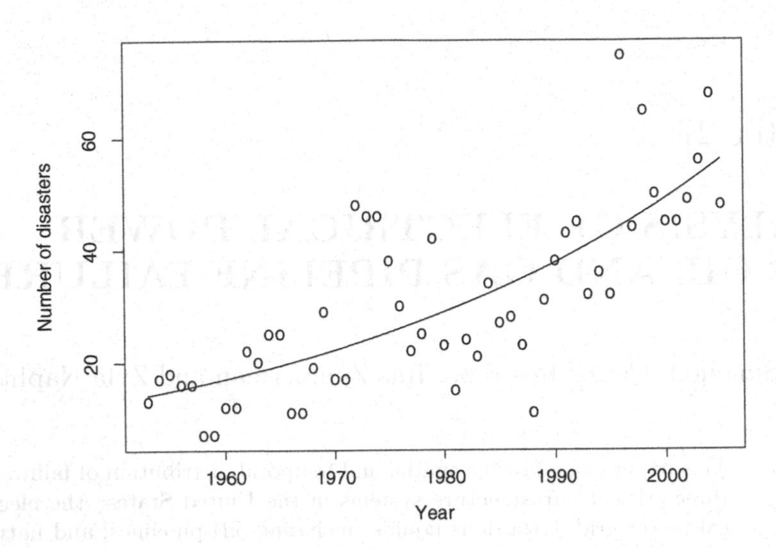

Figure 1. Federally-declared major U.S. disasters (1953 – 2005).

nearly ten days. Several refineries were also non-operational for similar time frames.

According to data released by the Federal Emergency Management Agency (FEMA), natural hazards in general (which include the most severe weather events) have been growing steadily over the past few decades. Figure 1 shows the annual number of federally-declared major disasters from 1953 through 2005, with a negative binomial regression fit superimposed on the counts. The regression model (which fits the data well) implies a 2.7% annual increase in major disasters over roughly 50 years.

Meanwhile, the energy infrastructure and society's dependence on the infrastructure continues to grow, making the ramifications of disruption much more serious. For example, the production of energy in the U.S. doubled between 1950 and 2000 [16] (calculated from [13, 14]).

Given its importance, understanding the extent of vulnerabilities in the energy sector and its resilience to disruptions is critical. An analysis of a hypothetical attack on New Jersey's systems alone found that "the electrical power system's resiliency to damage is the key to the extent and duration of any economic consequences of a terrorist attack, at least in New Jersey" [3] (p. 722).

2. Electrical Power Outages

The electricity infrastructure has become so central to our lives that we take it for granted. It is difficult to think of any daily activities that are not somehow related to electricity. Hence, understanding electrical power outages

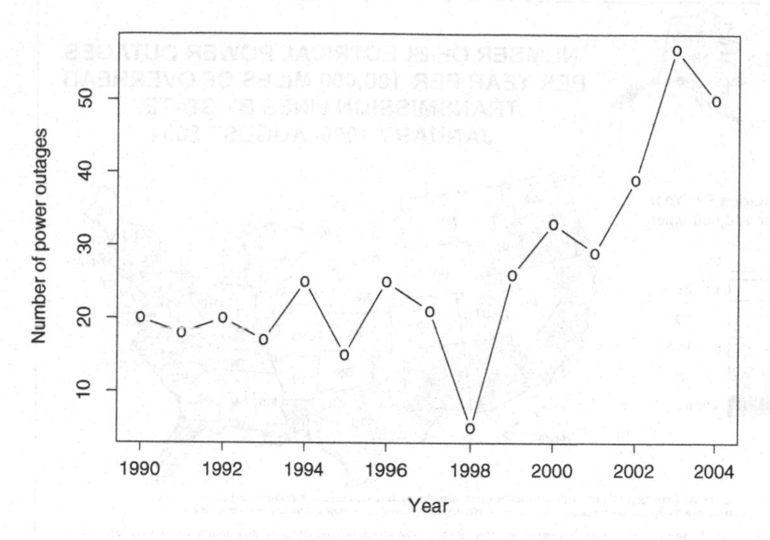

Figure 2. Electrical power outages (1990 – 2004).

and the sector's vulnerabilities is key to maintaining national security. This section examines electrical power outages in the United States using data for the period 1990 – 2004. The data were obtained from the Disturbance Analysis Working Group (DAWG) database, which is maintained by the North American Electric Reliability Council (NERC). The database includes information on 400 outages and is available online [4].

Figure 2 presents annual counts of electrical power outages for 1990 – 2004. It is apparent that other than in the anomalous year 1998, there has been a steady increase in the average annual number of outages. This is consistent with other analyses [7] that found increasing rates, particularly in outages that were confined to a single state.

Although the DAWG database has been used to portray various dimensions of outage patterns and trends [1, 12], analyses of the spatial distribution of these outages and their characteristics are less common. Maps like the one shown in Figure 3 help illustrate the spatial variation. Figure 3 provides the number of electrical power outages per 100,000 circuit miles of overhead transmission lines for January 1990 – August 2004 by state. Note that outages in different states that were related to each other are listed as separate outages.

Electrical power outages are not evenly distributed across the country. As one might expect, states with higher populations and energy use are likely to have more outages. Outages, however, can also vary from one region to another for several reasons, e.g., weather conditions, utility maintenance and investment policies, and the regulatory environment under which utilities operate. Weather events and equipment failure are the most common causes of outages, but the relative importance of different causes of outages has changed over the period

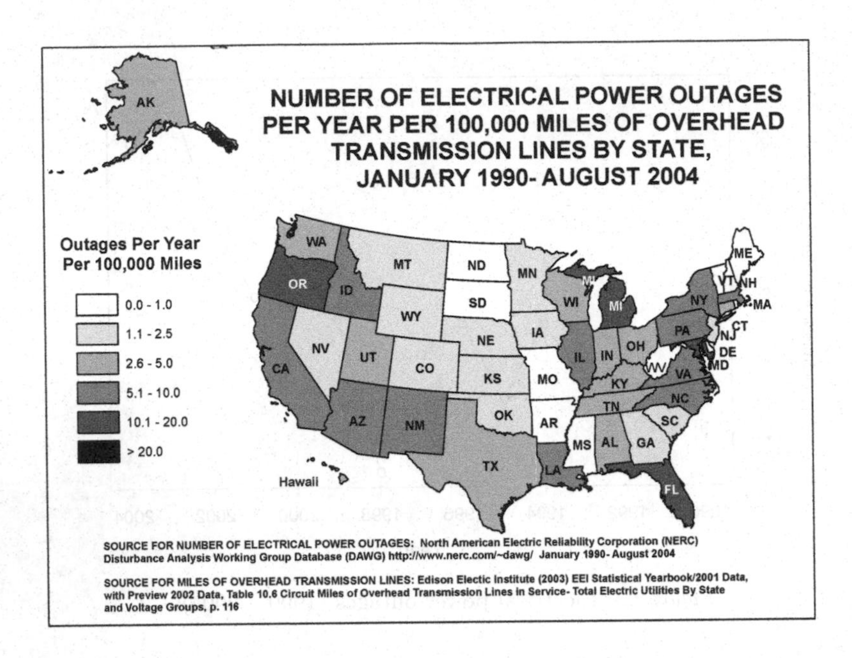

Figure 3. Electrical power outages per 100,000 miles of transmission lines.

under analysis in the United States. In the early 1990s equipment failure was the major cause of outages, but by the early 2000s weather events were the most common cause [11, 17]. This is consistent, of course, with the apparently increasing frequency of natural disasters noted in Section 1.

The states with the highest number of outages were California (56), Michigan (30), Florida (29), New York (26), Texas (22), North Carolina (22), Oregon (19) and Illinois (18). No outages were reported in Delaware, Maine, Mississippi, New Hampshire, North Dakota, Rhode Island, South Dakota, Vermont and West Virginia. Although it seems clear that state size and population are related to the frequency of outages, this is not the only effect, as larger states such as Ohio and Pennsylvania had fewer outages than smaller states such as Oregon.

The observed patterns can be explored more formally. Statistical analyses of incident counts are based on count regression models [9], since the response variable in each case is the number of outages or the number of incidents for each type of pipeline (hazardous liquids, natural gas transmission and natural gas distribution, respectively), in each state in a given year. The standard distributional model for data of this type is the Poisson random variable. Let Y_i be the number of outages (incidents) occurring in a given state during a given year. The Poisson random variable implies that the probability of observing y_i outages (incidents) is

$$P(Y_i = y_i) = \exp(-\mu_i + y_i \log \mu_i - \log y_i!),$$

where μ_i is the expected number of outages (incidents). The Poisson regression model posits a loglinear relationship between μ_i and a linear combination of the predictors,

$$\mu_i = \exp(\beta_0 + \beta_1 x_{1i} + \cdots + \beta_k x_{ki}).$$

In the context of this paper these predictors are indicator variables that identify the different states and the different years. Parameters of the model are estimated using maximum likelihood (analogous to using least squares for regression models based on normally distributed errors). The adequacy of the model can be assessed using the deviance statistic, a goodness-of-fit test that is compared to a χ^2 distribution.

In many cases, a more meaningful analysis occurs if the number of incidents is standardized using an appropriate size measure, as is done in Figure 3. For example, while a larger number of incidents would be expected in states with more miles of pipeline, this might not be as important from a risk management point of view as understanding the rate of incidents per (for example) 10,000 miles of pipeline. Similarly, examining the number of power outages per 100,000 circuit miles of overhead electric transmission lines corrects for uninteresting size effects (such state-by-state figures for 2000 are available in [2]). Modeling the rate is accomplished in the loglinear model by using the logarithm of the number of miles of pipeline or transmission lines as an offset (an additional predictor that is forced to have a slope equal to 1 in the model). So, if t_i is the number of pipeline or transmission line miles in a state, fitting the model

$$\mu_i = \exp(\beta_0 + \beta_1 x_{1i} + \cdots + \beta_k x_{ki} + \log t_i)$$

corresponds to modeling the rate of incidents or outages, rather than the count. All of the count regression models reported in this paper are standardized in this way. Other variables that could be used to correct for size effects include state population size, population density and energy consumption.

The Poisson random variable has the property that its variance is a function of only its mean, i.e., $V(Y_i) = \mu_i = E(Y_i)$. This can be too restrictive, particularly when there are differences in the expected number of incidents that are not accounted for by only the state and year, in that this unmodeled heterogeneity results in overdispersion relative to the Poisson distribution. An alternative model in such a circumstance is a negative binomial regression model (still using a loglinear model relating the mean to the predictors), since the negative binomial random variable has the property that $V(Y_i) = \mu_i(1 + \alpha\mu_i)$, with $\alpha > 0$, which is necessarily larger than the mean μ_i.

A Poisson regression model fitting time and geography main effects fits the 1990 – 2004 power outage data well (a deviance of 666.0 on 713 degrees of freedom, $p = .90$), and indicates strong time and geographical effects. The time trend is consistent with a roughly 8.5% annual increase in outages. States with unusually high numbers of outages per 100,000 miles of overhead transmission lines include California, North Carolina, New York, Oregon, and in particular Florida, Maryland and Michigan (note that this need not correspond exactly to the pattern in Figure 3, since the regression model takes the time effect into account). There is little apparent connection between outage rates and the size of the local power grid, indicating the lack of any economies or diseconomies of scale (Washington, DC, has an extremely high outage rate, but this is somewhat misleading given that it has only three miles of overhead transmission lines).

3. Pipeline Incidents

This section examines the spatial and temporal variation of failures in the hazardous liquid and natural gas pipeline infrastructure. Three data sets are analyzed; a more detailed description of these data sets is found in [8]. The first data set relates to hazardous liquid incidents, which include leaks in pipelines that carry petroleum, petroleum products and anhydrous ammonia. These substances are considered harmful to human health and to the environment. The second data set relates to natural gas transmission incidents, which refer to failures in large pipelines that transport natural gas from facilities that gather, process or store natural gas to large-volume customers and natural gas distribution systems. The third data set relates to natural gas distribution incidents, which refer to failures in the smaller-diameter natural gas distribution pipeline networks that supply natural gas to the final consumer [6]. The data sets are maintained by the Office of Pipeline Safety (OPS), which is part of the U.S. Department of Transportation's Pipeline and Hazardous Materials Safety Administration (PHMSA) [5].

It is important to keep in mind that oil and gas transmission and distribution systems also link production facilities, namely, refineries and power plants. As with power plants, refineries are heavily concentrated in certain geographical regions, with more than 50% of U.S. refineries located in only four states [15].

3.1 Hazardous Liquid Pipeline Incidents

Hazardous liquid pipeline incidents are decreasing over time. The overall trend for the period 1986 – 2005 is shown in Figure 4. The sharp increase after 2002 is a result of a change in the definition of what constitutes a reportable incident. Since 2002, spills as small as five gallons have had to be reported to OPS, rather than the 50 gallon limit used earlier.

The spatial distribution of hazardous liquid pipeline incidents also varies significantly from state to state. While some variability from year to year and state to state would be expected just from random fluctuation, a count regression model fit based on main effects for year and state can be used to assess whether the rates of hazardous liquid pipeline incidents differ significantly over time and space. A Poisson model, when fit to the period 2002 – 2005 (this time period is most relevant for current risk management, as it reflects the new definition of hazardous liquid incident), finds both effects highly statistically significant, and fits the data well (the deviance goodness-of-fit statistic is 155.7 on 150 degrees of freedom, with associated tail probability $p = .36$).

The time trend is consistent with a roughly 9% annual decrease in incidents per 10,000 miles of pipeline. Figure 5 illustrates the geographical

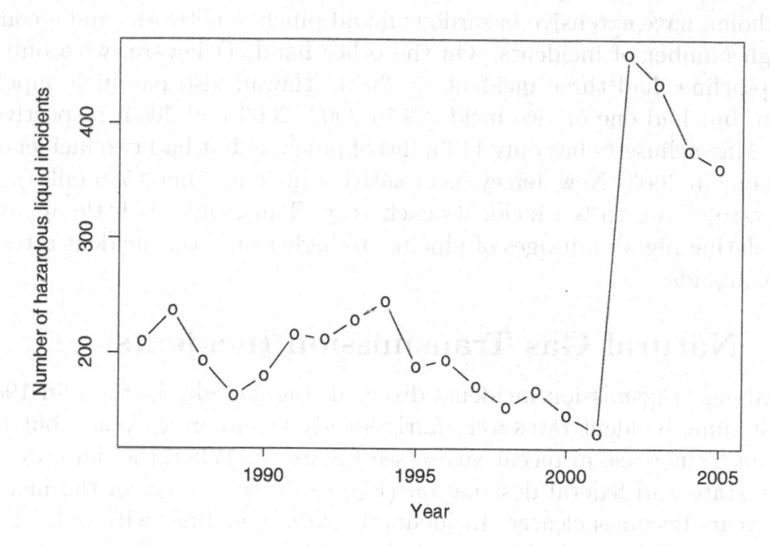

Figure 4. Hazardous liquid incidents (1986 – 2005).

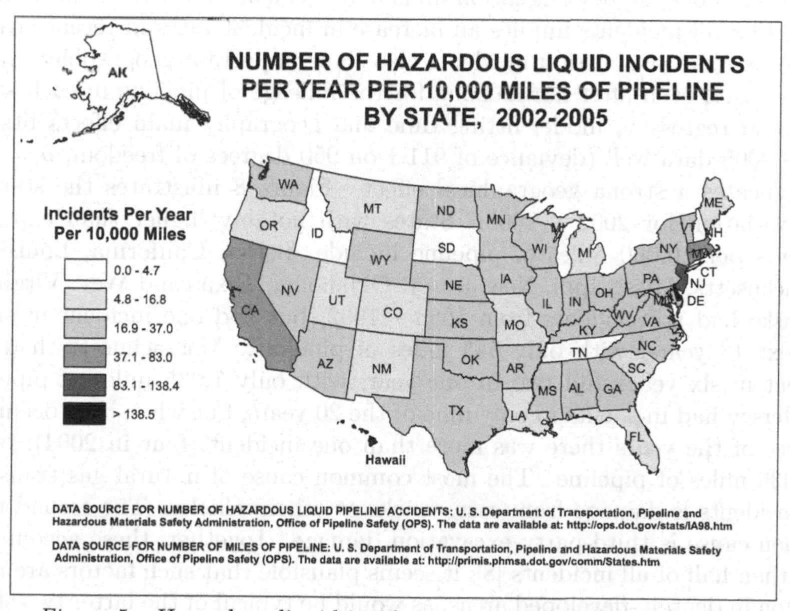

Figure 5. Hazardous liquid incidents per 10,000 miles of pipeline.

(state to state) variation. States with notably higher than expected pipeline incidents per 10,000 miles of pipeline are California, Delaware, Hawaii, Kansas, Massachusetts, New Jersey and Oklahoma. States such as California, Kansas and Oklahoma have extensive hazardous liquid pipeline networks and a consistently high number of incidents. On the other hand, Delaware, with only 61 miles of pipeline, had three incidents in 2004. Hawaii also has little pipeline (90 miles), but had one or two incidents in 2002, 2003 and 2004, respectively; similarly, Massachusetts has only 114 miles of pipeline, but had two incidents in 2002 and one in 2003. New Jersey has relatively little pipeline (556 miles), but a steady rate of two to ten incidents each year. Thus, there is little apparent pattern relating higher mileages of pipeline to higher or lower incident rates for hazardous liquids.

3.2 Natural Gas Transmission Incidents

Natural gas transmission incidents dropped dramatically in the mid 1980s. Since that time, incident rates were fairly steady for about 15 years, but they have begun to increase in recent years (see Figure 6). When the data are separated by state and federal designation (Figure 7), the source of the increase in recent years becomes clearer. Incidents involving pipelines with federal designations (i.e., offshore pipelines located outside state jurisdiction) show an increasing trend corresponding to a more than doubling of expected incidents annually after 2002, which accounts for much of the overall increase in incidents. This is supported by formal analysis: a Poisson regression model excluding incidents without a state designation finds little evidence for a time effect, while a model for all incidents implies an increase in incident rates in recent years.

Natural gas transmission incidents also show important geographical variation by state, even after normalizing for the mileage of pipeline in each state. A Poisson regression model fitting time and geography main effects fits the 1986 – 2005 data well (deviance of 911.1 on 950 degrees of freedom, $p = .83$), and indicates a strong geographical effect. Figure 8 illustrates the state to state variation for 2002 – 2005. States with notably higher than expected incidents per 10,000 miles of pipeline include Alaska, California, Louisiana, Massachusetts, Mississippi, New Jersey, Oklahoma, Texas and West Virginia.

Alaska had no incidents from 1986 – 1992, but had one incident in six of the next 13 years, with only 543 miles of pipeline. Massachusetts had one incident in six years and two in one year, with only 1,035 miles of pipeline. New Jersey had incidents in only nine of the 20 years, but when they occurred, in three of the years there was more than one incident (four in 2004), based on 1,436 miles of pipeline. The most common cause of natural gas transmission incidents is damage from cars, trucks or other vehicles. The second most common cause is third-party excavation damage. Together, these account for more than half of all incidents [8]; it seems plausible that such factors are more common in densely-developed areas, as would be typical of the latter two states (Massachusetts and New Jersey).

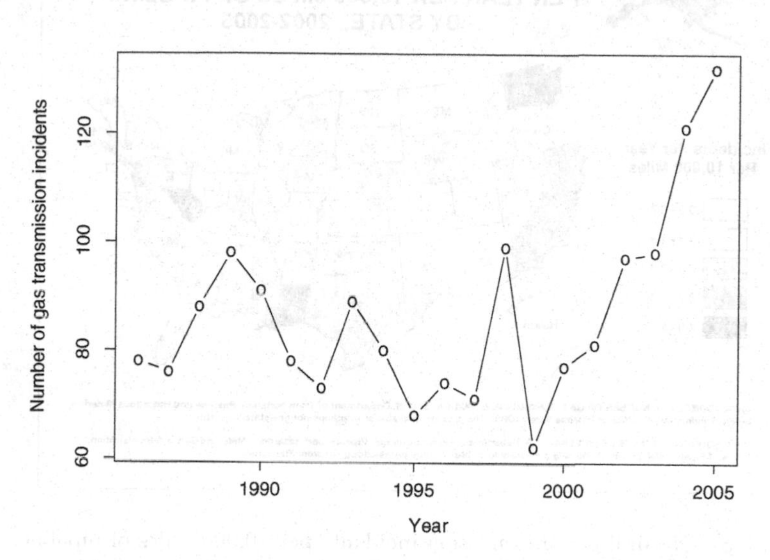

Figure 6. Natural gas transmission incidents (1986 – 2005).

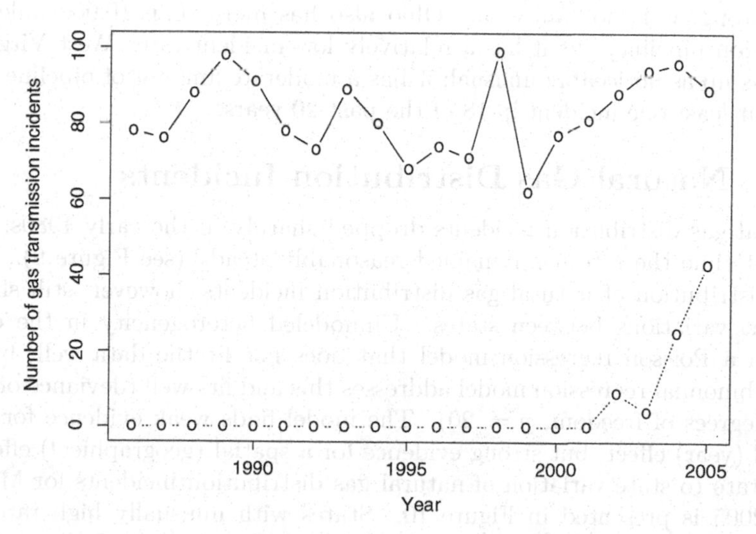

Figure 7. Natural gas transmission incidents (state: solid line; federal: dotted line).

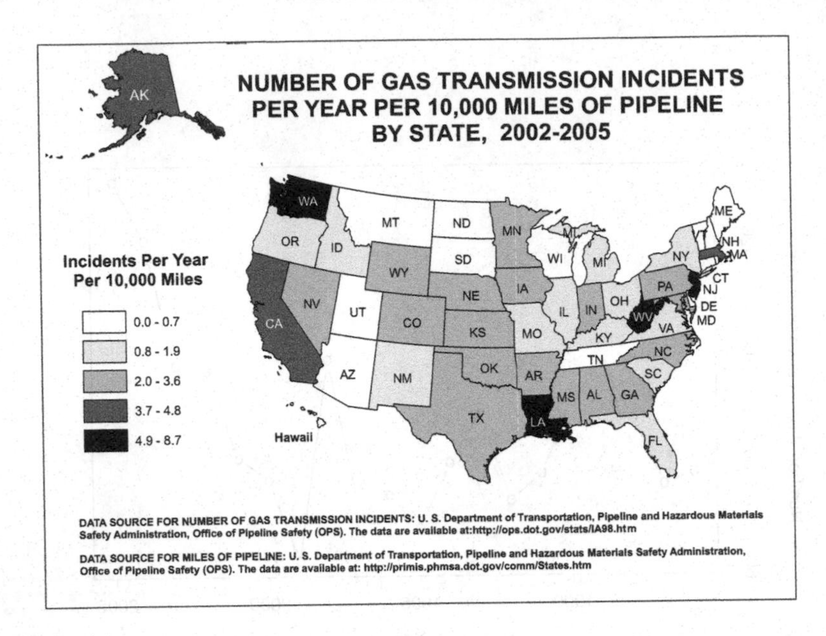

Figure 8. Natural gas transmission incidents per 10,000 miles of pipeline.

California, Louisiana, Mississippi, Oklahoma and Texas are among the states with the most pipeline mileage (in excess of 10,000 miles), implying evidence of diseconomies of scale — the states with the most transmission pipeline mileage also have higher-than-expected incidents per mile of pipeline. While this pattern is strong, it is not universal: Ohio also has more than 10,000 miles of transmission pipeline, but it has a relatively low incident rate. West Virginia also shows up as noticeably unusual; it has a moderate amount of pipeline, yet has had at least one incident in 18 of the past 20 years.

3.3 Natural Gas Distribution Incidents

Natural gas distribution incidents dropped sharply in the early 1980s, but since that time the rate has remained reasonably steady (see Figure 9). The spatial distribution of natural gas distribution incidents, however, still shows important variations between states. Unmodeled heterogeneity in the data results in a Poisson regression model that does not fit the data well, but a negative binomial regression model addresses this and fits well (deviance of 986 on 950 degrees of freedom, $p = .20$). The model finds weak evidence for any temporal (year) effect, but strong evidence for a spatial (geographical) effect.

The state to state variation of natural gas distribution incidents for March 2004 – 2005 is presented in Figure 10. States with unusually high rates of incidents include Alaska, Louisiana, Maryland, Maine, Missouri, Pennsylvania, Texas and Vermont. Maine and Vermont, with relatively low pipeline mileage, had only one or two incidents, but the incidents occurred in multiple years so

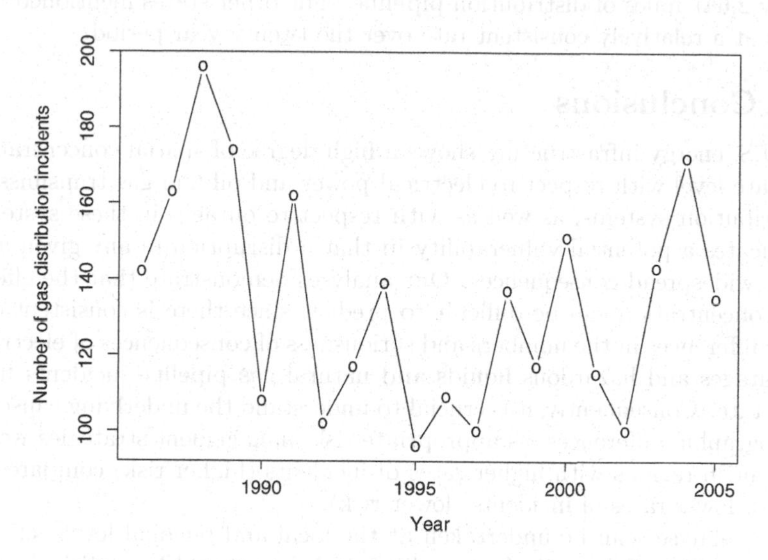

Figure 9. Natural gas distribution incidents (1986 – 2005).

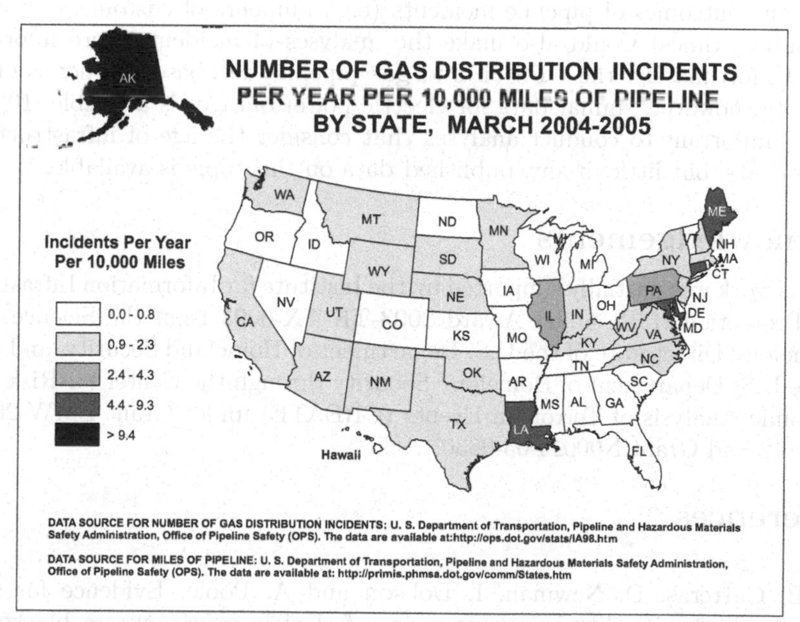

Figure 10. Natural gas distribution incidents per 10,000 miles of pipeline.

they cannot be viewed as isolated incidents. Alaska only had three incidents from 1986 – 1992, but has averaged more than five incidents annually since then, with only 2,647 miles of distribution pipeline. The other states mentioned had incidents at a relatively consistent rate over the twenty-year period.

4. Conclusions

The U.S. energy infrastructure shows a high degree of spatial concentration at the state level with respect to electrical power and oil and gas transmission and distribution systems, as well as with respect to outages in these systems. This indicates a potential vulnerability in that a disruption in any given area will have widespread consequences. Our analyses demonstrate that the effects of such concentration can be difficult to predict, since there is consistent evidence of differences in the numbers and seriousness of consequences of electrical power outages and hazardous liquids and natural gas pipeline incidents from state to state. Consequently, it is crucial to understand the underlying causes of these geographic differences, as appropriate risk management strategies would be different in regions with higher rates of incidents (higher risk) compared to those with lower rates of incidents (lower risk).

Similar analyses can be undertaken at the local and regional levels subject to the availability of data. Such spatially-based data would be a critical input to prioritizing areas for targeting resources in risk management efforts.

Incorporating data from the Canadian electrical power grid would be useful, given the interdependencies existing between the U.S and Canadian grids. Data about the outcomes of pipeline incidents (e.g., numbers of customers affected and outage times) would also make the analyses of incidents more informative. Unfortunately, the OPS oil and gas pipeline databases do not contain this data; however, similar data for electric power outages is available [10]. It is also important to conduct analyses that consider the age of infrastructure components, but little, if any, published data on this topic is available.

Acknowledgements

This work was partially supported by the Institute for Information Infrastructure Protection (I3P) under Award 2003-TK-TX-0003 from the Science and Technology Directorate of the U.S. Department of Homeland Security, and also by the U.S. Department of Homeland Security through the Center for Risk and Economic Analysis of Terrorism Events (CREATE) under Grant EMW-2004-GR-0112 and Grant N00014-05-0630.

References

[1] B. Carreras, D. Newman, I. Dobson and A. Poole, Evidence for self-organized criticality in a time series of electric power system blackouts, *IEEE Transactions on Circuits and Systems*, vol. 51(9), pp. 1733–1740, 2004.

[2] Edison Electric Institute, *Statistical Yearbook of the Electric Utility Industry*, Edison Electric Institute, Washington, DC, 2003.

[3] M. Greenberg, N. Mantell, M. Lahr, F. Felder and R. Zimmerman, Short and intermediate economic impacts of a terrorist-initiated loss of electric power: Case study of New Jersey, *Energy Policy*, vol. 35(1), pp. 722–733, 2007.

[4] North American Electric Reliability Council, Disturbance Analysis Working Group (DAWG) Database, Princeton, New Jersey (www.nerc.com/~dawg), 2006.

[5] Office of Pipeline Safety, Pipeline Statistics, Pipeline and Hazardous Material Safety Administration, U.S. Department of Transportation, Washington, DC (ops.dot.gov/stats/stats.htm), 2007.

[6] Pipeline and Hazardous Materials Safety Administration, Pipeline basics, U.S. Department of Transportation, Washington, DC (primis.phmsa.dot.gov/comm/PipelineBasics.htm), 2006.

[7] C. Restrepo, J. Simonoff and R. Zimmerman, Unraveling geographic interdependencies in electric power infrastructure, *Proceedings of the Thirty-Ninth Annual Hawaii International Conference on System Sciences*, p. 248a, 2006.

[8] C. Restrepo, J. Simonoff and R. Zimmerman, Vulnerabilities in the oil and gas sector, presented at the *First Annual IFIP WG 11.10 International Conference on Critical Infrastructure Protection*, 2007.

[9] J. Simonoff, *Analyzing Categorical Data*, Springer-Verlag, New York, 2003.

[10] J. Simonoff, C. Restrepo and R. Zimmerman, Risk management and risk analysis-based decision tools for attacks on electric power, to appear in *Risk Analysis*, 2007.

[11] J. Simonoff, R. Zimmerman, C. Restrepo, N. Dooskin, R. Hartwell, J. Miller, W. Remington, L. Lave and R. Schuler, Electricity Case: Statistical Analysis of Electric Power Outages, Technical Report 05-013, Center for Risk and Economic Analysis of Terrorism Events, Los Angeles, California, 2005.

[12] S. Talukdar, J. Apt, M. Ilic, L. Lave and M. Morgan, Cascading failures: Survival vs. prevention, *Electricity Journal*, vol. 16(9), pp. 25–31, 2003.

[13] U.S. Census Bureau, Table HS-1 – Population: 1900–2002, *Statistical Abstract of the United States*, U.S. Department of Commerce, Washington, DC, (www.census.gov/statab/hist/HS-01.pdf), 2003.

[14] U.S. Census Bureau, Table HS-43 – Energy supply and disposition by type of fuel: 1949–2002, *Statistical Abstract of the United States*, U.S. Department of Commerce, Washington, DC (www.census.gov/statab/hist/HS-43.pdf), 2003.

[15] R. Zimmerman, Critical infrastructure and interdependency, in *The McGraw-Hill Homeland Security Handbook*, D. Kamien (Ed.), McGraw-Hill, New York, pp. 523–545, 2006.

[16] R. Zimmerman and C. Restrepo, The next step: Quantifying infrastructure interdependencies to improve security, *International Journal of Critical Infrastructures*, vol. 2(2-3), pp. 215–230, 2006.

[17] R. Zimmerman, C. Restrepo, J. Simonoff and L. Lave, Risks and costs of a terrorist attack on the electricity system, in *The Economic Costs and Consequences of Terrorism*, H. Richardson, P. Gordon and J. Moore II (Eds.), Edward Elgar, Cheltenham, United Kingdom, pp. 273–290, 2007.